SOMALIA

AFRICAN BIBLIOGRAPHIC CENTER
SPECIAL BIBLIOGRAPHIC SERIES
NEW SERIES

Series Editor: *DANIEL G. MATTHEWS*

American-Southern African Relations: Bibliographic Essays
Mohamed A. El-Khawas and Francis A. Kornegay, Jr.

A Short Guide to the Study of Ethiopia: A General Bibliography
Alula Hidaru and Dessalegn Rahmato

Afro-Americans and Africa: Black Nationalism at the Crossroads
William B. Helmreich

African Bibliographic Center • Special Bibliographic Series
New Series • Number 4

SOMALIA

A Bibliographical Survey

Compiled by
Mohamed Khalief Salad

Greenwood Press

Westport, Connecticut • London, England

Ref.
Z
3507
. A375
1977
n.s.
no. 4

Library of Congress Cataloging in Publication Data

Salad, Mohamed Khalief.
   Somalia.

   (Special bibliographic series - African Bibliographic Center: new ser., no. 4)
   Bibliography: p.
   Includes index.
   1. Somalia—Bibliography. I. Title. II. Series: African Bibliographic Center.
Special bibliographic series; new ser., no. 4.
Z3507.A45 n.s. no. 4   [Z3526] [DT401]   016.96s
ISBN 0-8371-9480-6   [016.967'73]   76-51925

Library of Congress Catalog Card Number: 76-51925
ISBN 0-8371-9480-6

First published in 1977

Greenwood Press, Inc.
51 Riverside Avenue, Westport, Connecticut 06880

Printed in the United States of America

CONTENTS

SERIES FOREWORD

This comprehensive bibliography on Somalia is the second in a series of reference tools developed this year for publication in the Center's Special Bibliographic Series devoted to providing the user with as complete as possible guide to resources on the Horn of Africa.

Most of the attention in African affairs at this present juncture in time is focused on developments in Southern Africa even though considerable attention over the years has been given to study and research on Ethiopia. Somalia has always been considered an adjunct field of study because of the difficulty in obtaining data in English on that nation. The Center over the years in its journal *A Current Bibliography on African Affairs* has regularly featured literature resources on Somalia as well as publishing *Somalian Panorama* in this series in 1967 as an illustrative survey.

However, the compilation of works on the Horn of Africa published this year are compiled by nationals of those respective countries who obviously possess significantly more knowledge and sensitivity for the task than our regular Center personnel. The policy also fits in with the Center's encouragement and development of African librarians through cooperative and compilation arrangements.

In short, we consider this comprehensive bibliographical tool on Somalia not only as a valuable reference tool for study and research, but also as valuable in its current usage by those who will need much of the topical data contained within the pages of this volume.

Daniel G. Matthews
September 1976

FOREWORD

This bibliographical work on the Somali Nation is both unique and timely. It is unique because it is - to my knowledge- the first published work of its kind, and it is timely because of the pace of the recent development in this part of the world. This up-to-date compendium comprises book and journal, newspaper and cartographical materials.

As a comprehensive bibliography, the work is of relevance and significance not only for an expanding Somali clientele but for all those who have an interest, direct or indirect, in the area. In Somalia, there has been an enormous expansion in school enrollment since the onset of the revolutionary era and there has been a spirited literacy campaign and an overall cultural consciousness revival engineered by the official introduction for the first time of an orthography for the Somali language on 21st October 1972. Mr. Salad's work will doubtless be of great use to educators and translators. Foreign scholars, needless to say, will appreciate the bridging work which is commendably done by the author.

The bridging of the yawning gap in written materials related to the Somali Nation has taken the author over the last ten years. During this period he visited some of the major libraries in America and Western Europe which have valuable collections on Somalia. These visits have enhanced the author's quest for bibliographical accuracies and have further enabled him to consult with his professional colleagues. But it is the materials in the local libraries and museums which really form the backbone of this work, and it could hardly have been otherwise.

Dr. Ali Khalif Galied

General Manager
Jowhar-Sugar Enterprise (SNAI)
&
Former Director-General of the
Somali Institue of Public Adminis-
tration.Mogadiscio.Somalia.

30/5/76 Mogadiscio.
(Somalia).

INTRODUCTION

AN ESSAY ON THE COMPREHENSIVE BIBLIOGRAPHY
OF THE SOMALI NATION

By Mohamed Khalief Salad, Research Librarian
Central Bank of Somalia

Unlike earlier bibliographical works on Somalia which were mostly
incomplete, the present one is closer than any previous work to qualify
for comprehensiveness if viewed from the point of aggregate volumes and
the range of subject coverage. That it is the only bibliography compiled so far by a professional national is perhaps another point worthy
noting.

The work has successfully managed to encompass into its orbit quite a
robust and formidable literature; several thousands of titles (almost
4000) which comprise books as well as grey literature materials like
agriculture, geography, anthropology and politics and administration
are thoroughly covered. These subjects account for the greater part
of the work. The rest are sufficiently covered too. The language
areas are English, Italian, French, German and Somali. Books written
in Arabic are not included. This does mean a tolerable weakness.
Titles in Arabic about Somalia are comparatively few in number and are
not recorded systematically in any library. Now that Muslim Somalia
has joined the Arab League, one may genuinely expect an added interest
in the Arab writers of Somalia.

Furthermore, the arrangement and classification of materials done with
a view to assist the reader/researcher in finding books on his areas
necessitated a careful checking of as many titles as possible, since
this is the only way to ensure bibliographical accuracies.

Since a formidable literature on Somalia was kept by outside libraries,
collaboration with those depository libraries in the West was essential.
Thanks to a grant by UNESCO, the compiler has had an opportunity to
visit them. In Europe, those depository libraries are located in UK,
France and Italy. Germany and Russia also hold some invaluable collections on Somalia, mainly materials of historical importance - maps,
anthropology and exploration of Somalia. But these countries were not
visited. In addition to this, the compiler has paid a short visit to
Washington, D.C., under the auspices of the State Department in mid-
1966. Consultation with the vast literature on East African Region
kept by the Library of Congress was indispensable for comparative
study since some depository libraries in Europe did also hold same
documents. But still, there were materials uniquely held by the
Library of Congress.

The chief advantage of visits to libraries abroad was to acquaint the
researcher intimately with the works of Somalia proper, and to conduct
a physical checking for all bibliographical inaccuracies. It was
through these visits that the compiler has established personal

contacts with some scholars on Africana bibliographies. The unique
assistance and advice that they had imparted with the compiler has
given the latter an insight into the nature and complex task involved
in compiling a nation's bibliographical data.

It is important to note that the attempt to include in this work all
bibliographical data available on Somalia was difficult to achieve.
The element of "time gap" is now abridged. Thus, the work's time
chain represents two distinct periods in the history of the Somali
nation. It starts for that matter with exploration - cum colonial
period followed by post-colonial or independence era.

Another point equally important is that the work treats or relates not
only the present Somali Democratic Republic formed out of British and
ex-Italian Somalilands but other Somali territories and their constitu-
ent populations still under foreign administrations. These are French
Somaliland (Côte Francaise des Somalis), the Western Somaliland and the
NFD (The Northern Frontier Districts of Kenya) ruled respectively by
France, Ethiopia and Kenya.

Any compiler, national or foreigner who attempts to compile a genuine
bibliography of the Somali Nation is bound to disregard those artifi-
cial boundaries; the legacy of colonial partition of Africa is a con-
sequence of the Berlin Conference in 1884 with all the accompanying
injustices of the Scramble of Africa.

It was Mr. N.M. Viney, a British Colonial Administrator who while writing
a preface for his brief "Bibliography of British Somaliland" has put in
record the following passage of September 10, 1947:

"Authors of books about Somaliland and Somalis take as little regard of
political boundaries as do the Somalis themselves. So the list has
split over the borders of British Somaliland, southwards, east and
west and even overseas."

ACKNOWLEDGMENTS

The compiler is extremely grateful to numerous individuals and
institutions who have made valid and worthy contributions to this
bibliographical text on the Somali Nation. Without their suggestions
and ideas, it would have been very difficult to accomplish much.

However, I am particularly indebted to Mr. Abdullahi Haji Abdi,
Librarian of the Somali National Library for his professional guidance
and thoughtful review of the manuscript and also to Dr. Prof. Michele
Pirone, a scholar on African history and sociology, author of books
on Somalia and former Director of the University Institute (now,
National University of Somalia), mainly for his encouragement and
guidance to bibliographical sources in Italian as well as his introduction to Italian institutions which hold invaluable collections of
literature on Africa and which had carried out for a long time
research studies on Africa in general and Somalia in particular.

For collaboration, I am also grateful to authorities of those
institutions which either allowed me to make use of their library
facilities or sent to me lists of their bibliographical entries on
Somalia. The local ones are the Somali National Library, the National
University Library, the Library of the Museum of the Garesa, the
Somali National Bank Library, the British Council Library here in
Mogadiscio, the Ex-Parliament Library, private Library of Eng.
Ariberto Ferlani, later endowed to the University, and finally, the
United Nations Library here in Mogadiscio.

The foreign institutions are: The Library of Congress; The British
Museum; the Colonial Office Library; the Foreign Office Library; the
War Office Library; School of Oriental and African Studies, University
of London Libraries; Biblioteca Nazionale Centrale Vittorio Emanuele
II, Rome; Instituto Agronomico per l'Oltrmare, Florence; Instituto
Italiano per l'African, Rome; and lastly Bibliotheque National, Paris.

Furthermore, I am indebted to Mr. Abdullahi Waberi, specialist on
French Somaliland, in helping me to find bibliographical data on the
Côte Francaise des Somalis. I am equally indebted to my colleagues
at the Economic Research and Statistics Department, Somali National
Bank, for their help. They are Dr. Rudolf Seiler, IMF Expert and
Director of the Department, Dr. Isse Haji Musse, Dr. Abdullahi Haji
Mohamud Ereg, Dr. Ahmed Mohamed Basai, Dr. Ali Abdi Amalo, Dr. Mohamud
Mohamed Mohamud Guled, Mr. Habib Simba Habib, MissMarie Mureal Haji
Mudei, Mr. Abdi Sofe Abdulle, Mr. Said Ahmed Yusuf, Mr. Abdulkadir
Ismail Jama "Bruno" and Mr. Omar Jama Ali.

For typing and checking of the bibliography, I would like to express
my sincere and profound gratitudes to Mr. Ali Samantar Mohamed, owner
of the "Secretarial Service" in Mogadiscio and to Miss Amina Daud
Mohamed, a member of Somali History Commission.

                                    Mohamed Khalief Salad
                                    Mogadiscio, 2.4.1973

AGRICULTURE

1. Agricultural Research

AMMINISTRAZIONE FIDUCIARIA ITALIANA DELLA SOMALIA.

Studio sulle possibilita agricole
della Regione del Giuba.
Mogadiscio Novembre 1954.
23 pp.

AGNOLONI,MARIO.

Relazione sulle missioni in Somalia
per lo studio dei terreni dei
comprensori di Genale e Bulo Mererta.
Instituto Agronomico per l'Oltremare.
Firenze Dicembre 1966.
18 pp. tables. map.

ALBERTI,CARLO.

Ricerche sul capsico della Somalia:
Capsim frutescens."L. Annali Chimica
Applicata." 1939.
392-402 pp.

BARBACCI.

Sperimentazione agraria in Somalia:
Orto botanico a Mogadiscio:Azienda
Sperimentale a Genale."Agricoltura
Coloniale." Firenze 1922.
135 p.

BENEDETTO, P.

Notizie sulle coltivazioni
sperimentale di cotone condotte
nella stagione Der-Gilal 1928/29.
(S.A.I.S.)" Annali S.A.I.S." Genova 1929.

BETTINI,T.M.

Contributo alla conoscenza della
composizione chimica e del valore
nutritivo della flora somala.
Monograf.No.66. Istituto Agronomico
per l'Oltremare. Firenze 1941.

BIGI,F.

Nota sulla coltura dell'Anacardio e
dell'Avogado i Kenya e sui tentativi e le
prospettive di introduzione delle stesse in
Somalia." Rivista di Agricoltura Subtropicale e
Tropicale." Nos. 1-3. Firenze Gennaio-Marzo 1962.
4-20 pp.

BRANCA,A.

Primi risultati sperimentali
sulla introduzione di essenze
forestali in Somalia, nel periodo
1954-1958. "Rivista di Agricoltura
Subtropicale e Tropicale." Nos. 4-9
Firenze Aprile-Settembre 1960.
652-660 pp.

BROWN,DALTAS AND BERGER ASSOCIATES.

Design analysis and cost estimates:
Agricultural Research Center, Afgoi Somalia
for the Ministry of Agriculture and Animal
Husbandry. U.S.Aid Mission to Somali Republic.
tables.diags.

CARLISI,F.

Ricerche sul frutto della Cordeauxia Edulis:
Jeheb. "Annali Chimica Applicata." No. 12.   1937.

CENTRAL AGRICULTURAL RESEARCH STATION,AFGOI.

Available phosphorous and potassium
in Somali soils.   USAID/SOMALI REPUBLIC.
University of Wyoming Team.Mogadiscio July 1967.
10 pp. tables.

CUFINO,L.

I risultati scientifici della

Missione Stefanini-Paoli nella Somalia
Italiana.Meridionale. "Bollettino Societa
Geografica Italiana." Fasc. No. 10. Roma 1916.

ELECTROCONSULT.

Stazione di moltiplicazione
vegetale: progetto di pre-investmento.
Milano 1967.

FANELLI,L.

Il terreno della sponda sinistra
del Giuba all'analisi chimica.
Tipogr; Agnesotti. Viterbo 1907.
15 pp.

FILIPPO,LA ROSSA.

Studio sulla coltura della
palma da dattero in Migiurtinia.
Ministero dell'Agricoltura e Zootecnia.
Mogadiscio 1966.

FOOD AND AGRICULTURAL ORGANIZATION.

Agricultural Water Surveys: Somalia.
Final Report. Vol.I. (General).
FAO. SF/36/SOM. Rome 1968.
275 pp. maps, charts. tables.

Agricultural Water Surveys: Somalia.
Final Report. Vol.II.(Water Resources).
FAO. SF/36/SOM. Rome 1968.
197 pp. tables.charts.diagrs.

Agricultural Water Surveys: Somalia.
Final Report. Vol.III.(Landforms & Soils).
FAO. SF/36/Rome 1968.
236 pp. tables.

Agricultural Water Surveys:Somalia.
Final Report.Vol.IV.(Livestock and crop production).
FAO. SF/36/SOM. Rome 1968.
173 pp. map. tables.

Agricultural Water Surveys: Somalia.
Final Report.Vol.V (Engineering aspects of development).
FAO. SF/36/SOM. Rome 1968.
138 pp. maps, tables.

Agricultural Water Surveys:Somalia.
Final Report. Vol. VI.(Social and economic aspects of
                        development).
FAO. SF/36/SOM. Rome 1968.
179 pp. tables.

Installazione di una piantagione di palma
da datteri in Migiurtinia:Missione Preliminaria.
FAO. Roma Agosto 1967

Rice experiments at Afgoi:
Report to the Government of
Somalia. FAO. Report No. 2227.
Rome 1966.
11 pp. tables.

GANDOLFI, C.

Note sulle prove di coltura di
alcune varieta di cotone nel 1931.
"Annali S.A.I.S." Genova 1932.
99 p.

GUIDOTTI,R.

II Centro Agrario Sperimentale
di Alessandria. "Agricolture
Coloniale." Firenze 1930.
70 p.

INTERNATIONAL COOPERATION ADMINISTRATION.

Inter-River Economic Exploration:
(The Somali Republic) ICA.
Washington, D. C. January 1961,
XXXI, 346 pp. maps, diagrs. tables, charts.

JOHN H. STONE.

Recommendation for the Development of
an Agricultural Research Education Program
in the Somali Republic and the Feasibility
of Assistance by United States Aid through
a college contract. 1962.

JONES, B.T.

Bringing crops to a Somali desert.
"Commonwealth." No. 4. London 1960.
242-244 pp.

MAGNANENSI, P.

II primo esperimento di coltura del
tabacco al Centro Agrario di Alessandria.
"Agricoltura Coloniale," Firenze 1931.
567 p.

MAMELI, CALVINO E.

Sperimentazione agraria in Somalia.
"Agricoltura Coloniale." Firenze 1922.
355 p.

MANGANO, G.

Studio analitico di alcuni
terreni della Somalia Italiana
Meridionale. "Agricoltura Coloniale."
Firenze 1909.
19 pp.

MARIANI, G.

Considerazioni su problemi di
sperimentazione agraria e di
miglioramento genetico in Somalia.
"Rivieta di Agricoltura Subtropicale e
"Tropicale. Nos. 4-9. Firenze Aprile-Settembre 1960.
517-534 pp.

MISSIONE STEFANINI-PAOLI.

Ricerche idrogeologiche,botaniche ed
entomologiche fatte nella Somalia
Italiana (1931). Istituto Agricolo
Coloniale Italiano. Firenze 1916.
255 pp.

NISTRI, P.F.

Il Centro Agrario Sperimentale di
Genale nel 1933-34."Bonifica e
Colonizzazione." Vol. No. 4. Roma 1938.
118-119 pp.

NUTINI, G.

Studio sulla palma da dattero
in Migiurtina. AFIS. Mogadiscio 1953.

ONOR, G.

L'azienda agraria sperimentale
Governativa di Genale." Agricoltura
Coloniale." Firenze 1914.
234 p.

PEYRONE, B. AND DAL VESCO, G.

Ricerche sulla micoflora di alcuni
terreni agrari. "Allionia." No. 3. 1957.
113-132 pp.

PRINCIPI, I.

Osservazioni sui terreni agrari della Somalia
Italiana Meridionale. "Giornale di Geologia
Pratica." Anno XI. 1913.
77 p.

PRINCIPI, P.

Alcune osservazioni sui tipi di
terreno nella Somalia. "Rivieta di
Agricoltura Subtropicale e Tropicale."
Nos. 1-3. Firenze Gennaio-Marzo 1957.
36-42 pp.

RAPETTI, G.

Sul coefficiente di appassimento
transitorio dei terreni del Comprensorio
per la coltura del cotone.
"Annali S.A.I.S." Genova 1932.
109 p.

Note sulle prove di coltura di alcune
varieta di cotone nel 1932.
"Annali S.A.I.S." Genova 1932.
103 pp.

REPUBBLICA SOMALA.

Studio sulla coltura della palma da
dattero in Migiourtinia. Ministero
dell'Agricoltura e Zootecnia.
Mogadiscio 22 Ottobre 1966.
11 pp.

ROSSI, G. V.

Analisi chimica di alcuni terreni
del Benadir."Agricoltura Coloniale."
Vol. 3. No. 2. Firenze 1909.
116-130 pp.

SACCO, T.

Ricerche sul citrus paradis Mof. della
Somalia. "Rivista di Agricoltura Subtropicale
e Tropicale." Nos. 1-3. Firenze Gennaio-Marzo 1960.
88-89 pp.

Ricerche sul Citrus aurantium L. della
Somalia. "Rivista di Agricoltura Subtropicale
e Tropicale." Nos. 1-3. Firenze Gennaio-Marzo 1960.
100-105 pp.

S.A.I.S.

Note sulle prove di concimazione
del cotone: Gu 1931 e 1932.
Annali S.A.I.A." Genova 1932.
87-93 pp.

Note colturali riguardanti alcune varieta
di cotone coltivate nel 1933 in parcelle
sperimentale. "Annali S.A.T.S." Genova 1934.
35 p.

Note sulle prove di coltura di alcune
varieta di cotone (1935).
"Annali S.A.I.S." Genova 1935.

Determinazione del coefficiente di
appassimento per tre diversi tipi
di terreno. "Annali S.A.I.S." Genova 1934.
37 p.

Note sull'appassimento del cotone
1936. "Annali S.A.I.S." Genova 1936.
41 p.

SAPPA,F. AND MOSCA, A.M.

Premiers resultats de recerches sur la composition
de la mycoflore de quelques sols tropicaux en
climat aride (Somalie Italienne). "VII Congress
Internaz. Scienze del Suole." Paris 1956.

Ricerche sulla micoflora dei terreni della
savana spinosa Somala. "Allionia." No. 2.   1954.
247-257 pp.

SCURTI,

Relazione sui risultati ottenuti
nell'analisi dei vari campioni del
terreno del comprensorio della S.A.I.S.
"Annali della S.A.I.S" Bonavia. Genova 1930.
11-25 pp.

SOMALI REPUBLIC.

Vegetable trials 1964/65. Central Agricultural
Research Station (Afgoi). Mogadiscio May 1966.
141 pp. tables.ills.

Central Agricultural Research Station:
Progress Report. Mogadishu 1966.

TOMMASI, G.

Analisi terre delle Aziende di Villagio
Duca degli Abruzzi. "Annali della S.A.I.S."
Bonavia. Genova 1929.
7-18 pp.

U.S. AGENCY FOR INTERNATIONAL DEVELOPMENT.

Somali Republic: crop trails result.
Bonka Farmers Training Center. June 1964.
6 pp. ills. Tables.

WIXOM, CALVINI.

Soil and water conservation-Northern
Region Somali Republic. USAID.
Mogadiscio 1964.

WYOMING UNIVERSITY SOMALI PROGRAM.

Progress Report Research and Extension to
the Ministry of Agriculture Somali Republic.
(1st July-31st December 1968). Mogadiscio.
64 pp.

2.   Agriculture (General)

AMMINISTRAZIONE FIDUCIARIA ITALIANA DELLA SOMALIA.

Studi per l'attuazione di un
programma di collaborazione tecnica
per las valorizzazione della Somalia.
Direzione per lo Sviluppo Economico.
Mogadiscio II Agosto 1950.
8 pp.

Studio per la valorizzazione della zona
mesopotamica ad agricoltura seccagna.
Direzione per lo Sviluppo Economico.
Mogadiscio Settembre 1954.
7 pp.

Agriculture (other than livestock and natural pasture).
Mogadiscio 1951.
29 pp.

Organizzazione dell'Ispettorato per
l'Agricoltura e la Zootecnia e programma
di attivita per l'anno 1954. Stamperia AFIS.
Mogadiscio 1954.
29 pp. appendices.

Studi per opere di risanamento e valorizzazione
dei Descek del Giuba. Direzione per lo Sviluppo
Economico. Mogadiscio Settembre 1954.
8 pp.

Risposto al questionario della Banca
Internazionale per la Ricostruzione e lo
Sviluppo su problemi d'interese agricolo.
Direzione per lo Sviluppo Economico.
Mogadiscio Aprile 1956.
68 pp.

Opere a favore dell'agricoltura
Somala: Basso e Medio Scebeli.
Ufficio Speciale. Min.AA.EE. Roma.
18 pp. map. charts.

Opere a favore dell'agricoltura Somala:

Basso e Medio Scebeli. Istituto Agronomico
per l'Oltremare. Fasc. No. 3649. Firenze 1957.
25 pp.

AGRESTI, A.

L'agricoltura e la mano d'opera in
Somalia. "La Rivista d'Oriente." No. 2-3. Napoli.
37 p.

AGRICULTURAL DEVELOPMENT AGENCY.

Annual Report 1967. ADA. Mogadiscio 1968.
11 pp.

_____

Annual Report 1968. ADA. Mogadiscio
20 April 1969.
22 pp. appendices.

_____

Annual Report 1969. ADA. Mogadiscio
Februark 1970.
30 pp. appenices, tables.

AGLIETTI, B.

L'agricoltura fattore essenziale
dell'economia della Somalia. "Italiani
nel Mondo." No. I. Roma 1946.
6 p.

ANONYMOUS.

Per la messa in valore del Benadir.
"Rivista Coloniale." Roma 1917.
141 p.

_____

Ii problema agricolo e la manodopera
del Benadir. "Rivista Coloniale." Roma 1918.
503 p.

_____

Distruzione degli steli delle piante
di cotone nella Somalia Italiana.
Bollettino Informazione Economica del
Ministero delle Colonie." Roma 1925.
69 p.

_____

Ii grande problema Somala: SAIS.
"L'idea Coloniale." Roma 1926.

AGRICULTURE
201 p.

Lavori di bonifica compiuti dalla SAIS
nella regione "Scidle" della Somalia
Italiana, 1919-1927. Tipografia G. Bonavia. Genova.
393 pp. ills. tables.

La colonizzazione in Somalia. "Bollettino
Informazione Economica." Ministero delle
Colonie. Roma 1927.
636 p.

Concorsi a premio fra i Concessionari
della Somalia Italiana. "Rassegna Economica
delle Colonie." Toma 1930.
1020 p.

Il comprensorio di bonifica di Genale nella
Somalia Italiana. "Bollettino dell'Associazione
Cotoniera." No. 3. Milano 1931.
153 p.

Cenni sui consorzi di colonizzazione
della Somalia Italiana. "La Somalia
Italiana." No. 1-6. Mogadiscio 1934.
7 p.

I Consorzi di colonizzazione della Somalia
Italiana. "Rassegna Economica delle Colonie."
Roma 1935.
283 p.

Agricoltura Somala. "Rivista Italiana di
Essenze e Profumi." No. 4 Milano 1936.
76 p.

La valorizzazione agraria e la colonizzazione:
L'opera compiuta in Somalia. "Annali Africa
Italiana." Anno II. Vol. III. Roma 1939.
240 p.

ARFELLI, R.

Cooperazione e valorizzazione agricola in
Somalia. "Atti del VII Congresso Economico
Italo-Africano." Milano 1958.
109-111 pp.

————————

Problemi agricoli della Somalia. "Atti del
IX Convegno Economico Italo-Africano." Milano 1960.
97-100 pp.

BALDASSARRI, L.

Possibilita culturali su Giuba e sull'Uebi Scebeli.
"L'Italia Coloniale." Roma-Milano 1933.
67 p.

BARILE, P.

Consorzio di colonizzazione di
Genale:Vittorio d'Africa. "La Somalia
Italiana." Mogadiscio 1934.
54 p.

BARTOLAZZI, E.
La mostra dei tipi di trasformazione
fondiaria e dei principali prodotti
delle Colonie Italiane Somalia.
"Agricoltura Coloniale." Firenze 1933.

BARTOLOMEI, A.

Piccole imprese di colonizzazione in
Semalia. "Vie Imp." No. 5-6. 1926.
5 p.

BARTOLOMEI, G.G.

L'importanza agraria del Benadir.
"Agricoltura Coloniale." Firenze 1907.
149 p.

BECCARI, F.

Missione tecnica-agricola per la Somalia.
"Rivista di Agricoltura Subtropicale e
Tropicale." Nos. 7-9. Firenze 1959.
358-370 pp.

BIGI, F.

Agricoltura, vita della Somalia: Esame
tecnico della situazione e dei problemi
agricoli somali. "Africa." Roma 1950,
167 p.

Il problema agricola della Somalia: Esame
tecnico della situazione e dei problemi
agricoli somali. "I Quaderni di Africa."
Roma 1950.

Il problema del lavoro nelle aziende
agricole della Somalia. "Rivista di
Agricoltura Subtropicale e Tropicale."
Firenze 1954.

Missione Tecnico Agricola Per La Somalia:
Relazione e Monografie Agrarie Subtropicale
e Tropicale. No. 79. Istituto Agronomico
per l'Oltremare. Firenze 1960.
171-255 pp.

BOGGIA, C.

Nuovi orizzonti per l'avvenire coloniale
d'Italia: un grandioso progetto di valorizzazione
della Somalia Italiana. "Illustrazione Coloniale."
Milano 1923.

BONADONNA, T.

Agricoltura ed allevamenti in Somalia.
"L'allevatore." No. 4-9. 1964.
6 pp.

BOUTET, R.

Agricoltura e razze nella Somalia Italiana.
"Cooperazione Rurale." No. 2. 1939.

Prospettive agricole in Somalia.
"L'Agricoltura Italiana." No. 3.
Pisa 1950.

BOZZI, L.

La Somalia ed il suo sviluppo
agricolo: La valle del Giuba;
agricoltura indigena. Numero Speciale
"Rivista "Costruire". 1938.
76 p.

BUFFO, C.

L'impresa agricola in Somalia. "Bollettino
dell'Associazione Cotoniera." No. I. Milano 1930.

5 p.

CAPPELLINI, A.

Le risorse agricole della nuova Somalia.
"Etiopia." No. 9-10. Settembre-Ottobre 1937.
38 p.

CARNEVALI, G.

Indici del progresso economico della Somalia.
"Rivista di Agricoltura Subtropicale e Tropicale."
Nos. 7-9. Firenze Luglio-Settembre 1953.
203-213 pp.

CARNIGLIA, G.B.

II Giuba: Monografia delle Regioni della
Somalia. Giovanni de Agostini. Torino 1924.

La Vallata del Giuba: Monografie delle
Regioni della Somalia. Giovanni de Agostini.
Torino 1927.

CAROSELLI, F.S.

L'agricoltura nell'economia Somala.
"Rassegna Italiana Fascista." No. 184-184.
Roma 1933.
226 p.

Programmes and plans for rural development
in Somaliland. International Institute for
Differing Civilisation. The Hague 1953.

CHIUDERI, A.

Relazione su alcuni aspetti dell'agricoltura
Somalia. "Rivista di Agricoltura Subtropicale
e Tropicale" Nos. 1-3. Firenze Gennaio-Marzo 1959.
3-16 pp.

CONFORTI, E.

Problemi agricoli e di lavoro della Somalia
Italiana. "Atti II Congresso Studi Coloniali."
1947.
305 p.

Primi programmi di sviluppo agricolo da
attuare a mezzo del Fondo Valorizzazione
Somalia. Stamperia AFIS. Mogadiscio 1954.

10 pp.

Studi per opere di risanamento a valorizzazione
dei descek del Giuba. Istituto Agronomico per
l'Oltremare. Fasc. No. 1560. Firenze 1954.
8 pp.

Organizzazione attuale ed attivita
dell'Ispettorato dal 1950 al 1954.
Direzione per lo Sviluppo Economico.
Mogadiscio Settembre 1954.
35 pp. tables; appendices.

Relazione sulle possibilita agricole del territorio
del Nogal e consigliabili forme d'intervento per lo
sviluppo dell'agricoltura indigena. AFIS. Mogadiscio
Giugno 1954.
6 pp.

Programma per la valorizzazione agricola
di alcune zone del Nogal e l'incremento
della coltura della palma da dattero in
Migiurtinia. AFIS. Direzione per lo Sviluppo
Economico. Mogadiscio 1955.

Primi programmi di sviluppo agricola
secagna. Stamperia AFIS. Mogadiscio 1955.
8 pp.

Ispettorato dell'Agricoltura e Zootecnia:
Organizzazione ed attivita dell'Ispettorato
nel 1955. AFIS. Direzione per lo Sviluppo
Economico. Mogadiscio 1956.
73 pp. Map. charts.

Linee programmatiche orientative per lo
sviluppo economico agrario della Somalia.
AFIS. Direzione per lo Sviluppo Economico.
Mogadiscio 1956.

CORFITZEN, W.E. AND KINZY.

Agricultural Mission to Somalia. U.S.
Operations Mission to Italy. Rome 1950.

42 pp.

CORTESI, F.

Vegetazione e piante utili della
Somalia Italiana. "L'Oltremare." No. 3
Roma 1933.
123 p.

CORTINOIS, A.

Le richezze naturali della Somalia.
Genova 1935.

CRESPOLANI, R.

La Societa Romana di Colonizzazione
in Somalia. "L'Italia d'Oltremare."
Roma 1940.
191 p.

DAINELLI, G.

The agricultural possibilities of Italian
Somaliland."The Geographical Review." Vol. XXI.
New York January 1931.

DI LAURO, R.

Avvaloramento della vallata del Giuba.
"Illustrazione Coloniale." No. 9. Milano 1931.
35 p.

D'ANNIBALE, L.

Coltura e prodotti del medio Uebi
Scebeli."Illustrazione Coloniale."
No. 6 . Milano 1937.
146 p.

DE MARCO, G.

Valorizzazione di resorse somale.
(Societa "La Somalia").
"Agricoltura Coloniale." Firenze 1922.
10i p.

ESPOSITO, G.

L'aridicoltura ed i suoi sistemi in
Somalia. Instituto Agronomico per l'Oltremare.
Fasc. No. 3764. Firenze 1960.
23 pp.

FALCONE, A.

L'agricoltura in Somalia. "Atti del

I° Convegno Economico Italo-Africano."
Milano 1952.
218-222 pp.

FIORI, A.

Le costruzione agrarie nella Somalia
Italiana. "Agricoltura Coloniale." Firenze 1910.
405 p.

FILIPPO, LA ROSSA.

Riflessi sociali dell'agricoltura in
Somalia. Ministero dell'Agricoltura e
Zootecnia. Mogadiscio 1966.

_____

L'Agricoltura praticata lungo i fiumi
Giuba e Uebi Scebeli. Ministero dell'Agricoltura
e Zootecnia. Mogadiscio 1966.
26 pp.

FOLCO, A.

Rapida rassegna sull'andamento dell'agricoltura
metropolitana ed indigena della Somalia Italiana.
"La Somalia Italiana." Mogadiscio 1933.
19 p.

_____

L'agricoltura indigena della Somalia Italiana.
"Atti II Congresso Studi Coloniali." Vol. VI.
Napoli 1934.
968 p.

FOOD AND AGRICULTURAL ORGANIZAIT ION.

Planning for agricultural development:
Report to the Government of the Somali
Republic. FAO Technical Assistance Report.
No. 2578. FAO. Rome 1968.
7 pp.

FORLANI, A.

Ll cuore agricolo della Somalia:
Le realizzazione della SAIS.
"Africa." Roma 1950.
186 p.

FORMIGARI, F.

Bonifica e guerra in Somalia.
"Civilta Fascista." 1937.
509 p.

FRANCOLINI, B.

I concorsi agricoli fra i concessionari
della Somalia Italiana. "Agricoltura
Coloniale." Firenze 1930.
535 p.

FUNAIOLI, U.

Relazione su alcune zone agricolo di
Galcaio. Direzione per lo Sviluppo
Economico. AFOS. Mogadiscio 20 Luglio 1954.
8 pp.

Alcuni aspetti della bonifica di
Bulo Mereta (Basso Uebi Scebeli).
"Rivista di Agricoltura Subtropicale e
Tropicale." Nos. 7-9. Firenze Luglio-Settembre 1958.
355-379 pp.

La tecnica dell'uso della terra in Somalia:
Possibilita e limiti. (Conferenza tenuta il
12/5/1960 nella Germania Federale al Congresso:
"L'agricoltura nell'Africa Tropicale).
Istituto Agronomico per l'Oltremare.
Fasc. No. 3644. Firenze 1960.
17 pp.

Censimento trattori della Somalia al
31 Dicembre 1955. Istituto Agronomico
per l'Oltremare. Fasc. No. 4271. Firenze.
7 pp.

Bonifiche lungo l'Uebi Scebeli. "Rivista
di Agricoltura Subtropicale e Tropicale."
Nos. 4-9. Firenze Aprile-Settembre 1960.
492-504 pp.

Economia ed agricoltura della Somalia.
"Agriforum" No. 9. 1962.
283-286 pp.

GIORIO, C.

Importanza politico economico delle
aziende agricole in Somalia." Atti III
Convegno Economico Italo-Africano."

Milano 1954.

GOVERNO DELLA SOMALIA.

Il comprensorio di bonifica di Genale
nella Somalia Italiana. "Bollettino
dell'Associazione Cotoniera." Nos. 3. Milano 1930.
1197 p.

Lo sviluppo dell'agricoltura nella
Somalia Italiana. Mogadiscio 1934.

GOVERNO SOMALO.

Rapporto sulle possibilita di valorizzazione
delle fasce rivierasche della valle del Giuba.
Ministero Lavori Pubblici. Mogadiscio.

GROTTANELLI, V.L.

La colonizzazione agricola della Somalia
Italiana. "Rivista Italiana di Scienze
Economiche." Roma 1936.
597 p.

GUIDOTTI, R.

L'agricoltura in Somalia nel 1929.
G. Ramella. 1930.
10 pp.

HOLM, HENRIETTA M.

The Agricultural resource of Somalia.
U.S. Department of Agriculture. Foreign
Service. Washington, D. C. 1956.
20 pp.

INCONTRI,G.

Agricoltura e zootecnia in Somalia.
"Rassegna Nazionale Fascista Italiana."
Firenze 1915.

ISTITUTO AGRICOLO COLONIALE.

L'agricoltura e la colonizzazione
agricola nella Somalia Italiana.
Tipografia del Senato. Roma 1945.
79 pp.

L'agricoltura e la colonizzazione
agricola nella Somalia Italiana.
Tipografia del Senato. Roma 1947.
88 pp.

ISTITUTI AGRONOMICO PER L'OLTREMARE.

Numero dedicato alla Somalia. (Rivista di
Agricoltura Subtropicale e Tropicale.)
Firenze 1953.
193 pp.

KUO,L.T.C.

Somalia: background information.
Food and Agricultural Organization.
Rome June 1951.
10 pp.

LEONARDI,E.

Del possibilie sviluppo agrario della
Somalia Italiana."Atti I Congresso Italiani
all'Estero." Vol.I. 1908.
522 p.

LESSONA,A.

I grandi problemi coloniali:
Lo sfruttamento del Giuba. "Politica
Sociale." No. 3-4. Roma 1930.

LOCKWOOD SURVEY CORPORATION, LTD.

Agricultural and water survey,Somali
Republic. Vol.I. (General Report).
FAO & UNSF. Toronto 1966.

LUCCI, L.

Boscaglia e sabbia: progetti di valorizzazione
nel quadro E.R.P. 1950.
145 pp.

LUCHINI,R.

L'odierna situazione dell'agricoltura
metropolitana in Somalia. 1947.
33 pp.

MACCALUSO, C.

L'agricoltura nella Somalia Italiana
meridonale. "Bollettino Ministero Affari
Esteri."Roma 1908.
44 p.

———————

L'agricoltura nella Somalia Italiana
meridionale."Agricoltura Coloniale."
Firenze 1909.
184 p.

MALLARINI, A.G.

Nel nostro Egitto Somalo: I fiumi e
le terre della Somalia."Illustratione
Coloniale." No. I. Milano 1928.
22 p.

MANETTI, C.

Il concorso e la mostra dei
fabbricati rurali per la zona
di Genale. "Agricoltura Coloniale."
Firenze 1911.
114 p.

MANGANO,G.

Le imprese agrarie della Somalia
Meridonale. "Atti Congresso Espansione
Econom.Commer.Estero." 1923.
249 p.

MARIOTTINI,M.

Panorama delle bonifiche e delle
trasformazione agrarie in Somalia. "Rivista di
Agricoltura Subtropicale e Tropicale." Nos. 4-9.
Firenze Aprile-Settembre 1960.
217-234 pp.

MAUGINI,A.

Un altro grande esempio di bonifica
agraria nella Somalia: Genale.
"Agricoltura Coloniale." Firenze 1926.
409 p.

_____

La production de l'encens dans la
Somalie Italienne. "Atti VI Congress
Internazionale Agricol. Tropical e
Subtropical." Paris 1931.
71 pp.

_____

La Somalia Italiana. "Rivista di
Agricoltura Subtropicale e Tropicale."
Firenze 1947.
221 p.

_____

La colonizzazione della Somalia.
"L'Italia in Africa". Vol. XI.
Societa Editrice Arti Grafiche.
Roma 1948.

Valorizzazione agricola. (Somalia).
"Atti I Convegno Economico Italo-Africano."
Milano 1952.

Guardando al domani. "Rivista di Agricoltura
Subtropicale e Tropicale." Nos. 4-9.
Firenze Aprile-Settembre 1960.
670-685 pp.

MAURIGI, C.

Clima e agricoltura nella Goscia.
"Rivista Coloniale." Roma 1910.

MAZZOCCHI-ALEMANNI, N.

La regione del Giuba: un grande
problema di organizzazione. "Rivista
Coloniale." Fasc. No. 5-6. Roma 1920.
229 p.

Il problema del Giuba. "La Rassegna
del Mediterraneo." Roma 1925.
15 p.

Il nuovo problema del Giuba.
(Da per le nostre colonie).
Vallecchi, Istituto Agricolo Coloniale
Italiano. Firenze 1927.
237 pp.

Il problema del Giuba. "Atti I Congresso
Internazionali Studi Coloniali." Vol.VI. 1931.
406 p.

MENEGHINI, A.

Agricoltori ed agricoltura nel
Basso Giuba. Istituto Agronomico
per l'Oltremare. Fasc. No. 3809. Firenze 1955.
5 pp.

Piani di sviluppo economico a favore
delle regioni mesopotamiche in Somalia.
Rivista di Agricoltura Subtropicale e
Tropicale." Nos. 4-9. Firenze 1960.
505-516 pp.

MEREGAZZI, R.

Nuove iniziative agricolo-industriale
in Somalia. "Economia Nazionale." No. I. Milano 1928.
23 p.

MINISTERO AFFARI ESTERI(ITALIA).

Provvedimenti per la messa in valore delle
terre della Somalia Italiana. Direzione
Centrale Affari Coloniali. Tipografia Ministero
Affari Esteri. Roma 1911.

MISEROCCHI, M.

Dalla boscaglia somala al comprensorio
di Genale. "La Conquista della Terra." 1936.
455 p.

_____

Aspetti agricoli della Somalia.
"La Conquista della Terra." 1937.
17 p.

MISSIONE TECNICO AGRICOLA PER LA SOMALIA.

Deduzioni e considerazioni riferite ai
problemi ed alle condizioni specifiche della
Somalia (Parte seconde). Riprodotto a cura del
"CEASA". Firenze.
223-344 pp.

MONDAINI, G.

La Somalia Italiana ed i suci
problemi in un'opera sulla colonizzazione
dell'Est Africa."Rivista Coloniale." Roma 1909.
45 p.

MORI, A.

L'emigrazione Italiana al Benadir.
Atti I Congresso Italiani all''Estero."
Vol. I. 1908.
529 p.

NALDONI, N.

La colonizzazione Italiana della
Somalia. "L'Universo". No. 2. Firenze 1950.
197 p.

NISTRI, P.F.

Considerazioni e cenni retrospettivi
sulla colonizzazione del Giuba." Bonifica
e Colonizzazione." No. 2. Roma 1939.
227 p.

N.S.

La Colonizzazione della Somalia Italiana.
"Illustrazione Coloniale." No. 12. Milano 1934.
28 p.

OGNA, P.

Per una sistematica valorizzazione agricola
della regione del Giuba. "Illustrazione
Coloniale." No. 5 Milano 1925.
154 p.

O.M.

Il Giuba d'Italia." Illustrazione
Coloniale." No. II. Milano 1925.
358 p.

ONGARO, G.

Le risorse alimentari della nostra
colonia: Somalia. "Rivista di Commiss. e
Serviz. Amminist. Milit." 1936.
43 p.

ORSINI, G.P.

Le coltivazioni in Somalia. "Illustrazione
Coloniale" No. I. Milano 1929.
47 p.

PAVERI, F.F.

Note sul comprensorio di bonifica di
Genale nella Somalia Italiana."Atti III
Congresso Studi Coloniali." Vol. VIII. 1937.
587 p.

PEZZI,E.

ALcuni cenni sull'agricoltura e
pastorizia del territorio dei Gherire.
Mogadiscio 4 Giugno 1938.
17 pp. map. ills.

PECK, E.F.

Agriculture in the Somaliland Protectorate.
"East African Agricultural Journal". Nairobi 1943.

Annual report of the development of
Agriculture and Veterinary Services.
Hargeisa 1950.
29 pp.

POLLACCI, G.

Studio sulla Somalia Italiana Meridionale.
"Atti Istituto Botanica.Universita di Pavia."
Serie IV. Vol.VI. Pavia 1935.
158 p.

RENIER,S.

La colonizzazione del Comprensorio
di Genale nella Somalia Italiana.
Bottettino Societa Geografica Italiana."
No. 3-4. Roma 1936.
153 p.

REGIS,R.

Considerazioni per il potenziamento
e sviluppo dell'agricoltura della Somalia.
Atti del IX Convegno Economico Italo-Africano."
Milano 1960.
194-195 pp.

REPUBBLICA SOMALA.

Costruzione di una azienda governative
Somala in zona arida Migiurtinia. Dipartimento
Agricolo. Ministero dell'Agricoltura e Zootecnia.
Mogadiscio Dicember 1961.
17 pp. map. tables.

_____

Organizzazione ed attivita del Dipartimento
Agricolo dal I luglio 1960 al 30 giugno 1961.
Ministero Agricoltura e Zootecnia . Mogadiscio 1961.
33 pp.

REPUBLIC OF SOMALIA.

Report on the organisation and establishment
of the Ministry of Agriculture. United Nations
Public Administration Advisory Mission.
Mogadiscio June 1968.
31 pp.

ROMAGNOLI, L.

Appunti di geomorfologia Somala:
L'avanzamento della dune a Barcana.
Istituto Agronomico per l'Oltremare.
Fasc. No. 4. Firenze Dicembre 1964.
412-416 pp.

RONCATI, R.

Elementi di agraria, entomologia
agraria, patologia vegetale e inudstrie
agrarie. Ministero dell'Istruzione
Pubblica. Mogadiscio 1965.
207 pp. ills.

RUSSO, G.

Problemi di agricoltura tropicale:
Somalia Italiana."Agricoltura Coloniale."
Firenze 1931.
400 P.

SACCO, T.

Relazione sull'attivita svolta nella
Somalia Meridionale ed in Migiurtinia
nel periodo Gennaio-Marzo 1934.
Arti Grafiche Conti & Co. Roma.
7 pp.

SALAD ABDI MOHAMED.

Linee di politica agrario in Somalia.
"Rivista di Agricoltura Subtropicale e
Tropicale." Nos. 4-9. Firenze Aprile-Settembre 1960.
164-170 pp.

SENNI,L.

La valorizzazione del Giuba.
"Agricoltura Coloniale." Firenze 1929.
476 p.

SCASSELLATI-SFORZOLINI,G.

Condizioni agrarie del Benadir.
"Rivista Coloniale." No. 5. Roma 1914.
190 p.

L'agricoltura nella Somalia Italiana.
"Rassegna Economica delle Colonie." Roma 1930.
96 p.

SOMALILAND PROTECTORATE.

Department of Agricultural and Veterinary
Services (Annual Report 1955) Hargeisa.
36 pp.

SOMALI REPUBLIC.

Programme for 1964-1966. Ministry of
Agriculture and Animal Husbandry.

Mogadiscio June 1964.
30 pp.

SUKERT, E.

Opere a favore dell'agricoltura Somala nel
Basso e Medio Scebeli.   Istituto Agronomico
per l'Oltremare.   Fasc.No.3809.   Firenze 1960.
17 pp.

TOZZI, R.

Problemi di agricoltura indigena sul Giuba.
"Atti II Congresso Studi Coloniali."   Vol.VI. 1930.
923 pp.

_____

Manifestazioni agricole della Goscia.
"Agricoltura Coloniale."   Firenze 1941.
26 pp.

_____

Cenni sulla regione della Goscia.
"Agricoltura Coloniale."   No.11.
Firenze Novembre 1940.
462-468 pp. ills.

_____

Programma di attivita per incrementare
l'agricoltura Somala.   "Rivista di Agricoltura
Subtropicale e Tropicale."   Nos. 7-9.   Firenze 1953.
252-262 pp.

_____

Il Nuovo comprensorio agricolo
di Balad.   "Somalia d'Oggi."   No.2.
Mogadiscio 1957.

_____

Agricoltura tradizionale Somala e
problemi relativi di miglioramento.
Relazione Monografie Tropicale e
Subtropicale.   No.81.   Istituto Agronomico
per l'Oltremare.   Firenze 1961.
82 pp.

I sistemi tradizionali dell'agricoltura
irrigua in Somalia. "Rivista di Agricoltura
Subtropicale e Tropicale." Nos. 7-9.
Firenze Luglio-Settembre 1961.
266-278 pp.

UNIONE AGRICOLA COLONIALE ITALIANA.

Concorso per un progetto di un centro
colonico agrario in un concessione agricola
situata nel comprensorio di bonifica di Genale.
"Bollettino Eritrea." Asmara 1932.
1601 p.

VALLARINO,A.G.

La bonifica integrale della Somalia
Italiana. "La Conquista delle Terra." 1936.
338 p.

VALORI,F.

L'azienda agricola somala. "Bonifica e
Colonizzazione." No. 2. Roma 1939.
238 p.

VIDOTTO, M.

Notizie su alcuni provvedimenti a
favore dell'agricoltura indigena in
Somalia. "I Georgiofili." No. 2. 1941.
314 p.

WORZELLA,W.W. AND MUSSON,L.A.

Proposed program for agricultural
technical assistance for Somalia.
U.S. Operations Mission to Italy. Rome 1954.
17 pp. ills.

ZERBINATI, R.

Un miracolo del lavoro Italiano in
Somalia. "Le Vie d'Italia." No. 6.
Milano 1925.
641 p.

3.   Agronomy

AMMINISTRAZIONE FIDUCIARIA ITALIANA DELLA SOMALIA.

Studi sulla meccanizzazione agricola
applicata particolarmente alla coltivazione
del cotone e delle arachidi. Mogadiscio.
31 pp.

Studio sulla costituzione di centri di
motoaratura a Genale, Balad, Villabruzzi,
Afgoi,Margherita,Bardera e Dugiuma. Mogadiscio 1955.

BECCARI,F. AND ASCANI,F.

Ricerche orientative per l'isolamento di
criteri non empirici di valutazione del frutto
del banano: I° Correlazione fra contenuto in
zuccheri colorazione allo idio e durezza della
polpa nella coltivare Giuba nana. "Rivista di
Agricultura Subtropicale e Tropicale." Nos. 7-9.
Firenze Luglio-Settembre 1963.
251-265 pp.

BIGI,F.

Relazione e considerazioni sui risultati conseguiti
in Somalia dall'applicazione del banano congiunto al
tipo d'impianto a sesti stretti in quadro. Istituto
Agronomico per l'Oltremare. Fasc.No.4262. Firenze 1960.
6 pp.

BIGI,F. AND BOZZI,L.

Appunti sulla meccanizzazione agricola applicata
particolarmente sulla coltivazione del cotone e
delle arachidi. "Rivista Agricoltura Subtropicale
e Tropicale. "Nos. 7-9. Firenze Luglio-Settembre 1952.

Mechanical agricultural Survey, A.F.I.S.
Mogadiscio 1952.
32 pp.

FUNAIOLI,A.

In tema di concimazione del banano in
Somalia: I risultati di concimazione effettuata
nella regione del Basso Giuba. "Rivista di Agricoltura
Subtropicale e Tropicale. "Nos. 7-9. Firenze Luglio-
Settembre 1962.
381-394 pp.

MARIANI, G.

Consigli per la concimazione dei bananeti
a Genale. Istituto Agronomico per l'Oltremare.
Fasc.No.4289. Firenze 1955.
5 pp.

MONTEMARTINI,L.

Appunti sulla germinazione ed il primo
sviluppo delle piante di Palma dum
(Hyphaene nodulario)Somalia. "Giardini Palermo."
Vol.XIV. Palermo 1937.
7 p.

RAPETTI, G.

Sulle arature di esercizio e sui mezzi per
eseguirle in Somalia. "Annali S.A.I.S."
Genova 1931.
53 p.

REPUBBLICA SOMALA.

Diversificazione dell'agricoltura:
studio preliminare. Italconsult.
Roma Agosto 1965.
107 pp.

ROSSETTI,C.

La coltivazione Italiana agricola
del Benadir. "L'Italia Coloniale."
Roma-Milano 1900.

SUCKERT, E.

Informazione e considerazione su alcune piante
coltivate nella Somalia Italiana.
Il Cenacolo. Firenze 1934.
115 pp.

4. Banana

ARFELLI, R.

Somalia terra delle banane. "Agricoltura
Coloniale." No. 4. Firenze 1957.
50-56 pp.

BECCARI, F.

La produzione bananiera in Somalia:
Ciclo di conversazioni sulle principali
produzioni agricole nei paesi tropicali.
Istituto Agronomico per l'Oltremare.
Fasc.No. 2949. Firenze Aprile 1958.
5 pp.

BIGI,F.

Primi risultati dell'introduzione di nuovi
principi di tecnica nella bananicoltura Somala.
"Rivista di Agricoltura Subtropicale e Tropicale."
Nos. 10-12. Firenze Ottobre-Dicember 1962.
557-601 pp.

Attualita e prospettive delle bananicoltura
Somala nel quadro dei rapporti tra Italia
e Somalia. Estraz. "Africa." No. 5. Roma 1963.
11 pp.

BOTTAZZI, F.

Le banane frutto di alto valore alimentare.
Ministero delle Colonie. Monografia No. 2
Roma 1936.
31 pp.

BOZZI, L.

La produzione delle banane-fico:consigli agli
agricoltori della Somalia. Stamperia della Colonia.
Mogadiscio 1941.

CATOZZO,A.

La banana della Somalia. "L'Oltremare."
Roma 1930.
192-352 pp.

CERRI,P.G.
Alcuni aspetti della tecnica produttiva
del banano in Somalia. "Rivista di
Agricoltura Subtropicale e Tropicale."
Nos. 4-9. Firenze Aprile-Settembre 1960.
535-549 pp.

CIBELLI, E.

Le banane della Somalia:richezze
della nazione. "Italia Coloniale."
No. 12. Roma-Milano 1937.
186 p.

————————

L'oro vegetale dell'Impero:Banane.
"Espansione Coloniale." No. 13. Roma 1938.
51 p.

CIFERRI,R.

Identificazione e caratteristiche delle
razze di banano coltivate nella Somalia Italiana.
Atti Istituto Botanico. Univ. Pavia. Serie IV.
Vol.X. Pavia 1938.
73 p.

————————

Tipi e cicli di produzione bananiera della

Somalia nel triennion 1933-34 e 1935-36.
"Annali Tecnica Agraria." Fasc. No. 2. 1939.

————————

Problemi della produzione bananiera Somala:
un programma di lavoro."Rivista di Biologia Coloniale."
Fasc.No.3. Roma 1940.
223 p.

————————

Il banano nell'Africa Italiano e in Italia.
Centro Studi Coloniali. Firenze 1943.
257 pp.

CONFORTI, E.

Consigli pratici sulla coltura
del banano nel Comprensorio di Genale.
"Agricoltura Coloniale." Firenze 1938.
451 pp.

————————

Lo spostamento dei bananeti
di Afgoi sul Scebeli. "Somalia d'Oggi."
No.2. Mogadiscio 1956.
30 pp.

CONSIGLIO, G.

La banana della Somalia. "Africa."

Roma Luglio-Agosto 1952.
189 pp.

FIORESI, L.

L'industria del banano in Somalia.
Atti III° Congresso Studi Coloniali."
Vol.VIII. 1937.
568.

FOLCO, A. AND MAZZA,M.

Note pratiche sulla coltura della
Musa Chinesis var.Giuba nella Somalia Italiana.
"Agricoltura Coloniale." Firenze 1934.
573 pp.

FOOD AND AGRICULTURAL ORGANIZATION.

FAO Mission to Somalia: Preliminary report of
cost study of bananas 1963. Istituto Agronomico
per l'Oltremare. Fasc.No.4194. Firenze 1963.
9 pp.

_____

Banana Production: Report to the Government of Somalia.
United Nations Development Programme. FAO.TA.No.2186.
Rome 1966.
14 pp. map.

FRANCOLINI, B.

Nuovi dati sulla produzione ed el commercio
della banana in Somalia. "Agricoltura Coloniale."
Firenze 1931.
170 pp.

GOLATO, C.

Relazione della missione fatta in Somalia nei
comprensori bananicoli di Genale e del Giuba.
Istituto Agronomico per l'Oltremare. Fasc.No.4170.
Firenze 1964.
14 pp.

GIORIO, G.

Alcune considerazioni sulla produzione
bananiera in Somalia nell'attuale momento, Gennaio 1964.
Istituto Agronomico per l'Oltremare.
Fasc.No.4261. Firenze 1964.
8 pp.

MAINERI, B.

Le banane dell'A.O. nell'Italia ed all'Estero.
"Illustrazione Coloniale." No.9. Milano 1937.
76 pp

MANNI, E.F.

La banana somala dagli esperimenti
all'affermazione.   "Commercio Italo
Africano." (C.I.A.) No. 8. Geneva 1933.

MARINO, A.

La banane della Somalia Italiana.
"Rivista del Freddo." No. 8. 1929.
350 p.
_____

Problemi della produzione coloniale:
banane di Derna e banane Somale.
"Illustrazione Coloniale." No. 8. Milano 1934.
34 p.

MISSIONE TECNICO AGRICOLA PER LA SOMALIA.

Relazione del viaggio di studi riguardanti la
coltivazione del banano e di altre piante tropicali
nella Guinea,Costa d'Avorio,Giamaica,Colombia,Ecuador,
Stati Uniti d'America.Monografia No. 79. Istituto Agronomico
per l'Oltremare. Firenze 1960. (Somalia 170-252).
170-252 pp. ills.

PAOLETTI,A.

Il valore economico del banana:possibilita
di produzione nella Somalia Italiana.
"Agricoltura Coloniale."Firenze 1913.
281 p.

P.B.S.

Le banane della Somalia. "L'Italia Coloniale."
Roma-Milano 1933.
144 p.

ROCCHETTI,G.

La bananicoltura della Somalia.
Monografia. No. 75. Istituto Agronomico
per l'Oltremare. Firenze 1956.
68 pp.

_____

Attivita connesse in Somalia alla bananicoltura
industriale. "Rivists di Agricoltura Subtropicale
e Tropicale. "Nos. 7-9. Firenze Luglio-Settembre 1956.
311-325 pp.

ROMAGNOLI,MARIO.

Coltivazione del banano nella Somalia Italiana.
"Agricoltura Coloniale." No. 8. Firenze Agosto 1933.

362-373 pp.

Coltivazione del banano nella Somalia Italiana.
"Agricoltura Coloniale." No. 9 Firenze Settembre 1933.
433-446 pp.

S.A.C.A.

Le banane in Somalia. SACA. Roma 1935.
28 pp.

SACCA,ACCS AND SAG.

Questione bananiera in Somalia. Roma 1955.
28 pp.

S.A.I.S.

Il banano alla S.A.I.S. "Annali S.A.I.S."
Genova 1931
47 p.

SALVO,I.

Le banane della Somalia.
"Illustrazione Coloniale." Milano 1934.
II p.

SOCIETA AGRICOLTORI GIUBA.

Relzaione sull'industria bananiera sul
Basso Giuba. Istituto Agronomico per l'Oltremare.
Fasc.No. 4279. Firenze 1965.
17 pp.

Brevi notizie sulla coltura del
banano e sulle operazioni alle frutta
in esportazione. SAG. 1962.
5-16 pp.

SOCIETA AGRICOLA MORODI.

Composizione ed incidenza delle voci di costo
delle banane prodotte nel 1964 sul Giuba.
Istituto Agronomico per l'Oltremare.
Fasc. No. 4209. Firenze 1965.
10 pp.

SUKERT, E.

La banana in Somalia. "Notiz. Economica"
Governo Somala. Vol. V°. 1930.
273 pp.

5.   Botony

AGOSTINI,A.

Miceti della Somalia. "Atti Istituto
Botanico della Universita di Pavia."
Serie IV.Vol.IV. Pavia 193..
191 p.

BACCARINI,P.

Sopra alcuni Padaxon della Somalia.
"nuovo Giornale Botanico Italiano".
Nuova Serie.Vol. XXI. No. 2. 1914.

BOALER,S.B. AND HODGE,C.A.H.

Vegetation patterns in Somaliland.
"Journal of Ecology". No. 5. London 1962.
465-474 pp. ills.

BORZI,A.

Sulla flora della Somalia Meridionale
Italiana. "Bollettino Orto Botanico
di Palermo". Vol.VII. Fasc.No. 1-3. Palermo 1908.
29 p.

Nuova specie di Abutilon della Somalia
Italiana: Abutilon Agnesae. "Bollettino
Orto Botanico di Palermo".Vol.X. Palermo 1911.
127 p.

BOZZI,L. AND TRIULZI,G.A.

L'immobilismo della pastorizia Somala.
"Rivista di Agricoltura Subtropicale e
Tropicale". Nos. 4-9. Firenze Aprile-Settembre 1960.
403-410 pp.

CHEVALIER,A.

La Somalia francaise: sa flore et
ses productions vegetales, "Revue Botan.
Appl.Agr.Trop." Vol.XIX. No. 217. 1939.
663-687 pp. ills.

CHIARUGI,A.

Paleoxilologia della Somalia Italiana.
"Nuovo Giornale Botanico Italiano".
Vol. XL. 1933.
306 p.

CHIOVENDA, E.

Graminacee dell Harar e dei Somali raccolte da
L.Robecchi-Brichetti. "Annali Reale Istituto
Botanico di Roma". Vol. VI. Fasc. No. 2. Roma 1895.
14 pp.

Di alcune Graminacee della Somalia.
"Annali Botanica Prof. Pirotta". Vol. V.
Fasc. No. I. 1906.
59 p.

Le colleziono botaniche:risultati scientifici
della Missione Stefanini-Paoli nella Somalia Italiana.
Tipografia Galletti. Firenze 1916.
200 pp.

Materie prime di vegetali spontanei e
coltivabili nelle nostre colonie di Eritrea
e Somalia. Tipografia Unione Editirice. 1921.
23 pp.

Nuove specie di Solanum Somalo.
"Bollettino Societa Botanica Italiana",
Maggio 1925.

Contributo alla conoscenza della
flora Somala transjubense.
"Agricoltura Coloniale". Firenze 1926.
42-103 pp.

La collezione botanica di S.A.R. il Duca
degli Abruzzi alle sorgenti dell'Uebi
Scebéli. "Nuovo Giornale Botanico Italiano".
Nuova Ser. Vol. XXXVI. 1929.
360 p.

Studio sul materiale botanico raccolto
ed annotato dal Dr. Scassellati Sforzolini
(Scidle 1919/20)"Annali S.A.I.S. 1919/27".
Genova 1929.
163 p.

Flora Somala (parte III) raccolta Pollacci,
Maffei,CiferriPuccioni 1934/35. "Atti Istituto
Botanico Universita di Pavia". Serie IV.Vol.VII.
Pavia 1936.
117 p.

CIFERRI, R.

I rapporti floristici tra i distretti della
Somalia Italiana. "Nuovo Giornale Botanico Italiano".
No. 2. 1939.
344 p.

_____

Saggio di emerecologia b nelle comunita' vegetali
delle regioni irrigue della Repubblica Domenicana
(Antille) e del Benadir (Somalia Italiana).
"Atti Istituto Botanico Universita di Pavia".
Labor.Crittogamico. Serie No. V. Vol.VII. Pavia 1946.
35 p.

_____, CORRADI, R. AND BIGI, F.

Piante medicamentos e piante amuleto
usate degli indigeni del Basso Giuba.
"Rivista di Biologia Coloniale". Vol.I-VI.
Roma 1938.
401-433 pp.

COLLENETTE,C.L.

North Eastern British Somaliland.
"Kew Bulletin og Misc. Information."
No. 8. London 1931.
401-414 pp. ills, map.

_____

Botany of North Eastern British Somaliland.
"Geographical Journal". Vol.LXXVIII. London 1931.
119-121 pp.

ENGLER,A.

Taxaceae, Tyhaceae,Potagemonaceae. Zigophillaceae,
Burseraceae ,Anacardiaceae,Guttiferae,Ochnaceae,
ed altre in Harar et in Somalia a D.D. La Robecchi-Brichetti
et Riva Lectae. "Annali Istituto Botanico di Roma".
Vol.VII. Roma 1897-8.
13 p.

_____

Araceae,Liliaceae,Moraceae,Hydnoraceae,Chenopodiaceae,
Nyctaginaceae,Aizoaceae,Cruciferae,Moringaceae,
Crassulaceae,Saxifragaceae,Hamamelidaceae,
Geraniaceae,Oxalidaceae,Malpighiaceae,Gallitrichaceae,
Combretaceae,Primulceae,Plumbaginaceae,Sapotaceae,
Salvadoraceae,Lentibulariaceae,Dipsaceae in Harar
territorio Galla et Somalia a D.D. Robecchi-Brichetti
et Riva lectae. "Annali Istituto Botanico di Roma".
Roma 1901.

FIORI,A.

Piante del Benadir: manipolo I$^{\circ}$ e 2°.
"Bollettino Societa Botanica Italiana".
Roma 1912-13.

Missione scientifica Stefanini-Paoli nella
Somalia Meridionale 1913: Plantae somalenses
novae. "Bollettino Societa Botanica Italiana".
Roma 12 Giugno 1915.

FUNAIOLI,A.

Aspetti del problema della infestanti nella
regione del Medio Uebi Scebeli. "Rivista di
Agricoltura Subtropicale e Tropicale". Nos. 7-9.
Firenze Luglio-Settembre 1953.
319-340 pp.

GILLETT,J.B.

The plant formation of Western British Somaliland
and the Harar Province of Abyssinia. "Kew Bulletin
of Misc. Information". No. 2 London 1941.
37-199 pp. map, ills.

GILLILAND,H.B.

The vegetation of Eastern British Somaliland.
"Journal of Ecology". No. I. Vol.40.
London February 1952.
91-124 pp. ills, map.

GILG,E.

Thymalacaceae Somalenses a D.D.Robecchi-Bricchetti
et Riva in Somalia Lectae. "Annali Istituto Botanico
di Roma". Vol.VI.Fasc.No.2. Roma 1896.

GLOVER, P.E.

A Preliminary Report on Comparative Ages
of some important East African Trees in
Relation to their Habitats. "South African
Journal of Science". Vol.XXVI. 1930.

A provisional check-list of British and
Italian Somaliland trees,shrubs and herbs,
including the reserved areas adjacent to
Abyssinia.(Vol.I. with a foreword by G.T.Fisher).
Crown Agents for the Colonies. London 1947.
446 pp. ills.

The root systems of some British Somaliland
plants. (Part I)"East African Agricultural Journal".
October 1950.
98-113 pp. ills, diagrs.bibl.

The root systems of some British Somaliland
plants. (part II) "East African Agricultural Journal".
January 1951.
154-162 pp.

The root systems of some British Somaliland
plants. (Part III) "East African Agricultural Journal".
April 1951.
205-210 pp.

The root systems of some British Somaliland
plants. (Part IV). "East African Agricultural Journal".
July 1951.
38-45 pp.

GREENWOOD, J.E.G.W.

The development of vegetation patterns
in the Somaliland Protectorate.
"Geographical Journal". No. 123. London 1957.
465-473 pp.

HALLIER.

Convolvulaceae in Harar et in Somalia
a D.D. Robecchi-Bricchetti et Riva Lectae.
"Annali Istituto Botanico di Roma".
Vol. VII. Roma 1898.

HARMS, H.

Amyryllidaceae,Leguminosae,Meliaceae,
Passifiloraceae in Harar et in Somalia
a D.D. Robecchi-Bricchetti et Riva Lectae.
"Annali Istituto Botanico di Roma".
Vol.VI. Roma 1897.

HEMMING,C.F.   (COMPILER)

Somalia Range Management and Development:
a short list of Somali plant names (Grazing lands).
FAO. Rome 1971.
10 pp. (Somali and Botanical names).

HENNINGS,P.

Fungi Somalenses in expeditione Ruspoliana
a D.Riva Lecti. "Annali Istituto Botanico
di Roma". Vol.VI.Fasc.No. II. Roma 1895.

LANZA, D.

Sanseverinia rorida Lanz,nuove species Somalenses.
"Bollettino Orto Botanico di Palermo". Vol. IX.
Palermo 1910.
208 p.

LINDAU,G.

Acanthacee Somalenses a D.D. Robecchi-Bricchetti
et Riva in Harar et in Somalia lectae.
"Annali Istituto Botanico di Roma" Vol.VI.
Fasc.No. 2. Roma 1895.

LOESENER,T.H.

Caelastraceae in Harar et in Somalia
a D. Riva lectae. "Bollettino Istituto
Botanico di Roma". Vol.IX. Fasc.No. I. Roma 1899.

LO PRIORE,G.

Amaranthaceae a D.D.Robecchi-Bricchetti
et Riva in Somalia et in Harar Lectae.
"Annali Istituto Botanico di Roma". Vol.IX.
Roma 1899.

MACFADYEN,W.A.

Vegetation patterns in the semi-desert plains
of the British Somaliland. "Geographical Journal".
No.CXVI. London December 1950.
199-210 pp.

Soil and vegetation in British Somaliland.
"Nature". London 21st January 1950.

MATTEI,G.E.

Plantae novae italo-somalenses:
Repertorium specierum novarum Regnis vegetalis.
"Band IX". 1911.
250-310 pp.

MATTIROLO,A.

Podaxon Ferrandi: nuove specie della Somalia
Italiana. "Annali di Botanica del Prof.Pirotta".
Vol.XI. 1913.

MOGGI,G.

Dieci anni di esplorazione e di
ricerche botaniche in Somalia.
"Rivista di Agricoltura Subtropicale e Tropicale".
Nos. 6-9. Firenze 1960.
252-262 pp.

Missione botonaica in Somalia: relazione
itineraria e risultati principali.
"La Ricerca Scientifica" No. 7 Consiglio
Nazionale delle Ricerche. Roma 1960.
955-966 pp.

MULLER.

Lichenes Somalenses a Hildebrand in Africa
Orientale: Territorio Somaliland lecti.
"Flora". Milano 1885.
528 p.

PAMPANINI,R.

Missione scientifica Stefanini-Paoli nella
Somalia Meridionale 1912: Contributo alla
conoscenza della flora somala. "Bollettino
Societa Botanica Italiana". 14 Febbraio 1913.

PAOLI,G.

Intorno alla flora della Somalia Italiana
Meridionale. "Atti III Congresso Internaz.
Agricoltura Subtropicale e Tropicale".Vol.II.
Londra 1914.
501 p.

PICHI-SERMOLLI,R.E.G.

Arid Zone Programme: a report on the
plant ecology of the arid and semi-arid
zones of Tropical East Africa:Ethiopia,
Somaliland,Kenya and Tanganyika. UNESCO.
Florence July 1952.
89 pp. ills. appendices.bibl.

Una carta geobotanica dell'Africa Orientale
(Eritrea,Etiopia,Somalia). "Webbia". No. I.

Firenze 1957.

PIROTTA,R.

Le collezioni botaniche dell'Ing.Robecchi-Bricchetti.
"Bollettino Societa Geografica Italiana". Serie III.
Vol. IV. Roma 1891.
45 p.

SACCO,T.

Ricerche sulla Cassia Fistula L.della Somalia.
"Osmosi". No. 6. 1951.
8 p.

_____

Considerazioni botaniche e ricerche fisico-chimiche
sull'Ocium Basilicum Var.Hispidum Lam.della Somalia.
"Allionia". Vol.III.Fasc.No. I. Torino 1956.
I-6 pp.

_____

Sull'essenza di Lippia dauensis Chiov.della Somalia.
"Atti Convegno Studi e Ricerche sulle Essenze".
Reggio Calabria 1956.

_____

Considerzaioni botaniche e ricerche fisico-chimiche
sull'Ocimum Basilicum Var.Hispidum Lam.della Somalia.
Arti Grafiche P. Conti & C. Torino 1957.
6 pp. ills.

_____

Sull'essenza di Lippia dauensis Chiov.
della Somalia. Arti Grafiche P.Conti &
C. Torino 1957.
4 pp. ills.

_____

Ricerche sulla Cassia Fistula L. della Somalia.
"Rivista di Agricoltura Subtropicale e Tropicale".
Nos. I-3. Firenze Gennaio-Marzo 1958.
119-123 pp.

_____

II Cymbopogon Citratus Stapf nell'agricoltura
e nell'industria Somala. "Rivista di Agricoltura
Subtropicale e Tropicale". Nos. 10-12. Firenze
Ottobre-Dicembre 1959.
428-438 pp.

_____

Primi risultati sull'introduzione in Somalia
come pianta essenziera dell'Ocimum Basilicum
L.Var. Crispum Cam. "Rivista di Agricoltura
Subtropicale e Tropicale". Nos. I-3. Firenze
Gennaio-Marzo 1960.
76-80 pp.

SCHUMANK,K.

Tiliaceae,Sterculiaceae,Bigoniceae,
in Harar et in Somalia a D.D.Robecchi-Bricchetti
et Riva lectae. "Annali Istituto Botanico di Roma.
Vol.VII. Roma 1898.
32 p.

TERRACCIANO,A.

Contribuzione alla flora del paese dei Somali.
"Bollettino Societa Botanica Italiana". 1892.
421 p.

URBANI, I.

Turneraceae somalenses a D. Robecchi-Bricchetti
lectae. "Annali Istituto Botanico di Roma".
Vol. VI. Fasc. No. III. Roma 1896.

6. Cotton

AMMINISTRAZIONE FIDUCIARIA ITALIANA DELLA SOMALIA.

Relazione al Segretario Generale sul nuovo
scheme di ordinanza per la regolamentazione
della coltivazione,lavorazione industriale e
commercio del cotone in Somalia. Direzione
Sviluppo Economico. Mogadiscio 17 Maggio 1955.
33 pp.

ANONYMOUS.

Esperimenti di coltivazione di cotone.
"Rivista Coloniale" Roma 1903.
216 p.

_____

La coltivazione del cotone nel Benadir:
costo e reddito. "Rivista Coloniale."
Roma 1909.
469 p.

_____

Coltura ed industria del cotone. "Documenti di
Vita Italiana." No. 44. Roma 1955.
1477-80 pp.

AGRICULTURE
  BIGI,F.

Il cotone in Somalia. "Meridiano Somalo."
No. I. Mogadiscio Ottobre 1951.

_____

Recenti sviluppi e prospettive della
cotonicoltura in Somalia. "Rivista di
Agricoltura Subtropicale e Tropicale."
Nos. 7-9. Firenze 1953.
295-319 pp.

_____

Recenti sviluppi e prospettive della cotonicoltura
in Somalia. "Rivista Industrie Tessile e Cotoniere."
No. I. Milano 1954.

BORZI,A.

Cotone della Somalia. "Bollettino
Orto Botanico di Palermo." Vol. V.
Fasc. No. 3-4. Palermo 1906.
154 p.

BRANDALISE,A.

Coltivazione del cotone in Somalia. "Bollettino
Studi e Informazioni del Giardino Coloniale."
Vol. V. Palermo 1919.
66 p.

BRUNO,A.

Per la cotonicoltura nella Somalia Italiana.
"Bollettino Societa African d'Italia."
Fasc.No.12. Napoli 1913.
220 p.

CALVINO, M.

L'oro verde dell'Oltregiuba: Una sanseviera
gigantesca da fibre tessile. "L'Italia Coloniale."
Roma-Milano 1937.
249 p.

CARPANETTI,G.

Il cotone nella valle del Giuba.
"Agricoltura Coloniale". Firenze 1907.
51 p.

CONSORZIO AGRICOLO SOMALO.

La cotonicoltura nella zona delle concessioni
di Merca e Genale. "Bollettino dell'Associazione
Cotoniera." Fasc. No. 5. Milano 1930.

280 pp.

CORTINOIS, A.

Cotonicoltura e mezzi di trasporto nella
Somalia Italiana. "Rivista Coloniale." Roma 1908.
40 pp.

DORIA, T.

Il cotone in Somalia. "Illustrazione Coloniale."
Milano 1926.
119 pp.

DOUWES, H.

The cytological relationship of
"Gossypium somalense." "Gurke Journal of
Genetics." 1951.

EL-MARASHLY, M.S.

Il cotone in Somalia: versione italiana
a cura del Dr. Umberto Manzella. Camera di
Commercio Industria e Agricoltura della Somalia.
Stamperia AFIS. Mogadiscio 25 Gennaio 1955.
30 pp. ills.

FOLCO, A.

Note sulla campagna cotoniera 1933-34, nel
Comprensorio di Genale. "Agricoltura Coloniale."
Firenze 1934.
432 pp.

GASBARRI, L.

Studio per una nuova regolamentazione della
coltivazione, lavorazione industriale e commercio
del cotone in Somalia. AFIS. Mogadiscio 1955.

GOVERNO DELLA SOMALIA.

Documentazione della elaborazione dell-ordinanze
sul cotone e modifiche proposte dal Consiglio
Territoriale. Mogadiscio.

GUIDOTTI, R.

La coltivazicne del cotone nella Somalia Italiana
(zona di Genale). "Bollettino dell'Associazione
Cotoniera." No.11. Milano 1929.
722 pp.

LEVI, C.

Su alcuni caratteri tecnologici dei cotoni della
Somalia Italiana e dell'Eritrea. "Rassegna Economica
delle Colonie." Istituto Poligrafico dello Stato.
Roma 1932.
12 pp.

MALLARINI, A.G.

Progetto per una societa per la
coltivazione del cotone nel Benadir.
"Rivista Coloniale." Roma 1909.
428 pp.

MATTEI, G.E.

Sopra alcune specie di cotone indigeno
della Somalia Italiana. "Giardino Palermo."
Vol. II.   Fasc.No.IV.   Palermo 1916.
221 pp.

_____

Il cotone in Somalia. "Giardino Palermo."
Vol.VIII.   Palermo 1925.
38 pp.

MAUGINI, A.

La coltivazione del cotone nella Somalia
Italiana. Congresso Internazionale del Cotone
(Atti). 1932.

MAZZOCCHI, ALEMANNI N.

La regione del Giuba e la coltura del cotone
nella Somalia Italiana. "Illustrazione Coloniale."
No.13.   Milano 1920.
117 pp.

_____

Il cotone nel Benadir ed il problema
dell'irrigazione.
"Illustrazione Coloniale."
No.4.   Milano 1921.
131 pp.

ONOR, G.

Cotton possibilities in Italian Somaliland
and Jubaland (British East Africa).
"Atti III° Congresso Internaz. Agricoltura
Tropicale."
Vol. I. 1914.
240 pp.

RAPETTI,G.

Istruzione sulla coltura del cotone.
"Annali S.A.I.S." Genova 1932.
35 p.

ROMANENGO, F.

La coltivazione del cotone in Somalia.
(Zona Genale-Merca) "Bollettino dell'Associazione
Cotoniera." No. 9-11. Milano 1929.
578-724 pp.

SCAVONE,G.

Il cotone in Somalia: la tecnica colturale
in rapporto ai fattori ecologici. "Rassegna
Economica delle Colonie." Roma 1934.
933 p.

REPUBBLICA SOMALA.

Brevi notiziari agricoli sulla cotonicoltura.
Ministero Agricoltura e Zootecnoa. Mogadiscio.
5 pp. tables.

S.A.I.S.

Cotone 1930 in Somalia. "Annali S.A.I.S."
Genova 1930.
49 p.

SCASSELLATI-SFORZOLINI,G.

Appunti sulla coltivazione del cotone
nella Somalia Meridionale. Tipografia Gio.
Ramella. 1915.
18 pp.

WILD,C.E.

La coltivazione del cotone in Somalia e
l'azienda Italo-Somala. "Bollettino
dell'Associazione Cotoniera." Milano 1925.
321 p.

7. Forest

AMMINISTRAZIONE FIDUCIARIA ITALIANA DELLA SOMALIA.

Studio sulla palma da datteri
in Migiurtinia. AFIS. Direzione
per lo Sviluppo Economico.

Mogadiscio 12 Giugno 1953.
18 pp.

Relazione sui problemi dell'incenso
in Somalia e sulla organizzazione e
prima attivita delle Cooperative del
Consorzio. AFIS. Direzione per la
Sviluppo Economico. Mogadiscio II Giugno 1955.
12 pp.

ANONYMOUS

Ricerche sulla micoflora dei terreni
forestali Somali."Allionia." No. 2. 1954.
245-293 pp.

Il capok nella Somalia e la callotropis
nella Libia ed Eritrea. "Bollettino Informazione
Economica." Ministero delle Colonie. Roma 1923.
51 p.

Il capok somalo. "Illustrazione
Coloniale." No. I. Milano 1924.
30 p.

La coltivazione del capok in Somalia.
"La Somalia Italiana." No. 5. Mogadiscio 1925.
I p.

Il caucciu' e la nostra Colonia." La Somalia
Italiana." Anno IV. No. 2. Mogadiscio 1928.

L'incenso della Migiurtinia." La Somalia
Italiana" Anno IV. No. I. Mogadiscio 1928.

Prove di carbonizzazione del
legno nella Somalia Italiana.
"Il Legno". 1929.
286 p.

BARBACCI.

La boscaglia della zona dunosa del

Benadir ed i provvedimenti per la sua
tutela e per il rimboschimento delle dune
della costa. "Agricoltura Coloniale." Firenze 192i.
578 p.

BEGUINOT,A.

Frutti e semi della formazione a mangrovia
raccolti lungo la costa somala: Missione
scientifica Stefanini-Paoli nella Somalia
Italiana Meridionale."Bollettino Societa
Geografica Italiana." Fasc. No. I. Roma 1915.
1915 p.

_____

Sulla costituzione dei boschi di Mangrovie
nella Somalia Italiana. "Bollettino Societa
Geografica Italiana." Fasc. No. 3-4. Roma 1918.
295 p.

BOCCA,B.

Le mangrovie Somale e la loro messa in
valore. "Illustrazione Coloniale." No. 2.
Milano 1938.
37 p.

_____

La valorizzazione delle mangrovie Somale.
Atti III Congresso Internazionale di Chimica."
Roma 1938.
861 p.

BOZZA, C.

Incenso della Migiurtinia. "Materie Prime
d'Italia e delle Impero." No. 12. 1940.
492 p.

BRANCA,A.

Relazione sulla missione agraria
forestale in Migiutinia. Istituto
Agronomico per l'Oltremare. Fasc. No. 3133.
Firenze 1956.
II pp.

_____

Le piante spontanee della Somalia e loro
utilizzazione. "Rivista di Agricoltura
Subtropicale e Tropicale". Nos. 4-9.
Firenze Aprile-Settembre 1960.
608-651 pp.

BRILLI,P. AND MULAS,S.

Note su la Cordeauxia Edulis:Jeheb.
"Agricoltura Coloniale." Firenze 1939.
565 p.

CECON,G.

Prove con carburante nazionale proveniente
dalla Somalia. "Il Legno." 1930.
92 p.

CHIOVENDA,E.

La flora somala. (2 Vol.) Sind.Italiana
di Arti Grafiche. Roma 1929.
Vol. I. 436 pp. ills.
Vol. II. 482 pp. ills.

CIFERRI,R.

La vegetazione dell'Impero: Boschi e
prodotti forestali della Somalia.
L'Alpe" Nos. 13-14. 1937.
404 p.

Osservazioni sul genere Swietenia e
possibilita di acclimitazione del vero
mogano. (Swietenia Mahogani) nella regione
del Giuba. "L'Alpe". No. 4. 1938.
89 p.

CORNI,G.

Il carbone di legna somala come
carburante negli autotrasporti.
"Atti III Congresso Internazionale
Carbonio Carburante." 1937.

CORMIO,R.

Caratteristiche anatomiche e meccaniche
del legno Rhizophora Mucronata d'Oltregiuba
e sue applicazioni. Lignum. 1938.

La Rhizophora Mucronata dell'Oltregiuba.
Lignum Gennaio - Febbraio 1939.

L'Avicennia Marina dell'Oltregiuba.
Lignum 1939.

Caratteristiche anatomiche e meccaniche del
legno di Avicennia Marine (Forsk) dell'Oltregiuba
e sue applicazioni. "Atti VIII Congresso Internazionale
di Agricoltura Tropicale e Subtropicale". Vol. IV.
(C 108). Tripoli 1939.
16 pp.

DOWSON,V.H.W.

Date cultivation in British Somaliland:
Report to the Government of the Somaliland
Protectorate. Hargeisa 15 November 1947.
120 pp. bibl. ills.

_____

Report on date scheme: report to the governor
of the Somaliland Protectorate. Jibut 7 March 1954.
43 pp.

_____

Dates in Somaliland and Libya: Report to the
Thirty-Second Meeting of Date Growers' Institute.
Indio, California 23 April 1955.

ENGLER,A.

Ueber die Vegetationsverhaltnisse
des Somalilandes. "Sitzungsberichte
di Preussischen Akademie D. Wissenschaften."
Berlin 1904.
355-416 pp.

EDWARDS, D.C.

Report on the grazing areas of the Northern
Frontier District of Kenya (NFD). Department
of Agriculture and Forestry. Nairobi.

_____

A survey of the grazing areas of British
Somaliland. Hargeisa 1942.

FABRIUS, U.

Sulla valorizzazione dei cascami di
noce dum. "Rassegna Economica delle Colonie."
Roma 1933.
53 p.

FOOD AND AGRICULTURAL ORGANIZATION.

Date production. Expanded Program of
Technical Assistance. FAO Report No. 1731.
FAO. Rome 1963.

64 pp. ills. map.

GIORDANO,G.

Per la tutela del patrimonio forestale
in Somalia. "Monti e Boschi." 1950.
316 p.

GLEISBERG,CHR.

Forstwirtsschaftliche probleme des
Entwicklungs-landes Somalia. Afrika heute.
Bonn 21 Novembre 1964.
273-274 pp.

GOVERNO DELLA SOMALIA.

L'incenso della Somalia Italiana. "Bollettino
Informazione Economica." Ministero delle Colonie.
Roma 1925.
335 p.

GUIDOTTI,R.

Gomme e resine della zona di
Oddur nella Somalia Italiana.
Istituto Poligrafico dello Stato.
Roma 1932.
9 pp.

La mirra. "Rivista delle Colonie Italiane".
No. 4. Roma 1941.
489 p.

La palma dum nella Somalia Italiana.
Rassegna Economica delle Colonie."
Roma 1930.
10 p.

L'incenso della Migiurtinia. "Rivista
Italiana di Essenze e Profumi." Milano 1930.
18 p.

KLEMME,MARVIN.

Forestry and range management survey
Somalia, East Africa. U.S.Operations
Mission to Italy. Rome 1957.
23 pp. map.

A survey of forestry,grazing and
related land use in Somalia. International
Cooperation Administration.Mogadishu 1957.
54 pp.

LACHERADE,G.

Une plante cactoide du T.F.A.I.:
la stapelie. "Revue Pount." No. 5.
La Societe D'etudes de l'Afrique
Orientale. Djibouti 1968.

LAWRIE,J.J.

Acacias and the Somali.
Empire Forest Review". No. 3.
Vol. 33. London 1954.
234-238 pp.

LUCHINI,R.

Legnami utilizzabili della Somalia
Italiana. "Rivista di Agricoltura
Subtropicale e Tropicale. "Firenze 1948.
55 p.

MAMELI, C.E.

Sulla Cordeuaxia edulis (Jeheb) della
Somalia. "Atti Societa Progresso Scienza
Riunione XXV°". Vol. IV.   Roma 1937.
385 p.

MARASSI,A.

Della Cordeauxia edulis. "Agricoltura
Coloniale." Firenze 1939.
613 pp.

MARESCA,A.

Sulle essenze di Eucaliptus globulus
Labil. della Somalia e del Benadir.
"Rivista Italiana di Essenze e Profumi."
No. 10. Milano 1950.
498 p.

MATTEI,G.E.

Contributo alla flora della Somalia Italiana:
Centuria I e Centuria II. Orto Palermo.Vol.
VII. Fasc. Nos. 1-2-3. Palermo 1908.

————————————

Una nuova pianta a caucciu nel Benadir.
"Rivista Tecnica e Coloniale di Scienze

Applicate." No. 6. Bari 1911.
81p.

MAHONEY,FRANK.

A report of pilot project in range management
near Afmadu. United States Agency for International
Development. Mogadishu.
7 pp.

MAUGINI,A.

Il capok nella Somalia Italiana."Rivista delle
Colonie." Roma 1927/28.
161 p.

MOLL,F.

Il legname di Mangrovia:(Rhizophora mucranta).
"Il Legno." 1940.
295 p.

NELSON,N.T.

Range management in Somalia. United States Agency
for International Development. Mogadishu 1958.
45 pp.

NUTINI,G.

La palma da dattero in Migiurtinia. "Rivista di
Agricoltura Subtropicale e Tropicale." Nos. 1-3.
Firenze Gennaio-Marzo 1955.
67-77 pp.

ONOR,R.

La Cordeauxia edulis (Jeheb). "Agricoltura
Coloniale." Firenze 1911.
372 p.

ORNU',A.

La Cordeauxia edulis (Jeheb).
"Autarchia Alimentare." No. 6. 1938.
7 p.

PAOLI,G.

Contributo allo studio dei rapporti tra le acacie
e le formiche. Memor. Societa Entomologica Italiana.
Vol. IX. 1930.
131 p.

PAX,F.

Euphorbiaceae somalenses a D.D. Robecchi-Brichetti

et Riva in Harar et Somalia lectae. "Annali Istituto
Botanica." Vol. VI. Fasc. No. III. 1896.

PELLEGRINESCHI,V.

Incenso e resine della Migiurtinia.
"L'Idea Coloniale." No. 8. Roma 1937.
25 p.

PIROTTA,R.

Acacia Robecchi. "Bollettino Societa
Botanica Italiana." 1893.
61 p.

REVOIL,G.

Faune et flore des pays comalis:
(Afrique Orientale). Challamel.
Paris 1882.

ROVESTI,P.

L'incenso della Somalia Italiana.
"Rivista Italiana di Essenze e Profumi."
No. 12. Milano 1935.
350 p.

SACCO,T.

Due nuove specie per la Somalia:
Corchorus tridens L. ed Euphorbia
prostrata. "Webbia." No. 15. Firenze 1960.
5 p.

L'azienda di Uar Mahan: Considerazioni
floristiche primo contributo."Rivista di
Agricoltura Subtropicale e Tropicale."
Nos. 4-9. Firenze Aprile-Settembre 1960.
425-453 pp.

SCARFI,P.

Maidi,la prima resina Italiana.
"Rassegna d'Oltremare." No. 9. Genova 1936.
48 p.

SCASSELLATI-SFORZOLINI,G.

Piante cauccifere della Somalia
Italiana Meridionale. "Agricoltura
Coloniale." Firenze 1915.

SCERIF MUSSALLEM ALI.

La palma da dattero in Somalia.

"Rivista di Agricoltura Subtropicale
e Tropicale". Nos. 4-9. Firenze Aprile-
Settembre 1960.
661-665 pp.

SENNI,L.

La palma dum. "L'Alpe." 1930.
533 p.

_____

Visioni forestale della Somalia.
"Agricoltura Coloniale". No. 2.
Firenze Febbraio 1931.
55-65 pp. ills.

_____

Le condizioni forestale della Somalia.
Atti 2° Congresso Studi Coloniali."
Vol. VI. 1934.
1014 p.

_____

Gli alberi e le formazioni legnose
della Somalia Italiana. Istituto Agricolo
Coloniale Italiano. Firenze 1935.
305 pp. ills.

_____

L'utilizzazione delle mangrovie nella Somalia
per opere della S.A.Tannini d'Etiopia. "Atti
VIII Congresso Internazionale di Agricoltura
Tropicale e Subtropicale." 1939.

SOMALILAND PROTECTORATE.

Pastures of British Somaliland:
Review by Military Governor.
Cowasjee Dinshaw & Bros Ltd.
(Printers) Aden 1947.
45 pp.

SORRENTINO, L.

Boscaglia Somala. "Etiopia."
No. 5. 1937.
35 p.

SUKERT, E.

Considerazioni e proposte sui problemi
forestali in Somalia. Istituto Agronomico
per l'"Oltremare." Fasc. No. 3809." Firenze 1960.
5 pp.

TOZZI,R.

Principali essenze legnose della zona
del Giuba. "Agricoltura Coloniale."
No. 3. Firenze Marzo 1941.
119-125 pp. ills.

TRIULZI,G.A.

Somalia pastorale. III Fiera della
Somalia. (Numero Unico). Mogadiscio 1955.
28-31 pp.

TROPEA, C.

Panicum Bossi,nuova graminacea della
Somalia Italiana." Orto Palermo." Vol. X.
Palermo 1911.
100 p.

WIXOM,CALVIN.

Wire fence construction. United
States Agency for International
Development. Mogadiscio December 1963.
9 pp. ills.

Grassland use - past and present.
United States Agency for International
Development. Mogadiscio 1964.

Range management: Somali Republic.
USAID Report. Mogadiscio 1965.
39 pp.

ZAVATTARI,E.

Le caratteristiche della flora nei
territori posti tra lo alto Giuba ed
il lago Rodolfo. "Illustrazione Coloniale."
No. 9. Milano 1941.
13 p.

8.   Grain Crops

AMMINISTRAZIONE FIDUCIARIA ITALIANA DELLA SOMALIA.

Relazione sui risultati delle prove condotte
in Somalia nel 1953 con sementi di mais forniti
della A.M.S.A. Istituto Agronomico per l'"Oltremare.
Fasc. No. 3814. Firenze 1954.
10 pp.

ANONYMOUS.

Possibilita di utilizzazione della manioca
nel Benadir. "Bollettino Informazione Economica
del Ministero Colonie." No. I. Roma 1925.
71 p.

AUDISIO,G.

La manioca in Somalia. Istituto Chimico e
Farmaceutico. Stamperia AFIS. Mogadiscio 1955.
32 pp.

BIGI,F.

Note sulla coltura del granturco in Somalia e sui
risultati di alcuni esperimenti di coltivazione di ibridi.
Rivista di Agricoltura Subtropicale e Tropicale."
Nos. 4-6. Firenze Aprile-Settembre 1962.
40 pp.

BRANDOLINI,A.

Il mais in Somalia:prospettiva di miglioramento.
"Maydica." No. 2. Stazione Sperimentale di Maisoltura.
Bergamo Aprile 1959.
46-54 pp.

BROSS,H.

Grain study Somalia. U.S. Operations Mission
to Italy. Rome 1954.
13 pp.

CENTRAL AGRICULTURAL RESEARCH STATION, AFGOI.

How to grow sorghum in Somalia. USAID/SOMALI REPUBLIC.
University of Wyoming Team. Mogadiscio November 1968.
4 pp.

———————

Growing maize in Somalia. USAID/SOMALI REPUBLIC.
University of Wyoming Team. Mogadiscio November 1968.
4 pp.

———————

Sorghum (Dura) production in Somalia.
USAID/SOMALI REPUBLIC. University of
Wyoming Team. Mogadiscio September 1968.
9 pp.

FARIAS,G.

Relazione sull'attivita svolta dalla sezione di
Maisoltura di Afgoi negli anni 1959. Istituto
Agronomico per l''Oltremare. Fasc. No. 3182. Firenze 1959.

8 pp.

Considerazione sul miglioramento della coltura
del mais in Somalia. "Rivista di Agricoltura Subtropicale"
e Tropicale. Nos. 4-9. Firenze Aprile-Settembre 1960.
550-555 pp.

GERMAN,E.

Somalia Grain Study. International Cooperation
Administration (I.C.A.) Rome 1953.

MARIANI,G.

Possibilita di miglioramento dell'economia agricola delle
regioni ad agricoltura seccagna:direttive per una efficace
propoganda, corsi per L'addestramento del personale.
Istituto Agronomico per l"Oltremare. Fasc. No. 3809. Firenze 1960.
5 pp.

WIXOM, CALVIN.

Seeding feed grains and forage crops. U.S. Agency
for International Development. Mogadiscio January I, 1964.
4 pp.

9. Horticulture

ANONYMOUS.

La coltivazione del papaia nella
Somalia Italiana. "Bollettino Informazione
Economica del Ministero Colonie." Roma 1927.
577 p.

BRANCA,A.

Notizie sul pompelmo in Somalia.
Istituto Agronomico per l"Oltremare.
Fasc. No. 4294. Firenze 1965.
II pp.

CENTRAL AGRICULTURAL RESEARCH STATION, AFGOI.

A new citrus variety for Somalia: "the bearss lime":
A progress report. USAID/SOMALI REPUBLIC. University
of Wyoming Team. Mogadiscio June 1969.
6 pp. ills.

Bulb onion production. USAID/SOMALI REPUBLIC.
University of Wyoming Team. Mogadiscio October 1968.
3 pp. ills.

Grapefruit production in Somalia. USAID/SOMALI REPUBLIC.
University of Wyoming Team. Mogadiscio December 1968.
20 pp. ills. appendices.

CHIAROMONTE,A.

Per l'introduzione in Italia del pompelmo della Somalia.
"Rivista di Agricoltura Subtropicale e Tropicale."
Nos. 10-12. Firenze 1952.

GIORIO,G.

Analisi dei costi di produzione della papaina in Somalia.
"Rivista di Agricoltura Subtropicale e Tropicale."
Nos. 4-9. Firenze 1960.
571-574 pp.

G.B.

Aspetti della produzione di ortaggi
ed agrumi. "Somalia d'Oggi." No. 4.Mogadiscio 1957.
50 p.

MAZZARI,G.

La coltura dell'arancia nel comprensorio di
bonifica di Genale. L'Agricoltura Coloniale."
Vol.XXVI. Firenze Giugno 1937.

PARSI,O.

Esperienze sul valore di grani di leguminose
della Somalia nella alimentazione dei bovini.
"Atti Congresso Nazionale Latte." 1932.

SACCO,T.

I frutti del citrus hystrik DC Subsp acida
(Roxb) Bonavia var abyssinica (Riccobono)
Chiov. della Somalia. "Ricerche biometriche).
Nos. 4-6. Firenze Aprile-Giugno 1958.
247-259 pp.

─────────────────

II citrus histrix Dc Subsp acida
(Roxb) Bonavia var abyssinica (Riccobono)
Chiov. della Somalia. "Allionia." Vol. II.
Fasc. No. 2. Torino 1955.
419-428 pp.

TOZZI,R.

Prospettive della coltura dell'ananasso in Somalia.
"Somalia d'Oggi." No. 4. Mogadiscio 1957.
16-18 pp.

10. Irrigation

A.F.I.S.,
Elaborati tecnici e finanziari per la
creazione di un consorzio irriguo Somalo
nel basso Uebi. Stamperia A.F.I.S.
Mogadiscio 1955.
22 pp.

Studio di massima per l''adduzione delle
acque del Giuba al Descek Uamo: Lavori in
corso per la prima sistemazione del canale
di presa. Mogadiscio 6, Giugno 1955.

AGRICULTURAL RESEARCH STATION, AFGOI.

Irrigation development, United States.
Agency for International Development.
Mogadishu March 6, 1964.
63 pp. ills. Diagrs.

Irrigation plans, designs and fundamentals.
USAID/SOMALI REPUBLIC. University of Wyoming.
Laramie, Wyoming September 24, 1965.
59 pp. map, diagrs. tables.

ANSALDI, G.

Le acque del Giuba nell'agricoltura della
Somalia Italiana. "Rassegna Economica delle
Colonie." Nos. 5-6. Roma 1932.
520 p.

CARNIGLIA, MANFREDI and MORTARA.

La regolazione del Giuba: elemento fondamentale per lo sviluppo della Somalia.
Milano 1950.
10 pp.

CONFORTI, E.

Aspetti del problema idrico nell'agricoltura
della Somalia. "Rivista di Agricoltura
Subtropicale e Tropicale. "Firenze,
Luglio-Settembre 1953.

La Valle dell'Uebi Scebeli. Direzione
per lo Sviluppo Economico. Ispettorato
Agricoltura e Zootechnico. Stamperia A.F.I.S.
Mogadiscio 1955.
34 pp. Maps.

AGRICULTURE

DE ANGELIS, G.

La diga di Genale. "La Somalia Italiana".
No. 2. Mogadiscio 1926.

ESPOSITO, G.

La diga di Genale. "La Somalia Italiana."
No. 2. Mogadiscio 1926.

———————————

Quantitativo di acque occorrente ad
irrigare le varie colture principali
della Somalia. Istituto Agronomico per l''Oltremare.
Fasc. No. 3450. Firenze 1965.
18 pp.

FAVILIA, G.

Studio per l'adduzione delle acque del
Giuba al descech Uamo. A.F.I.S. Mogadiscio 1955.
7 pp.

———————————

Captazione e sfruttamento di acque superficiali
ad uso agricolo e pastorale in Somalia. "Rivista
di Agricoltura Subtropicale e Tropicale."
Nos. 4-9. Firenze Aprile-Settember 1960.
333-376 pp.

———————————

Nuovo comprensorio agricolo di Belet Uen-
utililizzazione parziale delle acque di piena
dello Scebeli. Mogadiscio.

MANFREDI, G.

La regolazione del Giuba elemento fondamentale
per lo sviluppo della Somalia." I$^{\circ}$ Convegno
Economico Italo Africano." Milano 1952.

———————————

La regolazione dei fiumi della Somalia.
"Africa." No. 2. Roma 1953.
50-51 pp.

MAZZOCCHI-ALEMANNI, N.

I nostri grandi problemi coloniali: lo
sbarramento del Giuba. "Agricoltura Coloniale."
No. 10. Firenze 31 Dicembre 1919.
387-426 pp. ills. map. charts.

POLACCI, G. CIFERRI, R. AND GALLOTTI, M.

Un metodo rapido per la determinazione
dell'acqua nelle banane verdi con osservazione
sulla campionatura dei caschi. "Atti Istituto
Botanica Universita di pavia." Serie IV°. Vol. IX° pavia 1937.
279 p.

SERRAZANETTI, R.M.

L'irrigazione nei paesi caldi (Somalia)
"Agricoltura Coloniale" Firenze 1931.
225 p.

SOMALI REPUBLIC.

Project report on irrigation of lands
under cotton and oil crops state farms
in the Republic of Somalia. 3 Volumes.
Technopromexport. Moscow 1964.
Vol.I. 432 pp. (explanatory notes) map. drawings, charts, tables.
Vol. II. 86 pp. map. drawings, charts. tables.
Vol. III. 86 pp. map drawings, charts. tables.

SUKERT, E.

Il problema dell'irrigazione in Somalia.
"Rivista di Agricoltura Subtropicale e
Tropicale." Nos. 4-9. Firenze 1960.
491-494 pp.

TOZZI, R.

Utilizzazione agricola delle acque del Giuba.
"Agricoltura Coloniale." Firenze 1941.

––––––––––––––

Contributo allo studio del regime idraulico del
fiume Scebeli per una piu razionale utilizzazione
delle piene. "Rivista di Agricoltura Subtropicale
e Tropicale." Nos. 7-9. Firenze 1960.

11. Land Tenure

ANONYMOUS.

Gli inizi della politica fondiaria
al Benadir secondo l'onorevole
De Martino. "Rivista Coloniale."
Vol. VI, Roma 1909.

––––––––––––––

Land tenure and Colonization.
"International Review of Agricultural
Economics." Vol. 75. 1917.
94-115 pp.

––––––––––––––

La concessione dei terreni agrari nella
Somalia. "Agricoltura Coloniale."
Firenze 1918.
253 p.

———————————

Disciplinare tipo per le Concessioni
di terreno a scopo agricolo nella
Somalia Italiana. "Agricoltura Coloniale."
Firenze 1927.
389 p.

———————————

Norme per le concessioni agricole
in Somalia. "Rassegna Economica delle
Colonie." Roma 1928.
296 p.

———————————

Modificazione all'Ordinamento per
le concessioni agricole nella Somalia
Italiana (R.D. del 24 Gennaio 1929).
"Rassegna Economica delle Colonie."
Roma 1929.

ARFELLI, R.

Problemi dell'agricoltura africana:
le proprieta in Somalia. "Atti del
VII Convegno Economico Italo-Africano."
Milano 1959.
68-70 pp.

BERTOLA, ARNALDO.

Sulla questione fondiaria in
Somalia. Stamperia Missione.
Mogadiscio 18 Gennaio 1959.
7 pp.

COLUCCI, M.

Sistemi di accertamento e di pubblicita
dei diritti fondiari nelle Colonie.
Istituto Superiore di Studi Coloniali.
Cesare Alfieri. Firenze 1934.

CUCINOTTA, E.

Proprieta fondiaria in Somalia.
Nuovo Digesto Italiano." Vol. X. 1939.
767 p.

DE SANCTIS, C.

Odissea dei concessionari in Somalia.
"Africa" No. 3. Roma 1947.
53 p.

FERRARI, G.

Il basso Giuba e le concessioni
agricole della Goscia. "Bollettino
Societa Geografica Italiana." Roma 1910.
1079-1203-1310 pp.

GOVERNO DELLA SOMALIA ITALIANA.

Disciplinare di concessione di terreno
a scopo agricolo con trasferimento della
proprieta. Direzione Affari della Coloniaazaione
e del Lavoro. Regia Stamperia della Colonia.
Mogadiscio 1939.
15 pp.

JORGENSON, HAROLD T.

Land tenure problems in the
Republic of Somalia.
International Cooperation Administration.
Mogadiscio 1960.
61 pp.

MANASSEI, T.

La ripartizione delle terre
concesse in Somalia. "Rivista
Coloniale." Roma 1910.
67 p.

MANETTI, C.

L'agricoltura nella Somalia
Italiana ed il nuovo ordinamento
fondiario. "Agricoltura Coloniale."
Firenze 1911.
114 p.

ISTITUTO AGRONOMICO PER L'OLTREMARE.

Principali leggi e decreti interessanti
il settore agrario (Aprile 1950-Aprile 1960)
in Somalia. "Rivista di Agricoltura Subtropicale
e Tropicale." Nos. 4-9. Firenze 1960.
686 -692 pp.

SANDONA', A.

Il regime fondiario e la colonizzazione
dell'Africa Italiana: Eritrea, Somalia,
Libia. Istituto Internazionale D'Agricoltura.
Roma 1917.
61 pp.

SCARPA, ANTONIO.

Della proprieta fondiaria in Somalia.
"Agricoltura Coloniale." No. 8.
Firenze Agosto 1923.
281-294 pp.

UNITED NATIONS TRUSTEESHIP COUNCIL.

Land legislation and land tenure in
Somaliland under Italian Administration.
Committee on the Rural Economic
Development of the Trust Territories.
New York 1951.

Land alienation and land and population
distribution in Somaliland under Italian
Administration. Committee on the Rural
Economic Development of the Trust
Territories. New York 1951.

Population, land categories and tenure
in Somaliland under Italian Administration.
Committee on the Rural Economic Development
of the Trust Territories. New York 1952.

12. Oil Seeds

AFFERNI,E.

Alcuni prodotti oleosi della
Somalia Italiana. "Rassegna Economica
Delle Colonie". Roma 1937.
785 p.

BALDASSARRI,L.

La coltura del cocco nella Somalia
Italiana. "Rassegna Economica delle
Colonie". Nos. 9/10. Roma 1932.
1034 p.

BIGI,F.

La coltura dell'arachide nella
Somalia Italiana. "Olearia." 1948.
582 p.

L'arachide nelle condizioni ambientali
della Somalia Italiana meridionale.
"Olearia." 1949.
339 p.

BRUNO, A.

La palma da cocco in Somalia.
"illustrazione Coloniale." No.6. Milano 1934.
36 pp.

CHIAROMONTE, A.

Il problema della sesamia nella Somalia
Italiana. "Rivista di Agricoltura Subtropicale
e Tropicale." Nos. 1-3. Firenze Gennaio-Marzo 1948.
42-47 pp.

GUIDOTTI, R.

Il cocco nella Somalia Italiana.
"Agricoltura Coloniale". Firenze 1930.
456 pp.

MAGNANENSI, P.

L'arachide sul lungo Giuba.
"Agricoltura Coloniale." Firenze 1931.
372 pp.

MAUGINI, A.

Studio analitico di alcuni semi
oleosi della Somalia Italiana.
"Agricoltura Coloniale." Firenze 1914.
171 pp.

MAZZARI, C.

La coltura dell'arachide nel comprensorio
di bonifica di Genale. "Agricoltura Coloniale."
Firenze 1937.
273-322-378 pp.

MONILE, F.

Prodotti e semi oleosi della Somalia
Italiana. "Commercio Italo Africano."
No.7. Genova 1933.

PAOLI, G.

Una pianta a seme oleosi della Somalia
Italiana (solanum Arundo). "Agricoltura
Coloniale." Firenze 1938.
253 pp.

RAPETTI, G.

Notizie sulla coltivazione dell'arachide.
"Annali S.A.I.A." Genova 1933.
47 pp.

La coltivazione delle arachidi nella Somalia
Italiana. Estraz. "Rassegna Economica
della Colonie." Istituto Poligrafico dello Stato.
Roma 1934.
19 pp.

TOZZI, R.

Le colture inondate del Giuba. "Atti II
Congresso Studi Coloniali." Vol. VI. 1934.
964 pp.

La coltura delle arachide nelle sciambe
indigene del Giuba. "Somalia Italiana."
Nos. 1-6. Mogadiscio 1931.
7 pp.

13. Plant Pathology

BECCARI, F.

I risultati di applicazioni su
vasta scala per la repressione
del marciume del rachide dei
regimi di banano.
"Rivista di Agricoltura Subtropicale
e Tropicalle."
Nos. 10-11. Firenze 1961.
410-423 pp.

_____

Relazione riassuntiva sulle ricerche
tendenti ad isolare un prodotto fungicida
efficace per la repressione del marciume
del rachide del regime di banano somalo.
Istituto Agronomico per l''Oltremare.
Fasc. No. 4267. Firenze 1961.
3 pp.

_____

Relazione sulle osservazioni compiute
a Genova il 6/7/1961 sul lotto sperimentale
di banane trattato contro il marciume del
rachide e trasportato in Italia con la
Motonaca Castelnuovo. Istituto Agronomico
per l''Oltremare. Fasc. No. 4266. Firenze.
4 pp.

_____ AND CERRI, P.G.

Ricerche e prove di lotta contro le
crittogame nocive al banano. (II).
Prove applicative sulle azione di alcune
fungicidi sintetici e di un fungistatico
antibiotico sulle degenerazioni patologiche
dei tagli del rachide e dei traumi del regime
di banano dopo la raccolta. "Rivista di
Agricoltura Subtropicale e Tropicale."
Nos. 10-12. Firenze Ottobre-Dicembre 1960.
752-762 pp.

_____

Ricerche e prove di lotta contro le
crittogame nocive al banano. (IV);
I risultati di una spediti in stiva refrigerata della
Somalia all'Italia. "Rivista di Agricoltura
Subtropicale e Tropicale." Nos. 1-3.
Firenze Gennaio-Marzo 1961.
52-73 pp.

_____

Ricerche e prove di lotta contro le
crittogame nocive al banano (V): Altre
prove applicative sull'azione di un
fungistatico antibiotico sulle alterazioni
patologiche dei tagli del rachide e dei
traumi del regime di banano dopo la raccolta.
"Rivista di Agricoltura Subtropicale e Tropicale."

AGRICULTURE

Nos. 1-3. Firenze Gennaio-Marzo 1961.
75-82 pp.

BECCARI,F. AND FENILI,G.A.

Relazione sulla missione di collegamento
compiuta dal 13 al 21 settembre 1960 dai
Dottori Beccari e Fenili presso l'Osservatorio
per le malattie delle piante per il Lazio e
presso l'Istituto di Entomologia agraria di
Catania. Istituto Agrnonomico per l'Oltremare.
Fasc. No. 4272. Firenze 1960.
4 pp.

_____AND GOLATO,C.

Ricerche orientative sull'azione in
vitro di un composto quaternario di
Ammonio e di un antibiotico su coltura
pure di patogeni del frutto di banano.
"Rivista di Agricoltura Subtropicale e
Tropicale." Nos. 1-3. Firenze Gennaio-Marzo 1964.
89-101 pp.

_____

Note sull'azione dell'antibiotico
Lagosin su colture pure di Gloeosporium
musarum Cooke e Massee. "Rivista di Agricoltura
Subtropicale e Tropicale." Nos. 4-6.
Firenze Aprile-Giugno 1963.
176-182 pp.

_____

Ricerche e prove di lotta contro le
crittogame nocive al banano. (I): prove
orientative sull'azione "in vitro di
alcuni fungistatici su colture pure di
Gloeosporium musarum" (Cooke Massee).
"Rivista di Agricoltura Subtropicale e
Tropicale." Nos. 10-12. Firenze Ottobre-Dicembre 1959.
411-427 pp.

_____

Ricerche e prove di lotta contro le
crittogame nocive al banano. (VI):
Intorno agli affotti macro e microscopici
della Nystatin del TCNB e del PONB in Latex
sintetico su coltura pure di "Gloeosporium
musarum" Cooke e Massee. "Rivista di Agricoltura
Subtropicale e Tropicale." Nos. 4-6.
Firenze Aprile-Giugno 1961.
163-181 pp.

BECCARI,F. AND OTHERS.

Un grave parassita fungino del banano
nuovo per la Somalia. "(Cercospora Musae Zimm.)"
"Rivista di Agricoltura Subtropicale e Tropicale."
Nos. 7-9. Firenze Luglio-Settembre 1963.
248-250 pp.

I risultati di una spedizione sperimentale
dalla Somalia all'Italia di banane in mani
trattate con un quaternario ed un antibiotico.
"Rivista di Agricoltura Subtropicale e
Tropicale." Nos. 10-12. Firenze
Ottobre - Dicembre 1964.
446-457 pp.

Ricerche e prove di lotta contro
le crittogame nocive al banano.
(III) Prove orientative in vitro
contro il "Gloeosporium musarum"
Cooke e Massee e di alcuni preparati
fungicidi di sintese destinati alla
prevenzione del marciume del rachide del
regime di banano. "Rivista di Agricoltura
Subtropicale e Tropicale." Nos. 10-12.
Firenze Ottobre-Dicembre 1960.
763-781 pp.

Ricerche e prove di lotta contro le
crittogame nocive al banano. Monografie
Agrarie Subtropicale e Tropicale. No. 82.
Istituto Agronomico per l'Oltremare.
Firenze 1961.
99 pp. tables. bilb.

BENEDETTO,P.

Notizie sugli esperimenti per
diagnosticare il male del raggrinzimento
del cotone: Stagione Der-Gilal 1929-30.
"Annali S.A.I.S." Genova 1930.
71p.

BIGI,F. AND CIFERRI,F.

Segnalazione della rosetta
dell'arachide nella Somalia Italiana.
"Agricoltura Coloniale." Firenze 1938.
105 p.

AGRICULTURE
CAPRA,F.

Una nuova specie di Macrotoma
Russois S. Straz. della Somalia
Italiana: Coleopter Prionidde.
"Bollettino Laboratorio Universita
Portici." Portici.

CASTELLANI,E.

La biologia del Gloeosporium in rapporto
alle condizioni colturali e di trasporto delle
banane. "Rivista di Agricoltura Subtropicale e
Tropicale. Nos. 7-9. Firenze Luglio-Settembre 1956.
339-356 pp.

―――――――――

Su alcune malattie da trasporto
delle banane. "Progresso Agricolo."
Vol. III. Bologna 1957.
674-680 pp

―――――――――AND OTHERS.

Prove preliminari sull'impiego della
Mycostantin contro il Gloeosporium
Musarum. "Notiziario Malattie delle Piante."
Nos. 43-44. Pavia 1958.
3 p.

CURZI,M.

Una nuova specie di Helmintosportum
in una malattia del banano segnalata nella
Somalia Italiana. "Atti R. Accademia dei
Lincei." Serie VI. Vol. XIV. 1931.
146 p.

―――――――――

De funghi et morbis africanis:
(II) De(pseudominis) plantarum
parasitis Somalie. "Bollettino Stazione
Patologia Vegetale." No. 8. 1934.
173 p.

GOLATO, C.

Una nuova malattia fogliare della
cipolla in Somalia. "Rivista di Agricoltura
Subtropicale e Tropicale." Nos. 4-6.
Firenze 1965.
140-142 pp.

―――――――――

Malattie delle piante coltivate in
Somalia. Biblioteca Agraria Tropicale.
Istituto Agronomico per l'Oltremare.
Firenze 1967.
147 pp. ills.

_____AND LAMBERTI,F.

Cercosporiosi della papaia in Somalia. "Rivista
di Agricoltura Subtropicale e Tropicale."
Nos. 10-12. Firenze Ottobre-Dicembre 1964.
468-469 pp.

_____

Cercosporiosi del ricino in Somalia.
Rivista di Agricoltura Subtropicale e
"Tropicale" Nos. 1-3. Firenze Gennaio-Marzo 1965.
78-81 pp.

MARCELLI,E.

Un alterazione delle banane provenienti
dalla Somalia causata da Gloeosporium
musarum. Laboratorio Crittogamico e
Osservatorio Fitopatologico di Pavia.
"Rivista di Ortofrutticola Italiana."
Nos. 1-2. Pavia 1953.
7 pp.

ROSSI, V.

Contributo allo studio della patologia
vegetale in Somalia. "Agricoltura Coloniale."
Firenze 1931.
522 p.

RUSSO,G.

Il raggriniziamento o arriciamento del
cotone nella Somalia Italiana. Relazione
e Monogr. Agricolo Coloniali. Istituto
Agricole Coloniale Italiano. Firenze 1935.

SAPPA,F.

Nuove specie di Aspergillus dei terreni
forestali Somalia. "Allionia." No. 2. 1954.
79-95 pp. And No.2, 1955, 247-257 pp.

VERONA,O. AND PINI,G.

Referti microbiologici su alcuni terreni
della Somalia. "Agricoltura Coloniale."
Firenze 1934.
516 p.

AGRICULTURE
VILARDEBO,A.

Observations sur le degre d'infestation des
bananiers du comprensoire de Genale per les
nematodes parasites. (Relazione) 1964.
5 pp.

14. Sugar Cane

ANFOSSI,A.

Notizie sulla Somalia: riguarda la
produzione saccarifera della SAIS.
"Bollettino Saccarifera Italiana." 1929.
161 p.

ANONYMOUS.

Un'impresa agricola italo-somalo di S.A.R.
il Duca degli Abruzzi. "Agricoltura Coloniale".
Firenze 1920.
430 p.

_____

La SAIS. "Rivista Coloniale".
Roma 1920.
584 p.

_____

L'impresa di S.A.R.: il Duca degli Abruzzi
in Somalia. "Esploratore Commerciale". No. 11-12.
Milano 1921.
132 p.

_____

L'azienda coloniale del Duca degli Abruzzi.
"L'Italia Coloniale"n. No. 2. Roma-Milano 1924.
27 p.

BERTONELLI, F.

L'opera di S.A.R.: Il Duca degli Abruzzi in
Somalia. (Conferenza letta alla "Leonardo da Vinci"
di Firenze il 29 Dicembre 1922.) "Agricoltura Coloniale".
No. 1. Firenze Gennaio 1923.
1-17 pp. ills.

BIGI,F.

Il miglioramento della produzione della canna
da zucchero in Somalia: Tentativi e risultati.
"Rivista di Agricoltura Subtropicale e Tropicale".
Nos. 10-12. Firenze Ottobre-Dicembre 1962.
602-667 pp.

BRUNO,L.

In memoria del Duca degli Abruzzi (SAIS).
Atti dello VIII Convegno Economico Italo-Africano.
Milano 1959.
35-36 pp.

DE ANGELIS,G.

Il progetto di colonizzazione del Duca
degli Abruzzi. "Illustrazione Coloniale".
No. 5. Milano 1920.
265 p.

FEDERAZIONE NAZIONALE CAVALIERI DEL LAVORO.

S.A.R. Luigi di Savoia: Duca degli Abruzzi-
Cavaliere del lavoro: l'opera di colonizzazione
in Somalia. Stab. Tipogr. C. Colombo. 1939.
16 pp.

FERRARA, A.

Problemi relativi alla coltivazione della canna
da zucchero. "Agricoltura Coloniale" Firenze 1928.
455 p.

FORLANI, A.

La canna di zucchero nell'A.O.I.
(Corso organizzazione tecnica agricoli).
Tipografia Ediz.Sallustiana. Roma 1936.
32 pp.

FUNAIOLI,A.

Concimazione azotata per canna da zucchero.
"Progresso Agricolo". No,8. Bologna 1955.

I lineamenti della oldierna tecnica di
coltivazione della canna da zucchero in Somalia.
"Rivista di Agricoltura Subtropicale e Tropicale".
Nos. 1-3. Firenze Gennaio-Marzo 1961.
36-51 pp.

GARBIN,G.

La produzione dello zucchero di canna nelle
Colonie Italiane: La possibilita dell'evoluzione
dell'industria. "Agricoltura Coloniale". Firenze 1926.
460 p.

GRASSELLI,B.A.

Sui risultati di alcune direttive colonizzatrice
(SAIS). "Rivista Coloniale". Roma 1926.

427 p.

MAINO,C.

La Somalia e l'opera del Duca degli Abruzzi.
Istituto Italiano per l'Africa. Roma 1959.
222 pp. ills.

MANASSEI,T.

La canna da zucchero in Somalia: E' possibile
tale coltivazione?. "Rivista Coloniale". Roma 1913.
145 p.

MARCELLO,A.

L'opera del Duca degli Abruzzi nel Benadir.
"Illustrazione Coloniale". No. II. Milano 1921.
421 p.

MEREGAZZI,R.

La Societa Agricola Italo-Somala.
"Rivista delle Colonie Italiane".
No. 5. Roma 1927-28.
655 p.

NEGROTTO CAMBIASO,F.

Inizi,sviluppi ed affermazioni della
Societa Agricola Italo-Somala: il contributo
della SAIS all'autarchia alimentare del paese.
"L'Autarchia Alimentare". No. 5. Roma 1938.
19 p.

PELLEGRINI,L.

Villabruzzi. "Le Vie del Mondo".
No. 4. Milano 1958.
353-366 pp.

PICCIOLI,A.

Il grande pioniere della Somalia:
Luigi di Savoia Duca degli Abruzzi.
L'impero Coloniale Fascista. De Agostini.
Novara 1936.
377 p.

RAPETTI, G.

L'opera della Societa Agricola Italo-Somala
in Somalia: Contributo su alcune aspetti della bonifica.
Istituto Agricolo Coloniale Italiano. Firenze 1935.
35 pp.

SAIS.

Programma e lavori della SAIS. Genova 1922.

L'attivita della SAIS nella colonia del Benadir.
"Rivista Coloniale". Roma 1923.
272 p.

Lavori di bonifica compiuti dalla SAIS nella
regione della Somalia Italiana 1919-1927.
Tipografia Bonavia. Genova 1929.

Annali della SAIS. Legatoria G. Bonavia.
Genova 1930.

Societa Agricola Italo-Somala.
Atti VIII Congresso Internazionale di
Agricoltura Subtropicale e Tropicale.
Vol. II. 1939.
639 p.

SCASSELLATI-SFORZOLINI,G.

I lavori agricoli dell'impresa SAIS di S.A.R.
il Duca degli Abruzzi nella Somalia Italiana.
Tipografia Mazzocchi-Borgo. S. Lorenzo 1922.

La Societa Agricola Italo-Somala in Somalia.
Monografia No. 12. Istituto Agricolo Coloniale
Italiano. Firenze 1926.
75 pp.

La SAIS. "Italia-Africa". Roma 1948.
63 p.

SOCIETA NAZIONALE AGRICOLA INDUSTRIALE.

Primo anno attivita SNAI: relazione del Presidente
Dott. Ahmed Dahir Hassan. SNAI. Mogadiscio Giugno 1964.
13 pp.

Relazioni e Bilancio al 31 Dicembre 1967.
Assemblea Ordinaria e Straordinaria del
27 Giugno 1968. SNAI. Giohar 29 Maggio 1968.
34 pp.

Relazioni e Bilancio al 31 Dicembre 1968.
Assemblea Ordinaria del 10 Luglio 1969.
(II convocazione). SNAI. Giohar 10 Luglio 1969.
20 pp.

SNAI: 1963-1969. 6 anni di attivita:
Relazione del Presidente Dr. Ahmed Dahir Hassan.
SNAI. Mogadiscio Aprile 1969.
17 pp.

II

ANTHROPOLOGY AND ETHNOGRAPHY

ABUD,H.M.

Genealogies of the Somali.
London 1896.

AMMINISTRAZIONE FIDUCIARIA ITALIANA DELLA SOMALIA

Censimento della popolazione Somala
12 Aprile 1951. Tipografia I. Failli.
Roma 15 Gennaio 1953.
87 pp.

ANONYMOUS

Rapport ethnographique suvles populations
de la Cote Francais des Somalia. "Revue Coloniale".
Vol.I. Paris 1901.
206-38 pp.

Le genti somale. "Africa Italiana".
Fasc. No. I. Roma 1956.
227 p.

A.S.

Donne e uomini della Somalia.
"Africa". No.8-12. Roma 1956.
227 pp.

BARDEY.

Traditions et divisions du Somali.
"Bulletin de la Societe d'Anthropologie de Paris".
Vol. VII. No.3. Paris 1884.

BARDI, B.

Stimmaufnahmen bei den Somal. "Signale für
die Musikalische Welt". Vol.LXXXIV. Berlin 1926-7.
469-90 pp.

BARTON, C.J.

Origins of the Galla and Somali tribes.
"Journal of East Africa Natural History Society".
No.91. Nairobi 1924.
6-11 pp.

_____AND JUXON,T.

Report on the Bajun islands. "Journal of
East Africa Natural History Society".
Nairobi March 1922.

BERNARDELLI,G. AND BERTONELLO,P.

Cenni monografici sul paese dei Gherire (etnografia).
Governo della Somalia. Mogadiscio 1937.
89 pp. ills.

BERNARD,M.

Description de la ceremonie de Te Moha:
Cote francaise des Domalis. "Journal de la
Societe des Africanistes". Vol. IV. 1934.
33-34 pp.

BERTIN, F.

Quelques signes de l'arabisation des noms
portes par les Issas. "Revue Pount". No. 3.
La Societe D'etudes de l'Afrique Orientale.
Djibouti 1967.

_____

L'Ougas des Issas. "Revue Pount" No. 5.
La Societe D'etudes de l'Afrique Orientale".
Djibouti 1968.

BIASUTTI, R.

La missione Stefanini-Paoli nella Somalia
Italiana. "L'Africa Italiana". Roma 1916.
209 p.

BONO,E.

Note sulle popolazioni della R.Residenza
di Bur Acaba. "La Somalia Italiana"/
No. 10-12. Mogadiscio 1928.

_____

La Residenza di Bur Hacaba. "La Somalia Italiana".
Anno VI. No. 4-6. Mogadiscio 1929.

ROBECCHI-BRICCHETTI,L.

Dal Benadir,lettere illustrate alla Societa
Antischiavista d'Italia. Milano 1904.

BRITISH MILITARY ADMINISTRATION. (Somalia).

British Somaliland and its tribes. Military
Government of British Somaliland. Berbera 1945.
16 pp.

BRITISH SOMALILAND PROTECTORATE.

Non-Somali census, April 26th 1931.

BUSINCO,L.

Genti della Somalia. "Etiopia".
No. 10-11. 1938.
107 p.

CANIGLIA,G.

Note di demografia politica della Somalia
Italiana. "Rivista Coloniale." Roma 1917.
565 p.

Note di demografia politica della Somalia Italiana.
"Rivista Coloniale". Roma 1918.
196 p.

Gogondovo: note di demografia politica
della Somalia Italiana. "Africa Italiana."
Roma 1918.
72 p.

Genti di Somalia. Zanichelli. Bologna 1922.
167 pp.

Genti di Somalia. Cremonese (Editore). Roma 1935.
162 pp.

Genti di Somalia. 2 edizione.
Cremonese (Editore). Roma 1937.

Il razzismo dei Somali. "Nazione Militare".
Roma 1940.
480-482 pp.

I Somali dell'Impero. Cremonese (Editore).
Roma 1942.
XVI, + 174 pp.

CASILLI D'ARAGONA,M.

Brevi note su alcuni giochi praticati
nella Somalia Italiana. "Rivista delle Colonie Italiane".
Roma 1941.
617 p.

CERULLI,E.

Nuovi appunti sulle nozioni astronomiche dei Somali.
"Rivista degli Studi Orientale". Vol. XIII. Roma 1924.
76-84 pp.

_____

Un gruppo Mahri nella Somalia Italiana.
"Rivista degli Studi Orientali". Vol. II.
Roma 1926.
25-26 pp.

_____

Le stazioni lunari nelle nozioni astronomiche
dei Somali e dei Danakil. "Rivista degli
Studi Orientale". Vol. XII. Roma 1929.

_____

Razzi e razziatori nella Somalia Settentrionale.
"Oriente Moderno". Vol. XI. 1931.
259-262 pp.

_____

Gruppi etnici negri nella Somalia.
"Archivo per l'Antropologia e l'Etnologia".
Vol. LXIV. No.8. Roma 1934.

_____

Scritti vari editi ed inediti. Vol. II.
(Diritto,Etnografia Linguistica, Come Viveva Una
Tribu Hawiyya). Stamperia AFIS. Mogadiscio 1959.
392 pp.

_____

Somalia. Vol. III. (La Tribu Somala, Lingua Somala
in Caraterri Arabi ed altri Soggi). AFIS. Roma 1959.

_____

Dalla Tribu allo Stato nell'Africa Orientale.
Roma 1962.

CHAILLEY.

L'habitation a la cote francaise des Somalis.
"Bulletin Istitut Francaise Afrique Noire".
Vol. XIV. Dakar Octobre 1952.
1490-1511 pp.

CHAPELON,R. AND ABALAIN,M.

Contribution a l'etude du "jouet-chameau"
en T.F.A.I. (Territoire Francaise des Afars et des Issas).
"Revue Pount". No. 4. La Societe D'etudes de l'Afrique
Orientale. Djibouti 1968.

CHAUFFARD,E.

Les populations indigenes du protectorat
francais de la Cote des Somalis et des
regions voisines. Giard et Briere. Paris 1908.

CIPRIANI,L.

Osservazioni antropologiche sulle popolazioni
migiurtine." I° Congresso Studi Coloniali".
Vol. III. Firenze 1931.
235 p.

CLARK, J.D.

Dancing masks from Somaliland. "Man".
Vol. LIII. London 1953.
49-51 pp.

CORONARO,E.

Le popolazioni dell'Oltregiuba. "Rivista Coloniale".
Roma 1925.
330 p.

CORSO,R.

Conoscere i nostri sudditi: le popolazioni
della Somalia. "L'Italia d'Oltremare. No. 4.
Roma 1937.
11 p.

_____

Donna Somala. "Il Mediterraneo".
No. 10. 1937.
23-28 pp.

_____

L'unita delle genti della Somalia.
"L'Italia d'Oltremare". Roma 1940.
300 p.

COSTA,C.

Le abitazioni dei Somali. "Le Vie d''Italia".
Vol. XXXIX. Roma 1933.
185 p.

_____

I Tungi della Somalia Italiana. "Le Vie d'Italia".
Vol. XI. 1934.

COSTANZO,G.A.

La formazione delle classi medie autoctone
nelle tre Somalie. Napoli 1955.

_____

The development of a middle class in British
Somaliland,French Somaliland and in Somalia under
Italian Trusteeship. "Compte Rendu de la XXIX Session
dell'Incidi'". Bruxelles 1956.

_____

Problemes de la coexistence de groupments ethnique
differents dans le territoire de la Somalie sous
tutelle italienne. "Compte Rendu de la XXX Session
dell'Incidi". Bruxelles 1957.

COX,P.Z.

Genealogical trees of the Aysa and Gadabursu tribes.
Aden 1894.

_____ AND ABUD,H.M.

Genealogies of the Somal including those
of Aysa and Gadabursi. Eye & Spottiswide Ltd.
London 1896.

CRAWFORD.

On the Ethnology of Abyssinia and adjoint
countries. "Transactions of the Ethnological Society".
Vol. VI. London 1868.
282-310 pp.

CRUTTENDEN,C.J.

Report on the Mijerthein tribe of Somali
inhabiting the district forming the north-east
point of Africa. "Journal of Bombay Asiatic Society".
Vol. VII. Bombay 1849.

_____

Memoir of the Western or Idoor tribes inhabiting
the Somali coast of north-east Africa.
"Journal of the Royal Geographical Society". Vol.XIX.
London 1849.
46-76 pp.

DELAFOSSE.

Les hamites de l'Afrique Orientale.
"L'Anthropologie". Vol.V. Grenoble 1894.
157-172 pp.

DE VILLARD,U.M.

Note sulle influenze asiatiche nell'Africa Orientale.
"Rivista degli Studi Orientali". Vol.XVII. Roma 1938.
303-349 pp.

DE VILLARD, U.M.

Note sulle influenze asiatiche nell'Africa Orientale.
"Rivista degli Studi Orientali". Vol.XVII. Roma 1938.
303-349 pp.

DE VILLENEUVE,A.

Etude sur une coutume somalie: les femmes cousues.
"Journal de la Societe des Africanistes. Paris 1937.
15-32 pp.

DUCATI,B.

Genti e linque somale delle nostre colonie.
Istituto Coloniale Fascista. Roma 1936.

DUNCAN,W.M.M.

Extracts from Jubaland and the
Northern Frontier District. Stamperia
della Colonia. Mogadiscio 1944.
51 pp.

ELLIOTT,E.

Jubaland and its inhabitanta.
"Geographical Journal".Vol.XXXI.London 1913.
554-61 pp.

FAUROT,L.

Sur les "tumuli" du territoire d'Obock.
"Revue d'Ethnographie et des Traditions Populaires".
Vol. V. Paris.
6 p.

FETTARAPPA-SANDRI,C.

Genti della Somalia. "Annali Istituto
Orientale di Napoli" Vol. VIII. Fasc. No. 3.
Napoli 1936.
III p.

FRANCOLINI,B.

Arte indigena somala.   "L'Oltremare".
No. 2. Roma 1933.
881-884 pp.

————————

I Somali dell'Harar. "Annali Africa Italiana".
Anno I. Vol. III-IV. Roma 1938.
IIII p.

GALAAL,M.H.I.

The terminology and practice of
Somali weather lore,astronomy.Mogadiscio 1968.
77 pp.

GASPARINI,J.

Somalia Italiana: le popolazioni
fra il Gheledi e lo Sciaveli.
G. Bertero. Roma 1912.
27 pp.

GOLDSMITH,K.L.G. AND LEWIS,I.M.

A preliminary investigation of the blood
groups of the 'Sab' Bondsmen of Northern
Somaliland. "Man". Vol.IVIII.   London 1958.
188-190 pp.

GROTTANELLI,V.L.

Asiatic influences on Somali culture.
"Ethnos". No. 4. 1947.
153-181 pp.

————————

Influssi indonesiani nella cultura materiale
dei Somali. "Rivista di Antropologia". 1944-47.
435-436 pp.

————————

I Bantu del Giuba nelle tradizioni dei Wasegua.
"Geografia Helvetica". Vol. VIII. 1953.
249-260 pp.

————————

Pescatori dell'Oceano Indiano. Cremonese (Editore).
Roma 1955.
409 pp.

HAYWOOD,C.W.

The Bajun Islands and Birikau.
"Geographical Journal". Vol. LXXXV. London.
62 p.

HEINITZ,H.

Ueber die Musik der Somali.
"Zeitschrift Musikwissenschaft.". Vol. II.
Leipzig 1920.
257-263 pp.

HUNT, J.A.

Genealogies of the Tribes of British
Somaliland & Mijertein.(General Survey of
British Somaliland 1943-44). Burao 26th June 1944.
32 pp.

_____

British Somaliland and its Tribes.
"East African Pamphlet". No. 377. London 1945.

IMPERATORI,G.

Sulle origini dei Somali.
"L'Oltremare. Roma 1933.
130 p.

ISTITUTO CENTRALE DI STATISTICA.

Censimento della popolazione italiana
e straniera della Somalia, 4 Novembre 1953.
I.C.S. Roma 1958.
170 pp. map, tables.

JOUSSEAUME,F.

Sur l'infibulation ou mutilation des organes
genitaux de la femme chez les peuples des bords
de la Mer Rouge et du golfe d'Aden.
"Reve d'Anthropologie". Vol. IV. Paris 1889.

_____

Reflections anthropologiques a propos
des Tumulus en silex tailles des Somalis
et des Danakil. "Revue d'Anthropologie".
Vol. VI. Paris 1895.
393-413 pp.

KELLER,C.

Reisestudien in den Somaliländern.
"Globus". Vol. LXIX. Zurich 1896.
361-367 pp.

KING, J.S.

On the practice of the female circumcision
and infibulation among the Somali and other
nations of north-east Africa. "Journal of
the Anthropological Society". Bombay 1888.

The practice of female circumcision and
infibulation among the Somal. "Journal of
the Anthropological Society". Vol. II.
Bombay 1890.
2-6 pp.

LAVISON,R.

Note su la transhumance des Issas de la
Cote Francasise des Somalis. "Revue Pount".
No. 1. La Societe D'etudes de l'Afrique Orientale.
Djibouti Octobre 1966.

LESTER,P.

Contribution a l'anthropologie des Somalis.
"Bulletin et Memoires Societe d'Anthropologie."
Paris 1927.
175-187 pp.

LEWIS,I.M.

The Social Organization of the Somali.
(MS. B.Litt. Oxford Thesis) Bodleian Library.
Oxford 1953.

Peoples of the Horn of Africa: Somali, Afar and
Saho. (Ethnographical Survey of North East Africa).
Part I. International African Institute. London 1955.
200 pp. map.

The Somali lineage system and the total genealogy:
a general introduction to basic principles of Somali
political institutions. Report of C.D. and W. Scheme
R.632 (Anthropological Research). Hargeisa 1957.
II, + 139 pp. bibl.

La Comunita (Giamia) di Bardera sulle rive del Giuba.
"Somalia d'Oggi". No. I. Mogadiscio 1957.
36 p.

Historical aspects of genealogies in Northern
Somali Social Structure. "Journal of African History".
Vol.III. No. I. London 1962.
35-48 pp.

Force and fission in Northern Somali
Lineage Structure. "American Anthropologist".
Vol. 63. 1961.
94-112 pp.

Clanship and contract in Northern Somaliland.
"Africa". Vol.XXIX. London.
274-293 pp.

Marriage and the family in Northern
Somaliland. East African Institute of
Social Research. Kampala 1962.

The origins of the Galla and Somali.
"Journal of African History". Vol. VII.
No. I. London 1966.
27-46 pp.

A Study of Pastoralism and Politics among
the Northern Somali of the Horn of Africa.
(2nd reprint). International African Institute.
Oxford University Press. London 1967.
IX, + 320 pp. ills.maps.diagrs.

The Galla in Northern Somaliland.
"Rassegna Studi Etiopici" Vol. XV. Roma
21-38 pp.

LIPPMANN,A.

Guerriers et sorciers en Somalie:
recit de sejour. 1921-30. Hachette. Paris 1953.
254 pp.

MALLET,R.

Djibouti: problemes ethniques et politiques.
"Revue de Defence Nationale". Paris Decembre 1966.
1942-1955 pp.

MARIN,G.

Somali games. "Journal of the Royal Anthropological Institute."
London 1931.
499-512 pp.

MASSARI, C.

Su alcune caratteristiche craniometriche
dei Somali. "Societa Italiana per il Progresso
della Scienze". Vol. I. Roma 1951.
3 p.

_____

Maschere di danza degli Uaboni. "Archivio per
l'Antropologia e Etnologia. Roma 1950-51.

MOHAMED,S.OSMAN.

Migrazioni e urbanismo in Somalia.
"Africa". No. 7-8. Roma 1952.

DE MONFREID, H.

Les guerriers de l'Ogaden. N.R.F. 1936.

MORGANTINI,A.M.

Quelques resultats preliminaries des releves
concernant les populations somalie effectuees
en 1953. Roma 1955.

_____

Contributo alla conoscenze demografica della
Somalia sotto l'amministrazione fiduciaria Italiana.
Roma 1954.

MORI,A.

Gli albori del Benadir. "Rivista Coloniale.
Roma 1915.
455 p.

MULLER,R.

Les populations de la Côte Francaise des Somalis.
"Cahiers de l'Afrique et de l'Asie". Editions Peyronnet.
Paris 1959.
45-102 pp.

NADA.

Mptes pm tje Somali. Native Affairs Department.
Ann. S. Rhodesia. 1948.
85-92 pp.

PANCERI.

Le operazioni che nell'Africa si praticano
sugli organi genitali. "Archivio per l'Antropologia
e l'Etnologia". Roma 1873.
353 p.

PARENTI,R.

I Bagiuni: contributo alla conoscenza delle
popolazioni della Somalia Italiana Meridionale.
"Rassegna Studi Etiopici". Vol. V. Roma 1946.
156-190 pp.

————————————

Antropologia della Somalia Meridionale:
risultati della missione Puccioni.
"Archivio per l'Antropologia e l'Etnologia".
Vol. LXXII-LXXIX. Roma 1940.

————————————

Gli Uaboni. "Rivista Biologia Coloniale".
Vol. IX. 1948.
66-90 pp.

————————————

Sull'antropologia della Somalia Meridionale.
Pisa 1949.

PARKINSON, J.

Customs in Western British Somaliland.
"Journal of the Royal Anthropological Institute."
Vol. XXXV. London 1936.
241-245 pp.

PAULITSCHKE, P.H.

Beiträg zur Ethnographie und Anthropologie der
Somal, Galla und Harrar. Frohber. Leipzig 1886.

————————————

I Somali dell'occidente. "Bollettino Sezione
Fiorentina Societa Africana d'Italia" Napoli 1889-90.

————————————

Ethnographie Nordost - Afrikas: Die materielle
Kultur der Danakil, Galla und Somal. Reimer. Berlin 1893.
338 pp.

Praehistorische Funde aus dem Somaliland.
"Mitteilungen Anthrop. Gesellschaft." Vol. XXVII.
Vienna 1898.
15 p.

PICCOLI, M.

Indagini antropologiche ed etnografiche sulle
popolazioni della Somalia. "Rassegna Sociale Africana Italiana".
No. 12. Napoli 1939.
1337 p.

Aspetti della vita indigena nella Somalia Italiana.
"Rassegna Sociale Africana Italiana". No. 2. Napoli 1940.
134 p.

PIRONE, M.

Le popolazione dell'Ogaden. "Archivio per l'Antropologia
e l'Etnologia". Vol. LXXXIV. Roma 1954.

Le maschere di Bur Eybi. "Somalia d'Oggi".
No. 2. Mogadiscio 1957.
30 p.

Appunti di sociologia generale: (Parte Terzo)
Sguardo alla societa somala e ai suoi problemi
in generale. "Istituto Universitario della Somalia.
Mogadiscio 1965.
62 pp.

PUCCIONI, N.

Ricerche antropometriche sui Somali.
"Archivio per l'Antropologia e l'Etnologia".
Vol LXI. Fasc. No. IV. Roma 1911.

Appunti sull'antropometria dei Somali.
"Rivista d'Antropologia". Fasc. No. II-III.
Roma 1911.

Appunti sulla distribuzione geografica delle
popolazioni della Somalia. "Bollettino R. Societa

Geografica Italiana". Fasc. No. III-Iv. Roma 1919.
149 p.

———————

Studi sui materiali e sui dati antropologici
e etnografici raccolti della Missione Stefanini
Paoli nella Somalia Meridionale Italiana. Tipografia
M.Ricci. Firenze 1919.
154 pp.

———————

Studi sui materiali e sui dati antropologici
e etnografici raccolti della Missione Stefanini
Paoli nella Somalia Meridionale Italiana. Tipografia
M.Ricci. Firenze 1920.
333 pp.

———————

Carta della distribuzione delle principali
cabile somale. "Atti VIII Congresso Geografico Italiano".
Vol. Ii. Firenze 1921.
458 p.

———————

La Somalia del Nord. "Le Vie d'Italia".
No. 12. Milano 1927.

———————

Le genti somale. "Atti I Congressi Studi Coloniali".
Vol. III. Firenze 1931.
230 p.

———————

Antropologia ed Etnografia delle genti della Somalia.
Vol. I. (Antropometria). (R.Societa Geografica Italiana):
Zanichelli. Bologna 1931.
384 pp. tables.

———————

Tipi di industria litica raccolti nella Somalia
Italiana della Missione della Reale Societa Geografica
Italiana. "Archivio per l'Antropologia e l'Etnologia".
Vol. LXIII. Roma 1933.
259 pp.

———————

La missione della Reale Accademia d'Italia
nel Giuba e nell'Oltregiuba. "Annali Africa Italiana".
No. 1-3. Roma 1935.
157 p.

Missione antropologica ed etnografica nel Giuba
e nell'Oltregiuba gennaio-aprile 1935. Reale Accademia
d'Italia. Roma 1936.

Paesaggi della Somalia Meridionale.
"Le Vie d'Italia". Milano Gennaio 1936.

Caratteristiche Antropologiche ed Etnografiche
delle popolazioni della Somalia. "Bollettino Societa
Geografica Italiana". Roma 1936.
209 p.

Osservazioni sugli Uaboni. "L'Universo".
No. 6. Firenze 1936.
431. p.

Antropologia ed Etnografia delle genti della Somalia.
(R. Societa Geografica Italiana). Zanichelli. Bologna 1936.
140 pp. tables.

Giuba e Oltregiuba. Sansoni. Firenze 1937.
145 pp.

Le popolazioni indigene della Somalia Italiana.
(a Cura del Ministero delle Colonie).
Capelli. Bologna 1937.
115 pp.

Osservazioni sui Bagiuni. "Bollettino della Sezione
Fiorentina della Societa Africana d'Italia". Napoli. 1937.
1-41 pp.

RADLAUER.

Anthropometrische Studien an Somali. (Haschia)
"Archiv.fur Anthropolog." Vol. XIII. 1915.
451 p.

RE'VOIL,G.

Notes d'archeologie et d'etnographie recueillis
dans le Somal. "Revue d'Ethnographie". Vol. I.

Paris 1882.
5 p.

REVERE,A.

Costumi e caratteri dei Somali.
"Illustrazione Coloniale" No. 12. Milano 1932.
21 p.

SALKELD,R.E.

Notes on the Boni hunters of Jubaland.
"Man". London 1905.

SERGI,G.

Africa, antropologia della stripe camitica.
Bocca. Torino 1897.
426 pp.

SMITH,R.H.

The Tribes of British Somaliland.
Caxton Press. London 1941.
12 pp. tables.

STEFANINI, G.

Tribu e villagi in Somalia. "Bollettino Societa
Geografica Italiana". Vol. XXXI. Roma 1924.
73 p.

_____AND PUCCIONI, N.

Notizie preliminari sui principali risultati della missione
R. Societa Geografica Italiana in Somalia 1924. "Bollettino
R. Societa Geografica Italiana". Roma 1926.
12 p.

TASCHDJIAN,E.

Stammesorganisation und Eheverbote der Somalis.
"Anthropos". Vol. XXXIII. 1938.
1-2 pp.

VITALE,M.A.

Genti di Somalia sul mare. "Congresso Internaz.
Etnografia folklore del mare". 1954.
731-747 pp.

WAR OFFICE.

British Somaliland and its Tribes.
London 1945.

WALKER,H.

The tribes of Somaliland and reserved area Ogaden.
(MS. Tylor Library, Oxford).

WERNER,A.

The Bantu coast tribes of the east Africa
protectorate. "Journal of the Royal Anthropological
Institute". Vol. XLV. London 1915.
327-328 pp.

III
ARMY AND COLONIAL WAR OPERATIONS

ANONYMOUS.

La Somalia Italiana e l'eccidio di Lafole.
"Rivista Marittima". Roma 1897.
30 p.

La conquista della Somalia Britannica.
"Agricoltura Coloniale". No. 8. Firenze Agosto 1940.
309-311 pp.

L'action militaire en Côte Francaise des Somalis;
de 1939 a 1945. "Revue Historizue de l'Armes'.
No. 1965-2. Paris.

Numero special consacre a l'oeuvre de l'Eveche
de Djibouti. "Vivante Afrique". Mai 1967.
55 pp.

ALBERTI, G.

In Somalia contro il Mullah pazzo. "Rassegna Italiana".
Roma 1935.
547-556 pp.

BATTERSBY, H.F.P.

Richard Corfield of Somaliland. 1914.
XIX, + 259 pp.

CANTU', G.

La nostra Marina nella Somalia. Arti Grafiche S. Belforte.
Livorno 1911.

CAROSELLI, F.S.

Ferro e fucco in Somalia: Venti anni di lotta contro
il Mullah e i Dervisci. Sind. Arte Grafiche. Roma 1931.
330 pp.

CATALUCCIO, F.

Il conflitto Italo-Etiopico. Istit. per gli
Politici Internaz. Milano 1936.
550-590 pp.

CERREETTI, E.

Col l'esercito Italiano in A.O. Mondadori. Milano 1937.
798 pp.

CHAMIER, J.A.

Operations in British Somaliland, 1903.
United Service Institution. Vol. 54. Bombay 1924.
103-109 pp.

CIMMARUTA, R.

Ual-Ual. Mondadori. Milano 1936.
240 pp.

COMANDO DEL CORPO DI STATO MAGGIORE.

Azione militare nella Somalia Italiana - Dallo scontro
di Bahalle (15 Dicembre 1907) alla fine del 1910.
Lab. Tipo. della Stato Maggiore. Roma 1911.
II pp.

CORMACK, R.P.

Some medical aspects of the campaign in Somaliland
and Ethiopia 1941. "East African Medical Journal".
Nairobi November 1943.

CORSI,C.

La guerra nelle Colonie 1914-1918. Tipografia Unione Ed.
Roma 1918.

DE MONFREID, H.

La guerra nell'Ogaden. Genio Ed. Milano 1937.
232 pp.

────────────

Les guerriers de l'Ogaden. Gallimard. Paris 1936.

DE VECCHI, G.

Dubat - Gli arditi neri. Mondadori. Milano 1936.
239 pp.

DOWER, K. C.

The first to be freed: a record of the campaign

and British Military Administration in Eritrea and
Somalia 1941-1943. Ministry of Information. H.M.S.O.
London 1944.
70 pp. ills. map.

FALZONE, S.

Mohamed Abdileh e l'azione anglo-italiana in Somalia.
"Bollettino Societa Africana d'Italia". Vol. XXI.
Napoli 1902.
161-175 pp.

FERRANDO, L.

L'opera della R. Marina in Eritrea e Somalia.
Roma 1928.

FOREIGN OFFICE.

Correspondence relating to the Rising of Mullah Mohamed
Abdullah in Somaliland and consequent Military Operations,
1899-1902. London 1901-1903.

———————————

Military Report on Somaliland. London 1907.

———————————

The Red Sea and Gulf of Aden Pilot. London 1909.

———————————

Military Report on British Somaliland. London 1925.

FOX, F.

Death and censure of Richard Corfield. "National Review".
Vol LXI. London 1914.
1019-30 pp.

FRANCHINI, N.

Ogaden. Cappelli Ed. Bologna 1937.
139 pp.

FRUSCI, L.

In Somalia sul Fronte Meridionale.
Cappelli Ed. Bologna 1936.
163 pp.

GATTESCHI, C.

La Somalia Italiana e le operazioni militari
dell'anno 1908. "Rivista di Fanteria". Roma 1935.
727-746 pp.

GRANDE,A.

Vigilia di avanzata sul fronte somalo. "Civilta Fascista".
No. 10. Roma 1936.

GRAZIANI, R.

Fronte Sud. Mondadori. Milano 1938.
348 pp.

HAMILTON, J.A.L.

Somaliland. Hutchinson & Co. London 1911.
XV, + 366 pp. Map.

HARDEN, H.S.S.

Campaigning against the Mad Mullah in Somaliland.
"Can.Milit.Inst". 1907.
9-21 pp.

HOWARD, C.A.I.

Operations in British Somaliland 1920. United Service
Institution. Vol. 53. 1923.
201-18 pp.

JARDINE, D.J.

The Mad Mullah of Somaliland. (Forward by Viscount Milner).
Herbert Jenkins Ltd. London February 1923.
XIV, + 336 pp. maps. ills.

––––––––––––––––

Mad Mullah of British Somaliland.
"Blackwood's Magazine". Vol. CCVIII. Edinburgh 1920
108-121 pp.

––––––––––––––––

Il Mullah del Paese dei Somali.
(Traduz. Ital. a cura di M.Quercia). Societa Italiana
Arti Grafiche. Roma 1929.
277 pp.

JENNINGS, J.W. AND ADDISON, C.

With the Abyssinians in Somaliland. Hadder and Stongton.
London 1905.

LAUREATI, L.

La Marina Italiana in Somalia. "Rivista di Cultura Marinara".
No. 3-4. 1950.

MACNEILL,M.

In pursuit of the mad Mullah: service and sport
in Somaliland Protectorate. Pearson C.A. London 1902.
XI, + 313 pp.

MICALETTI, R.

Nell'Ogaden con gli ascari libici. Sculola Tipogr. Marchigiana.
Senigallia 1938.
169 pp.

MINISTERO DELLA DIFESA.

Vademecum della Somalia (per ufficiali e sottoufficiali).
Corpo di Stato Maggiore. dell'Esercito. Roma 1949.
207 pp. ills. maps.

MORDAL,J.

Blocus a Djibouti. "Historia-Magazine".
No. 23. Paris Mars 1968.
635-644 pp.

OWEN, F.C.

The Somaliland Operations, June 1903 to
May 1904. "Journal of the United Services Institution".
Vol. XLIX. Bombay 1905.
169-182 pp.

PALIERI, M.

Note per la storia del R. Corpo Truppe Coloniali
della Somalia Italiana. Schioppo Ed. Torino 1929.
40 pp.

PARI, M.

Esperimenti di traino con cammelli della Somalia.
Tipogr. Ed. Voghera. Roma 1914.

PESENTI, G.

La rassegna eroica: Cenni storici sui gloriosi
caduti in terra di Somalia. Stamperia della Colonia.
Mogadiscio 1929.
40 pp.

———————

Danane nella Somalia Italiana. "L'Erioica" Milano 1932.
140 p.

PIGOTT, G.E.

Somaliland Operations. "Army Ser. Corps Quarterly".
Vol. No. 3. London 1911.
246-271 pp.

PO.G.

Un cinquantennio di storia coloniale: La partecipazione delle R.R.Navi per la stipulazione del protettorato sulla Somalia settentrionale 1889. "Rivista Marittima". Roma 1939.
50-59 pp. ills.

POMILIO, M.

Coi Dubat - Fronte Sud. Vallecchi Ed. Firenze 1937.
202 pp.

SANDRI, S.

Sei mesi di guerra sul Fronte Somalo. Bertarelli Arti Grafiche. Milano 1936.
177 pp.

SAVA, F.

Ospedale da campo in Somalia. Bemporad. Firenze 1937.
218 pp.

SWAYNE, E.J.E.

Final Report on the Operations conducted in Somaliland from the 18th January 1902 to the 1st November 1902. "London Gazetter". London 2 September 1904.
5623-5673 pp.

VOLTA,S.

Graziani a Neghelli. Vallecchi Ed. Firenze 1936.
205 pp.

WALSH,L.P.

Under the Flag, and Somali Coast Stories. London 1932.

WAR OFFICE.

Precis of information concerning Somaliland. H.M.S.O. London 1902.

─────────────

Official History of the Operations in Somaliland, 1901-04. H.M.S.O. London 1907.
273 pp.

WATERFIELD, G.

Morning will come. London 1944.

ZERES.

From the outposts: a day's work with the Somaliland Constabulary. "Blackwood's Magazine". Vol. CXIX. Edinburgh 1918.
481-489 pp.

1. Animal Husbandry

ADANI,C.

Dall'allevamento del bestiame nella
Somalia Italiana e del suo trasporto
in Italia. "Atti II° Congresso Italiani
all'estero." 1911.
1715 p.

AMMINISTRAZIONE FIDUCIARIA ITALIANA DELLA SOMALIA.

Studio per la valorizzazione delle attivita
zootecnica. Direzione dello Sviluppo Economico.
Ispettorato Agricoltura e Zootecnia. Stamperia AFIS.
Mogadiscio Dicembre 1954.
16 pp.

Livestock genetics study in
Somalia. (E.C.A.) Mogadiscio 1951.
ANONYMOUS.

Bestiame in Somalia. "La Somalia Italiana."
No. 12. Mogadiscio 1927.

BATTAGLINI, U.

Esperimenti di incroci dell'ariete
Carakul con pecore di razza somala.
"Rivista di Zootecnia." No.6. Firenze 1937.
231 p.

BETTINI, T.M.

Il cavallo Nogali in Somalia.
"Agricoltura Coloniale." Firenze 1939.
273 p.

Relazione preliminare su di una missione
zootecnica in Somalia. Istituto Agronomico
Africa Italiana. Firenze 1939.
21 pp.

Problemi zootecnici della Somalia. "Atti
Reale Accademia Geogr." No. 4. Firenze 1939.
501 p.

Problemi delle valorizzazione zootecnica
della Somalia Britannica."Agricoltura Coloniale"
No. I. Firenze Gennaio 1940.
31-32 pp.

Sulla groppa degli zebu della Somalia.
"Agricoltura Coloniale." No. 3
Firenze Marzo 1940.
101-107 pp. ills.

L'allevamento del bestiame in Migiurtinia.
"Agricoltura Coloniale." No. 5
Firenze Maggio 1941.
177-194 pp. ills.

L'allevamento del bestiame in Migiurtinia.
"Agricoltura Coloniale" No.6.
firenze Giugno 1941.
225-232 pp. ills.

Sulla valorizzazione zootecnica della
Somalia."Atti II Congresso Studi Coloniali."
Firenze 1947.
313 p.

Memorandum sull'introduzione della Somalia di
tori migliorati e su altre iniziative zootecniche.
Istituto Agronomico per l'Oltremare.
Fasc. No. 508. Firenze 1950.
7 pp.

La conferenza internazionale di Lucknow
sull'allevamento animale in condizioni tropicali
e subtropicali. "Rivista di Agricoltura Subtropicale
e Tropicale." Nos. 7-9. Firenze Luglio-Settembre 1950.

Relazione sulle ricognizioni eseguite in alcune
regioni della Somalia ai fini della scelta di una
zona da destinare azienda zootecnica sperimentale.
AFIS. Mogadiscio 1950.

Problemi zootecnici della Somalia.
"Rivista di Agricoltura Subtropicale
e Tropicale." Nos. 4-9.   Firenze Aprile-Settembre 1960.
235-243 pp.

BOZZI,L. AND TRIULZI,G.A.

Osservazioni sugli animali domestici
allevati in Somalia. "Rivista di Agricoltura
Subtropicale e Tropicale" Nos. 7-9. Firenze 1953.
266-294 pp.

_____

Gli animali domestici allevati
in Somalia. AFIS. Mogadiscio 1954.
34 pp.

CARUSILLO,G.

Patrimonio zootecnico della Somalia,
sue risorse e possibilita d'incremento.
Governo della Somalia. Ministero Affare
Sociale. Dipartimento Veterinario. Mogadiscio 1958.
8 pp.

CHILDS, S.A.

Improvement of the livestock industry-
Somali Republic. FAO. TA. Report Nol 1191.
Rome 1960.

_____

Report to the Government of Somalia in
the improvement of the livestock industry.
FAO Technical Assistance Programme. 1960.
19 pp.

CLAXTON, H.W.

Three main problems of British
Somaliland."The Crown Colonist."
January 1939.

CONGIU,S.

I caprini Somali, studio biometrico.
"Zootecnia e Veterinaria." No. I. Milano 1952.
409-415 pp.

_____

Indagini su alcuni costituenti
normali del latte di zebu Somalo.
"Annali della Societa di Medicina ed
Igiene Tropicale della Somalia."
Vol. I. Mogadiscio 1953.

89-96 pp.

Indagini sulla resa al macello, sulla
distribuzione ponderale e sulle correlazioni
fra le diverse parti del corpo del
dromedario Somalo. "Zootecnia e Veterinaria."
No. 6. Milano Giugno 1953.
188-191,pp.

Indagini sulla resa al macello, sul
peso vivo,sulla distribuzione tra le
diverse parti del corpo nella popolazione
caprina Somala." Zootecnia e Veterinaria."
No. II. Milano Novembre 1954.
359-367 pp.

Studio preliminare sulla migliore
ubicazione dei pozzi e di una azienda
zootecnica del Benadir. Stamperia AFIS.
Mogadiscio Gennaio 1955.
4 pp.

COZZI,P.

Gli zebu della Somalia. "Rivista di
Agricoltura Subtropicale e Tropicale."
Nos. 1-3. Firenze Gennaio - Marzo 1965.
61-77 pp.

L'allevamento del bestiame in Somalia.
"Rivista di Agricoltura Subtropicale e
Tropicale." Nos. 4-6. Firenze Aprile-Giugno 1965.
123-139 pp.

CROVERI,P.

Esperimenti di reditto alla macellazione dei
bovini,caprini e ovini Somali."Rivista
Freddo." No. 3. 1919.
93 p.

ELECTROCONSULT.

Infrastrutture per l'allevamento
di una zona pilota: progetti di
pre-investimento. Milano 1967.

FERRARI, G.

A proposito delle "Note Zootecniche" di
T. Manassei. "Rivista Coloniale." Roma 1910.
431 p.

FERRIO, M.

Il popolo pastore della Somalia ed il
suo bestiame: note di zootecnica somala.
Tipogr. Bono. Moncalvo. 1927.

_____

Studio per una istituenda stazione
zootecnica per la Somalia Italiana
nella zona di Genale. Casalmonferrato. 1934.

FIORI, A.

Foraggi della Somalia. Istituto
"Agricolo Coloniale Italiano." Monogr.
No. 72. Firenze 1944.

_____

Piante foraggere raccolte in Somalia
dal Dr. T.M. Bettini durante la sua missione
1938-39. Istituto Agricolo Coloniale.
Italiano. Firenze 1941.

_____ AND BETTINI, T.M.

Contributo alla conoscenze di alcuni pascoli
della Somalia Italiana. Istituto Agricolo
Coloniale Italiano. Firenze 1941.

FOOD AND AGRICULTURAL ORGANIZATION.

Agriculture and Water Surveys: Somalia's livestock
development survey. F.A.O. UNDP Programme. Rome 1967.
59 pp. map.

GADDI, S.

I due tori del Dott.B.: Progetti E.C.A. per
la Somalia. "Africa." No. 11. Roma 1950.
279 p.

GADOLA, A.

La pastorizia somala e l'azione
svolta dall'Italia. "Africa." No.s 5-6.
Roma 1948.
133-159 pp.

GIORIO,C.

Il cammello della Somalia settentrionale.
"Rassegna Economica delle Colonie."
Roma 1930.
351 p.

GLENDAY,V.G.

Improving Somaliland livestock
and pastures."The Crown Colonist."
January 1940.

GOVERNO DELLA SOMALIA.

Censimento del bestiame al 1º Febbraio 1920.
"Bollettino Informazione Ministero Colonie."
Roma 1923.
822 p.

KNUT SCHMIDT,NIELSON.

Il cammello (realta e leggenda).
Somalia d'Oggi. No. 2. Mogadiscio 1957.
31-36 pp.

LUCHINI,R.

Sulla produzione in latte delle bovine
Somale. "Rivista di Agricoltura Subtropicale
e Tropicale." Firenze 1947.
202 p.

MAGRI,G.

Il miglioramento della pastorizia somala
attraverso l'attivita di aziende zootecniche
(l'aziende di Uar Maham). "Rivista di Agricoltura
Subtropicale e Tropicale." Nos. 4-9.
Firenze Aprile-Settembre 1960.
411-423 pp.

MANASSEI,T.

Note zootecniche:appunti di un viaggio in
Somalia. "Rivista Coloniale." Roma 1910.
357 p.

MARES,R.G.

Animal husbandry, animal industry and
animal disease in the Somaliland
Protectorate. "British Veterinary Journal."
Vol. 110. Nos. 10-11. London October-November 1954.

MASCHERONI,E.

Zootecnica Somala. "LeVie d'Italia."
Milano 1935.
852 p.

II bestiame della Somalia.
"Agricoltura Coloniale." Firenze 1936.
39 p.

McCOLLOCH, D.C.

Livestock Survey Somalia, East Africa.
U. S. Operations Mission to Italy.
Rome 1954.
40 pp. And 1957.   15 pp.

Livestock Survey Somalia, East Africa.
International Cooperation Administration.
(I.C.A.) Mogadiscio 1960.

PROVENZALE,F.

L'allevamento del bestiame nella
nostra Somalia. Tipogrf. Nazionale di
G. Bertero. Roma 1914.
485 pp.

RAPETTI,G.

L'attivita zootecnica della S.A.I.S.
"Atti I congresso Studi Coloniali." Vol. VI.
Firenze 1934.
309 p.

SCASSELLATI-SFORZOLINI, G.

L'impresa zootecnica della Somalia
Italiana Meridionale. Tipogr. della
Camera dei Deputati. Roma 1913.
245 pp.

SOMALI REPUBLIC.

Progress report of the Livestock
Development Agency (year of establishment).
Mogadiscio December 31st, 1966.
26 pp. tables. appendices.

Progress report of the Livestock
Development Agency for 1967.
Mogadiscio 31st December 1967.
48 pp.

Livestock Development Agency 1968.
Mogadiscio 6 February 1969.
38 pp.

TARANTINO, G.B.

Il latte di cammella. "La Somalia
Italiana." No. 12. Mogadiscio 1928.

Il cammello somalo. "Rivista di
Zootecnica." No. 70. Anno IV%.
Firenze 1928.
254 p.

Lo zebu somalo. "Illustrazione
Coloniale." No.7. Milano 1929.
25 p.

La zebra della Somalia Italiana.
"Rassegna Economica delle Colonie." Roma 1929.
544 p.

Gli asini di Martina Franca e di Pantelleria
in Somalia. "Rivista Zootecnica."
Firenze Giugno 1931.

Il toro Schwitz-Sardo in Somalia.
"Rivista Zootecnica." Firenze 1933.
11 pp.

Il cammello da sella (Recub)
della Somalia.
"Revista Zootecnica." Firenze 1934.
39 p.

L'allevamento bovina nella Somalia
Italiana. Querimonia. 1934.
10 p.

_____

L'allevamento bovino nella Somalia
Italiana. "Critica Zootecnica". Roma 1934.

_____

L'alimentazione dei bovini nella Somalia
Italiana. "Rassegna Economica delle
Colonie". Roma 1934.
97 p.

_____

L'alimentazione del bestiame bovino
nella Somalia Italiana. "Rassegna Economica
delle Colonie." Roma 1934.

_____

L'industria zootecnica nella Somalia
Italiana."Critica Zootecnica." Roma 1934.

_____

Miglioramento e sfruttamento del bestiame
bovino in Somalia. "Atti II Congresso Studi
Coloniali." Vol. VI. Firenze 1934.
1021 p.

_____

Incremento del patrimonio bovino
somalo. "Rassegna Economica delle
Colonie." Roma 1935.
121 p.

TRIULZI,G.A.

Studio sulla localizzazione di una
azienda zootecnica in zona di Hortacaio.
Stamperia AFIS. Mogadiscio 7 Maggio 1953.
4pp.

_____

Documenti e relazioni relative
all'impianto dell'azienda zootecnica di
Uar Mahan. Istituto Agronomico per l'Oltremare.
Fasc. No. 3399. Firenze 1956.

_____ AND BASSONI,A.

Relazione zootecnica e idrologia
del Mudugh: 1952-1953. Stamperia AFIS.
Mogadiscio 1953.
27 pp.

2. Entomology

ANONYMOUS

Disposizioni per la difesa delle
piante industriali nella Somalia
Italiana. "Rassegna Economica delle
Colonie." Roma 1929.
150 p.

Programma delle ricerche da eseguirsi
nella concessione della S.A.I.S. sugli
insetti delle piante coltivate. "Agricoltura
Coloniale." Firenze 1926.
24 p.

BECCARI, F.

Antomofauna Somala: Linee programmatiche
e.considerazioni. "Rivista di Agricoltura
Subtropicale e Tropicale." Nos. 7-9
Firenze Luglio-Settembre 1953.
341-355 pp.

Studio per una regolamentazione ed
organizzazione fitosanitaria in Somalia.
Direzione per lo Sviluppo Economico.
Ispettorato Agricoltura e Zootecnia.
Stamperia AFIS. Mogadiscio Dicembre 1954.
18 pp.

Organizzazione fitosanitaria per le
cooperative autoctone in Somalia.
Istituto Agronomico per l'Oltremare.
"Fasc." No. 2492. Firenze 1955.

Organizzazione fitosanitaria poderi
modello Alto Giuba. Istituto Agronomico
per l'Oltremare. "Fasc." No. 4284
Firenze 1955.

Studio in merito all esecuzione di trattamenti antiparassitari
su bananeti di una superficie complessiva di ettari 3000 a
Genale, Afgoi e Chisimaio. Istituto Agronomico per l'Oltremare.
"Fasc." No. 4260 Firenze 1958.
12 pp.

Studio per l'organizzazione di
"unita di disinfestazione" nella regione
mesopotamica ad agricoltura seccagna.
Stamperia AFIS. Mogadiscio Maggio 1955.
12 pp.

I risultati di una missione in Somalia per
lo studio dei problemi connessi alle
infestazione coccidiche sul banano. "Rivista di
Agricoltura Subtropicale e Tropicale."
Nos. 1-3. Firenze Gennaio-Marzo 1958.
12-45 pp.

Cautele fitosanitarie indispensabili alle
dogane somale: primo elenco di agenti patogeni
temibili. "Rivista di Agricoltura Subtropicale e
Tropicale." Nos. 4-8. Firenze Aprile-Settembre 1960.

_____ AND OTHERS.

Insetti dannosi alle coltivazioni in
Somalia: cenni biologici e consigli per
la lotta. Tipogr.Missione Catto.ica.
Mogadiscio 1953.
42 pp. ills.

_____ AND SCAVAZZO, R.

I risultati di trattamenti nematocidi
eseguiti in Somalia su materiale
moltiplicativo del banano prima
dell'impianto.
"Rivista di Agricoltura Subtropicale e Tropicale."
Nos. 4-6. Firenze 1966.
20 pp. ills. bibl.

BEZZI,M.

Ditteri raccolti nella Somalia
Italiana Meridionale: Missione
Stefanini-Paoli."Redia"Vol.X. 1915.
19 p.

BIGI,F.

Sui parassiti dell'arachide nella
Somalia e negli altri Territori
dell'A.O. "Olearia." 1949.
901 p.

_____

Gli ambienti, i parassiti e le malattie
del cotone in Africa Orientale: Eritrea,
Etiopia, Somalia. "Rivista di Agricoltura
Subtropicale e Tropicale." Nos. 4-6.
Firenze Aprile-Giugno 1954.
49 pp.

BOZZI,L. AND SOZIO,S.

Notizie utili per la lotta antiacridica
in Somalia. AFIS. Mogadiscio 1950.
12 pp.

BUSURY,SHERIF MOHAMED AND FRANKLIN,W.W.

Use of insecticides. Afgoi Agricultural
Research Station. Ministry of Agriculture
and Animal Husbandry. Mogadiscio 1964.
15 pp.

CASTELLANI,E.

Problemi fitopatologici della bananicoltura
somala.   Istituto Agronomico per l'Oltremare. Monogr.No. 73.
Firenze 1955.
81 pp.

CENTRAL AGRICULTURAL RESEARCH STATION,AFGOI.

Cotton insects in the Somali Republic: a preliminary
report. USAID/SOMALI REPUBLIC. University of
Wyoming Team. Mogadiscio April 1968.
8 pp.

_____

Citrus insect control in Somalia.
USAID/SOMALI REPUBLIC. University
of Wyoming Team. Mogadiscio June 1967.
13 pp. ills. tables. appendices.

_____

A Progress report insect and
weed control for sorghum in the
Somali Republic. USIAD/SOMALI REPUBLIC.
University of Wyoming Team. Mogadiscio
August 1969.
5 pp.

CHIAROMONTE,A.

Considerazioni entomologiche sulla coltura
del cotone nella Somalia Italiana. "Atti V
Congresso Internaz. Agricoltura Tropicale." 1930.
452 p.

_____

Note intorno alla biologia dei Coleoptera
piu dannosi per la coltivazione del cotone
nella Somalia Italiana. "Atti I Congresso
Internaz. Studi Coloniali." Vol. VI. 1931.
449 p.

_____

Note intorno alla biologia degli Orthoptera,
Isoptera,Thysanoptera,Hemiptera piu dannosi
per la coltivazione del cotone nella Somalia
Italiana." Atti I Congresso Studi Coloniali."
Vol. VI. 1931.
428 p.

_____

L'inutilita della disinfestazione al calore
del seme di cotone prodotto in lungo come
mezzo di lotta preventiva control la Platyedra
nella Somalia Italiana. "Atti I Congresso Studi
Coloniali." Vol. VI. 1931.
461 p.

_____

Considerazioni entomologiche sulle principali
colture della Somalia Italiana." Atti V Congresso
Internaz. di Entomologia." Vol. II. 1932.
495 p.

_____

Considerazioni entomologiche sulla
coltura degli alberi da frutto nella
Somalia Italiana. "Agricoltura Coloniale."
Firenze 1933.
383 p.

_____

Considerazioni entomologiche sulla coltura
della canna da zucchero in Somalia.
"Agricoltura Coloniale." Firenze 1933.
220 p.

_____

Considerazioni entomologiche sulle
colture dei cereali in Somalia.
"Agricoltura Coloniale." Firenze 1933.
484 p.

_____

Considerazioni entomologiche nella coltura
delle piante da ombra,da frangivento,ecc.
nella Somalia Italiana. "Agricoltura
Coloniale." No. 12. Firenze Dicembre 1933.
584-587 pp.

_____

Considerazioni entomologiche sulle colture
delle piante da foraggio nella Somalia.
"Agricoltura Coloniale." Firenze 1933.
431 p.

_____

Considerazioni entomologiche sulla coltura delle
piante Oleaginose in Somalia.
"Agricoltura Coloniale." Firenze 1934.
38 p.

_____

Considerazioni entomologiche sulla coltura
delle piante da fibra della Somalia Italiana.
"Agricoltura Coloniale." Firenze 1934.
193 p.

_____

Note intorno alla biologia degli insetti
piu importanti per la coltivazione delle
principali piante economiche (escluso cotone)
della Somalia Italiana: Orthoptera,Isoptera,
Thysanoptera, Hemiptera,Lepidoptera,Coleoptera
Himenoptera e Diptera. "Atti II Congresso Studi
Coloniali." Vol. VI. 1934.
1067-1081-1101 pp.

_____

L'anguillulosi del banano nella Somalia
Italiana."Agricoltura Coloniale." Firenze 1943.
128 p.

_____

L'achaea catella Guen. della Somalia.
Esraz. "Atti VIII Congresso Entomologico."
Stockholm 1950.

———————

Per una piu adeguata condotta contro
le cavallette in Somalia. "Rivista di
Agricoltura Subtropicale e Tropicale."
Nos. 10-12. Firenze 1950.

———————

Recenti progressi nella lotta contro
le cavallette. "Rivista di Agricoltura
Subtropicale e Tropicale." Nos. 4-6.
Firenze 1950.

———————

La riunione del Desert Locust Control
Advisory Committee di Nairobi. "Rivista
di Agricoltura Subtropicale e Tropicale."
Nos. 7-9. Firenze 1950.

———————

Materiale per la revisione e il
completamento del "Prodromo di Entomologia
Agraria della Somalia Italiana". Rivista
di Agricoltura Subtropicale e Tropicale."
Firenze 1952.

———————

La riunione in Etiopia del Desert Locust
Survey Advisory Committee di Nairobi.
"Rivista di Agricoltura Subtropicale e
Tropicale." Nos. 1-3. Firenze Gennaio-Marzo 1954.

———————

La riunione in Uganda del Desert Locust
Survey Advisory Committee di Nairobi.
"Rivista di Agricoltura Subtropicale e
Tropicale." Nos. 4-6. Firenze Aprile-Giugno 1954.

———————

La prima sessione del Comitato FAO di
lotta contro la cavaletta del deserto
nell'Africa Orientale. "Rivista di Agricoltura
Subtropicale e Tropicale." Nos. 4-6.
Firenze Aprile-Giugno 1957.

———————

Gli insetti dannosi alle piante oleaginose

della Somalia. "Estraz. della Rivista Olearia." 1964.
9 p.

DEL GUERCIO,C.

Afidi raccolti nella Somalia Italiana.
Meridionale. "Redia." Vol. XI. 1916.
299-321 pp.

_____

Note ed osservazione di entomologia agraria:
il disderco del cotone in Somalia ed i suoi
parassiti "Agricoltura Coloniale." Firenze 1918.
5 p.

_____

Il ligeide del cotone in Somalia
(Oxicarenus Hyalipennis,Costa) ed
i suoi sporozoari. "Agricoltura Coloniale."
Firenze 1918.
747 p.

EMERY,G.

Formiche raccolte da Don Euqenio dei
Principi Ruspoli nell'ultimo suo viaggio
nelle regioni dei Somali e dei Galla.
"Annali Museo Civico Storia Naturale di
Genova." Serie II. Vol. XVIII. Genova 1897.

EVERARD,A.C.T.

Ground Reconnaissance in the Alula
Area (21-31 August 19610. Report to
the Director, Desert Locust Survey, Nairobi.
Hargeisa 5 September 1961.
7 pp.

FOOD AND AGRICULTURAL ORGANIZATION.

Desert Locust Control: Report to the
Government of Somalia. Expanded Program
of Technical Assistance. FAO Report No.
1987. Rome 1965.
29 pp. tables.

_____

Locust Control Progress Report No. 8.
1953 "GU" campaign. (Italian Trusteeship
Territory of Somaliland). FAO. Rome
17 August 1953.

GANS, C. AND OTHERS.

Notes on a Herpetilogical collection from the
Somalia. Musee Royale de l'Afrique Centrale.
Annon. 134. Belgique 1965.
93 pp.

GESTRO, R.

Osservazioni sopra le Hispide raccolte
durante l'ultimo spedizione Bottego.
"Annali Museo Civico Storia Naturale di
Genova." Serie 2. Vol. XVIII. Genova 1898.

Contributo allo studio delle Paussidi
della Somalia. "Bollettino Societa
Entomologica Italiana." Vol. LVI.
Genova 1924.
17 p.

Paussidi raccolti dal Marchese S.
Patrizi nell'A.O. (Somalia). "Annali
Museo Civico Storia Naturale di Genova."
Vol. LI. Genova 1925.
31 p.

GIGLIO,TOSSE E.

Ortotteri raccolti nella Somalia
Italiana Meridionale. "Redia". Vol. XII.
1917.
279 p.

GIULIANI, F.

Dieci anni di lotta anticrittogamica
in Somalia. "Rivista di Agricoltura
Subtropicale e Tropicale." Nos. 4-9.
Firenze Aprile-Settembre 1960.
588-607 pp.

G.T.

Nemici del cotone nella Somalia
Italiana. "Agricoltura Coloniale."
FIRENZE 1919.
439 p.

HUSTACHE,A.

Curclionides noubeaux du Museum
de Trieste appartennants a la faune
Somalo-ethiopienne. "Atti Museo Civico
Storia Naturale di Trieste." Vol. XIV.
Trieste 1938.

73 p.

JANNONE,C. AND OTHERS.

Ricerche sul comportamento della
cocciniglia del Banano (Aspidiotus destructor)
al suo arrivo in Italia. (Vol. I). Ricerche
dell'Osservatorio per le Malattie delle piante
di Genova. Relaz. e Monogr. Subtropicale e
Tropicale. No. 83. Istituto Agronomico per
l'Oltremare. Firenze 1962.
132 pp. ills. tables.

LAMERE,A.

Une spece nouvelle de Notohophisis
de L'A.O. (Somalia). "Annali Museo
Civico Storia Naturale di Genova."
Serie III. Vol. VI. Genova 1915.
197 p.

MAGRETTI, P.

Di alcune specie di Imenotteri
raccolte dall'Ing. Robecchi-Brichetti
nel paese dei Somali. "Annali Museo Civico
Storia Naturale di Genova." Serie II.
Vol. XIX. Genova 1898.

Imenotteri della seconda spedizione di
Don Eugenio Ruspoli nel paese dei Somali
e dei Galla. "Annali Museo Civico Storia
Naturale di Genova." Serie II. Vol. IX.
Genova 1898.

OBENBERGER,J.

Buprestides recueillis dans l'Afrique
Orientale Tropicale par le Marquis S.
Patrizi (Somalia). "Annali Museo Civico
Storia Naturale di Genova." Serie III.
Vol. IX. Genova 1920-22.
317 p.

PAOLI,GUIDO.

Prodromo di entomologia agraria della
Somalia Italiana: Relazione di una
Missione compiuta al Villagio Duca degli
Abruzzi in colloborazione col Dr. Alfonso
Chiaromonte dell'Istituto Agricolo Coloniale
Italiano. Tipografia Mariano Ricci.
Firenze 1931-33.
426 pp. ills.

Caratteri diagnostici dell'empoasca
e descrizioni di nuove specie.
"Atti X Congresso Internazionale
di Zoologia." 1932.
1046 p.

Intorno ad una recente publicazione
sulle cause nemiche delle piantagioni
di cotone in Somalia. "Agricoltura
Coloniale." Firenze 1935.
15 p.

PENSO,G.

Su due Anguilluline parassite dei
banani nella Somalia Italiana. "Agricoltura
Coloniale." Firenze 1939.
355 pp.

PIC,M.

Un Anthicus nouveau de la Somalie
recueilli par M.le Lieut.C.C. Citerni.
"Annali Museo Civico Storia Naturale di
Genova." Serie III. Vol. I. Genova 1904.
92 p.

ROCCATI,R.

Appunti di entomologia agraria in Somalia:
parte I. Istituto Agronomico per l'Oltremare.
Fasc. No. 4280. Firenze 1954.
27 pp.

RAINEY,R.C. AND WALOFF,Z.V.

Desert Locust Migrations and
Synoptic Meterology in the
Gulf of Aden Area. "Journal of
Animal Ecology." London 1948.
101-112 pp.

Preliminary Surveys of the potential
outbreak areas of the Desert Locust on
the coast of Western British Somaliland.
Anti-Locust Research Centre. Nairobi 1949.

RUI,D. AND GIRALDI,G.

Ricerche sul comportamento della
cocciniglia del cocco e della banano
al suo arivo in Italia. Ricerche
dell'Osservatorio per le Malattie delle

Piante. Verona.
132 pp.

RUSSO,G.

Il deperimento delle piantagioni
di cotone nella Somalia Italiana:
Cause, mezzi di cura. "Agricoltura
Coloniale." Firenze 1932.
3-74-132 pp.

─────────────

Principali cause nemiche delle
piantagioni di cotone nella Somalia
Italiana. "Agricoltura Coloniale."
Vol. XXVIII. Firenze 1934.
561 p.

S.A.I.S.

Prove di disinfestazione del
seme di cotone S.2. "Annali
S.A.I.S." Genova 1935.
43 p.

SCIACCHITANO,I.

Nuova specie di Gordioideo
della Somalia. "Monitore Zoologico
Italiano." No. 3-4. Universita di
Firenze. Firenze 1961.
146-148 pp.

SOZIO,A.S.

La lotta contro la cavalletta del
deserto in Somalia. "Rivista di
Agricoltura Subtropicale e Tropicale."
Nos. 7-9. Firenze 1953.

SACCO,T.

Possibilita d'incremento della
vetiveria zizanoides Stapf. della
Somalia come pianta essenziera. "Rivista
di Agricoltura Subtropicale e Tropicale."
Nos. 1-3. Firenze Gennaio-Marzo 1960.
81-87 pp.

SCHUTTERER,H.

Zur Kennitnis der Schadling und
Krankheiten der Kulturpflanzen in
Somalia. Instit. fur die Auslandische
Landwirtschaft. 1964.

3.   Fish and River Hydro-Biology

ARCANGELI,A.

Isopodi terrestri raccolti in Somalia dal
Dr. G. Russo. "Laboratoria di Zoologia Generale
ed Agraria dell'Universita di Portici". Vol. XXVI.
Portici 1932.
47 p.

BACCI,G.

Studi vari sui Molluschi. "Annali Museo Civico
Storia Naturale di Genova". Vol.LVII. Genova 1939.
333 p.

───────────────

Studi vari sui Molluschi. "Annali Museo Civico
Storia Naturale di Genova". Vol. LXI. Genova.
194 p.

BISACCHI, J.

Una nuova specie Assiminea della Somalia Italiana.
"Annali Museo Civico Storia Naturale di Genova".
Vol. LVI. Genova 1934.
263 p.

CARNIGLIA,G.B.

Note sulla pesca dei mari della Somalia Italiana.
"Somalia Italiana". No. I-3. Mogadiscio 1930.
10 p.

CIFERRI, R.

Le associazioni del litorale marino della Somalia Meridionale.
"Rivista di Biologia Coloniale". Roma 1939.
5 p.

COZZOLINI, A.

Osservazioni etologiche sulla Chelonemydas delle coste
della Somalia Italiana. "Rivista di Biologia Coloniale".
No. 8. Roma 1938.
241 p.

DELLA CROCE,G.

La Madreperia. "Somalia Italiana". No. I-3.
Mogadiscio 1930.
14 p.

DE MORI,A.

L'ambra grigia (Somalia). "Rivista Italiana di

Essenze e Profumi''. No. I. Milano 1931.
23 p.

DE TONI,G.B.

Alghe della Somalia raccolte da L. Cufino.
''Africa Italiana''. Roma 1920.
134 p.

FRASER-BRUNNER, A.

Local and scientific names of the fishes collected
on the Coast of the Trust Territory of Somalia.
F.A.O. Expanding Program. No. 52/8/5222. Rome 1952.
19 pp. (Scientific,English,Somali terms).

_____AND OGILVIE.

Exploratory fishery survey in Somalia. U.S. Operations
Mission to Italy. Rome 1953.
83 pp.

FUNAIOLI,U. AND RONCATI,R.

La pesca tradizionale nel Basso Uebi Scebeli (Somalia).
''Rivista di Agricoltura Subtropicale e Tropicale''.
No. 4-6. Firenze 1964.
250-272 pp.

GIANFERRARI,L.

Nuovi orizzonti sui Ciprindi di Callis (Somalia).
''Atti Societa Scienze Naturali di Milano''.
Vol. LXXVI. No. 2. Milano 1937.
198 p.

(R) GOVERNO DELLA SOMALIA ITALIANA.

La pesca nella Somalia Italiana. ''Rassegna Economica
delle Colonie''. Roma 1929.
426 p.

_____

La Madreperla della Somalia Italiana. ''Rassegna Economica
delle Colonie''. Roma 1930.
722 p.

GUIGLIA,D.

Spedizione Patrizi nel Basso Giuba ed Oltregiuba
1934 (Pesci). ''Annali Museo Civico Storia Naturale di Genova''.
Vol. LVIII. Genova 1939.
27 p.

ISNARDI,G.

La pesca in Somalia. "Illustrazione Coloniale".
No. 2. Milano 1930.
27 p.

JOHNSON, L.R.

Fisheries Reconnaissance in Somalia, East Africa.
U.S. Operations Mission to Italy. Rome 1956.
29 pp.

LINO,E.

La pesca in Somalia. "Africa". Fasc. No. 9-10. Roma 1951.
289 p

LOTHAR,F.

Spedizione biologica in Somalia dell'Universita di
Firenze 1959: Risultati Zoologici (V.Mollusca).
"Monitore Zoologica Italiano". Vol.LXXIX. No. 1-2. 1961.
39-45 pp.

MASI,L.

Descrizione du due Fillopodi Anostraci della
Somalia Italiana. "Annali Museo Civico Storia
Naturale di Genova". Vol. LII. Genova 1928.
93 p.

MOAL,R.A. AND GRATEAU.

Peche en T.F.A.I. (Territoires Francaise des Afars et
des Issas). "Revue Pount". No. 3. La Societe D'etudes
de l'Afrique Orientale. Djibouti 1967.

NINNI,E.

Per la pesca in Libia,Eritrea e Somalia.
Officina Grafiche Ferrari. Venezia 1921.
78 pp. ills.

PARENZAN,P.

Pesci delle acque sotterranee della Somalia.
"Bollettino di Pesca,Pescicoltura e Idrobiologia".
Vol. XIV. 1938.
795 p.

Pesci,pesca e pescosita dell'Uebi Scebeli e del Giuba
in Somalia. "Collani Scient. e Documenti dell'Africa
Orientale". Vol. IV. Ministero Africa Italiana. Ufficio
Studi. Roma 1941.
13-30 pp.

SEGUENZA,G.

Viaggio Antinori,Beccari ed Issel nel Mar Rosso e
tra i Bogos "Crostacei",Intorno ad alcuni cirripedi
raccolti nel Mar Rosso. "Annali Museo Civico Storia
Naturale di Genova". Genova 1873.
8 p.

SERRA MENICHEDDA,F.

La pesca e l'industria peschereccia in Somalia:
Appunti ricavati dalla relazione sui servizi della Marina
Mercantile in Somalia per l'anno 1930. BICP. 1940.
17 p.

TORTONESE,E.

Pesci marini della Somalia Italiana raccolti
dal Marchese Negrotto Cambiaso."Atti Reale
Accademia Ligure di Scienze e Lettere". No. 2. 1941.
109 p.

VINCiGUERRA,D.

Vari studi Ittiologici (Somalia). "Annali Museo Civico
Storia Naturale di Genova.". Vol. XXXIII. Genova 1893.
448 p.

_____

Vari studi Ittiologici (Somalia). "Annali Museo Civico
Storia Naturale di Genova". Serie II. Vol. XV. Genova 1895.
19 p.

_____

Vari studi Ittiologici (Somalia). "Annali Museo Civico
Storia Naturale di Genova". Serie II. Vol. XVII. Genova 1897.

_____

Vari studi Ittiologici (Somalia). "Annali Museo Civico
Storia Naturale di Genova". Serie III. Vol. V. Genova 1913.
293 p.

_____

Vari studi Ittiologici (Somalia). "Annali Museo Civico
Storia Naturale di Genova". Serie III. Vol. IX. Genova 1922.

_____

Vari studi Ittiologici (Somalia). "Annali Museo Civico
Storia Naturale di Genova". Vol. LII. Genova 1928.

_____

Vari studi Ittiologici (Somalia). "Annali Museo Civico
Storia Naturale di Genova". Vol. LV. Genova 1932.

40 p.

Contributo alla conoscenze della fauna ittiologica
dell'Uebi Scebeli. "Annali Museo Civico Storia
Naturale di Genova". Serie II. Vol. IX. Genova 1922.
378-389 pp.

ZOLEZZI,G.

Descrizioni di tre nuovi pesci del Giuba
raccolti dalla Missione Ittiologica in
Africa Orientale Italiana. BICP.Vol. XV. Fasc. No. 2. 1939.

Pesci del Giuba e dell'Uebi Scebeli raccolti
dalla Missione Ittiologica in Africa Orientale
Italiana. "Collani Scient. e Documenti dell'Africa Orientale".
Vol. IV. Ministero Africa Italiana. Ufficio Studi. Roma 1941.
33-49 pp.

ZUCCO,G.

La Spata Wahlberg, Kraus del Giuba (Mollusco).
"Bollettino Informazione Economica".
Ministero delle Colonie. Roma 1925.
789 p.

4.   Game and Wild Life

AMMINISTRAZIONE FIDUCIARIA ITALIANA DELLA SOMALIA.

Ordinamento per l'esercizio della caccia nel
territorio della Somalia. Stamperia AFIS.
Mogadiscio 1951.
32 pp.

BELFANTI,S.

Un valeno di frecce: Uabaio usato in
Abissinia,Somalia. R. Istituto Lomb. Scienze
Lettere. Serie II. Vol. LXIX. Fasc. No. XVI-XX. 1936.
960 p.

BLATHWAYT, R.

Hunting the lion and rhinoceros: a talk
with Mr. H. W. Seton-Karr. "Travel". Vol.III.
London 1898.
174.182 pp.

EDYE,J.S.

Sport in India and Somali: with hints to
young Shikares. Gale Polden. London 1895.
170 pp.

GHIKA,N. AND COMANESTI, D.

Cina mois au pays des Somalis. Georg & Co.
Geneve 1896.
223 pp.

(R) GOVERNO DELLA SOMALIA.

La caccia al dik dik nella Somalia Italiana.
"Rassegna Economica delle Colonie". Roma 1929.
629 p.

Regolamento generale sulla caccia nella Somalia
Italiana (Decreto Governator. No. 7842 del 25-11-1929).
"Rassegna Economica delle Colonie". Roma 1930.
153 p.

GLYN,F. AND BARON WOLVERTON.

Five Months Sport in Somaliland.
London 1894.

HASKARD,D.

Lion shooting in Somaliland.
"Travel Explorations". Vol. 2. London 1909.
342-347 pp.

HERBERT,A.

Two Dians in Somaliland. Thomas Nelson & Sons Ltd.
London 1908.
252 pp.

Two Dianas in Somaliland: the record of a
shooting trip. John Zane. London and New York 1908.
306 pp.

HOYOS,E. (Junior).

Zu den Auliham Reise und Jagderlebnisse im Somaliland.
Gerold & C. Vienna 1884.
185 pp.

KINGDO,J.

Big Game in Somaliland. United Service Institution.
Vol. 52. (India) 1922.
402-411 pp.

LOWTHER,H.C.

Lion hunting beyond the Haud.
"19th Cent". September 1895.
474-493 pp.

MAINWARING,H.G.

A soldier's shikar trips: with photographs
of Somaliland by Maj. Bhonam Christie. London 1920.
213 pp.

MELLIS,C.J.

Lion-hunting in Somaliland: an account of
a pig-sticking, the African wart hog. London 1895.
186 pp.

MORSE,A.H.E.

Lion hunting in Somaliland. "W.W. Magazine".
Vol. 46. London 1922.
505-514 pp.

NEUVILLE,H.

Notes sur le onabe poison de fleches de
l'Afrique Orientale et sur la tribe des Mitgen.
"L'Anthropologie". Vol. XXVII. Paris 1916.
369-386 pp.

PAGENTAND,V.

Routes of shooting expeditions in Northern
Somaliland. London 1894.

PEARCE, F.B.

Rambles in lion Land: three months leave
passed in Somaliland. Chapman & Hall. London 1898.
260 pp.

PEASE,A.E.

Travel and Sport in Africa.
(3 Vols). London 1902.

PEEL,C.V.A.

Somali: being an account of two expeditions into the
far interior. London 1900.

POTOCKY,Z.J. (Count).

Sport in Somaliland: being an account of a hunting
trip in that region. (Transl. from the Polish by J. Curtin).
Row Sand Ward Ltd. London 1900.

140 pp.

SHORTHOSE,W.T.

Sport and adventure in Africa: a record of
12 years of big game hunting, campaigning
and travelling in the wilds of tropical Africa. 1923.
316 pp. Maps.

STOCKLEY,V.M.

Big game shooting in India, Burma and
Somaliland. Cox H. London 1913.
XII, + 282 pp.

SWAYNE,H.G.C.

Seventeen Trips through Somaliland:
A record of exploration and big game
shooting, 1885-1893. Rowland Ward & Co.
London 1895.
377 pp. Maps, ills.

A Woman's Pleasure Trip in Somaliland.
J. Wright. Bristol 1907.
XII, + 172 pp. maps.

TEDESCO ZAMMARANO,V.

Come ho rintracciato l'Ammodarcas Clarkei
a 4° nord e 45° 30° est di Greenwich.
"Bollettino Societa Geografica Italiana".
Roma 1919.
367 p.

Impressioni di caccia in Somalia. Italiana.
1° Edizione. Alfieri & Lacroix. Roma 1920.
198 pp.

Impressioni di caccia in Somalia Italiana.
2° Edizione. Agnelli. Milano 1929.
208 pp.

Hic sunt leones: Un anno di esplorazione
e di caccia in Somalia. Societa An.Libreria Italiana.
Roma 1924.
312 pp. maps.

Il sentiero delle belve. Mondadori (Editore).
Milano 1929.
343 pp.

Fauna e caccia. (a cura Ministero delle Colonie).
Sindacato Ital. Arti Grafiche. Roma 1930.
222 pp.

WOLWERTON,

Five Months sport in Somali-Land.
Chapman & Hall. London 1894.
108 pp.

ZICCARDI,F.

Il cacciatore: Caccia Grossa e turismo
in Somalia. "Africa". Roma 1950.
175 p.

ZUCCO, G.

Il cuocio marino e la cattura degli squali.
"Bollettino Informazione Economica Ministero delle Colonie".
Roma 1927.
579 p.

5. Insects

ANONYMOUS.

L'allevamento del baco da seta (Bombix mori)
nella Somalia Italiana. "Somalia Italiana".
No. 1-3. Mogadiscio 1932.
32 p.

Somalia: esperimenti di bachicoltura.
"Bollettino Informazione Economica". No. 5-7.
Ministero delle Colonie. Roma 1915.
367 p.

BOUVIER,E.D.

Sur un nouvel Apus de la Somalis Capture
par le Cap. Bottego. "Annali Museo Civico
Storia Naturale di Genova." Genova 1899.
5 p.

BRENSKE,E.

Risultati biologici della missione Bottego
al Giuba: Melolonthini e Rutelini.
"Annali Museo Civico Storia Naturale di Genova".
Serie II. Vol. XV. Genova 1895.

DI CAPORIACCO, L.

Alcuni Aracnidi di Somalia. "Bollettino del
Laboratoria di Zoologia Generale ed Agraria". Vol. XXXXI.
Universita di Portici. Portici 1941.
295 p.

MUSEO CIVICO DI STORIA NATURALE DI GENOVA.

Risultati zoologici della missione Bottego al Giuba:
Rincoti,Formiche,Staphylinidae,nuove specie di
Curculionidae,Coleotteri,Imenotteri,Plataspidinae,
Anthicidae e Pseudoanthicidae,Dytiscidae e Gyrinidae.
"Annali Museo Civico Storia Naturale di Genova".
Serie II. Vol.XVII. Genova 1895.

PAVESI,P.

Aracnidi somali e galla raccolti da Don
Eugenio Ruspoli. Vol. I. Tipografia Sordomuti. 1883.

PEEL, C.V.A.

On a collection of Insects and Arachnids made in
1895 and 1897 (Somaliland) with descriptions of
New Species. "Proceedings of the Zoological Society.
London 1900.
4-63 pp.

ROSSI, V.

Baco da seta nella Somalia Italiana.
Ministero delle Colonie. Istituto Poligrafico
dello Stato. Roma 1931.
5 pp.

II baco da seta nella Somalia Italiana.
"Rassegna Economica delle Colonie". Roma 1931.
116 p.

SERRAZANETTI,M.

L'allevamento dei bachi da seta nella Somalia Italiana.
"Rassegna Economica delle Colonie". Roma 1930. 316 p.
And in "Agricoltura Coloniale". Firenze 1930. 53 p.

SIMONETTA,A. AND FUNAIOLI,U.

Spedizione biologico in Somalia 1959.
(III Parte,Risultati Zoologici:Insectivora).

Istituto Zoologico Universita degli Studi di Firenze.
Firenze 1960.
7 pp.

6.   Mammals

DE BEAUX,O.

Vari studi sui mammiferi (Somalia).
"Atti Societa Scienze e Lettere di Genova".
Fasc. No. III. Vol. III. Genova.
149 p.

Vari studi sui mammiferi (Somalia).
"Atti II Congresso Studi Coloniali".
Vol. III. 1934.
124 p.

Vari studi sui mammiferi (Somalia).
Annali Museo Civico Storia Naturale di Genova".
Vol.LXXIII. Genova 1934.

Vari studi sui mammiferi (Somalia).
"Annali Museo Civico Storia Naturale di Genova".
Vol. LVIII. Genova 1939.
150 p.

DRAKE-BROKMAN,R.E.

Mammals of Somaliland. London 1910-12.
201 pp.

ELLIOT,D.G.

List of mammals from Somaliland obtained by
the Field Columbian Museum's Expedition.
Field Columbian Museum's Publications. No. 19.
Chicago 1897.
109-155 pp.

FUNAIOLI,U.

I mammiferi della Somalia: Cenni al loro interese nel'economia del paese. "Rivista di Agricoltura Subtropicale e Tropicale". No. 7-9. Firenze Luglio-Settembre 1959. 335-355 pp.

_____

Statut actuel des ongules in Somalia. "Mammalia". Vol.XXVI. Paris 1960. 97-111 pp.

_____ AND SIMONETTA,A.

A propos du grand Koudou on Somalie. "Mammalia". No. 3. Paris 1962. 450-451 pp.

PECK,E.F.

Salt intake in relation to Cutaneous Necrosis and Arthritis of One-humped camels (Camelus dromedarius) in British Somaliland. "Vet.Record". Vol. 51. London 1939. 1355-60 pp.

PETAZZI,E.

Per la protezione del dik dik. "Somalia Italiana". No. 3. Mogadiscio 1929.

SIMONETTA,A. AND FUNAIOLI,U.

Spedizione biologica in Somalia 1959: Parte II. (Risultati Zoologici: Carnivora). Istituto Zoologico Universita degli Studi di Firenze. Firenze 1960. 31 pp.

SOLDI,P.

Note di osservazione sui mammiferi dell'Alta Somalia anni 1951-1953. Istituto Agronomico per l'Oltremare. Fasc. No. 3170. Firenze 1953. 7 pp.

THOMAS,E.O.

On a collection of mammals obtained in Somaliland by Maj. H.H. Dunn, R.A. M.C. with descriptions of allied specimens from other localities. "Annals and Magazine of Natural History". Vol.XIV. London 1904.

TOSCHI,A.

Missione del Prof. Scortecci in Somalia nel 1955. (Mammiferi).
"Atti della Societa Italiana di Scienze Naturali".
Vol. 92. No. 2. Milano 1956.
121-128 pp.

7. Ornithology

ARCHER,G. AND GODMAN,E.M.

The birds of British Somaliland and the Gulf of Aden:
Their life histories, breeding habits, and eggs.
(2 Vol). Gurney and Jackson. London 1937.
290-626 pp. map. ills.

BANNERMAN,D.

On a collection of birds made in Northern Somaliland
(By G. W. Bury). "Annali Museo Civico Storia Naturale
di Genova." Genova 1910.
291-327 pp.

ELLIOT,D.G.

Catalogue of a collection of birds obtained by the
recent expedition into Somaliland authorized and
equipped by the Field Columbian Museum.
(description of new species). Publications of Field
Columbian Museum No. 17. Ornithol. Series No. 2.
Chicago 1897.
29-67 pp.

FUNAIOLI,U. AND ROCCHETTI,G.

Il guano di pipistrelli della Somalia Meridionale.
"Rivista di Agricoltura Subtropicale e Tropicale".
No. 7-9. Firenze 1963.
292-298 pp.

HAWKER,R.M.

On two new birds from Somaliland. "Bulletin of
British Ornithological Club". Vol. IIV. London May 1898.

_____

On the results of a collecting tour of three months
in Somaliland. "Bulletin of British Ornithological Club".
London 1899.
52-81 pp. map. ills.

HEUGLIN, (M.THEODOR VON).

Ornithologie Nordost-Afrikas,der Nilquellen-und
Kusten-Gebiete des Rothen Meers und des Nordlichen
Somali-Landes. Fischer. Kassel 1869-1873.

LORT,P.E.

On Birds observed in the Goolis Mountains in
Northern Somaliland. Field Columbian Museum.
Chicao 1896.
62-87 pp.

———————————

Narrative of a Visit to Somaliland in 1897 with
Field Notes on the Birds obtained during the Expedition.
Field Columbian Museum. Chicago 1898.
382-425 pp. ills.

MOLTONI,E.

Vari studi ornitologici (Somalia). "Atti Societa
Scienze Naturali di Mialno". Vol. LXXII. Milano 1933.

———————————

Vari studi ornitologici (Somalia). "Atti Societa
Scienze Naturali di Milano". Vol. LXXV. Milano 1936.
307p.And Vol. LXXIV Milano 1935. 333 p.

———————————

Vari studi ornitologici (Somalia).
"Annali Museo Civico Storia Naturale di Genova".
Vol. LVIII. Genova 1939.
85 p.

SALVADORI,T.

Vari studi ornitologici (Somalia). "Annali Museo Civico

Storia Naturale di Genova". Vol.XVI. Serie II. Genova 1896.
43 p.

———————————

Vari studi ornitologici (Somalia). "Annali Museo Civico
Storia Naturale di Genova". Vol. XVIII. Serie II. Genova 1898.

———————————

Vari studi ornitologici (Somalia). "Annali Museo Civico
Storia Naturale di Genova". Vol. V. Serie III. Genova 1913.
304 p.

Vari studi ornitologici (Somalia). "Annali Museo Civico
Storia Naturale di Genova". Vol:VI. Genova 1915.
72 p.

SHARPE,R.B.

On a collection of Birds made by Dr. Donaldson Smith in
Northern Somaliland. "Proceedings of tne Zoological
Society,London". London 1895.
457-520 pp.

On a collection of Birds made by Dr. Donaldson Smith in
Northern Somaliland. "Proceedings of the Zoological
Society ot London". Vol. II. London 1901.
298-316 pp.

TONELLI,R.

Ixodidea del Fezzan e della Somalia Italiana raccolta
dal Prot. Zavattari e dal Prof.G.Tedesc...i. "Atti Societa
Scienze Naturali di Milano." Vol.LXXV. Milano 1936.
243 p.

TOSCHI,A.

Uccelli del Giuba. "Rivista Italiana di Ornitologia".
Vol.VI. Serie II. 1936.

8.   Reptile

BORELLI,A.

Studi vari sugli scorpioni. "Annali Museo Civico
Storia Naturale di Genova". Serie III. Vol. VIII.
Genova 1920.
359 p.

Studi vari sugli scorpioni. "Annali Museo Civico
Storia Naturale di Genova". Vol. LI. Genova 1925.
316 p.

_____

Studi vari sugli scorpioni. "Annali Museo Civico
Storia Naturale di Genova". Vol. LII. 1928.
9 p.

BOULENGER,G.A.

Some list of Reptiles and Batracians. "Annali Muesseo
Civico Storia Naturale di Genova". Serie II. Vol. XII.
Genova 1891.
13 p.

_____

Some list of Reptiles and Batracians. "Annali Museo
Civico Storia Naturale di Genova". Serie II.VOI. XVII.
Genova 1897.
5-15-275 pp.

_____

Some list of Reptiles and Batracians. "Annali Museo
Civico Storia Naturale di Genova". Serie II.
Vol. XVIII. Genova 1898.

_____

Some list of Reptiles and Batracians. "Annali Museo
Civico Storia Naturale di Genova". Serie III.
Vol. IV. 1910. Genova.
308-310 pp.

_____

Some list of Reptiles and Batracians. "Annali Museo
Civico Storia Naturale di Genova." Serie III.
Vol. V. Genova 1913.
329 p.

CALABRESI,E.

Vari studi sui rettili e gli anfibi della Somalia
Italiana. "Atti Societa Toscana di Scienze Naturali".
Vol. LXVI. Pisa 1927.

PARKER, H.W.

Two collections of Reptiles and Amphibians from
British Somaliland. London 1932.
335-367 pp.

The lizards of British Somaliland. "Bull. Mus. Zool".
Harvard 1942.

The snakes of Somaliland and the Sokotra Islands. 1949.

SCORTECCI,G.

Vari studi sui Rettili ed Anfibi della Somalia Italiana.
"Atti Societa Scienze Naturali di Milano". Vol.LXVIII.
Milano 1929.

Gli Ofidi velenosi dell'Africa Italiana.
Istituto Sieroterapico Milanese. Milano 1939.
292 pp. ills.

SILVESTRI,F.

Studi vari sui Chilopodi (Somalia). "Annali Museo
Civico Storia Naturale di Genova". Serie II.
Vol. XVII. Genova 1897
55-301 pp.

9.   Veterinary

ANONYMOUS

L'Istituto Sierovaccinogeno di Merca.
"Bollettino Informazione Economica.
Ministero Colonie." Roma 1925.
495 p.

Campagna vaccinatorie contro la peste
bovina nella R. Residenza di Brava, Gelib
Margherita e nell'Oltregiuba. "La Somalia
Italiana." No. I. Mogadiscio 1926.

———————

Campagna vaccinatoria del bestiame nelle
regioni del "Doi" e del "Bai". "La Somalia
Italiana. Mogadiscio" 1927.

———————

Svolgimento della campagna vaccinatoria del
bestiame nella zona di Bur Acaba. "La Somalia
Italiana." No. Mogadiscio 1928.

———————

Il servizio veterinario in Somalia. "Annali
Africa Italiana." Anno III. Vol. I. Roma 1940.
851 p.

APPLETON,A.F.

Report on Veterinary Work of Somaliland
Expedition. "East Africa Pamphlet." No. 319. 1904.

AUGUADRA,P.

Caso di Leishmaniosi nel cane in Somalia.
"Annali della Societa di Medicina e Igiene
Tropicale della Somalia." Vol. 2. Mogadiscio 1958.
179-181 pp.

———————

Contributo alla Orchiectomia del dromedario.
"Annali Societa di Medicina ed Igiene. Tropicale
della Somalia." Vol. 2. Mogadiscio 1958.
5 10 pp.

———————

Grippe o influenze del dromedario somalo.
"Annali Societa di Medicina ed Igiene
Tropicale della Somalia." Vol. 2. Mogadiscio 1958.
99-105 pp.

———————

Contributo alla conoscenze della necrobacillosi
dei ruminanti selvatici. "Clinica Veterinaria. Vol. 85" Milano 1962.
609-613 pp.

———————

Contributo alla profilassi e alla terapia
della tripanosi in Somalia e nel Congo con
l'impiego dell'Antrycide,del Naganol e del
Berenil. "Clinica Veterinaria." Vol. 86. Milano 1963.
8 pp.

BORSETTI,ARTURO

Osservazioni su di una infezione di peste equina
negli animale della Societa Agricola Italo-Somala.
"Agricoltura Coloniale". No. 9. Firenze Settembre 1924.
290-299 pp. tables.

BRITISH VETERINARY TEAM.

Report on livestock diseases in Northern
Somaliland October 1969-March 1971. Ministry of
Rural Development. Mogadiscio 1971.
19 pp.

CARUSILLO,G.

La Tripanosoniasi dei bovini in Somalia.
Ministero della Sanita Veterinario e Lavoro.
Dipartimento Veterinario. Mogadiscio 1958.
14 pp.

_____

Risultati della difesa sanitaria del bestiame
in Somalia. "Rivista di Agricoltura Subtropicale
e Tropicale." Nos. 4-9. Firenze Aprile-Settembre 1960.
464-468 pp.

_____

La lotta contro le malattie ingettive
degli animali. "Notiziario Sanitaria della
Somalia." Vol. I. Fasc. No. 2. Mogadiscio
Settembre-Ottobre 1962.
51 52 pp.

_____

La tripanosomiasi dei bovini in Somalia.
"Rivista di Agricoltura Subtropicale e Tropicale."
Firenze Novembre Dicembre 1963.

_____

La tripanosomiasi dei bovini in Somalia.
Scuola Tipografia Missione Cattolica. Mogadiscio.
(English-Italian).

CONGIU,S.

La profilassi della peste bovina in Somalia:

Controlli di infettivita del virus capra
sopra i bovini Somali. "Annali della Societa
Medicina ed Igiene Tropicale della Somalia."
Vol. 2. Mogadiscio 1958.
183-195 pp.

CONGIU,S. AND SOBRERO,L.

La setaria equina e la sua microfilaria
nell'asino somalo. "Annali della Societa
Medicina ed Igiene Tropicale della Somalia."
Vol. 2. Mogadiscio 1958.
37-41 pp.

CROVERI,P.

Sull'azione svolta dalla direzione dei servizi
zootecnici e dall'Istituto Sierovaccinogeno
della Somalia Italiana dal 1915 al Giugno 1918.
G. Bertero. Roma 1919.
124 pp.

_____

Osservazioni sulla biologia della Glossina Pallidipes
della Somalia Italiana e sulla trasmissione agli
animali domestici della Tripanosi detta "Ghendi".
"Annali d'Igiene." No. 7. 1919.
448 p.

CROVERI,P. AND SALVESTRONI,B.

Osservazioni sull'ematologia normale e
patalogica dei bovini somali e specialmente
riguardo alla pests bovina ed alla "Ghendi"
(Triponosomiasi): Note di tecnica sierovaccinatoria
antipestosa. "Agricoltura Coloniale." Firenze 1921.
421 pp.

COZZI, PAOLO.

Riorganizzazione dei Servizi Veterinari e valorizzazione
del patrimonio Zootecnico della Somalia. Comunita
Economica Europea. Direzione Generale del Fondo
Europeo di Sviluppo. Bruxelles Aprile 1964.
57 pp.

DI DOMIZIO, G.

I tripanosomi patogeni del bestiame nella
Somalia Italiana con particolare riguardo
al "Trypanosoma congolense". "Rinnovamento
Medico." Vol. VII. Napoli 1929.

_____

A proposito delle Glossine nella Somalia
Italiana. "III Congresso Nazionale Medico
Coloniale." Tripoli 1930.

_____

A proposito delle Glossine nella Somalia
Italiana. "Bollettino Societa Italiana
Medica ed Igiene Coloniale." Vol. II. 1931.

DI DOMIZIO,A. AND TARANTINO,G.B.

Sul Tripanosoma Brucei nei Dromedari della
Somalia Italiana. "Atti II Congresso Studi
Coloniali." Vol. VIII. Firenze 1934.
208 p.

_____

Sul Tripanosoma Brucei nei Dromedari della
Somalia Italiana. "Atti Congresso Studi Coloniali."
Vol. VII. 1936.

FALCONE,A.

L'Istituto Sierovaccinogeno della Somalia
Italiana. Istituto Poligrafico dello Stato.
Roma 1931.

GIRADON,C.A.

Alcune note sulla Strangilosi del
cammello in Somalia. "Mil. Medico Veterinario."
No. 6. 1940.
447 p.

_____

Contributo allo studio della lotta
contro le tripanosi del cammello in Somalia.
"Rivista Militare Medica Veterinaria." No. 3. 1940.

GADOLA,A.

Zootecnica,Profilassi ed Igiene Zootecnica
in Africa Orientale (Somalia). Istituto
Superfiore di Sanita. Roma 1947.
39 pp.

HASSAN ABDI EIBACAR.

Rapporto sul carbonchio ematico nella regione
del Nord. "Notiziario Sanit. della Somalia."
Vol. I. Fasc. II. Firenze 1962.
53-54 pp.

_____

Prospettive e nuovi programmi di sviluppo
Veterinari e Zootecnici in Somalia. Ministero
dell'Agricoltura e Zootecnia. Stamperia del
Governo. Mogadiscio.

MARTOGLIO,F.

Le epizoozie predominanti nella Somalia
Italiana e la loro profilassi. "Bollettino
Societa Italiana Medicina e Igiene Coloniali."
Vol. II. 1911.

———————————

Le epizozzie predominanti nella Somalia
Italiana e loro profilassi. Off. Poligrafico
Italiano. 1911.
17 pp.

———————————

La peste bovina e le tripanosomiasi nella
Somalia Italiana. U.T.E.T. Torini 1911.

———————————

La peste bovina e le tripanosomiasi
nella Somalia Italiana. A. I. Sperimentale.
Vol. XXI. 1911.

MOGGRIDGE,J.Y.

Some observations on the seasonal spread
of Glossina Pallidipes in Italian Somaliland
with notes on G. Brevipalpis and G. Austeni.
"Bulletin of Entomological Research." Vol. 27.
Part. 3. London September 1936.
449-466 pp. ills.

MOHAMED ALI NUR.

Considerazioni e confronti sull'attivita
svolta dal Dipartimento Veterinario negli
anni 1961-1962" Notiziario Sanitario della
Somalia." Vol. I. Fasc. No. 2. Mogadiscio
Settembre-Ottobre 1962.
47-50 pp.

OECONOMICUS.

Ricerche zootecniche,veterinarie sugli animali
domestici della Somalia. "Bollettino Mensile
Camera di Commercio della Somalia." Nos. 8 9.

PELLEGRINI,D.

Alcune osservazioni sulla Schistosomiasi

bovina in Somalia (Basso Giuba). "Rivista di
Parassitologia." Nos. 13-14-15. 1952.

PELLEGRINI,D. AND ROETTI,C.

Un'Epizoozia da Tripanosoma Brucei nel cammello
in Somalia. "La Clinica Veterinaria." Milano 1939.
263 p.

ROSETTI,A.

Osservazioni su di una infeszione di
peste equina negli animali della S.A.I.S.
"Agricoltura Coloniale." Firenze 1924.
289 p.

ROSSETTI, G.

Veterinari in Somalia: aspetti ed
importanza della assistenza zootecnica.
"Africa" No. 9. Roma 1950.
207 p.

_____

L'opera dei Veterinari in Somalia. "Annali
della Societa di Medicina ed Igiene Tropicale."
Vol. I. Mogadiscio 1953.
137 152 pp.

ROSETTI,G. AND CONGIU,S.

Ricerche zootecniche veterinarie sugli animali
domestici della Somalia. A.F.I.S. Ispettorato
Veterinario. Mogadiscio 1955.
203 pp.

SOBRERO,L.

La Spirochetosi Aviare in Somalia: Studio
Sperimentale della Malattia (Profilassi) No. 2.   1954.

_____

Su una miasi del cane in Somalia.
"Rivista di Parassitologia." No. I. 1955.

_____

Bulinus (physopsis) abyssinicus ospite
intermedio di Schistosoma Haematobium
in Somalia: Ricostruzione del ciclo di vita del
parassita. "Rendiconto dell'Accademia Nazionale
dei Lincei." Serie VIII. Vol.XXII. No. 4. Roma 1957.

_____

Alterazione del fegato nella Schistosomiasi
dei bovini somali. "Annali della Societa di
Medicina e Igiene Tropicale della Somalia."
Vol. II. Mogadiscio 1958.
85-89 pp.

L'attivita dell'Istituto Sierovaccinogeno
Somalo dal I° Aprile 1950 al 31 Marzo 1959;
"Rivista di Agricoltura Subtropicale e Tropicale."
Nos. 4-9. Firenze 1960.

Animali domestici ospiti naturali di
Schistosoma bovis in Somalia. "Rivista
di Parassitologia". No. I. 1960.

SOBRERO,L. AND CONGIU,S.

Manifestazione delle peste bovina in
Somalia." Archivio Italiano di Scienze
Mediche Tropicali e di Parassitologia."
No. I. Roma 1957.

Tripanosi naturale dei caprini somali.
"Zooprofilassi." No. 9.   1955.

SOMALI REPUBLIC.

Powers and duties of the staff of the
Department of Animal Health and Production.
Ministry of Agriculture and Animal Husbandry.
Mogadiscio 1966.

TARANTINO,G.B.

Tripanosi del dromedario in Somalia.
"La Clinica Veterinaria." Milano 1929.
77 p.

Una Enzoozia da Dengue (Somalia).
"La Clinica Veterinaria." Milano 1929.

Prima constatazione di carbonchio ematico
nei bovini della Somalia Italiana." Bollettino
Societa Italiana Medicina e Igiene Coloniale."
Cooperativa Parmense. 1931.
4 pp.

Ulteriore esperienze di Chemiotepapia
nella Tripanosomiasi nella Somalia Italiana.
Tipogrf. Parmense. 1931.

Insetti nocivi all'allevamento del bestiame
nella Somalia Italiana. Istituto Poligrafico
dello Stato.   Roma 1933.
19 pp.

Tripanosomiasi animali esistenti nel
Comprensorio della S.A.I.S.: profilassi
e trattamento curativo."Scienze Mediche
Coloniali." Vol. VI. Tripoli 1934.
430 p.

Avvelenamento alimentare,potere tossico
delle piante giovani di dura." La Clinica
Veterinaria." Milano 1935.
10 pp.

Potere tonico delle giovani piante
di dura (Somalia). "La Clinica Veterinaria."
Milano 1935.
66 p.

10. Zoology (General)

ANONYMOUS.

La fauna somala. "Somalia Italiana".
No. 11. Mogadiscio 1927.

BLYTH,E.

Report on a Zoological Collection (Speke's)
from the Somali Country. "Journal of the Asiatic
Society of Bengal". Vol. XXIV. No. 291. Calcutta 1855.

CHERCHI, M.A.

Tesori faunistici della Somalia.
"Le Vie del Mondo". No. I. Milano 1956.
79-88 pp.

FUNAIOLI,U.

Fauna e caccia in Somalia. Tipografia Missione Cattolica.
Mogadiscio 1957.
92 pp. ills. map.

L'aspetto attuale del problema faunistico venatorio
in Somalia. "Rivista di Agricoltura Subtropicale e
Tropicale". No. 1-3. Firenze Gennaio-Marzo 1958.
98-113 pp.

GIRARDON,C.A.

Risorse faunistiche della Somalia.
"Africa". No. 12. Roma 1948.
312 p.

GESTRO,R.

Collezioni zoologiche del Tenente Citerni.
"Bollettino Societa Geografica Italiana".
Vol. V. Roma 1904.
8-13 pp.

HEUGLIN, M. THEODOR VON.

Forschungen uber die fauna Rothen Meeres
und der Somali-Kuste. "Peterman's Geogr. Mitteilungen".
January 1861.
II 32 pp.

MUSEO CIVICO STORIA NATURALE DI GENOVA.

Risultati zoologici della missione Bottego al Giuba.
"Bollettino". Serie II. Vol.XV. Genova 1895.

PAOLI,G.

Sulla fauna entomologica della Penisola dei Somali
e sui rapporti zoogeografici. "Atti II Congresso
Studi Coloniali". Vol. III. Napoli 1934.
165 p.

PEEL,C.V.A.

Somaliland. Robinson & Co. Bloomsbury 1900.
345 pp.

SCIACCHITANO,I.

Spedizione biologica in Somalia dell'Universita
di Firenze (1959). "Monitore Zoologico Italiano".
No. 3-4. Istituto di Zoologia dell'Universita di Firenze.
Firenze 1961.
185 186 pp.

SCORTECCI,G.

Un viaggio di studi nella Somalia Settentrionale.
"Rivista delle Colonie Italiane". Vol.XXXIX. Roma 1932.
13 p.

Viaggio di esplorazione biologica sulle montagne
della Migiurtinia. Pagano. Genova 1953-55.
195 pp.

———————————

Viaggio di esplorazione biologica sulle montagne
della Migiurtinia compiuto con il contributo
del Consiglio Nazionale delle Richerche. No. 25.
"Bollettino dell'Istituto Biologico". Universita
di Genova. Genova 1955.
43-105 pp.

———————————

Itinerario di un viaggio di esplorazione biologica
in Migiurtinia compiuto con il contributo del Consiglio
Nazionale delle Ricerche. "Atti della Societa Italiana
di Scienze Naturali del Museo Civico Storia Naturale
di Milano". Milano 1956.
113-120 pp.

SIMONETTA,A.

Ricerche sulla fauna della Somalia: Nota I.
(Relazione sulla prima fase delle ricerche).
"Ricerca Scientifica". Vol. III. No. 4. Serie 2. 1963.
307-316 pp.

———————————AND FUNAIOLI,U.

Spedizione biologica in Somalia 1959: Risultati zoologici.
(I contributi, parte narrative) Istituto Zoologico.
Universita degli Studi di Firenze. Firenze 1960.
6 pp.

SPARTA' , A.

Ricerche biologiche compiute da febbraio a maggio 1938
durante la campagna idrografica in Somalia.
R.C. Talass. 1938-39.

ZICCARDI, F.

Dimenticato nell'archivio di un cacciatore
un progetto per la valorizzazione della fauna, Somalia.
"La Voce della Africa". No. 13. Roma 1960.

ECONOMICS

1. Banking and Money

BANCA D'ITALIA.

La Banca d'Italia nelle terre italiane
d'Oltremare. (Somalia Page 89-103). Roma 1940.
89-103 pp. graphs. ills.

Relazione sul Lavoro della Filiale e sulla
Attivita Economica e Bancaria del Territorio: Anno 1953.
Filiale di Mogadiscio. Mogadiscio 1954.
112 pp. tables.

BUONOMO,M.

Lo Scellino Somalo: Una moneta stabile.
Bancaria. (Estr). Roma 1965.
52 pp.

CAMERA DI COMMERCIO,AGRICOLTURA ED INDUSTRIA DELLA SOMALIA.

Il Credito Somalo nel 1955. "Bollettino Mensile Camera
di Commercio". No. 4-5. Mogadiscio 1956.

CIANCIMINO,F.

La cassa per la circolazione monetaria della Somalia:
Origini e caratteristiche-funzionamento. "Africa".
No. I. Roma 1952.
222-228 pp

CASSA PER LA CIRCOLAZIONE MONETARIA DELLA SOMALIA.

I° Esercizio Sociale: 18 Aprile 1950-31 Dicembre 1951.
Istituto Poligrafico dello Stato. Roma 1952.
134 pp. graphs.

2° Esercizio Sociale: I Gennaio-31 Dicembre 1952.
Istituto Poligrafico dello Stato. Roma 1953.
47 pp. graphs.

Disposizioni relativi alla CASSA PER LA CIRCOLAZIONE MONETARIA
DELLA Somalia. Istituto Poligrafico dello Stato. Roma 1955.
14 pp.

3° Esercizio Sociale: I Gennaio-31 Dicembre 1953.
Istituto Poligrafico dello Stato. Roma 1954.
43 pp. graphs.

———————

4° Esercizio Sociale: I Gennaio-31 Dicembre 1954.
Istituto Poligrafico dello Stato. Roma 1955.
65 pp. graphs.

———————

5° Esercizio Sociale: I Gennaio-31 Dicembre 1955.
Istituto Poligrafico dello Stato. Roma 1957.
51 pp. graphs.

———————

6° Esercizio Sociale: I Gennaio-31 Dicembre 1956.
Istituto Poligrafico dello Stato. Roma 1957.
55 pp. graphs.

———————

7° Esercizio Sociale: I Gennaio-31 Dicembre 1957.
Istituto Poligrafico dello Stato. Roma 1958.
57 pp. graphs.

———————

8° Esercizio Sociale: I Gennaio 31 Dicembre 1958.
Istituto Poligrafico dello Stato. Roma 1959.
77 pp. graphs.

———————

9° Esercizio Sociale: I Gennaio-31 Dicembre 1959.
Istit to Poligrafico dello Stato. Roma 1960.
109 pp. graphs.

CREDITO SOMALO.

Bilancio 1954: I° Esercizio. Mogadiscio 5 Marzo 1955.
14 pp.

———————

Bilancio 1955: 2° Esercizio. Mogadiscio II Febbraio 1956.
20 pp.

———————

Report of the first years of credit operations by the
Somali Credit Bank in favour of Somali Farmers and
artisans. AFIS. Mogadiscio 1955.

———————

Relazione Annuale e Bilancio 1958. Mogadiscio 1959.
19 pp.

———————————

Bilancio Esercizio 1959: all'esame del Consiglio
di Amministrazione e del Collegio dei Sindaci.
Mogadiscio 1960.

———————————

Statement of condition 1962. Mogadiscio March 1963.

———————————

Statement of condition 1963. Mogadiscio March 1964.
(Blingual: English-Italian).

———————————

Statement of condition 1963 and 1964.
Development Loan Section. Mogadiscio.

———————————

Bilancio 1964. Mogadiscio 1965.

———————————

Bilancio 1965. Credito Somalo. Mogadiscio.

———————————

Development Loan Section Credito Somalo:
Final report and recommendations. U.S. Agency for
International Development. Checchi & Company.
Washington, D. C. September 1965.
87 pp. graphs.

FORMENTINI.

Memorie e note sulle Somalia: 1948 1950.
Banca d'Italia. Mogadiscio 1959.
336 pp.

GRAZIOSI,A.

Caratteristiche strutturali del sistema bancario
in Somalia. "Il Risparmio". Anno XII. Fasc. No. II.
Casa Editrice Dott. A. Giuffre. Milano 1965.
II pp.

PALAMENGHI CRISPI, F.

Il nuovo sistema monetario della Somalia.
"Mondo Aperto". Anno V No. 2. Aprile 1951.

———————————

Storia del Somalo. "Africa d'Oggi". No. 4 5.
Roma 1953.
1-2 pp.

ROSSETTI,C.

Il regime monetario delle colonie italiano.
E. Loescher. Roma 1914.
143 pp.

SANTAGATA,E.

Il Credito Africano e l'Italia (La Cassa per La
Circolazione Monetaria della Somalia)
Il Credito Somalo. "Africa". No. 12. Roma 1954.

SOMALI COMMERCIAL BANK.

Bulletin (Special Issue). Tipo Lito Missione.
Mogadiscio October 197i.
39 pp. ills. graphs.

SOMALI DEVELOPMENT BANK.

Final Report of Richard G. Leonard: Adviser, 1966 1970. Mogadiscio.
April 1970.

———————————

Annual Report and Statement of Condition 1969.
Mogadiscio March 1970.
10 pp.

———————————

Report by the Board of Directors of the Somali Development
Bank covering the period from 1st January to 31st December
1970. Tipo-Lito Missione. Mogadiscio April 1971.
30 pp. graphs. Ills.

———————————

Rapporto del Consiglio d'Amministrazione della Banca
Somala di Sviluppo per il periodo 1mo Gennaio al
31 Dicembre 1970. Tipo-Lito Missione. Mogadiscio Aprile 1971.
26 pp. ills. graphs.

———————————

Third Annual Report January-December 1971.
Tipo-Lito Missione. Mogadiscio June 1972.
34 pp graphs.

———————————

Terzo Rapporto Annuale Gennaio-Dicembre 1971. Tipo-Lito
Missione. Mogadiscio Giugno 1972.

25 pp. graphs.

SOMALI REPUBLIC (OFFICIAL).

Proposals for the establishment of the Somali Post
Office Savings Bank. Department of Posts and Telecommunications.
Mogadiscio 1968.

SOMALI SAVINGS AND CREDIT BANK.

Bulletin-Year 1971 & First Half Year (January-June 1972).
Mogadiscio. No. 2. November 1972.
21 pp. tables.

(BULLETINS)

SOMALI NATIONAL BANK

Bulletin No. 1. March 1965. Mogadiscio 1965.
78 pp. graphs. (Bilingual: English-Italian)

Bulletin Nos. 2-3. June September 1965. Economic
Research and Statistics Department. Mogadiscio 1965.
106 pp. (Bilingual: English-Italian)

Bulletin No. 4. December 1965. Economic Research
and Statistics Department. Mogadiscio 1965.
102 pp. (Bilingual: English-Italian)

Bulletin Nos. 5-6. March-June 1966. Economic Research
and Statistics Department. Mogadiscio 1966.
96 pp. (English-Italian).

Bulletin Nos. 7-8. September-December 1966.
Economic Research and Statistics Department.
Mogadiscio 1966.
73 pp. (Bilingual: English-Italian)

Bulletin No. 9. March 1967. Economic Research and
Statistics Department. Mogadiscio 1967.
75 pp. (Bilingual: English-Italian)

Bulletin Nos. 10-11. June-September 1967. Economic
Research and Statistics Department. Mogadiscio 1967.
75 pp. (Bilingual: English-Italian)

Bulletin No. 12. December 1967. Economic Research
and Statistics Department. Mogadiscio 1967.
75 pp. (Bilingual: English-Italian)

Bulletin Nos. 13-14 March - June 1968. Economic Research and
Statistics Department. Mogadiscio 1968.
55 pp. (Bilingual: English-Italian).

Bulletin No. 15 September 1968. Economic Research
and Statistics Department. Mogadiscio 1968.
55 pp (Bilingual: English-Italian)

Bulletin No. 16. December 1968. Economic Research
and Statistics Department. Mogadiscio 1969.
55 pp. (Bilingual: English-Italian)

Bulletin Nos. 17-19 September 1969. Economic Research
and Statistics Department. Mogadiscio 1969.
37 pp. (Bilingual: English-Italian)

Bulletin No. 20. December 1969. Economic Research
and Statistics Department. Mogadiscio 1969.
37 pp. (Bilingual: English-Italian)

Bulletin Nos. 21-22 January-June 1970. Economic Research
and Statistics Department. Mogadiscio 1970.
61 pp. (Bilingual: English-Italian)

Bulletin Nos. 23-24 July-December 1970. Economic Research
and Statistics Department. Mogadiscio 1971.
59 pp. graphs (Bilingual: English-Italian)'

Bulletin Nos. 25-26 January-June 1971. Economic Research
and Statistics Department. Mogadiscio 1971.
71 pp. graphs (Bilingual: English-Italian)

Bulletin Nos 27-28 July-December 1971. Economic Research
and Statistics Department. Mogadiscio 1971.
71 pp. graphs (Bilingual: English-Italian)

Bulletin Nos. 29-30 January-June 1972. Economic Research
and Statistics Department. Mogadiscio 1972.
72 pp. graphs.   **(ANNUAL REPORTS)**

Report and Balance Sheet: Financial Year:
1st July 1960 to 31st December 1961 Economic
Research and Statistics Department.
(Stabilimento Topografico Fausto Failli, Roma).
Mogadiscio 1962.
454 pp. graphs.

Relazione e Bilancio: Esercizio 1° Luglio 1960
31 Dicembre 1961. (Stabilimento Tipografico Fausto Failli,Roma).
Mogadiscio 1962.
464 pp. graphs.

Rapport et Bilan: Excercise 1er Juillet 1960 - 31 Decembre 1961.
Banque Nationale de Somalie. Mogadiscio 1962.
480 pp. graphs.

Report and Balance Sheet: 2nd Financial Year.
(1st January to 31st December 1962) Economic Research
and Statistics Department. Mogadiscio 1963.
256 pp. graphs.

Relazione e Bilancio. 2 Esercizio 1° Gennaio-31 Dicembre 1962.
Mogadiscio 1963.
368 pp. graphs

Rapport et Bilan. 2e Excercise du 1er Janvier au 31 Decembre 1962.
Banque Nationale de Somalie. Mogadiscio 1963.
284 pp. graphs.

Report and Accounts. 3rd Financial Year.
1st Jan-31st Dec. 1963. Economic Research and
Statistics Department. Mogadiscio 1964.
45 pp.

Relazione e Bilancio. 3° Esercizio. 1° Genn-31 Dic. 1963.
Economic Research and Statistics Department. Mogadiscio 1964.
47 pp.

Report and Accounts. 4th Financial Year.
1st Jan-31st Dec. 1964. Economic Research and
Statistics Department. Mogadiscio 1965.
75 pp.

Relazione e Bilancio. 4° Esercizio.
1 Genn-31 Dic. 1964. Economic Research and
Statistics Department. Mogadiscio 1965.
87 pp.

Report and Balance Sheet. 5th Financial Year.
1st Jan-31st Dec. 1965. Economic Research and
Statistics Department. Mogadiscio 1966.
75 pp. (Bilingual: English-Italian)

Report and Balance Sheet. 6th Financial Year.
1st Jan-31st Dec. 1966. Economic Research and
Statistics Department. Mogadiscio 1967.
54 pp. (Bilingual: English-Italian).

Report and Balance Sheet. 7th Financial Year.
1st Jan-31st December 1967. Economic Research
and Statistics Department. Mogadiscio 1968.
55 pp. (Bilingual: English-Italian)

Report and Balance Sheet. 8th Financial Year.
1st Jan-31st Dec. 1968. Economic Research and
Statistics Department. Mogadiscio 1969.
58 pp. (Bilingual: English-Italian)

Report and Accounts. 9th Financial Year.
1st Jan-31st Dec. 1969. Mogadiscio 1970.
54 pp.

Relazione e Bilancio. 9 Esercizio 1 Gennaio-31 Dicembre 1969.
Economic Research and Statistics Department. Mogadiscio 1970.
60 pp.

Annual Report and Statement of Accounts. 1970.
10th Financial Year. 1st Jan-31 Dec. 1970.
Economic Research and Statistics Department. Mogadiscio 1970.

21 pp.
(ECONOMIC REPORTS)

_____

Economic Report 1963-1964. Economic Research and
Statistics Department. Mogadiscio 1965.
98 pp.

_____

Relazione Economica 1963-1964. Economic Research and
Statistics Department. Mogadiscio 1965.
107 pp.

_____

Economic Report 1965. Economic Research and Statistics
Department. Mogadiscio 1969.
142 pp. (Bilingual: English-Italian)

_____

Constitutive Law. Somali National Bank.
Mogadiscio 1961.
24 pp.

2. Economic and Social Conditions (General)

AMMINISTRAZIONE FIDUCIARIA ITALIANA DELLA SOMALIA.

Exigences economiques du territoire de la
Somalie a l'expiration du mandat de tutelle.
Rome 1958.

AGRESTI,A.

Prospettive economiche della Somalia.
"La Rivista d'Oriente". No. 10. Napoli 1935.

ALEXANDER,J.J.

A primer of economic development. McMillan and Company.
New York 1962.

ALFANI,A.

Problemi somali. "Rassegna d'Oltremare".
No. 9 Genova 1936.
46 p.

ALLEGRINI,A.

Lavoro e capitale in Somalia. "Africa" No. 6.
Roma 1953.

175-176 pp.

AMADIO,W.

L'Oltre Giuba: un anno nel nuovo territorio.
"L'Esploratore Commerciale". Milano 1926.
204-214 pp.

AMBASCIATA DELLA SOMALIA (ITALIA).

La Somalia: cenni geografici ed economici.
"Osservatore Economico del Medio Oriente e del Nord Africa".
No. 6. Roma 1962.
11-12 pp.

_____

La Somalia paradiso venatorio. "Osservatore Economico
del Medio Oriente e del Nord Africa". No. 7. Roma 1962.
12-13 pp.

AMBASCIATA D'ITALIA (MOGADISCIO,SOMALIA)

Breve note sulla Somalia. Ambasciata d'Italia.
Mogadiscio Gennaio 1969.
42 pp. appendices, tables.

ANONYMOUS.

Some economic products of Somaliland. Imperial
Inst. Vol.12. 1914.
11-27 pp.

_____

Notizie sulla popolazione,sul patrimonio zootecnico
e sulla produzione agricola della Somalia Italiana.
"Bollettino Informazione Economica del Ministero delle Colonie".
Roma 1925.
488 p.

_____

Somalia: some photographic representation of
Italy's actions. Istituto Agricolo Coloniale.
Firenze 1946.

ills: plates.

_____

Economia Somala 1950-51. "Africa". No. 9-10.
Roma 1951.

_____

Rassegna della Somalia. "Eurafrica". Roma 1957.
14-16 pp.

_____

La Somalia dell'avvenire. "Rassegna di Espansione Commerciale".
No. 3-4. Milano 1957.
55-58 pp.

_____

Rassegna economica della Somalia. "Eurafrica". No. 6.
Roma 1957.
14-16 pp.

_____

Economia della Somalia: Un decennio di commercio
con l'estero 1946-1956. "Bollettino Camera di Commercio
della Somalia." No. 7-12. Mogadiscio 1957.
1-3 pp.

_____

L'economia della Somalia. "Il Globo". No. 23.
Roma Gennaio 1960.
_____

La Somalia: storia ed economia. "L'Osservatore Economico
del Medio Oriente e del nord Africa". No. 13. Roma Luglio 1962.
10-11 pp..

_____

La Republique de Somalie et ses perspectives de development:
elevage et agriculture sont les deux activities fondamentales
de la Somalie. "Industries et Travaux d'Outer-mer". No. 107.
Paris 1962.
830-834 pp.

_____

Côte Francaise des Somalis. "Marches Tropicaux et
Mediterraneeens". No. 1050. Paris 25 Decembre 1965.
3287-3380 pp.

ASSOCIAZIONE FRA I COMMERCIANTI INDUSTRIALI DELLA SOMALIA
ITALIANA.

La Somalia: errori e deficienze. "Espansione Coloniale". Roma.
8 p.

BANCA INTERNAZIONALE PER LA RICOSTRUZIONE E LO SVILUPPO.

La economia del Territorio della Somalia sottoposto
alla Amministrazione Fiduciaria dell'Italia.
Washington, D. C. 1957.
95 pp.

BARTOLOMEI,A.

La Somalia e il suo sviluppo. "Vie dell'Impero".
No. 4. 1926.
5 p.

BATTISTELLA,R.

Panoroma economico della Somalia. "Bollettino d'Informaz.
Comm. dei Prezzi e dei Protesti Cambiari". Mogadiscio 1939.
59-65 pp.

_____

Aspetti e problemi dell'economia somala.
"Lo Stato". 1940.
61 p.

BERTONE,G.

La Somalia Italiana e la sua valorizzazione.
F. Giannini e D Figli. Napoli 1926.
90 pp.

BIGI,F.

Situazione e prospettive economiche della Somalia
alla vigilia dell'indipendenza. "Africa". No. 3.
Roma Maggio-Giugno 1960.
133-138 pp.

_____

Relazione sulle realizzazioni e prospettive della
participazione italiana allo sviluppo economico della Somalia.
"Atti V Convegno sui rapporti economici e commerciali con il
1 Continente Africano". "Africa". No. 5. Roma 1961.
239-243 pp.

BONO,S.

Basi e propettive dell'economia Somala.
"Le Vie del Mondo". No. 4. Milano 1962.
334-348 pp.

BOTTONI,G.

La Somalia Italiana offre vaste possibilita di sfruttamento:
"Le Vie d'Italia". Milano 1922.
49 p.

BROCKMAN,R.E.D.

Economic resources of British Somaliland. "Atti III Congresso
Internazionale di Agricoltura Subtropicale e Tropicale".
Vol. II. 1941.
488-500 pp.

BRUSASCA,G.

Produttivita: premessa dell'indipendenza somala.
"Africa d'Oggi". Roma 1952.

CAMERA DI COMMERCIO INDUSTRIA E AGRICOLTURA DELLA SOMALIA.

Relazione Economica per la Commissione delle
Quattro Potenze. Mogadiscio 31 Dicembre 1947.
95 pp.

_____

La congiuntura economica della Somalia in occasione
della sua indipendenze e dell'Unione con la
Regione Ex-Britannica. Mogadiscio 1960.
13 pp.

_____

Il progresso dell'economia della Somalia dal 1950.
"Atti del VI Convegno Italo-Africano". Milano 1957.
171 p.

CAPPELLO,E.

Rapporti economici tra la Somalia Italiana e
l'Etiopia (Relazione). Trieste 1928.
14 pp.

CARNEVALI,G.

Lineamenti del progresso economico della Somalia.
"Rivista di Agricoltura Subtropicale e Tropicale".
No. 7-9. Firenze 1953.

_____

Indici del progresso economico della Somalia.
"Rivista di Agricoltura Subtropicale e Tropicale".
Firenze 1954.

CAROSELLI,F.S.

La Somalia nell'economia dell'Impero.
"Rassegna Economica delle Colonie". Roma 1940.
669 p.

_____

Programmes and plans for rural development in
Somaliland. L'AJA. 1953.
10 pp.

CERINO,A.

Necessita economiche della Somalia e valore
dell'apporto italiano. "Italiani nel Mondo".

No. 1. Roma 1957.
11-12 pp.

CHIARAMONTE,A.

La Somalia Italiana Meridionale e le sue
possibilita di valorizzazione economica.
"Annali Societa Agraria della Provincia di Bologna".
Vol. LX. Bologna 1933.
197 p.

CHIESI,G.

Per la messa in valore della Somalia Italiana Meridionale
e Benadir. Tipografia La Stampa Commerciale. Milano 1903.
24 pp.

_____

Per la messa in valore della Somalia Italiana Meridonale.
"Atti I Congresso Italiani all'Estero". Roma 1908.
499 p.

_____

Note per lo sfruttamento agricolo,commerciale,
industriale del Benadir. Tipografia La Stampa Commerciale.
Milano 1903.
24 pp.

_____

La potenzialita economica della Somalia.
"Rivista Coloniale". Roma 1908.
576 p.

CIBELLI,E.

Il re dei vegetali nell'economia dell'Impero Italiano.
"Rassegna d'Oltremare". No. 12. Genova 1937.

COLONIAL OFFICE.

Annual report of the social and economic progress of
the people of Somaliland, 1937. H.M.S.O. London 1939.
33 pp. map.

CONFORTI,E.

La Somalia naturale ed economico-agrario. III Fiera della
Somalia. Numero Unico. Mogadiscio 24 Settembre-9 Ottobre 1955.
16-23 pp.

_____

Linee programmatiche orientative per lo sviluppo
economico agrario della Somalia. Istituto Agronomico

per l'Oltremare. "Fasc. No. 3648." Firenze 1956.
131 pp.

CORIO.

Il problema del Giuba. "L'esploratore Commerciale".
Milano 1889.

CORRINI,G.

Per il Benadir e la sua messa in valore.
Tipografia Unione Coop. Editrice. Roma 1906.

CORTINOIS,A.

Le richezze naturali della nostra Somalia: agricoltura
prodotti agricoli, l'allevamento del bestiame.
"Agricoltura Coloniale". Firenze 1908.
238-247 pp.

_____

Africa Orientale: le richezze naturali della Somalia Italiana.
Genova 1935.
62 pp.

CUFINO,L.

Segni precursori di attivita nella Somalia Italiana.
"Bollettino Societa Africana d'Italia". Fasc. No. V-VII.
Firenze 1914.

DI LAURO,R.

Il Giuba economico. Fratelli Bocca. Torino 1931.
22 pp.

E.C.

Sulla valorizzazione della Somalia Italiana.
"Bollettino Associazione Cotoniera". No. 11. Milano 1913.

EBLAN,J.

Basic data on the economy of the Somali Republic. U. S.
Department of Commerce. Overseas Reports. OBR 65-8. Washington,
D. C. 1965.
13 pp. tables, map.

FANELLI,A.

Alcune osservazioni sull'economia agraria indigena somala.
Biblioteca Studi Coloniali. Vol. VIII. Ed. Cya. Firenze 1939.
87 pp.

FERNAND,V.

Proposals for a pilot project for the development
of coastal fishing in Somalia. United Nations
Development Programme. Mogadiscio 1969.
27 pp.

FESTA,A.

Saline nell'A.O.I.'Materie prime dell'Italia
e dell'Impero''. 1938.
343 p.

FILIPPO, LA ROSA

La bananicoltura come fattore economico-sociale di
primaria grandezza. Ministero dell'Agricoltura e
Zootecnia. Mogadiscio 1966.
26 pp.

FOOD AND AGRICULTURAL ORGANIZATION.

Survey of Food Shortage: Report to the Government
of the Somali Republic. FAO/EPTA. Report No. 1471.
Rome 1961.
30 pp. tables.

FRANCOLINI,B.

Migiurtinia: note di geografia economica.
''Rivista delle Colonie Italiane''. Roma 1936.
31-44 pp.

_____

Nuova vita economica nella Somalia Italiana.
''Atti II Congresso Regionale di Studi Coloniali''.
Vol. VI. Napoli 1934.
903 pp.

_____

Esperimenti agricolo-industriali in Somalia.
''L'Oltremare''. Roma 1931.
313 pp.

FRATTINI,G.

Possibilita economiche della Somalia.
''Materie Prime Italia e dell'Impero''. 1936.
288 p.

GABDILLON,P.

Amenagement et mise en valeur de la cote Francaise
des Somalis. ''Memoires et comptes rendues de
travaux 1931''. Societe des Ingenieurs civils de
France.

GANZIN,M.

Report on the food situation and famine in Somalia.
Food and Agricultural Organization. Accra 16 November 1960.

GARCINA,A.

La decadenze della Somalia e le sue possibilita
di ripresa immediata. "Atti II Convegno Studi Coloniali".
Firenze 1947.
301 p.

GASBARRI,L

Linee fondamentali di sviluppo economico nel settore
agrario in Somalia. "Rivista di Agricoltura Subtropicale
e Tropicale" No. 4-9. Firenze Aprile-Settembre 1960.
171-197 pp.

GAVIN,R.

La situazione economique et sociale en Somalie sous
tutelle Italienne. (Relazione I. L. O.) Geneve 1952.

GIGLIO,C.

Lo sviluppo economico della Somalia.
"L'Oltremare". Roma 1932.
16 p.

Le possibilita economiche della Somalia.
"Gerarchia". No. 8. Roma 1935.

GIORDANO,A.

La valorizzazione economico della Somalia. "Rivista Pol. Ec".
Fasc. VII-VIII. 1936.

GIORIO,C.

Importanza politica economica delle aziende
agricole in Somalia. "Atti III Convegno Italo-Africano".
Genova 1954.
108 p.

Considerazioni ed osservazioni sull'economia Somala.
"Atti del VI Convegno Economico-Italo-Africano".
N Milano 1957.
179 p.

GORINI,P.

I prodotti animali dell'Oltregiuba: importanza

relativa ed assoluta;produzione,incetta,smercio.
"Agricoltura Coloniale". Firenze 1926.
209 p.

GRISOLINI,H.

Il progresso politico economico della Somalia sotto
l'Amministrazione Fiduciaria Italiana. "Rassegna
Espansione Commerciale". No. 9-10. 1954.
39-42 pp.

INTERNATIONAL BANK FOR RECONSTRUCTION AND DEVELOPMENT.

The economy of the Trust Territory of Somaliland.
Report of a Mission organized by IBRD at the request
of the Government of Italy. Washington, D. C. January 1957.
99 pp. appendices.

_____

The economy of Somalia. Department of Operations Africa.
Washington, D. C. May 28 1964
30 pp.

_____

Current economic position and prospects of Somalia.
African Department. Washington, D. C. October 2, 1967.
33 pp.

ISTITUTO COLONIALE ITALIANO.

Per il Benadir e la sua messa in valore.
"Rivista delle Colonie Italiane". Roma 1906.

ITALIAN TRUSTEESHIP ADMINISTRATION FOR SOMALIA.

Economic requirements of the territory of Somalia on
the expiration of the trusteeship mandate. Istituto
Poligrafico dello Stato. Rome June 1958.
27 pp.

KARP, M.

The economics of Trusteeship in Somalia. African
Studies Program. Boston University Press. Boston 1960.
185 pp. map. diagrs. graphs.

KITTERMASTER,H.B.

British Somaliland. "Journal of the African Society".
Vol. XXVII. London 1928.
329-337 pp.

_____

The development of the Somalis. "Journal of the

African Society". London July 1932.
234-244 pp.

KRAMER,M.

Die entwicklungschemen Somalia. "Neue Afrika".
Vol. 5. No. 11. Munchen 1963.
411--412 pp.

LEGNANI,D.

Sguardi economici d all'Oltregiuba. "Illustrazione Coloniale".
No. 11. Milano 1927.

LESSONA,A.

Politica indigena ed economia in Somalia
"Agricoltura Coloniale". No. 5. Firenze Maggio 1935.
225-237 pp.

LORD JEMAY.

Africa: Somaliland 1914-1920. "The Economic Forum".
Luxemborg 1965.

LUNA

L'avvenire della Somalia (intervista con l'On.Bettiol).
"Eurafrica". No. 5. Roma 1954.

LUPATELLI,L.

Prospettive somale. Italia in Africa.
Ass. Naz. Combat. Red. "Africa". Roma 1948.
25 p.

MAFFI,Q.

La collaborazione dei Somali allo sviluppo della
Somalia Italiana. "Africa". No. 10. Roma 1954.

Il convegno italo-africano di Milano:
i rapporti Italia-Somalia. "Africa". No. 4-5.
Roma 1956.

MAHONEY,F.

Problems of community development in Somalia:
The pastoral nomads. U. S. Operations Mission to
Italy. Mogadishu 1961.

Community Planning. USAID Report. Mogadishu 1963.
38 pp.

MAINARDI,G.

L'economia agricolo-pastorale della Somalia.
"Atti dell'VIII Congresso Internazionale di
Agricoltura Subtropicale e Tropicale". Vol. II.
Roma 1938.
446 p.

MAINERI,B.

La gomma dell'Oltregiuba e l'economia nazionale.
"Illustrazione Coloniale". No. 7. Milano 1926.
228 p.

MALLARINI,A.

Il presente e l'avvenire del Benadir e delle
regioni somale e galla vicine. "Rassegna Nazionale".
Firenze 1897.
504-519 pp.

_____

La Somalia Italiana Meridionale in rapporto alla
economia nazionale. "Atti Convegno Nazionale Coloniale".
Napoli 1927.
197 p.

_____

Il Benadir. Cosa e? Che puo fruttare al
capitale nostrano. "Rivista Ligure Scienze,
Lettere, Arti. Genova 1910.
21 p.

_____

Libia,Eritrea e Somalia di fronte all'Economia Nazionale.
"Rassegna Nazionale". Firenze 1913.
22 p.

MANFREDI,G.

I Miliardi nella sabbia della Somalia.
"Eurafrica". No. 4. Roma 1957.
21-22 pp.

MANGANO,G.

Che cosa vale il Giubaland? "La Rassegna del Mediterraneo".
Fasc. No. 38. Roma 1924.

MARC. G.

Comptes economiques de la Côte Francaise des Somalis.
Institut National de la Statistique et des Etudes
Economiques Paris 1961.

MARTUCCI,G.

I rapporti con la Somalia. "Atti del VIII
Convegno Economico Italo-Africano". Milano 1959.
132-133 pp.

MAUGINI,A.

Somalie sous tutelle italienne: aspects economiques.
Institut Internat. Civilisations Differents.
Bruxelles 1952.

———————————

Lineamenti dell'economia rurale della Somalia.
"Rivista di Agricoltura Subtropicale e Tropicale".
Firenze 1953.

MC-KAY,V. AND RINGWOOD,O.K.D.

Poverty of resources in Italian Africa.
"Foreign Policy Reports". Vol. 21.
January 1940.
280 p.

MILKAUD.

Social development in the Somali Republic.
Mogadishu 1961.

(R) MINISTERO AA.EE.

Provvedimenti per la messa in valore delle
terre della Somalia Italiana. Direzione
Affari Coloniali. Roma 1911.

MOHAMED ABDI NUR.

Problemi Economici di attualita per la Somalia.
"Atti del VII Convegno Economico Italo-Africano".
Milano 1958.
60-62 pp.

MORGANTINI,A.M.

Le condizioni di vita dei Somali: "Annali e Commenti
dei dati storici piu recenti. "Africa". Roma 1952.

———————————

La situation economiques de la Somalie sous tutelles
italiennes en 1958 et 1959. "Civilisations". No. 1
Vol. X. Bruxelles 1960.
117 p.

MURRI,F.

Il latifondo somalo. "Africa" No. 3. Roma 1951.
90 p.

NISTRI, P.F.

L'osservatorio di economia agraria della Somalia.
"Rassegna Economica Africa Italiana". 1937.
1286.

O.E.C.E.

Le Development economique du Territoire sous
tutelle Italianne de la Somalie. Paris Juillet 1955.

ODONE,A.

Somalia's economy prospect and problem.
"Civilisation". Vol.2. No. 4. Bruxelles 1961.
444-448 pp.

ONGARO,G.

Le caratteristiche economiche delle regioni dell'altipiano
somalo (Harar,Ogaden,Sidamo,Boran,Bale e Liban).
"Commercio". No. 4. Roma 1936.

ONOR,R.

La Somalia Italiana: eseame critico dei problemi di
economia rurale e di politica economica della Colonia.
Edit. Fratelli Bocca. Torino 1925.
362 pp.

PAOLI,G.

Relazione sulle risorse naturali della Somalia Italiana.
"Atti Convegno Nazionale Coloniale". Roma 1931.
419 p.

PAPINI,L.

L'economia somala verso una nuova fase.
"Africa". No. 12. Roma 1948.
305 p.

PETAZZI,E.

Cifre vere sulla Somalia. "L'Oltremare".
Roma 1929.
11 p.

La Somalia economica. "L'Italia Coloniale".
Roma-Milano 1933.
42 p.

PHILIP,K.

Remarks concerning the economic development
of Somalia. Mogadishu September 1965.
112 pp. tables

PICCIOLI,A.

La valorizzazione economica della Somalia.
"L'Italia Coloniale". Roma-Milano 1933.
178 p.

POMILIO,M.

Sintesi economica della Somalia. "Commercio".
No. 12. Roma 1934.

PRESIDENZA DEL CONSIGLIO DEI MINISTRI.

Dati sulla Somalia (Realizzazione sociali ed
economici nei primi 5 anni di attivita).
"Documenti di Vita Italiana". No. 36. Roma 1954.
2811. p.

Progressi e realizzazioni in tutti i settori
della vita politica sociale ed economia della Somalia.
"Documenti di Vita Italiana". No. 62. Roma 1957.
4883 4890 pp.

I progressi nel settore sociale, miglioramento nel
tenore di vita, istruzione, politica sanitaria.
"Documenti di Vita Italianai". No. 132. Roma 1962.
10317 10323 pp.

RAVA,M.

Lo sviluppo economico della Somalia.
"La Rassegna Italiana". Roma 1933.
184 185 pp.

REPUBLIQUE FRANCAISE.

Cote Francaise des Somalis. Service d'Information.
Paris 1954.
VII, + 93 pp.

ROCCHETTI,G.

Cenni alle condizioni, ambienti, alle risorse agricole,
forestali,zootecniche della Somalia: Ciclo di Converszaioni
sulle produzioni agricole dei territori di oltre mare
associati al MEC. Istituto Agronomico per l'Oltremare.
Fasc. No. 3642. Firenze 1960.

19-23 pp.

ROSSI, E. U.

Profilo storico ed economico della Somalia.
"Communicazione dell'VIII Convegno Economico Italo Africano".
Milano 1959.
184-189 pp.

_____

Profilo storico ed economico della Somalia.
Nuova Grafica Romana. Roma 1959.
37 pp. map. tables. appendices.

SALVATI,C.

La potenza di produzione della Somalia.
"Rivista delle Colonie e d'Oriente".
Bologna 1925.
386 p.

SALVI,M.

Banane: chiave di volta dell'economia Somala.
"Africa d'Oggi". No. 10-12. Roma 1952.

SCASELLATI SFORZOLINI, G.

La coltivazione del cotone e l'allevamento del bestiame
nella Somalia Italiana Meridionale. "Atti III Congresso
Internazionale di Agricoltura Subtropicale e Tropicale".
Vol. 1. Firenze 1914.
246 p.

SERRA ZANETTI,R.

Basi economiche della Somalia Italiana.
La Rapida. Bologna 1923.

SESTINI,A.

Problemi della trasformazione economico della Somalia
in una recente pubblicazione. "Rivists Geografica Italiana".
Anno LXVIII. Fasc. No.2. Roma 1961.
10 p.

SOMALILAND PROTECTORATE (OFFICIAL).

Report of the Committee of Inquiry into Pauperism
in British Somaliland. British Military Administration.
Government Press. Hargeisa 1945.
27 pp. tables.

SOMALI REPUBLIC (OFFICIAL)

Investment Guide for Somalia. Ministry of Planning and

Coordination. (German Planning and Economic Advisory Group).
Mogadishu August 31 1968.
54 pp. (27 appendices.).

Index of Cost of Living 1966 and Household Expenditure
Survey 1966. Statistical Department. Ministry of Planning
and Coordination. Mogadishu October 1967.
9 pp.

Rehabilitation programme drawn up by the Working Committee
set up by His Excellency the Prime Minister to recommend
measures essential to repair damages caused by the flood.
Ministry of Information. Government Press. Mogadiscio.
28 pp.

Situazione delle zone alluvionate nella Regione
del Benadir: Relazione. Mogadiscio 30 Dicembre 1961.
28 pp.

Rapporto ad interim sull'attuale situazione della carestia 1965.
Comitato Nazionale per i Soccorsi di Emergenza.
Mogadiscio Maggio 1965.
85 pp.

L'attivita del governo dall'indipendenza ad
oggi (1 Luglio 1960 - 31 Dicembre 1963).
Stamperia del Governo. Mogadiscio 1963.
199 pp.

Government activities from independence until
Today (July 1, 1960-December 31, 1963).
Government press. Mogadiscio 1963.

Prospects for Economic Development in Somalia:
Preliminary Report. A.E.S.D. Rome July 1962.
117 pp. graphs. tables.

SOMALI DEMOCRATIC REPUBLIC.

Beautiful Somalia. Ministry of Information and
National Guidance. Mogadishu 14 August 1972.
78 pp. map. ills.

Two years of progress: Somalia under the Revolution.
Ministry of Information and National Guidance.
Mogadishu October 1971.
247 pp. ills. map.

General Information: Somalia Today. (Illustrated)
The Ministry of Information and National Guidance.
State Printing Agency. Mogadishu October 1970.
179 pp. ills. Game map.

General Information: Somalia Today. (Illustrated).
Ministry of Information and National Guidance.
311 pp. ills. tables. game map.

The Revolution; in one year transforms Somalia.
Ministry of Information and National Guidance.
Mogadiscio 1970.
36 pp. ills.

Beautiful Somalia. Ministry of Information and
National Guidance. Jeune Afrique. Paris 1971.
86 pp. map. ills.

S.A.I.S.

Relazione presentata dalla SAIS nel 1948 alla
Commissione Quadripartita di Inchiesta sulle
Ex Colonie Italiane; Mogadiscio 1948.

TOZZI,R.

Cenni sull'economia familiare indigena della
regione della Goscia. "Agricoltura Coloniale".
No. 4. Firenze 1941.'
148 p.

Cenni sull'Agricoltura e l'economia degli
indigeni nel Basso Giuba. Istituto Agronomico
per l'Africa Italiana. Firenze 1941.
39 pp.

VALORI,F.

Possibilita economiche della Somalia.
"Rivista Politica Economica".

Roma Marzo 1950.

VEDOVATO,G.

L'avvenire economico della Somalia indipendente.
"La Communita Internazionale". No. 3. Anno XXVII.
Firenze Luglio-Settembre 1960.

VECCHI,B.V.

Nel Sud dell'Impero: Ambiente, problemi economie, risorse.
Fratelli Bocca. Milano 1937.
216 pp.

V.G.M.

La Somalia dell'avvenire. "Rassegna di Espansione Commerciale".
No. 3-4. Milano 1957.
55-58 pp.

WIAN,G.

L'avvenire della Somalia e il concorso italiano.
"Italiani nel Mondo". No. 2. Roma 1959.
19-21 pp.

ZICCARDI,F.

Lo sforzo italiano in Somalia. "Africa". No. 2.
Roma Marzo-Aprile 1961.
65-70 pp.

Lo sviluppo economico della Somalia e l'apporto
dell'ASES. "Africa". No. 3. Roma 1961.
115-120 pp.

ZOLI,C.

Il problema economico della vallata del Giuba.
"L'Universo". No. 11. Firenze 1927.

ZUCCO,G.

La Somalia Italiana economica. "Rivista Italiana e Am."
No. 11. 1924.

3. Economic Development Plans

AMMINISTRAZIONE FIDUCIARIA ITALIANA DELLA SOMALIA.

Piani di sviluppo economico della Somalia:
Anni 1954-1960. Istituto Poligrafico dello Stato.
Roma 1954.
135 pp. maps; diagrs.

Plans de developpement economique de la Somalie:
Annees 1954-1960. Istituto Poligrafico dello Stato.
Rome 1954.
94 pp. maps; diagrs.

AGENZIA SVILUPPO ECONOMICO SOMALIA. (ASES)

Consuntivo 1957. Mogadiscio 26 Marzo 1958.
62 pp.

Tendenze problemi e programmi economici della
Somalia 1957-1958. Istituto Agronomico per
l'Oltremare. "Fasc". No. 3137. Firenze 1958.
30 pp.

Tendenze problemi e programmi economici della
Somalia 1958-1959. Istituto Agronomico per
l'Oltremare. "Fasc". No. 3637. Firenze 1959.
25 pp.

Tendenze problemi e programmi economici della
Somalia 1959-1960. Istituto Agronomico per
l'Oltremare. "Fasc". No. 3739. Firenze 1960.
35 pp.

ANONYMOUS.

Il piano quinquennale di sviluppo economico somalo.
"Costruttori Italiani nel Mondo". Vol. X. No. 207.
9-16 pp.

BREUIL, H.

British Somaliland Protectorate Development Plan.
Hargeisa 1950.

CORFITZEN, G.

Plans and Schedules for Somalia Economic Development.

U.S. Operations Mission to Italy.   Rome 1954.
34 pp.

FONDO VALORIZZAZIONE SOMALIA.

Relazione del Con-Direttore Italiano al Comitato
per lo Sviluppo Economico della Somalia sulla
attivita del Fondo Valorizzazione Somalia dal
28 Giugno 1954 al 10 Maggio 1958.   Mogadiscio 1958.
189 pp.

_____

Report of the Italian Co-Director to the Committee
for the Economic Development of Somalia on the
activities of Somalia; from June 28 June 1954, up
to May 1958.   Mogadiscio 1958.
189 pp.

GERMAN PLANNING AND ECONOMIC ADVISORY GROUP (SOMALIA).
Report on the Progress of Development Projects in
the Somali Republic.   Mogadiscio December 31st, 1966.
64 pp. graphs.

_____

The Progress of the first Five Years of the
Somali Republic 1963-1967.   Mogadishu 1967.

_____

Report on the Progress of Development Projects in
the Somali Republic.   Mogadishu July 20th 1967.
63 pp. graphs.

_____

Report on the Progress of Development Projects in
the Somali Republic, December 31st 1968.
Mogadishu October 1969.

_____

The Progress of Development Projects in Somalia.
Frankfurt am Main.
18 pp.

_____

Report on the Progress of Development Projects in
the Somali Republic, December 31st 1969.
Mogadishu and Frankfurt, April 1970.
105 pp.

GOVERNO DELLA SOMALIA ITALIANA.

Somalia: Luglio 1931--Luglio 1934:   Opere Pubbliche

e servizi pubblici.   Stamperia della Colonia.
Mogadiscio 1934.

MALAGODI, G.F.

Linee programmatiche per lo sviluppo economico
e sociale della Somalia.   Ministero AA.AA.   AFIS.   Roma
1953.
270 pp.

MOHAMED JAMA (HABASHI).

Economic Survey of Somalia 1955-1967.
Mogadishu 1968.
90 pp.

MORGANTINI, A.M.

Somalie sous tutelle italienne: Schema de l'Economie
et chronique economique 1950-55.   "Civilisations"
No. 3.   Vol. VI.   Bruxelles 1956.

SOCIETA NAZIONALE AGRICOLA INDUSTRIA.

Appunto per la progettazione di un piano regionale
di sviluppo agricolo ed industriale del Basso Giuba.
Milano 1 Dicembre 1967.
29 pp.

SOMALI INSTITUTE OF PUBLIC ADMINISTRATION.

Report of the SIPA Special Seminar on "What went wrong
with the Somali first five year economic plan 1963-
1967", held at SIPA Mogadiscio, Nov. 18-25, 1967.
Mogadiscio 1967.
55 pp.

SOMALILAND PROTECTORATE.

Review of Development 1955-1957.
Stationery Office.   Hargeisa June 1957.
77 pp.

_____

Annual Review of Development 1957-58.
Stationery Office.   Hargeisa 1958.

SOMALI REPUBLIC.

Prospects for Economic Development in Somalia:
Preliminary Report.   Association Europeenne De
Societes D'etudes Pour Le Development (A.E.S.E.D.)
Rome July 1962.
117 pp.

_____

Ministerial Organisation and first 5 Years Development
Plan 1963-1967. Ministry of Agriculture and Animal
Husbandry. Mogadiscio 1963.

First Five-Year Plan 1963-1967. Planning and
Co-ordination Committee for Economic and
Social Development. Mogadiscio July 1963.
162 pp.

Primo Piano Quinquennale 1963-1967. Comitato di
Pianificazione e Coordinamento dello Sviluppo
Sociale ed Economico. Mogadiscio Luglio 1963.
199 pp.

The Progress of the First Five Year Plan of the
Somali Republic 1963-1976. Planning Directorate.
Mogadiscio 16 June 1965.
15 pp.

Address by H.E.The Prime Minister Abdirashid Ali
Scermarke on the occasion of the Release of the
Somali Republic's First Five-Year Plan. Mogadiscio
1963.
20 pp.

Mid-Term Appraisal of the First Five-Year Plan
of Somalia. Ministry of Planning and Co-ordination.
Mogadiscio October 1966.
192 pp.

Short Term Development Programme 1968-1970.
Ministry of Planning and Co-ordination.
Mogadiscio August 1968.
170 pp.

Mid-Term Appraisal of the Short-Term Development
Plan 1968-1970. (German Planning and Economic Advisory
Group). Ministry of Planning and Co-ordination.
Mogadishu January 1970.

Development Programme 1971-1973.
Ministry of Planning and Co-ordination.
Mogadishu 1971.
231 pp.

Development Programme 1971-73: Progress of
implementation 1971 and Programme of 1972.
Ministry of Planning and Co-ordination.
Mogadiscio January 1972.
37 pp.

4.   Finance and Foreign Aid

KAMIL, A.M.

Les incidences de la fiscalite sur la vie economique
du T.F.A.I. (Territoire Francaise des Afars et des
Issas). "Revue Pount". No. 4. La Societe D'etudes de
l'Afrique Orientale. Djibouti 1968.

AMMINISTRAZIONE FIDUCIARIA ITALIANA DELLA SOMALIA.

Studio sulle finanze pubbliche. Mogadiscio 1955.

Bilancio di previsione per l'anno finanziario 1957.
Stamperia del Governo. Mogadiscio 1957.
135 pp.

ANONYMOUS.

Provvidenze governative a favore della coltivazione
agraria nella Somalia Italiana. "Rassegna Economica
delle Colonie". Roma 1930.
531 pp.

Istituzione del credito agrario nella Somalia Italiana.
"Rassegna Economica delle Colonie". Roma 1930.

Il bilancio preventivo del futuro stato Somalo.
"Eurafrica". No. 3. Roma 1956.
20-21 pp.

Provvidenze governative per la Somalia.
"Eurafrica". Nos. 1-2. Roma 1959.

27-28 pp.

BODRERO, P.

Il problema tributario della Somalia Italiana.
Monogr. No. 1. Misistero delle Colonie.
G. Bertero. Tipografia Nazionale. Roma 1917.
110 pp.

BRITISH MILITARY ADMINISTRATION (SOMALIA).

Financial Report of the Deputy Controller of
Finance and Accounts for the year ended 1 July 1946
to 30 June 1947. BMA. Government Press. Mogadishu
1947.
41 pp.

CAMERA DI COMMERCIO INDUSTRIA ED AGRICOLTURA DELLA
SOMALIA.

Relazione: effetti dei recenti provvedimenti fiscali
sulla situazione economia del paese. Mogadiscio Aprile
1966.
13 pp.

CASSA PER LE ASSICURAZIONI SOCIALI DELLA SOMALIA.

Bilancio consuntivo dell'esercizio 1966.
CASS. Mogadiscio 5 Luglio 1967.

_____

Rendiconto delle entrate e delle uscite dal
1° Gennaio al 31 Dicembre 1970. CASS. 1971.
21 pp.

_____

Bilancio di previsione per l'anno 1971.
CASS. Mogadiscio Settembre 1971.

_____

Piano economico generale di previsione dell'esercizio
1972. CASS. Mogadiscio Settembre 1971.
28 pp.

_____

Bilancio di previsione per l'anno 1972.
CASS. Mogadiscio Settembre 1972.

DE VECCHI, C.M.

Relazione sul progetto di bilancio della Somalia
Italiana per l'esercizio finanziario 1925-26.

Tipografia Bettini (Edit).   Mogadiscio 1924.

_____

Relazione sul progetto di bilancio della Somalia
Italiana per l'esercizio finanziario 1926-27.
Tipografia Bettini.   Mogadiscio 1925.
134 pp.

_____

Relazione sul progetto di bilancio della Somalia
Italiana per l'esercizio finanziario 1927-28.
Stamperia della Colonia.   Mogadiscio 1926.

ENTE NAZIONALE BANANE DELLA SOMALIA.

Proposte di finanziamento per opere infrastrutturali
a favore della bananicoltura Somala.   ENB.   Firenze 4
Ottobre 1971.
12 pp. map.

FRENCH SOMALILAND.

Budget des recettes et des depenses du service local
pour l'exercise 1950.   Charles-Lavauzelle.   Paris 1950.
196 pp.

GOVERNO DELLA SOMALIA.

Tabella delle Aliquote: legge 16 Novembre 1957.
No. 15.   Ministero per gli Affari Finanziaru.
Dipartimento Tributi.   Ufficio delle Imposte Dirette.
Stamperia del Governo.   Mogadiscio 1959.
80 pp.

_____

Bilancio di previsione per l'esercizio finanziario 1960.
Stamperia del Governo.   Mogadiscio 26 Dicembre 1959.
110 pp.

_____

Relazione del Ministero per le Finanze sui Bilanci
Preventivi Ordinario e Speciale dell'Esercizio
Finanziario 1963.   Ministero delle Finanza.
Mogadiscio 1962.
34 pp.

_____

Attivita economica finanziaria del Governo della
Somalia dal 1° Luglio 1960 al 31 Dicembre 1963.
Ministero delle Finanze.
39 pp.

The Somali Government 1965-66 United Nations Expanded
Programme of Technical Assistance Request and 1965
United Nations Regular Programme Request.   Somali
Government.   Mogadishu 5 June 1964.
59 pp.

Request of the Government of the Republic of Somalia to
the United Nations Development Programme for technical
assistance under the expanded programme for 1967-68 and
under the United Nations and the International Labour
Organisations regular programmes for 1967.   Ministry of
Planning and Co-ordination.   Mogadiscio 1966.
56 pp.

Relazione del Ministero delle Finanze sul bilancio
di previsione per l'esercizio finanziario 1966.
Mogadiscio 1965.
21 pp.

Budget for the financial year 1967.   State Printing
Agency.   Mogadiscio 1966.
247 pp.

Bilancio di previsione per l'esercizio finanziario
1967.   Stamperia di Stato.   Mogadiscio 1966.
247 pp.

Financial statement for the year ended 31st December
1968.   Chief Accountant Sub-Treasury Office.   Hargeisa
20th May 1969.
51 pp.

Financial statement for the year ended 31st December
1969 and report thereon by the Account General.
Ministry of Finance.
(Blingual: English-Italian)

Financial statement for the year ended 31st December 1
1970 and report thereon by the Accountant General.
Ministry of Finance.   94 pp.   Blingual: English-Italian

Tariffs of customs duties and accessory fees. Customs
Service. State Printing Agency. Mogadiscio.
28 pp. (Blingual: English-Italian)

(R)   GOVERNO DELLA SOMALIA ITALIANA.

Ordinamento Fiscale.   Stamperia della Colonia.
Mogadiscio 1926.
27 pp.

LANESSAN, J.L. DE

Rapport sur un credit pour l'organisation de la
colonie d'Obock (1840-85).

LUSIGNANI, G.B.

Relazione sui contributi a favore dei concessionari
della Somalia Italiana nell'ultimo quinquiennio 1931-
1936.   "Atti III Congresso Studi Coloniali".   Vol.
VIII.   Firenze 1937.
593 pp.

MARANGONI, G.

Il credito agrario nella Somalia Italiana.
Torino 1935.

MEHMET, O.

Effectiveness of foreign aid - the case of Somalia.
"Journal of Modern African Studies." Vol. 9, No. 1,
1971.
31-37 pp.

MEREGAZZI, R.

Le entrate proprie della Somalia Italiana.
"Economia Nazionale". No. 2. Milano 1928.
8 p.

MONDAINI, G.

La partecipazione degli indigeni all'onere tributario
dell'Africa Italiana. (Part III) Somalia Italiana
1905-1936. "Rassegna Economica Africa Italiana".
Ottobre 1939.
1136-1141 pp.

MINISTERE DES AFFAIRES ETRANGERES.

Assistance Economique a la Somalie independente.
Rome Juin 1959.
29 pp.

MINISTERO AFFARI ESTERI.

Assistanza economica alla indipendenza somala.
Rome 1959.
29 pp.

R.B.

La cassa di risparmio di Torino ed il credito agrario
in Somalia. "La Somalia Italiana". Nos. 1-6.
Mogadiscio 1933. "Rivista delle Colonie Italiane".
Roma 1933.
720 pp.

SOMALILAND PROTECTORATE (OFFICIAL)

Financial instructions for the Somali Coast
Protectorate. 1899.
16 pp.

_____

Grants-in-aid of the administration of the Somaliland
Protectorate: arrangement for financial control.
Colonial Office. (CMND 9666) H.M.S.O. London 1955.
7 pp.

_____

Financial statement for the year ended 31st March 1959
and report thereon by the Accountant General.
Hargeisa 1959.
137 pp.

_____

Estimates for 1960-61. The Financial Secretary.
Hargeisa 1959.
139 pp.

TOMASELLI, A.

The Somali Taxation System. (Training Course for
District Commissioners Organized under the Auspices of
the Ministry of Interior). University Institute of
Somalia. Mogadiscio.
56 pp.

UNITED NATIONS ORGANIZATION.

Technical Assistance Programme, the trust territory of
Somaliland under Italian Administration. New York, 1952.

_____

Programma di Assistenza Tecnica per il territorio della

Somalia sotto Amministrazione Fiduciaria Italiana.
(Parta primo).   New York 1952.
153 pp. tables.

Financing of the Economic Development Plans of the
Trust Territory of Somaliland under Italian Administration.   New York 29 January 1957.
128 pp.

Report on the consolidation of the budgets of the
Northern and Southern regions of Somalia.
(Prepared for the Gov. of Somalia by R.O. Khalid).
United Nations Programme for Technical Assistance.
New York 25 April 1961.
22 pp.

Technical Assistance Program in Somalia: List of
Experts of the United Nations and of the Specialised
Agencies having served or serving in Somalia.
Office of the Resident Representative of the United
Nations. Mogadiscio October 1965.
29 pp.

Republic of Somalia: Status of Implementation of the
United Nations Programmes EPTA, REGULAR, REGIONAL
INTER-REGIONAL & SPECIAL FUND Projects 1963-1964.
(Comparative Statements of Approved & Delivered
Programmes).   Office of the Resident Representative of
the United Nations. Mogadiscio 15 September 1965.
42 pp.

Somalia: Terms of Reference of Projects of International Assistance in the Somali Republic 1967-1968.   Office
of the Resident Representative of the United Nations.
Mogadiscio May 1967.
76 pp.

Third Revised Summary of External Aid to the Republic
of Somalia.   Office of the Resident Representative of
the United Nations Development Programme.   Mogadiscio
June 1966.
22 pp.

Fourth Revised Summary of External Aid to the Republic
of Somalia. Office of the Resident Representative of
the United Nations Development Programme. Mogadiscio
May 1967.
22 pp.

_____

Sixth Revision: Summary of External Aid to the Republic
of Somalia. Office of the Resident Representative of
the United Nations Development Programme. Mogadiscio
March 1969.
24 pp.

_____

List of personnel of the United Nations and its
Specialized Agencies in the Somali Democratic Republic.
Office of the Resident Representative of the United
Nations Development Programme. Mogadishu August 1971.
22 pp.

_____

Annual Report for 1970 for the Inter-Agency Consultative
Board. Office of the Resident Representative of UNDP.
Mogadiscio 23 March 1971.
19 pp.

_____

Annual Report on Development Assistance to the Somali
Democratic Republic. Office of the Resident Representative of the United Development Programme. Mogadiscio
March 1971.
66 pp.

_____

U.S.A.I.D. (UNITED STATES AGENCY FOR INTERNATIONAL
DEVELOPMENT)

A Report on U.S. Economic Assistance to the Somali
Republic. "USAID" No. 1 of Series 1963. Mogadiscio
1963.
56 pp.

_____

Rapporto sull'Assistenza economica degli Stati Uniti
verso la Repubblica Somala. "USAID" No. 1 di Serie
1963. Mogadiscio 1963.
56 pp.

_____

Assistance to the Somali Republic. Mogadishu 1966.
25 pp.

VALERY, V.

Il credito agrario in Somalia. "L'Oltremare".
Roma 1929.
302 pp.

5. Industry and Manufacturer

AMMINISTRAZIONE FIDUCIARIA ITLAIANA DELLA SOMALIA.

Consigli pratici sulla scuoiatura degli animali
da macello e sulla preparazione delle pelli grezze
destinate al commercio. Ufficio Agricoltura e
Zootecnia. Ufficio Sanitario. Ispettorato Veter.
Stamperia AFIS. Mogadiscio 1951.
22 pp. ills.

ANONYMOUS.

Le cortecce tannanti della Somalia Italiana.
"Bollettino Informazione Economica".
Ministero delle Colonie. Roma 1922.
432 p.

_____

L'Oleificio della S.A.I.S. "Bollettino Informazione
Economica". Ministero delle Colonie. Roma 1925.
266 pp.

_____

La farina di banana. "Rivista di Agricoltura". 1934.
584 p.

_____

L'attivita delle saline di Dante nella Somalia.
"Rassegna Economica delle Colonie". Roma 1934.
434 p.

_____

L'attrezzatura industriale della Somalia.
"Azione Coloniale". Roma Maggio 1939.

AZAN, G.

Prospettive e necessita dell'industria casearia in
Somalia. "Somalia d'Oggi". No. 4. Mogadiscio Dicembre
1957.
51 p.

BIGAZZI, G.P.

La centrale del latte in Somalia.
"Rassegna d'Oltremare". No. 1-2. Genova 1938.
14 p.

BRAVO, G.A.

Su alcuni vegetali concianti della Somalia e
dell'Oltregiuba. "Bollettino Ufficio R. Stazione
Sperimentale Industria Pelli e Materie Concianti".
No. 6. Torino-Napoli 1932.
189 p.

─────────────

Il tannino delle mangrovie somale ed il suo
impiego in conceria. "Conceria". No. 6. 1938.
19 p.

BRIATI, R.

Le fibre tessili in Somalia. "Atti III Convegno Italo-
Africano". Milano 1954.
100 p.

BUONOMO, G.

Dante: il paradiso del sale. "Illustrazione
Coloniale". No. 9. Milano 1925.
284 p.

BRUNO, A.

Prodotti secondari della bananicoltura.
"Rassegna Economica delle Colonie". No. 10.
Roma 1942.
523 p.

CASILLI D'ARAGONA, M.

Artigianato somalo: i tessitori. "Azione Coloniale".
Roma Novembre 1939.

COLOMBO, M.

Il sale di Ras Hafun: programmi della
societa Saline somale. "Africa". Roma 1950.
184 p.

COMISAL, S.P.A.

Progetto di uno stabilimento per la pesca
e la conservazione del pesce in Somalia. Genova 1962.

COMITATO SVILUPPO ECONOMICO DELLA SOMALIA.

L'America coopera al progetto del Comitato
per il miglioramento dei pellami.
6 pp.

CONFORTI, E.

Utilizzazione della sovraproduzione e dei sottoprodotti
del banano nel Comprensorio di Genale. "Atti II
Congresso Studi Coloniali". Vol. VIII. 1937.
664 p.

CONSORZIO CONSULENTI TECNICI SALINE HAFUN (Somalia).

Preventivo per lo studio e la progettazione della
salina di Hafun (Somalia). CCTSH. Somalia.
34 pp.

CONSORZIO NAZIONALE PRODUTTORI ZUCCHERO.

Il primo Zuccherificio coloniale italiano.
"Bollettino Industria Saccarifera Italiana."
Genova 1928.

CREDITO SOMALO.

Programma per lo Sviluppo Produttivo ed Industriale
della Somalia 1956-1958. Mogadiscio Febbraio 1956.
65 pp.

_____

Feasibility study for tomato paste manufacturing in the
Republic of Somalia. Thomas M. Miner & Associates, Inc.
Chicago May 1968.
90 pp. tables.

Feasibility study for a vegetable oil industry
in the Republic of Somalia. Thomas H. Miner &
Associates, Inc. Chicago May 1968.
93 pp. tables.

FABRIUS, U.

L'estrazione dell'olio essenziale di M Lemongrass
della Somalia. "Rassegna Economica delle Colonie".
No. 9-10. Roma 1931.
8 p.

FERRARA, A.

Contributo alla conoscenza delle materie tanniche
della Somalia. Congresso Internazionale di
Silvicoltura. 1926.

_____

Lo stabilimento governativo per la sgranatura
e l'imballagio del cotone di Vittorio d'Africa.
"Agricoltura Coloniale". Firenze 1930.
7 p.

_____

Le industrie rurali indigene della Somalia Italiana.
Leo Olski. Firenze 1931.
31 pp.

_____

Le industrie rurali indigene della Somalia Italiana.
"Atti I Congresso Studi Coloniali". Vol. VI. 1931.
378-389 pp.

FERRETTI, U.

Se possa sorgere in Somalia un'industria delle carni.
"Rivista Freddo". No. 9. 1930-31.
377-2 pp.

FIORAVANTI, E.

L'artigianato della Somalia. "Africa". No. 9. Roma
1953.
237-238 pp.

_____

Artigianato Somalo. "Atti del III Convegno Economico
Italo-Africana". Milano 1954.
112-113 pp.

FOOD AND AGRICULTURAL ORGANIZATION.

Hides, skins and leather industries, Somali Republic.
(By Halilovic, A.) FAO Report No. 1989. Rome 1965.

_____

Hides, skins and leather development centre:
plan of work. FAO. Project No. 1. Mogadiscio
January 1968.
13 pp.

FRANCOLINI, B.

Industrie della Somalia Italiana: la pesca nelle
acque migiurtine. "Illustrazione Coloniale".
No. 10. Milano 1930.

GERMAN PLANNING AND ECONOMIC ADVISORY GROUP (SOMALIA).

Summary of a preliminary study concerning the former

Solar Plant near Hordio-Hafun.   Magadishu 1966.

_____

Feasibility report on the production of a
banana powder in Somalia.   Wirtschaftsprufer.
Frankfurt au Main.

_____

Feasibility Report on Fibre-Production of
Banana Trunks.   Mogadishu May 1965.

_____

Feasibility study on the Cement Production in Somalia.
Mogadishu Dicember 1966.

_____

Present Situation and Future Development of the
Energy Sector in the Somali Republic.   Mogadishu June
1969.
128 pp.

_____

Improvements in the Public Electricity Supply of
the Somali Democratic Republic 1971-73.
Mogadishu June 1970.
77 pp.

GIORDANO, A.

Industrie, artigianata e ricerche minerarie in Somalia.
"L'Ec.Italiana".   1937.
537 p.

GOLDING, E.W. AND STODHART, A.H.

An Energy Survey in the Somaliland Protectorate.
British Electrical & Allied Industries Research
Association.   Leatherhead 1954.
28 pp. ills. maps, diagrs.

G.R.

L'industria del tonno in Migiurtinia.
"Azione Coloniale".   Roma 10 Ottobre 1940.

INTERNATIONAL LABOUR ORGANIZATION

Report to the government of the Republic of Somalia on
the development of handicrafts and small-scale
industries.   ILO/TAP SOMALIA R/2.   Geneve 1963.
112 pp.

INDUSTRIE CHIMICHE SOMALE

Relazione Consiglio d'Amministrazione e
Bilancio Esercizio Finanziario 1969;
Atti della Societa I.C.S. Mogadiscio Giugno 1970.
59 pp. tables.

Progettazione Finale. I.C.S. Mogadiscio Aprile 1967.
30 pp.

L.B.

Gli impianti delle saline di Dante in Somalia.
"Illustrazione Coloniale". No. 6. Milano 1938.
33 p.

LEVI, C.

Fibre di cocco della Somalia. "Bollettino Reparto
Fibre Tessili Vegetali della R. Stazione Sperimentale
per l'Industria della Carta". Torino-Napoli Febbraio
1937.
55 p.

LINO, E.

Cenni sui materiali da costruzione della Somalia.
Mogadiscio 1956.
12 pp.

Prospettive per un impianto di fornace da laterizi
formati a mano in Somalia: Studio Tecnico Economico
e Progetto di Massima di una fornace tipo.
AFIS. Mogadiscio 1955.
23 pp.

LUSINI, G.

Le saline somale. "Africa". No. 8. Roma 1949.

MARIANI, G.

L'impiego di autogassogeni in Somalia. "Atti III
Congresso Studi Coloniali". Vol. VIII. Firenze
Aprile 1937.
637 p.

LA SOCIETA' MIGIURTINIA.

Possibilita e sviluppo della industria della
pesca in Somalia. (Africa) Commercio Italo-Africano.
Genova 1952.
214 p.

MIRANDA, A.

Un polo di sviluppo dell'economia somala:
caratteristiche e prospettive delle nuove
saline di Hafun. "Il Chimico Nuovo". Anno 1.
No. 12. Roma Dicembre 1971.
10-16 pp. ills.

MIRANDA, M.

Un po' di storia delle saline di Hordio-Hafun.
"Il Chimico Nuovo"﹐ Anno 1. No. 12.
Roma Dicembre 1971.
16-17 pp. tables.

MOHAMED SAID SAMANTAR.

Hafun: un obiettivo della cooperazione italo-somalo.
"Il Chimico Nuovo". Anno 1. No. 12. Roma Dicembre
1971.
9 p.

PASQUALUCCI.

Le risorse industrializzabili della Somalia Italiana:
prospettive d'opportunita. "Rivista Coloniale". No.
4. Roma 1921.
129 p.

P.B.

Il primo zuccherificio coloniale italiano (S.A.I.S.)
"Bollettino Industria Saccarifera Italiana. Genova 1927.
1927.
563 p.

PETAZZI, E.

Puo in Somalia sorgere un'industria delle carni?.
"La Somalia Italiana". No. 4-6. Mogadiscio 1929.

PISTOLESE, G.E.

Cautele dell'industria in Somalia: Industrializzazione
della Somalia. "Africa." No. 9. Roma 1950.
250 p.

POLCARO, B.

L'iniziativa privato nel compo agricolo-industriale
(Il Consorzio di Genale). "Costruire". Numero
Speciale. 1938.
84 p.

PROGRAMMA PER LOS VILUPPO PRODUCTTIVO ED INDUSTRIALE
DELLA SOMALIA.

1956-1958: Relazione illustrative e piano operativo
di attuazione. 1956.
65 pp.

RAPETTI, G.

Impiego dell'alcool nelle trattrici della S.A.I.S.
"Atti II Congresso Studi Coloniali". 1935.
324 p.

ROGGERO, R.V.

Meat Processing: The Kisimayu Packing Plant.
Ministry of Industry and Commerce. Mogadishu July 1966.

S.A.I.F.A.

Piante tessili - Utilizzazione del Banano da
frutto come piante tessile. Vittorio d'Africa.

SANUDO, M.

Le saline di Hafun. "Le Vie d'Italia e dell'America
Latina". Milano 1931.
532 p.

SOCIETA ELETTRO-INDUSTRIALE ITALO-SOMALA.

Sistema di impianti elettrici della Cita di Mogadiscio:
Previsioni di sviluppo nel periodo 1965-1974. Studio
Preliminare. Italconsult. Roma Luglio 1964.
55 pp. tables. graphs. map.

_____

Mogadishu electric power system: Estimated development
from 1965 to 1974: Preliminary Study. Italconsult.
Rome 1964.
50 pp. tables. graphs. maps.

SOCIETA' SOMALA PER L'INDUSTRIA DELLA PESCA.

Progetto di uno stabilimento per la pesca e la
conservazione del pesca in Somalia.
COMISAL. Genova.
22 pp.

SOMALI REPUBLIC (OFFICIAL).

Investment opportunities in cotton textiles.
Department of Industrial Development. Ministry of
Industry and Commerce. Mogadiscio 1961.
28 pp.

_____

Investment opportunities in dry cleaning plants.
Department of Industrial Development. Ministry
of Industry and Commerce. Mogadiscio 1961.
59 pp.

Investment opportunities in candy and confectionary
factories and stores. Department of Industrial
Development. Ministry of Industry and Commerce.
Mogadiscio 1961.
48 pp.

Investment opportunities in glue manufacturing plants.
Department of Industrial Development. Ministry of
Industry and Commerce. Mogadiscio 1961.
89 pp.

Investment opportunities in leather products
manufacturing plants. Department of Industrial
Development. Ministry of Industry and Commerce.
Mogadiscio 1961.
115 pp.

Investment opportunities in tire recapping. Department
of Industrial Development. Ministry of Industry and
Commerce. Mogadiscio 1961.
12 pp.

Investment opportunities in women's leather shoe factories. Deaprtment of Industrial Development. Ministry
of Industry and Commerce. Mogadiscio 1961.
174 pp.

Investment opportunities in concrete plants.
Department of Industrial Development. Ministry of
Industry and Commerce. Mogadiscio 1961.
14 pp.

Investment opportunities in paint manufacturing.
Department of Industrial Development. Ministry of
Industry and Commerce. Mogadiscio 1961.
11 pp.

Investment opportunities in slaughter houses and
meat packing plants. Department of Industrial
Development. Ministry of Industry and Commerce.
Mogadiscio 1961.
17 pp.

Investment opportunities inllaundry and toilet soap
plants. Department of Industrial Development.
Ministry of Industry and Commerce. Mogadiscio 1961.
103 pp.

Investment opportunities in brick, clay roof and floor
tiles. Department of Industrial Development. Ministry
of Industry and Commerce. Mogadiscio 1961.
35 pp.

Investment opportunities in terrazzo floor tile plants.
Department of Industrial Development. Ministry of
Industry and Commerce. Mogadiscio 1961.
158 pp.

Investment opportunities in tanning plants. Department
of Industrial Development. Ministry of Industry and
Commerce. Mogadiscio 1961.
145 pp.

Investment opportunities in furniture factories.
Department of Industrial Development. Ministry of
Industry and Commerce. Mogadiscio 1961.
75 pp.

Investment opportunities in man's leather
shoe factories. Department of Industrial Development.
Ministry of Industry and Commerce. Mogadiscio 1961.
130 pp.

Feasibility report on the establishment of Industrial
Estates at Mogadishu, Chisimaio, Hargeisa and Berbera.
Ministry of Industry and Commerce.
(Associated Consulting Engineers (ACE) Ltd). Banglore

Town.   Karachi October 1963.
107 pp.

———————————

Business Establishments in Mogadiscio 1966-1967.
Statistical Department. Ministry of Planning &
Coordination. Mogadiscio March 1969.
61 pp.

———————————

Industrial Production 1967. Statistical Department.
Ministry of Planning & Coordination. Mogadiscio
October 1968.
27 pp. tables.

———————————

Industrial Production 1968. Statistical Department.
Ministry of Planning & Coordination. Mogadiscio
January 1970.
13 pp. tables.

———————————

Meat Factory in Kisimayu-Somalia.   1969.
40 pp. ills.

———————————

Industrial Production 1970. Statistical Department.
Ministry of Planning and Coordination. Mogadiscio
March 1972.
45 pp. tables, appendices.

VEO, A.

Le industrie rurali della Somalia.
L'OLTREMARE". Roma 1932.
380 p.

WIAN, G.

Le industrie ittiche in Somalia e la collaborazione
italiana. "Italiani nel Mondo". No. 18. Roma 1959.
11-13 pp.

6.   Labor Economics and Conditions

ANONYMOUS.

Contratti agricoli per il comprensorio di Genale.
"Rassegna Economica delle Colonie". Roma 1929.
793 p.

Situazione attuale della manidopera agricola in
Somalia. "La Somalia Italiana Fascista". No. 1-6.
Mogadiscio 1934.
14 p.

Somalia: Gewerkschaftsweseh. "Neues Afrika".
Munchen 1961.
250-261 pp.

BIGI, F.

Il problema del lavoro nelle aziende agricola della
Somalia. "Revista di Agricoltura Subtropicale e
Tropicale". No. 10-12. Firenze Ottobre-Dicembre 1954.
374-387 pp.

CASSA PER LE ASSICURAZIONI SOCIALI DELLA SOMALIA.

Relazione al Sig. Ministero della Sanita e Lavoro
sull 'attivita della Cassa per le Assicurazioni
Sociali della Somalia dal 1 Luglio 1960 al 31 Dicembre
1963. CASS. Mogadiscio 14 Maggio 1964.
39 pp.

Anche una piccola ferita puo ridurti cosi, se non
ti disinfetti in tempo. (Brochure). CASS. Stamperia
dello Stato. Mogadiscio Ottobre 1972.
31 pp. ills.

CAVICCHIONI, A.C.

La mano d'opera nella Somalia Italiana.
"Rassegna Contemporanea." Serie II. 1914.

CONFEDERAZIONE SOMALA DEI LAVORATORI.

Per una storia del sindacalismo Somalo:
1959-1963. Quattro anni di attivita della C.S.L.
Mogadiscio.
24 pp.

FILESI, T.

Il sindacalismo in Somalia. "Africa". No. 3.
Roma Maggio-Giugno 1961.
123-136 pp.

FUNAIOLI, U.

La Somalia: Centro Studi CISL. "Cours de formation
Syndacalistes africains". Firenze 1962-63.
38 pp.

GAUDIO, A.

Vagabondaggio lungo la costa dei Somali.
"L'Universo". Firenze 1957.
264-300 pp.

GAVIN, R.

Report on labour conditions in Somalia.
International Labour Office. Geneve 1951.

GROTTANELLI, V.L.

La questione della mano d'opera nella Somalia Italiana.
"Rivista Italiana di Scienze Economiche". 1936.
669 p.

INTERNATIONAL LABOUR OFFICE.

Report of a Mission to Somalia under Italian Administration. I.L.O. Geneve 22 May 1951.
46 pp.

_____

Report to the Government of Somalia on the Possibility
of Extending the Social Insurance Scheme. I.L.O.
Geneve 1959.
87 pp.

_____

Report to the Government of Somalia on Manpower
Assessment and Planning. I.L.O. Tap.
Somalia L.5. Geneve 1970.
192 pp. tables.

MANGANO, G.

Della mano d'opera nelle nostre colonie:
Somalia Italiana. "Atti II Congresso Italiano
all 'Estero". Roma 1911.
1669 p.

MAUGINI, A.

Contratti per la mano d'opera indigena nella Somalia.
"Atti V Congresso Internazionale di Agricoltura
Subtropicale e Tropicale". Anversa 1930.
43 p.

RAPETTI, G.

Contratto di colonia per la mano d'opera indigena alle
dipendenze della S.A.I.S. "Atti II Congresso Studi
Coloniali". Vol. VI. 1935.

293 p.

Il contratto di colonia adottato dalla S.A.I.S.
"Rassegna Economica delle Colonie". Roma 1935.
16 p.

RAVA, M.

Il problems della mano d'opera in Somalia.
"Bonifica e Colonizzazione". Roma 1937.

SOMALI REPUBLIC (OFFICIAL)

Utilisation of manpower in the public service in
Somalia. (By Nigam, S.B.L. and Eaton, B.A.) Scmali
Government Press. Mogadishu 1964.

The Manpower Situation in Somalia:
(Report submitted to the Government of Somalia by)
(S.B.L. Nigam, I.L.O. Manpower Assessment & Planning
Adviser). Ministry of Health and Labour. Department
of Labour. Government Press. Mogadiscio 1965.
311 pp. tables. charts. diagrs. graphs.

Manual for labour inspectors. Ministry of Health
and Labour. Department of Labour. Mogadiscio 1967.
130 pp.

Manuale per ispettori del lavoro. Ministero della
Sanita e Lavoro. Departimento del Lavoro. Mogadiscio
1967.
130 pp.

The employment and unemployment situation in the
industrial and commercial sectors during 1967.
"Employment and Unemployment Series. No. 3.
Department of Labour. Ministry of Health and Labour.
Mogadiscio 1968.
24 pp.

Manpower Survey (Establishment Enquiry) in Dusa Mareb.
Ministry of Health and Labour. Department of Labour.
Manpower Unit. Mogadiscio 1969.
15 pp. map. tables. appendices.

Manpower Survey (Establishment Enquiry) in Galcaio.
Ministry of Health & Labour. Department of Labour.
Manpower Unit. Mogadiscio 1969.
16 pp. map. tables. appendices.

Manpower Survey (Establishment Enquiry) in Giamama.
Ministry of Health & Labour. Department of Labour.
Manpower Unit. Mogadiscio 1969.
19 pp. map. tables. appendices.

Manpower Survey (Establishment Enquiry) in Kisimayo.
Ministry of Health & Labour. Department of Labour.
Manpower Unit. Mogadiscio 1969.
24 pp. map. appendices. tables.

Manpower Survey (Establishement Enquiry) in Garoe.
Ministry of Health & Labour. Department of Labour.
Manpower Unit. Mogadiscio 1969.
14 pp. map. tables. appendices.

Manpower Survey (Establishment Enquiry) in Gardo.
Ministry of Health & Labour. Department of Labour.
Manpower Unit. Mogadiscio 1969.
15 pp. map. tables. appendices.

Manpower Survey (Establishment Enquiry) in Bosaso.
Ministry of Health & Labour. Department of Labour.
Manpower Unit. Mogadiscio 1969.
16 pp. map. tables. appendices.

Manpower Survey (Establishment Enquiry) in Bulo Burti.
Ministry of Health & Labour. Department of Labour.
Manpower Unit. Mogadiscio 1969.
15 pp. map. tables. appendices.

Manpower Survey (Establishment Enquiry) in Belet-Uen.
Ministry of Health & Labour. Department of Labour.
Manpower Unit. Mogadiscio 1969.
16 pp. map. tables, appendices.

Manpower Survey (Establishment Enquiry) in Las Anod.
Ministry of Health & Labour. Department of Labour.
Manpower Unit. Mogadiscio 1969.
7 pp. map. tables. appendices.

Manpower Survey (Establishment Enquiry) in Gabileh.
Ministry of Health & Labour. Department of Labour.
Manpower Unit. Mogadiscio 1969.
7 pp. map. tables, appendices.

Manpower Survey (Establishment Enquiry) in Las-Koreh.
Ministry of Health & Labour. Department of Labour.
Manpower Unit. Mogadiscio 1969.
18 pp. map. tables. appendices.

Manpower Survey (Establishment Enquiry) in Burao.
Ministry of Health & Labour. Department of Labour.
Manpower Unit. Mogadiscio 1969.
17 pp. map. tables. appendices.

Manpower Survey (Establishment Enquiry) in Hargeisa.
Ministry of Health & Labour. Department of Labour.
Manpower Unit. Mogadiscio 1969.
22 pp. map. tables. appendices.

Manpower Survey (Establishment Enquiry) in Berbera.
Ministry of Health & Labour. Department of Labour.
Manpower Unit. Mogadiscio 1969.
20 pp. map. tables. appendices.

Manpower Survey (Establishment Enquiry) in Borama.
Ministry of Health & Labour. Department of Labour.
Manpower Unit. Mogadiscio 1969.
15 pp. map. tables. appendices.

Manpower Survey (Establishment Enquiry) in Erigavo.
Ministry of Health & Labour. Department of Labour.
Manpower Unit. Mogadiscio 1969.
15 pp. map. tables. appendices.

Manpower Survey (Establishment Enquiry) in Afgoi.
Ministry of Health & Labour. Department of Labour.
Manpower Unit. Mogadiscio 1969.
20 pp. map. tables. appendices.

Manpower Survey (Establishment Enquiry) in Mogadiscio.
Ministry of Health & Labour. Department of Labour.
Manpower, Unit. Mogadiscio 1969.
41 pp. map. tables. appendices.

Manpower Survey (Establishment Enquiry) in Brava.
Ministry of Health & Labour. Department of Labour.
Manpower Unit. Mogadiscio 1969.
17 pp. map. tables. appendices.

Manpower Survey (Establishment Enquiry) in Balad.
Ministry of Health & Labour. Department of Labour.
Manpower Unit. Mogadiscio 1969.
18 pp. map. tables. appendices.

Manpower Survey (Establishment Enquiry) in Merca.
Ministry of Health & Labour. Department of Labour.
Manpower Unit. Mogadiscio 1969.
23 pp. map. tables. appendices.

Manpower Survey (Establishment Enquiry) in Giohar.
Ministry of Health & Labour. Department of Labour.
Manpower Unit. Mogadiscio 1969.
23 pp. map. tables. appendices.

Manpower Survey in Government Sector.
Ministry of Health & Labour. Department of Labour.
Manpower Unit. Mogadiscio 1969.
28 pp. map. tables.

Quarterly Labour Statistics Bulletin.
No. 1. (January–March 1972). Statistical Section
of the Labour Department. Ministry of Labour & Sports. Mogadiscio.
41 pp. tables.

Quarterly Labour Statistics Bulletin.
No. 2. (April-June 1972). Statistical Section of the
Labour Department. Ministry of Labour & Sports. Mogadiscio.
September 1972.
42 pp. tables.

Job description for Senior Officials and Inspectors in the
Department of Labour. Ministry of Justice, Religion and Labour.
Mogadiscio 1971.
25 pp.

STORTI, B.

Situazione di fatto e prospettive del movimento
sindacale in Somalia ai fini dello sviluppo
economico del paese. "Atti del IX Convegno Economico
Italo0Africano". Milano 1960.
198-199 pp.

7. Trade and Commerce

AMMINISTRAZIONE FIDUCIARIA ITALIANA DELLA SOMALIA.

Incenso della Migiurtinia. "Bollettino Mensile Camera
di Commercio". No. 3-6. Mogadiscio 1955.

AMBASCIATA D'ITALIA (SOMALIA)

Somalia: Guida per gli esportatori italiani.
(a cura dell'Ufficio Commerciale dell'Ambasciata d'Italia).
Tipo-Litografia Missione Cattolica. Mogadiscio.
173 pp. ills.

ANONYMOUS.

I commerci del Benadir. "I.C.I." 1907.
13 p.

L'incenso della Somalia. "La Somalia Italiana".
Anno II. No. 4. Mogadiscio 1925.

La produzione e il commercio delle banane nella
Somalia Italiana. "Rassegna Economica delle Colonie".
Roma 1929.
970 p.

Il commercio dell'incenso nella Somalia Italiana.
"Rassegna Economica delle Colonie". Roma 1930.
1144 p.

Il commercio dell'incenso in Aden. "Rassegna Economica
delle Colonie". Roma 1932.

Istituzione del Comitato economico per la Somalia:
La Somalia alla Fiera di Tripoli. "La Somalia Italiana".
Mogadiscio Gennaio-Giugno 1932.

Il movimento commerciale marittimo della Somalia Italiana
durante 1932. "Rassegna Economica delle Colonie." No. 9-10.
Roma 1933.

L'incenso della Migiurtinia: come sara regolato
il suo commercio. "Rivista Italiana di Essenze e Profumi".
No. 6. Milano 1934.
168 p.

La prima fiera internazionale della Somalia.
"Africa". Roma 1952.
140 p.

L'incenso ricchezza profumata della rupi migiurtinie.
(Numero Unico). III Fiera della Somalia Settembre-Ottobre 1955.
Mogadiscio 1955.
38-39 pp.

Un decennio di commercio coll'estero 1946-1956.
"Bollettino Mensile Camera di Commercio".
No. 7-12. Mogadiscio 1956.

Numbero dedicato alla Repubblica Somala in occasione
della IX Fiera Internazionale di Mogadiscio.
"Mondo Afro-Asiatico". Anno V. No. 8.
Roma Settembre 1967.
35 pp. ills. photos.

(R) AZIENDA MONOPOLIO BANANE.

Accordi per la refrigerazione e maturazione
delle banane. "Rivista Freddo". No. 1. 1937.

BARTOLUCCI, A.

La Fiera della Somalia. "Somalia d'Oggi".
No. 4. Mogadiscio 1957.
39 pp.

BARZELLOTTI, F.L.
L'Italia e i commerci dell'Africa Orientale.
Civeli. Firenze 1885.

BASCO.

Il commercio in Somalia. "Africa".
No. 13. Roma 1927.
223 p.

BECCARI, F.

Shema di regolamento per la produzione e l'esportazione
delle banane della Somalia. Istituto Agronomico per l'Oltremare.
"Fasc". No. 1440. Firenze 1954.

———————

Problemi di trasporto e di commercio della banana Somala.
Istituto Agronomico per l'Oltremare. "Fasc". No. 1138.
Firenze 1955.
27 pp.

———————

Relazione incontro A.M.B. per il monopolio, produzione
e trasporto delle banane della Somalia. Istituto Agronomico
per l'Oltremare. "Fasc". No. 1438. Firenze 1955.
6 pp.

———————

Pro-memoria per il progetto di ordinanza esportazione
banane Somale. Istituto Agronomico per l'Oltremare.
"Fasc". No. 4290. Firenze 1956.

BIGI, F.

Significato ed importanza del commercio bananiero Italo-Somalo.
"Rivista di Agricoltura Subtropicale e Tropicale".
No. 7-9. Firenze Luglio-Settembre 1962.
335-373 pp.

———————

Significato ed importanza del commercio bananiero Italo-Somalo.
Istituto Agronomico per l'Oltremare. Firenze 1962.
43 pp. ills.

BRITISH MILITARY ADMINISTRATION.

Export and Import Licence Regulations and
Exchange Control. Government Press.
Mogadiscio October 25, 1949.
16 pp.

Report on the first two years of agricultural
marketing section. Mogadishu.
35 pp. tables.

BRUSA, A.

Il traffico bananiero, la R.A.M.B. e l'autarchia.
"Rassegna d'Oltremare". No. 7. Genova 1938.
14 p.

CAMERA DI COMMERCIO, INDUSTRIA E AGRICOLTURA DELLA SOMALIA.

Relazione in occasione della visita dell'On. Brusasca
giugno 1950. Stamperia AFIS. Mogadiscio 1950.

Annuario 1953/54. Mogadiscio 1954.
174 pp.

Annuario 1954/55. Mogadiscio 1955.
107 pp.

III Fiera della Somalia. (Numero Unico).
Mostra Mercato dell'artigianato africano.
Mogadiscio 24 Settembre-9 Ottobre 1955.
69 pp.

IV Fiera Internazionale della Somalia.
2 Mostra Mercato dell'artigianato africano.
Mogadiscio 1957.
103 pp.

Annuario 1958.   Mogadiscio 1958.
94 pp.

Annuario 1959.   Mogadiscio 1959.
119 pp.

V Fiera Internazionale della Somalia: Catalogo
Ufficiale Mogadiscio 28 Settembre-12Ottobre 1959.
Mogadiscio 1959.

Annuario 1960.   Mogadiscio 1960.
51 pp.

Statuto e Regolamento.   Mogadiscio 1960.
35 pp.

Annuario 1961.   Mogadiscio 1961.
52 pp. ills.

Catalogo Ufficiale: 6 Fiera Internazionale
della Somalia.   Mogadiscio 28 Settembre-12 Ottobre 1961.
Mogadiscio 1961.

Annuario 1962.   Mogadiscio 1962.
77 pp. ills.

Annuario 1967.   Mogadiscio 1967.

Xa Fiera Internazionale della Somalia: Programma
28 Settembre-12 Ottobre 1969.   Sezione Fiere, e
Mostre e Turismo.   Mogadiscio 1969.
12 pp.

10th International Fair of Somalia: Programme
28th September-12 October 1969.   Fair and Tourism Section.

Mogadiscio 1969.
12 pp.

———————

Directory 1972. Mogadishu 1972.

CASILLI D'ARAGONA, M.

Note sull'economia della Somalia Italiana:
Parte I Commercio e Traffico. "Rassegna Economica
delle Colonie". Roma 1939.
952 p.

———————

Sistema tradizionale di pesi e misure in uso
nei territori della Somalia Italiana. "Rassegna Economica
delle Colonie". Roma 1939.
183 p.

CASTALDI, A.

La mostra delle pelli e delle fibre coloniali
(A.O.). "Costruire". 1935.
75 p.

CAS

CATTELLANI, G.

L'avvenire coloniale d'Italia nel Benadir:
Manuale per il commercio e l'Emigrazione.
Tipografia Giannini. Napoli 1897.

CAVALLINI, G.

Gli impianti frigoriferi della nuova navi bananiere
della R.A.M.B. "Rivista del Freddo". No. 5. 1933.
147 p.

CESARI, C.

Le possibilita commerciali ed agricolo che apportera
l'Oltregiuba. "Bollettino Lloyd Triestino". No. 8.
Trieste 1925.
5 p.

CHAMBRE DE COMMERCE DE DJIBOUTI.

Annuaire 1914. Impr. Saint Lazare.
Dire Daua 1914.
85 pp.

CIBELLI, E.

L'organizzazione produttivo commerciale del
Monopolio banane. "Botanica e Colonizzazione".
Roma 1938.
382 p.

─────────────

Azienda monopolio: creazione fascista.
"Rassegna Economica delle Colonie".
No. 11. Roma 1937.

─────────────

I nuovi compiti del Monopolio Statale Bananiero.
"Autarchia Alimentare". No. 2.
51 p.

CONF. NAZIONALE FASCISTA COMMERCIANTI.

I nostri mercati coloniali: Tripolitania,
Cirenaica, Eritrea, Somalia. Cameria dei Deputati.
Roma 1930.

CONFORTI, E.

L'esportazione delle banane dalla Somalia Italiana
dagli inizi ad oggi e suoi futuri sviluppi.
(Prefazione del Prof. Armando Maugini). Istituto Agricolo
Coloniale Italiano. Monograf. No. 51. Firenze 1939.
66 pp. tables.

CUFINO, L.

Il commercio della Somalia Italiana.
"L'esploratore Commerciale". Milano 1912.

DONATI, C.

Le pelli in Somalia. "La Somalia Italiana".
No. 4-6. Mogadiscio 1930.

─────────────

Il commercio delle pelli nella Somalia Italiana.
"Rassegna Economica delle Colonie". Roma 1930.

FABRIZI, C.

Il commercio della Somalia (dal Vol. Lezioni di
Tecnica del Commercio 1937-38). Casa Editrice Milano.
Padova 1939.
167 pp.

FALCONE, A.

La banana della Somalia: produzione, prezzi, esportazione.
Tipografia Falcioni. Roma 1950.

FIORESI, L.

Le banane ed il loro commercio. "Rivista del Freddo".
No. 5. 1937.
157 pp.

FONZI CURCIANI, C.

Brevi note illustrative al compionario delle merci
che principalmente vengono importate nel Benadir.
Tipografia La Stampa. Commerciale. Milano 1909.
23 pp.

FOREIGN OFFICE. (OFFICIAL)

Reports on the trade of the Somali Coast 1886, 1891-92,
1893-1894, 1898-1899, 1899-1900, 1900-1901, 1901-1902, 1903-04
(Dipl. Cons. Reps) 10 Part. London 1886-1905.

FRANCOLINI, B.

La Somalia alla Fiera di Tripoli. "L'Oltremare".
Roma 1931.
141 p.

_____

Le promesse della Somalia Italiana: Commercio bananiero.
"illustrazione Coloniale". No. 8. Milano 1931.
34 p.

GIL ACCOLTI, F.

La competitivita delle banane somale sul mercato italiano
nel periodo compreso fra il 1966 ed il 1970 (maggio).
"Rivista di Agricoltura Subtropicale e Tropicale".
No. 4-9. Firenze Aprile-Settembre 1970.
161-170 pp.

GIROSI, A.

Come e perche e nato la fiera. "Africa d'Oggi".
Roma Ottobre-Dicembre 1952.

GOVERNO DELLA SOMALIA.

Ordinamento sugli scambi commerciali con l'estero e
sul regime valutario. Ministero per gli Affari Economici.
Mogadiscio 1956.
24 pp.

_____

Statistica del commercio con l'estero: Anno 1952.
Ufficio Studi e Statistica. Mogadiscio 1953.
134 pp.

_____

Statistica del commercio con l'estero: Gennaio-Dicembre 1954.
Servizio di Statistica. Gabinetto dell'Amministrazione.
Stamperia AFIS. Mogadiscio.
112 pp.

_____

Statistica del commercio con l'estero: Gennaio-Dicembre 1955.
Servizio di Statistica. Gabinetto dell'Amministrazione.
Stamperia AFIS. Mogadiscio 1956.
102 pp.

_____

Statistica del commercio con l'estero: Anno 1956.
Servizio di Statistica. Dipartimento degli Studi.
Ministero per gli Affari Sociali. Stamperia del Governo.
Mogadiscio 1957.
108 pp.

_____

Statistica del commercio con l'estero: Gennaio-Dicembre 1957.
Servizio di Statistica. Mogadiscio 1958.
157 pp.

_____

Statistica del commercio con l'estero: Anno 1958.
Servizio di Statistica. Mogadiscio 1959.
178 pp.

_____

Statistica del commercio con l'estero: Gennaio-Dicembre 1960.
Servizio di Statistica. Mogadiscio 1961.
188 pp.

_____

Statistica del commercio con l'estero: Gennaio-Dicembre 1961.
(delle Regioni Meridionali). Ufficio Centrale di Statistica.
Mogadiscio 1962.
199 pp.

_____

Statistica del commercio con l'estero: Gennaio-Dicembre 1962.
(delle Regioni Meridionali). Ufficio Centrale di Statistica.
Mogadiscio 1963.

202 pp.

_____

Statistica del commercio con l'estero: Gennaio–Dicembre 1963.
(delle Regioni Meridionali). Ufficio Centrale di Statistica.
Mogadiscio 1964.
185 pp.

_____

Foreign Trade Returns Year 1964. Statistical Department.
Planning Directorate. Mogadiscio December 1965.
240 pp. (Bilingual: English-Italian)

_____

Foreign Trade Returns Year 1965. Statistical Department.
Ministry of Planning & Co-ordination. Mogadiscio December 1966.
(Bilingual: English-Italian).

_____

Foreign Trade Returns Year 1966. Statistical Department.
Ministry of Planning and Co-ordination. Mogadiscio December 1966.
(Bilingual: English-Italian).

_____

Foreign Trade Returns Year 1967. Statistical Department.
Ministry of Planning & Co-ordination. Mogadiscio October 1969.
(Bilingual: English-Italian).

_____

Foreign Trade Returns Year 1968. Statistical Department.
Ministry of Planning and Co-ordination. Mogadiscio May 1970.
(Bilingual: English-Italian).

_____

Foreign Trade Returns Year 1969. Statistical Department.
Ministry of Planning & Co-ordination. State Printing Press.
Mogadiscio March 1971.
221 pp. (Bilingual: English-Italian).

_____

Foreign Trade Returns Year 1970. Statistical Department.
Ministry of Planning and Co-ordination. Mogadiscio August 1971.
437 pp. (Bilingual: English-Italian)

_____

Foreign Trade Returns Year 1971. Statistical Department.

Ministry of Planning and Co-ordination. Mogadiscio July 1972.
487 pp. (Bilingual: English-Italian).

Foreign Trade Classification. Statistical Service.
Mogadiscio 1964.
86 pp.

Informazione sulle attivita economiche in Somalia.
Ministero dell'industria e Commercio. Mogadiscio 1968.
85 pp.

GOVERNO DELLA SOMALIA ITALIANA.

Indicazione illustrative dei campioni dei prodotti della
Colonia inviati alla Fiera di Milano del 1922.
Stamperia della Colonia. Mogadiscio 1922.
50 pp.

ISTITUTO COLONIALE ITALIANO.

Brevi note illustrative al campionario delle principali
n merci d'importazione ed esportazione dal Benadir.
"Rivista delle Colonie Italiane." Roma 1909.
20 p.

INTRONA, S.

Somalia 1953 alla Fiera del Levante. "Africa". No. 9.
Roma 1953.

KENYA EXPORT PROMOTION COUNCIL.

Report on the Kenya Trade Delegation to Somalia 1968.
Nairobi 1968.
25 pp.

LABROUSSE, H.

Les negociants marseillais a Chekh Said a la fin
du XIXe siecle. "Revue Pcount". No. 3. La Societe
D'etudes de l'Afrique Orientale. Djibouti 1967.

L.C.

Una ricognizione commerciale dei porti del mar Rosso
e di quelli africani dell'oceano Indiano da Gibuti
a Zanzibar. "Bollettino Societa Geografica Italiana".
Roma 1911.

LEFEVRE, R.

Le pelli della Somalia Italiana. "L'Oltremare".
Roma 1932.

―――――――――

Lo sviluppo commerciale della Somalia Italiana.
"Commercio". No. 9. Roma 1932.

LEVI, P.

La Societa del Benadir e il sottoscritto.
Tipografia della Tribuna. Genova.
21 pp.

LOADER.

Rapport commercial sur la cote orientale d'Afrique.
Paris 1851.

MAHONEY, F.

Livestock marketing in the Somali Republic.
(USAID Report). Mogadishu December 1963.
27 pp. tables. bibl.

MANNU, G.

Le ricchezze della Somalia, il commercio
dell'incenso migiutino. Monografie Commerciale
Ind. Italo-Africano. Genova 1933.

MARINO, A.

Frigoriferi in colonia: le nostre banane.
"Illustrazione Coloniale". No. 6. Milano 1930.
25 p.

MEREGAZZI, R.

Il movimento commerciale marittimo della Somalia.
"Economia Nazionale". No. 4. Milano 1928.
51 p.

(R) MINISTERO AFFARI ESTERI.

Movimento commerciale del Benadir. Roma 1907.
43 pp.

(R) MINISTERO DELLE COLONIE.

Somalia Italiana: Statistiche doganali per l'anno
finanziario 1911-1912. G. Bertero. Roma 1913.

―――――――――

Notizie sui commerci della Somalia Italiana:
movimento commerciale durante l'esercizio 1912-1913.
Tipografia Nazionale di G. Bertero. Roma 1914.
48 pp. tables.

Notizie sui commerci della Somalia Italiana.
G. Bertero. Roma 1914.
77 pp.

MONILE, F.

Il problema dell'incenso. "Commercio Italo-Africano".
No. 3. Genova 1934.
32 p.

NERI, L.F.

18 mesi di attivita della R. Azienda Monopolio banane.
"Rassegna d'Oltremare". No. 8. Genova 1937.
8 p.

OECONOMICUS.

Economia della Somalia 1946-1956: Un decennio di
commercio con l'estero. "Bollettino Mensile Camera
di Commercio della Somalia". No. 7-12. Mogadiscio 1957.

PAPINI, L.

Gli scambi commerciali fra l'Italia, Eritrea, Somalia
e Libia in regime di occupazione britannica.
"Rivista di Pol. Econ". 1947.
13 pp.

PARODI, E.

La banana e la sua ascesa commerciale.
"Rivista del Freddo". No. 11. 1936.
355 pp.

PETTAZZI, E.

Il consumo del riso in Somalia. "La Somalia Italiana".
No. 3. Mogadiscio 1929.

La produzione ed il commercio dell'incenso nella Migiurtinia.
"Rassegna Economica delle Colonie." Roma 1929.
1171 p.

L'esportazione del granoturco della Somalia ed il
commercio italiano. "La Somalia Italiana".
No. 1-3. Mogadiscio 1930.
3 p.

QUEIROLO, E.

Banane in Somalia: problemi di trasporto.
"Echi e Commenti". No. 1. Roma 1935.

REALE AZIENDA MONOPOLIO BANANE.

Un biennio di attivita della R. Azienda
Monopolio Banane. A.I.N.A. Roma 1938.
172 pp.

_____

Il monopolio delle banabe nel quadro dell'autarchia
economica e dei trasporti nazionali.
"Annali Africa Italiana". No. 4. Roma 1942.
997 p.

_____

L'Organizzazione Statale Italiana per la produzione,
il trasporto, e la vendita delle banane. "Atti VIII
Congresso Agricoltura Tropicale e Subtropicale".
(Tripoli 1938) 1941.
606 p.

R.B.

L'incenso migiurtini: Obblighi della Societa
Commerciale Coloniale. "L'Oltremare". Roma 1934.
287 p.

PRESIDENZA DEL CONSIGLIO DEI MINISTRI.

Scambi commerciali tra l'Italia e la Somalia:
L'interscambio e le sue caratteristiche.
Ufficio Informazione. "Documenti di Vita Italiana".
Roma 1961.
9347-9352 pp.

_____

Scambi commerciali tra l'Italia e la Somalia.
"Osservatore Economico del Medio Oriente e del Nord Africa".
No. 2. Roma 1962.
17-18 pp.

REPUBLIQUE ITALIENNE.

Statistique du Commerce Exterieur de la Somalie 1950-55.

Ministere des Affaires Etrangeres. Rome 1955.
30 pp.

─────────────

Statistiques du Commerce Exterieur de la
Somalie 1950-56. Ministere des Affaires Etrangeres.
Rome 1956.
30 pp.

─────────────

Statistiques du Commerce Exterieur de la
Somalie 1950-57. Ministere des Affaires Etrangeres.
Rome 1958.
34 pp.

─────────────

Statistiques du Commerce Exterieur de la
Somalie 1958. Ministere des Affaires Etrangeres.
Rome Juillet 1959.
34 pp.

─────────────

Statistiques du Commerce Exterieur de la
Somalie 1959. Ministere des Affaires Etrangeres.
Rome Juin 1960.
36 pp.

ROCCHETTI, G.

Gli scambi commerciali della Somalia. "Rivista di
Agricoltura Tropicale e Subtropicale e Subtropicale". Firenze
Ottobre-Dicembre 1955.

─────────────

Produzione e commercio con l'estero in Somalia
nel periodo 1950-59. "Rivista di Agricoltura Subtropicale
e Tropicale". No. 4-9. Firenze Aprile-Settembre 1960.
198-216 pp.

ROSSETTI, C.

I commerci del Benadir: Tre note sulla Citta di Mogasiscio.
1906.

ROSSI, U.

Il commercio delle banane. "Atti VIII Convegno Economico
Italo-Africano". Milano 1959.
131-132 pp.

SCASSELLATI SFORZOLINI, G.

Il problema cotoniero italiano (Somalia).
"Rivista Coloniale". Roma 1923.
267 p.

SOCIETA ANONIMO COMMERCIALE ITALIANA PER IL BENADIR.

Pubblicazioni varie per la liquidazione della Societa.
Tipografia Bellini F.B. Milano 1902-1903-1905.

SOLFERINI, A.

Relazione sul problema dell'incenso in Somalia e sulla
organizzazione e prime attivita delle Cooperative del
Consorzio. AFIS. Mogadiscio 1955.

SOMALILAND PROTECTORATE.

Annual Trade Report of Somaliland Protectorate for the
year ended 31st December 1951. The Modern Press.
Aden March 21, 1952.
67 pp.

_____

Annual Trade Report of Somaliland Protectorate for the
year ended 31st December 1952. Customs and Excise Department.
Berbera June 20, 1953. (D.L. Patel Press Ltd. Nairobi).
27 pp.

_____

Annual Trade Report of Somaliland Protectorate for the
year ended 31st December 1953. Customs and Excise Department.
Berbera April 2, 1954.
31 pp.

_____

Annual Trade Report of Somaliland Protectorate for the
year ended 31st December 1955. Customs and Excise Department.
Berbera April 16, 1956.
54 pp.

_____

Annual Trade Report of Somaliland Protectorate for
the Year ended 31st December 1958. The Pioneer Press.
Hargeisa 1959.
70 pp.

_____

Annual Trade Report of Somaliland Protectorate for the

year ended 31st December 1959. The Pioneer Press.
Hargeisa 1960.
72 pp.

_____ (SOMALI REPUBLIC).

Foreign Trade Statistics (Northern Region). January-December 1960
Central Statistical Service. Mogadishu 1961. (2nd April)
64 pp.

_____

Annual Trade Report for the year ended 31st December 1962.
(Northern Region). Customs and Excise Department.
Berbera July 11, 1962.
57 pp.

VECCHI, B.V.

Nel Nord Somalo: L'Incenso. "Numero Speciale della
Rivista "Costruire". Roma 1938.
71 pp.

_____

La prima fiera della Somalia. "Africa".   No. 10-11.
Roma 1952.

VENUTE, S.J.

Import Tariff system of the Somali Republic
as of April 1963. Department of Commerce.
Washington Overseas Business Report.

VERAX.

Il traffico bananiero ed i suoi peonieri.
"L'Italia d'Oltremare". No. 6. Roma 1938.
152 p.

VITALE, M.A.

La Mostra dell'Amministrazione Italiana in
Somalia. "Rassegna Espansione Commerciale".
No. 9-10. Milano 1950.

VILL.

Banane: Orientamenti merceologici per l'importazione
esportazione con l"Africa. "La Voce dell'Africa".
No. 17. Roma 1959.

VITALE, M.A.

Incenso e debiti. "Africa". No. 9. Roma 1955.
262 p.

EDUCATION

AFER.

Educazione di base in Somalia.
"Africa". No. 9. Roma 1954.
244 p.

AMMINISTRAZIONE FIDUCIARIA ITALIANA DELLA SOMALIA.

Lezioni sugli insegnamenti fondamentali per
gli alunni del II Corso (Anno Scolastico 1951-52).
Mogadiscio 29 Febbraio 1952.

———————

Piano quinquennale per lo sviluppo dell'istruzione
pubblica del Territorio 1951-56. Stamperia AFIS.
Mogadiscio 1953.
56 pp.

———————

Progetto di piano della organizzazione scolastica
della Somalia fino al 1960. AFIS. Mogadiscio Febbraio 1956.

ANONYMOUS.

L'istruzione primaria in Somalia. "L'Oltremare".
Roma 1953.
244-245 pp.

AWES,M.M. AND ABDULLAHI,M.

Informazioni sugli studenti Somali in Italia.
Roma 1966.
11 pp.

BAGLIONI,E.

L'istruzione tecnica in Somalia. "Africa". No. 10.
Roma 1954.
269-270 pp.

BATTISTELLA,R.

L'Italia per le genti di colore:
la scuola dei Sultanelli a Mogadiscio.
"L'Italia d'Oltremare". Roma 1940.
219 p.

BRITISH SOMALILAND PROTECTORATE.

Education Department. Annual Survey,1955.
Hargeisa 1966.

20 pp.

Triennial Survey 1955-1957. Educational Department.
Stationery Office. Hargeisa.

BROWN,E.H.

National Teacher Education Center. (Afgoi).
12 pp. map. ills.

COMELLA,F.

La scuola in Somalia. "Azione Coloniale".
Roma 21 Dicembre 1919.

COSTANZO,G.A.

Una scuola per l'autogoverno. "Meridiano Somalo".
Mogadiscio 1951.

Evolution de la femme dans la Somalie sous
tutelle italienne. Institut Internationale des
Civilisations Differentes. 31 Session.
Bruxelles 17-20 Septembre 1958.
24 pp.

L'educazione, chiave di sviluppo della Somalia.
"Africa". No. 3. Roma Maggio-giugno 1960.
139-145 pp.

DAWSON,G.G.

Education in Somalia. "Comparative Education Review"
October 1964.

DORATO,M.

L'istruzione professionale in Somalia.
"Africa". No. 1. Roma 1958.
15-18 pp.

EATON,G.E.

Survey of education and training in the
Somali Republic to meet the personnel needs of
the public services. Government Press.
Mogadishu, March 1965.
28 pp.

FERRY,R.

Esquisse d'une etude ethnique du lycee de

Djibouti en 1963-1964. "Revue Pount". No. 1
La Societe D;etudes de l'Afrique Orientale.
Djibouti Octobre 1966.

GAZZINI,M.

Giovani della Somalia. "Africa" No. 11.
Roma 1953.
291-294 pp.

Student somali in Italia. "Africa". No. 3-4.
Roma 1954.
101-102 pp.

GOVERNO DELLA SOMALIA.

Convegno didattico per maestri elementari:
la scuola,la famiglia,la societa. (Merca 25-26 Gennaio 1958)
Ministero Affari Sociali. Dipartimento Pubblica Istruzione.
Stamperia del Governo. Mogadiscio 10 Ottobre 1958.

GRANDJEAN,H.

Deux missions educatives en Somalie Italienne.
"International Review of Education". Vol. IV. No. 4.
Hamburg 1958.
409-422 pp.

HALANE,M.O.

L'organisation scolaire. "Presence Africaine".
No. 3. Paris 1961.
164-167 pp.

MAGNINO,L.

Universita a Mogadiscio. "Africa"/ No. 1-2.
Roma 1955.
269-270 pp.

MELE,F.

La scuola in Somalia. "Africa". Fasc. No. 50.
Roma 1951.
161 p.

MEREGAZZI,R.

Quaderni della pubblica istruzione. AFIS. Mogadiscio 1954.
181 pp.

MICACCHI, R.

L'enseignement aux indigenes dans les Colonies
Italiennes,dependentes directement de la Couronne.

Instit.Col.Internationale. Bruxelles 1931.
475 596 pp.

MORENO,M.M.

Problemi culturali della Somalia.
''Africa. Roma 1952.
235 p.

NATIONAL TEACHER EDUCATION CENTRE(NTEC)

College of Education. NTEC. Afgoi February 1969.
43 pp.

PACE,A.

Questioni di politica educativa
in Somalia. ''Somalia d'Oggi''. No. 2.
Mogadiscio 1956.
2 p.

Appunti per l'istruzione educativa
del popolo somalo. ''Somalia d'Oggi'' No. 2.
Mogadiscio 1956.
18 p.

PIRONE,M.

Somalie sous tutelle italienne: Developpement de
l'education, de l'instruction et de la culture de
la population somalie. ''Civilisations''. Vol. VII.
No. 1. Bruxelles 1957.

PUCCIONI,D.

L'istruzione degli Africani in regime
di Trusteeship. Roma 1950.
45 pp.

II problema dell'istruzione dei nativi.
''Africa''. No. 8. Roma 1950.
179 p.

SOMALI REPUBLIC.

Survey of education and training in the Somali
Republic to meet the personnel needs of the
Public Services. Establishment and Personnel
Directorate. Presidency Council of Ministers.
Mogadiscio March 1965.
29 pp. appendices.

Project for school building programme
in Somalia. Ministry of Education.
Mogadiscio 1965.

Statistical Tables 1965-1966. Ministry
of Education. Mogadiscio August 1966.

Statistical Tables for 1966-1967.
Ministry of Education. Mogadiscio October 1967.
102 pp. tables.

UNESCO/UNICEF Project for training in-service teachers
in the North held in Hargeisa and Sheik from 14 May, 1966
to 7 July 1966. Ministry of Education Regional Department
of Education. Hargeisa 1966.

Somali students studying abroad (position as in December 1966).
(Report prepared for the Government of Somalia by S.B.L. Nigam
I.L.O. Manpower Assessment and Planning Adviser). Ministry of
Planning and Co-ordination. Manpower Section. Mogadiscio.
December 1966.
153 pp. tables.

Handing over report submitted by H.E.Hon.Kenadid
Ahmed Yusuf,Out-going Minister of Education. Ministry
of Education. Mogadiscio July 1967.
21 pp.

Somali students studying abroad (position as on 31.12.1967).
Ministry of Planning & Co-ordination. Manpower Section.
Mogadiscio July 1968.
61 pp. tables.

Annual Report 1967. Ministry of Education.
Mogadiscio February 1968.
32 pp.

Somali-German Project;teachers in-service
training course on adult education held in
Mogadiscio from April 5 to June 8 1967.
Ministry of Education. Mogadiscio 1967.

UNESCO-UNICEF Project for Teacher Training at Mogadiscio:
Syllabus and Text for the Intensive Course for one year
to up-grade Headmasters and Teachers of Elementary Schools.
1968-1969. Mogadiscio 1968.

UNESCO-UNICEF Project; nine months course for
training in-service teachers of adult women education
centres in the North, held in Hargeisa July 1968-April 1969.
Ministry of Education. Regional Department of Education.
Hargeisa 1969.

Technical education and manpower in Somalia; an investigation
to be conducted with special regard to the Technical Institute
of Burao. (Prepared by Heinze Guenther Klein and Herman W.
Schoenmeier) Ministry of Education. Mogadiscio 1969.

SOMALI DEMOCRATIC REPUBLIC.

Annual Report 1969. Ministry of Education.
Mogadiscio February 1970.
26 pp. tables. appendices.

Statistical Survey of Education in Somalia 1969-1970.
(with back data on selected topics). Ministry of Education.
Mogadiscio, May 1970.
104 pp. tables.

Annual Report 1970. Ministry of Education.
Mogadishu May 20th 1971.
44 pp. appendices. tables.

National University of Somalia Development
Prospectives. (English Summary). Ministry of
Planning & Co-ordination. Mogadiscio October 1971.
24 pp.

Universita Nazionale Somala: studio delle prospettive
di sviluppo. Ministero della Pianificazione e Coordinazione.
Mogadiscio Ottobre 1971.
103 pp. tables.

Statistics of Education in Somalia 1970-1971.
Ministry of Education. Mogadiscio 20 March 1971.
40 pp. tables.

Statistics of Education, 1971-1972.
Ministry of Education. Mogadiscio May 1972.
50 pp. tables.

———————————

Current Statistical Trends in Somali Education.
Ministry of Education. Mogadishu 7th November 1971.
104 pp. tables.

———————————

Handbook for Teaching Adult V Classes.
National Adult Education Center. Ministry of
Education. Mogadiscio December 1971.

———————————

Manuale per l'insegnamento agli adulti. Centro Nazionale
per l'Educazione degli Adulti. Ministero della Pubblica
Istruzione. Mogadiscio Dicembre 1971.

———————————

A description of the Short-Term Development
Programme 1971-73. Ministry of Education. Mogadiscio.
22 pp. tables.

———————————

Annual Report 1971. Ministry of Education.
Mogadiscio May 30th 1972.
40 pp. tables.

———————————

National Adult Education Center. Ministry of
Education. Mogadiscio.
12 pp. ills. tables. (English-Italian).

TORELLI,D.

L'attivita delle scuole elementari in Somalia.
"Somalia d'Oggi". No. 4. Mogadiscio 1957.
30-35 pp.

UNESCO.

L'instruction publique en Somalie sous administration
italienne. Rapport du Conseiller Technique envoye par
l'UNESCO. Geneve Juin 1953.
117 pp.

———————————

L'instruction publique en Somalie sous administration
italienne. Rapport du Conseiller Technique envoye par

l'UNESCO. Geneve Mars 1956.

UNITED NATIONS.

List of Fellowships awarded in Somalia under the United
Nations Expanded Programme of Technical Assistance and
Regular Programme of the United Nations and the Specialised
Agencies 1957-1965. Office of the Resident Representative
and Director of Special Fund Programmes in the Somali Republic.
Mogadiscio 31st December 1965.
77 pp. tables.

VANNELLA,G.G.

Gli allievi della Polizia somala.
"Eurafrica". No. 4. Roma 1953.

VILLARI,L.

Somalia-Lo sviluppo dell'istruzione.
"Bollettino Legislaz. Scolastica Comparata.
No. 3. 1954.
122 p.

VILLORESI,M.

La scuola in Somalia. "Africa". No. 3
87 p.

GEOLOGY AND GEOGRAPHY

1. **Carthography (Arranged in a chronological order)**

1808.

Map of Western Somaliland. Scale: 1:1,000,000.
E. Stanford. London 1808.

1857.

Karte der Somali-Kuste und des Golfs von Aden
zur Ubersicht der Ergebnisse von T. von Heuglin's
Reise Septr. bis Decr. 1857. Maasstab. 1:2,500,000.
Petermann's "Geographische Mitteilungen". Band 6.
Tafel 18. Gotha 1860.

1876/1881   MOKTAR,com.te MOHAMED.

Carte du Cap Guardafui et ses environs.
E'chelle 1:40.000. "Bulletin de la Societe
Kediviale de Geographie". Ser. 1. Fasc. 9 et 10.
Le Caire.   1876/1881.

1882   PURDY.

Itineraire de Berenice a Berbera par Purdy.
E'chelle 1:5000.000. "Bulletin de la Societe
Kediviale de Geographie" Ser. 2. Le Caire. 1882.
431 pp.

1883.

Map of Somali Land and Harar. Italian and
Egyptian Surveys. Scale Geographical miles,50.
Gov. Photozinco Office. Poona 1883.

1885.

J. Menge's Reisen auf das Hochplateau der Somali
Halbinsel im Januar und Dezember 1884.
Massstab: 1:300.000. Petermann's "Geographische Mitteilungen".
Band 31. Tafel 20. Gotha 1885.

1889   AMORETTI.

Piano di Obbia. (Edizione Provvisorio). Scala 1:2000.
Ministero della Guerra. 1889.

1891.

Carta del Paese dei Somali. Scala 1:3,000.000.
(In A.E.Q. Mario's). La Colonia Eritrea e i
suoi Commerci. Fratelli Bocca. Torino 1891.

1892 MENGES,J.

Prequi'ile des Somali: Itineraires de J. Menges,
G. Nurse et L.Bricchetti-Robecchi 1890-91.
E'chelle de 1:10,000.000. "L'Annee Cartographique".
Deuxieme Supplement. 1892.

1892/93 CORA,G.

La Somalia tra Berbera ed i Bur Dap (Nogal)
esplorata dal Cap. Baudi di Vesme (1890) e
posizioni geografiche determinate nella Somalia
dalle spedizioni James, Swaine, Paget, Hooper.
Note Cartografiche con due carte. "Cosmos".
Ser. II. Vol. XI. Fasc. No. 8-9.
244 pp.

1893 DALLA VEDOVA,G.

Itinerario da Obbia ad Alula di Robecchi-Bricchetti.
Scala 1:5000.000 costruita e disegnata su schizzi
e rilievi del viaggiatore. Edizione Reale Societa
Geografica Italiana. Roma 1893.

1893 DALLA VEDOVA,G.

Itinerario dell'Ing. Luigi Robecchi-Bricchetti
attraverso la Somalia. Scala 1:1.000.000 redatta sulle
note del viaggiatore. Edizione Reale Societa
Geografica Italiana. Roma 1893.

1893 DALLA VEDOVA,G.

Itinerario dell'Ing.Luigi Robecchi-Bricchetti
attraverso la Somalia. Scala 1"1.000.000 redatta sulle
note del viaggiatore. Societa Geografica Italiana.
Edizione a colori di L.Salomone. Roma 1893.
Tavola 1º - Da Merca ad Obbia
Tavola 2º - Da Obbia allo Scebeli
Tavola 3º - Dallo Scebeli a Berbera
Tavola 4º - Quadro d'unione. Scala 1:4.000.000.

1894.

Sketch of the Routes in Somali Land travelled by Lts.
H.C. Lowther and C.F.S. Vandeleur in 1894.
Scale 1:443,520 or one inch=7 statute miles.
Southampton 1894.

1894 MENGES,J.

J. Menges' Reisen auf das Hochplateau der Somali
Halbinsel in den Jahren 1884 und 1892. Massstab: 1:3000,000.
Petermann's "Geographische Mitteilungen". Band 40.
Tafel 16. Gotha 1894.

1894.

Map showing Boundaries of the British Sphere with
France and Italy in Somaliland. Scale: 1 inches=32 miles.

Southampton 1894.

1895.

Hunting Map of Northern Somaliland. Scale: 20 miles to 1 inch.
Rowland Ward. London 1895.

1896.

Reiseroute des Fursten D. Ghika Comanesti im
Somal-Lande,1895 und 1896. Bearbeitet von DR.P. Paulitschke.
Massstab 1:2,000,000. Petermann's "Geographische Mitteilungen".
Band 42. Tafel 18. Gotha 1896.

1898.

Reiseroute des Grafen E. Wickenburg im Somalilande 1897.
Bearbeitet von Prof. P. Paulitschke. Massstab 1:1,000.000.
Petermann's "Geographische Mitteilungen". Band 44.
Tafel 5. Gotha 1898.

1898 MAGNAGHI,A.

La carta nautica costruita nel 1325 da Angiolino Dalorto.

1898.

Expedition Ghika au Pays des Somalis (du mois d'Octobre 1895
jusqu'en mars 1896) fait d'apres les releves du prince
Demetre Ghika par le Prof. Dr. Philippe Paulitschke.
E'chelle 1:1,000.000. Georg & Co. Geneve et Bale 1898.

1899   AMADEI,R.

Somalia Italiana. (5 tavole). Istituto Cartografico
Italiano. 1899.

1902 WAR OFFICE.

Map of a portion of Somaliland.
Scale 1:1,000.000 or 1.014 inches to 16 miles.
Intelligence Division. War Office. London December 1902.
(Another edition, revised October 1906).

1902 WAR OFFICE.

Sketch Map of Somaliland. Scale 1:3,000.000.
War Office. London 1902. Another Edition 1907.
(Reprint with corrections. C oured. 1919).

1903.

Map of the Nogal Valley and a part of the Haud: Somaliland.
Scale; approximately 1''=71/2 miles. Intelligence Branch.
Upper Sheik. Somaliland. 1903.

1906   ISTITUTO GEOGRAFICO MILITARE.

Da Ras Casar alla foce del Giuba. Scala 1:4.000.000.
Istituto Geografico Militare. Firenze 1906.

1906 ISTITUTO GEOGRAFICO MILITARE.

Carta dei possedimenti e protettorati europei
della Somalia. Scala 1:2,500.000. Istituto Geografico
Militare. Firenze 1906.

1907 ROSSETTI,C.

Carte dimostrative di colonie a paesi coloniali.
No. 2. Colonia del Benadir. Tip. Unione Coop. Editrice.
36 pp.

1908-09 MEUNIER,A.

Carte de la Côte Francaise des Somalis.
E'chelle de 1:500.000. Dressee par A. Meunier.
Service Geographique des Colonies. Paris 1908-09.

1907.

Somalia Italiana ed Inglese. Scala 1:300.000.
Topographical Section. General Staff. 1907.

1909.

French Somaliland. Scale 1:1,000.000. or 1.014 inches
to 16 miles. Geographical Section. General Staff.
London 1909.

1909 R.NAVE STAFFETTA.

Foce del Giuba. (Idrografia). Scala 1:10.000. 1909.

1909 FERRARI,G.

Il basso Giuba Italiano. Carta in 2 fogli.
Scala 1:200.000. Corpo di Stato Maggiore. 1909.

1909 FERRARI, G.

Giumbo e la foce del Giuba. Scala 1:10.000. 1909.

1910 ISTITUTO IDROGRAFICO DELLA R. MARINA.

Da Brava a Chisimaio: Carta Nautica. 1910.

1910/13 ISTITUTO GEOGRAFICO MILITARE.

Carta della Somalia Italiana. Firenze 1910/13.

1910 ZACCARINI,G.

Carta della Somalia al 200.000 (12 fogli). Servizio
Cartografico del Ministero dell'Africa Italiana. 1910.

1910-13 ZACCARINI,G.

Carta della media e bassa Goscia al 50.000. Ministero
dell'Africa Italiana. 1910-13.

1910.

Carta magnetica del Benadir: Scala 1:4.000.000.
Ministero AA/EE. Roma 1910.

1910.

Nuova foce del Giuba. Scala 1:10.000. 1909.

1910 ISTITUTO IDROGRAFICO DELLA R. MARINA.

Da Brava a Chisimaio: Carta Nautica. 1910.

1910/13 ISTITUTO GEOGRAFICO MILITARE.

Carta della Somalia Italiana. Firenze 1910/13.

1910 ZACCARINI,G.

Carta della Somalia al 200.00 (12 fogli). Servizio
Cartografico del Ministero dell'Africa Italiana. 1910.

1910/13 ZACCARINI,G.

Carta della media e bassa Goscia al 50.000. Ministero
dell'Africa Italiana. 1910-13.

1910.

Carta magnetica del Benadir: Scala 1:4.000.000.
Ministero AA/EE. Roma 1910.

1910.

Nuova foce del Giuba. Scala 1:25.000. (Carta Nautica). 1910.

1910.

Ancoraggio di Illig. (Carta Nautica). 1910.

1910.

Ancoraggio di Mogadiscio. (Carta Nautica). 1910.

1910 ISTITUTO GEOGRAFICO MILITARE.

Carta dimostrativa della Somalia Italiana.
Scala chilometrica di 1:2000,000. Istituto
Geografico Militare. Firenze 1910.

1910 MINISTERO AA/EE.

Carta magnetica del Benadir. Scala 1:4.000.000.
Ministero AA.EE. Roma 1910.

1910 MARCONI,A.

Carta della Somalia. Scala 1:200.000.
(12 tavole). Istituto Geografico Militare. Firenze 1910.

1910.

Da Brava a Uarchech. (Carta Nautica). 1910.

1911/12 ZACCARINI,G.

Carta della regione dell'Uebi Scebeli presso Merca
al 50.000. Servizio Cartografico del Ministero
dell'Africa Italiana. Roma 1911-12.

1911 MARCONI,A.

Somalia Italiana Meridionale. (1 solo foglio a colori).
Commando di Corpo di Stato Maggiore. Roma 1911.

1911 MINISTERO AA.EE.

Raccolta Cartografica Somalia Italiana 1889-1911.
Roma 1911.
371 pp.

1911 MINISTERO AA.EE.

Missione per la frontiera Italo-Etiopico.
6 fogli alla Scala 1:500.000. Istituto Geografico
Militare. Firenze 1911.

1911 PARDO.

Somalia Italiana: Il Giuba tra Lugh e Bardera.
Riduzione originale del Tenente Marconi.
Scala 1:500.000.Direzione Generale. Ministero
AA. Coloniali. 1911.

1912 CHECCHI,M.

Intinerari e distanze. Scala 1:2,000.000.
Governo della Somalia Italiana. Mogadiscio 1912.

1912   CHECCHI,M. AND MARCONI,A.

Somalia Italiana: Zona di influenza commerciale.
Scala 1:4.000.000. Governo della Somalia Italiana.
Mogadiscio 1912.

1912 CHECCHI,M. AND MARCONI,A.

Circoscrizioni amministrativi e militari nella
Somalia Italiana Meridionale. Scala 1:2.000.000.
Governo della Somalia Italiana. Mogadiscio 1912.

1912 CHECCHI, M.

Pianta di Mahaddei. Scala 1:4.000.
Governo della Somalia Italiana. Mogadiscio 1912.

1912 CHECCHI,M.

L'amministrazione italiana nella Somalia.
Scala 1:2.000.000. Ministero Esteri. Direzione
Centrale Affari Coloniali. Roma 1912.

1912 CARCOFORO,E. AND CHECCHI,M.

Somalia Italiana: popolazioni esistenti nel territorio
di juova occupazione. Scala 1:1.000.000. Governo della
Somalia Italiana. Mogadiscio 1912.

1912 CARCOFORO,E.

Carta della Somalia Italiana Meridionale.
(opere pubbliche eseguite dal 1910 in poi).
Scala 1:1.000.000. Governo della Somalia Italiana.
Mogadiscio 1912.

1912 CARCOFORO,E.

Regioni di nuova occupazione. Scala 1:1.000.000.
Governo della Somalia Italiana. Mogadiscio 1912.

1912 CARCOFORO,E.

Carta dimostrativa della Somalia Italiana, Meridionale.
Scala 1''1.000.000. Governo della Somalia Italiana.
Mogadiscio 1912.

1912 MINISTERO AA.EE.

Somalia Italiana. Scala 1:2.000.000. Ministero Esteri.
Ufficio Studi Coloniali. Roma 1912.

1912 MARCONI,A.

Carta dimostrativa della Somalia Italia Meridionale.
Scala 1:1.000.000. Ministero Affari Esteri. Roma 1912.

1912 MINISTERO DELLE COLONIE.

Rilievi in Libia ed in Somalia. Instituto Geografico
Militare. G. Bertero. Roma 1912.
55 pp.

1912 MINISTERO AA.EE.

Schizzo del territorio dipendente dalla residenze
di Bardera. Scala 1:400.000. Ministero Affari Esteri.
Direzione Centrale Affari Coloniali. Roma 1912.

1912 MINISTERO AA.EE.

Campo sperimentale di Genale: 1 esperimento di
colonizzazione bianca. Scala 1:50.000. Ministero Esteri.
Ufficio Studi Coloniali. Roma 1912.

1912 ISTITUTO GEOGRAFICO MILITARE.

Brava - Soblalle - Avai. Schizzo dimostrativo.
Scala 1:100.000. Istituto Geografico Militare.
Firenze 1912.

1912 STEFANINI,G.

Carta geologica della Somalia Italiana Meridionale.
Scala 1: 1.500.000. G.Giardi. Firenze 1912.

1912 STEFANINI,G.

Schizzo geologico della zona mogadiscio,Mahaddei,
Uanle Uen, Bur Acaba,Baidoa. Scala 1:500.000.
G.Giardi. Firenze 1912.

1912 STEFANINI,G.

Schizzo geologico della regione Baidoa, Lugh, Bardera.
Scala 1:500.000. G. Giardi. Firenze 1912.

1912.

Somalia Italiana: Circoscrizioni giudiziarie delle
regioni meridionali. Scala 1:4.000.000.

1912 GOVERNO DELLA SOMALIA ITALIANA.

La regione dell'Uebi Scebeli presso Merca.
Scala 1:50.000. Governo della Somalia Italiana.
Istituto Geografico Militare. Firenze 1912.

1912 PALAZZO,L.

La carta magnetica del Benadir. Ministero
delle Colonie. G. Bertero. Roma 1912.
12 pp.

1912 ALBERTAZZI.

Porto di Brava. Scala 1:7.500. Governo della
Somalia Italiana. Mogadiscio 1912.

1914 MINISTERO DELLE COLONIE.

Mostre coloniale di Genova: Rilievi in Libia ed
in Somalia a cura dell'Istituto Geografico Militare.
G.Bertero. & C. Roma 1914.
54 pp.

1914 STEFANINI,G.

I problemi geografici della Somalia meridionale e le
nuove carte dell'Istituto Geografico Militare.
"Rivista Geografica Italiana". Roma 1914.
471 p.

1914 RUSSO,E.

Pozzi esistenti nel territorio Galgial.
Scala 1:100.000. Ministero delle Colonie.
Ufficio Cartografica. Roma 1914.

1916 MARCONI,A. AND DARDANO,A.

Somalia Italiana Meridionale. Scala 1:1,000.000.
Ministero delle Colonie. Roma 1916

1917 MARCONI,A.

Somalia Settentrionale. Scala 1:2,000.000.
Ministero delle Colonie. Roma 1917.

1918 MARCONI,A.

Somalia e paesi limitrofi. Scala 1:4,000.000.
Ministero delle Colonie. Roma 1918.

1919.

Carta: distribuzione geografica delle popolazioni
della Somalia. "Bollettino della Reale Societa
Geografica Italiana". Serie V. Vol. VIII. No. 3-4. Roma 1919.

1921 MINISTERO DELLE COLONIE.

Etiopia sud-orientale. Carta alla scala 1:2.000.000.
Governo della Somalia Italiana. Ministero delle Colonie.
Servizio Cartografico. Roma 1921.

1921   EGIDI,S.

Costruzione di una carta a piccola scala della
Somalia del Sud. "Atti VIII Congresso Geografico Italiano".
Vol. II. Firenze 1921.
456 p.

1921 PUCCIONI,N.

Carta della distribuzione delle principali cabile somale.
"Atti VIII Congresso Geografico Italiano". Vol. II.
Firenze 1921.
458 p.

1922 WAR OFFICE.

British Somaliland. Provisional Scale 1:1,000.000.

War Office. London 1922.

1923 MINISTERO DELLE COLONIE.

Le regioni del basso e medio Giuba. Scala 1:200.000.
Ministero delle Colonie. Ufficio Cartografico. Roma 1923.

1925 CARCOFORO,E.

Carta della Somalia. Scala 1:200.000. Ministero
delle Colonie. Ufficio Cartografico. Roma 1925.

1927 MINISTERO DELLE COLONIE.

Oltregiuba. 3 fogli a Scala 1:400.000. Ministero
delle Colonie. Ufficio Cartografico. Roma 1927

1930 GOVERNO DELLA SOMALIA ITALIANA.

Carta della Somalia Italiana del Cap. Giovanni
Zaccarini. 22 fogli. Scala 1:400.000. Ministero
delle Colonie. Servizio Cartografico. Roma 1930.

1931-47 WAR OFFICE.

Anglo-Italian Boundary. Somaliland.
(Confine fra le Somalia Italiana ed Inglese).
Scale 1:50,000. War Office. Air Photographs by RAF.
London 1931-47. (GSGS No. 3918)

1934 MINISTERO DELLE COLONIE.

Somalia: carta dimostrativa. Scala 1:2.000.000.
Ministero delle Colonie. Servizio Cartografico. Roma 1934.

1933 STEFANINI,G.

Saggio di una carta geologica dell'Eritrea e della
Somalia e dell'Etiopia. Scala 1:2.000.000.
Istituto Geografico Militare. Firenze 1933.
195 pp.

1933.

Geological Map of British Somaliland.
Scale 1:1,000.000. Government of Somaliland
Protectorate. 1933.

1934 ZACCARINI,G.

Lavori cartografici in Somalia: Criteri e metodi
seguiti, risultati raggiunti. "Atti II Congresso
Studi Coloniali". C Vol.III. Napoli 1934.
36 pp.

1934 WAR OFFICE.

Somaliland. Scale 1:250,000.   War Office. London 1934.

1934 WAR OFFICE.

Map illustrating the Anglo-Italian exchange of notes
on 22nd November 1933 relating to the Boundry between
Kenya and Italian Somaliland. Scale 1:1,000.000.
War Office. London 1934. (G.S.G.S. No. 3934).

1935 MINISTERO DELLE COLONIE.

Somalia. Carta dimostrativa alla scala di 1:2,000.000.
Ministero delle Colonie. Servizio Cartografico. Roma 1935.

1935 AMER MUSTAFA.

Some unpublished Egyptian maps of Harar.
"Bulletin Societe Geographie E'gypte". 1935.

1936 STEFANINI,G.

Saggio di una carta Geologica dell'Eritrea,della
Somalia e dell'Etiopia. Scala 1:2,000.000.
Firenze 1936.
1-179 pp.

1938 ISTITUTO GEOGRAFICO MILITARE.

Belet Uen. Carta alla Scala 1:1.000.000.
Istituto Geografico Militare. Firenze 1938.

1939 LEFEVRE,R.

L'Africa Orientale nella cosmografia patristica
e nella cartografia genovese del 300.
"Rivista di Diritto Coloniale". Roma Febbraio 1939.
215-33 pp.

1940.

French Somaliland. Scale 1:200,000.
(Copied from original French map dated 1939).
War Office. London 1940. (G.S.G.S. No. 4166).

1946 INSTITUT GEOGRAPHIQUE NATIONAL.

Carte geologique de la Côte Francaise des Somalis.
PARIS 1946.

1946 INSTITUT GEOGRAPHIQUE NATIONAL.

Carte au 1/200.000 de la Côte Francaise des
Somalis, et Index des noms contenus dans la carta.
Paris 1946.

1947.

Frontier of British Somaliland and the French Somali Coast.

Scale 1:50,000. Ordanance Survey Office. War Office.
Southampton. London 1947. (G.S.G.S.No. 4075).

1949 MINISTERO AA.EE.

Somalia. Carta dimostrativa fisico-politica
(ristampa aggiornata a tinte altimetriche).
Scala 1:2.000.000. Ministero Affari Esteri. Ufficio
Servizio Cartografico. Roma 1949.

1949.

Croquis de la Côte Francaise des Somalis au
1000.000. Dresse et dessine par le Bureau
Cartographique de la Côte Francaise des Somalis,
en 1943. Imprime par E.A. Survey Group a Nairobi en
Avril 1943. Reproduit par l'Institut Geographique
National. Septembre 1947. Institut Geographique
National. Paris 1949.

1952 WAR OFFICE.

Somaliland. Scale 1:250.000 Second edition.
London 1952 (G.S.G.S. No. 3927)

1952.

Somaliland Protectorate: Preliminary plot.
Scale 1:50,000. (approx). Directorate of
Military Surveys. Directorate of Colonial Surveys.
Teddington 1952. (D.C.S. No. 27).

1952.

Somaliland Protectorate: Preliminary plot.
Scale 1:125,000. (approx). Directorate of
Military Surveys. Directorate of Colonial Surveys.
Teddington 1952. (D.C.S. No. 39)

1953-63   MINERARIA SOMALA.

Sezioni Geologiche Dimostrative. Scala 1:250.000.
All. No. 4. "Relazione sull'attivita svolta negli
anni 1953-1963". Mineraria Somala. Mogadiscio Maggio 1963.

1953-63 MINERARIA SOMALA.

Carte Indice. Scala 1:1.000.000. All. No. 1
"Relazione sull'attivita svolta negli anni 1953-1963".
Mineraria Somala. Maggio 1963.

1953-63 MINERARIA SOMALA.

Carta Fotogeologica. Scala 1:250.000. All. No. 2.
"Relazione sull'attivita svolta negli anni 1953-1963".
Mineraria Somala. Maggio 1963.

1953-63 MINERARIA SOMALA.

Carta Geologica. Scala 1:250.000. All. No. 3.
"Relazione sull'attivita svolta negli anni 1953-1963".
Mineraria Somala. Maggio 1963.

1953-63 MINERARIA SOMALA.

Rilievi Sismici. Scala 1:500.000. All. No. 6.
"Relazione sull'attivita svolta negli anni 1953-1963".
Mineraria Somala. Maggio 1963.

1953-63. MINERARIA SOMALA.

Rilievo Gravimetrico. Scala 1:1.000.000. All. No. 5.
"Relazione sull'attivita svolta negli anni 1953-1963".
Mineraria Somala. Maggio 1963.

1953-63 MINERARIA SOMALA.

Profili dei Pozzi Esplorativi. Scala 1:5.000. All. No. 8.
"Relazione sull'attivita svolta negli anni 1953-63".
Mineraria Somala. Maggio 1963.

1953-63 MINERARIA SOMALA.

Carta Indicativa dei Principali Elementi Strutturali
(messi in luce dai rilievi geologico-geofisici). All. No. 7.
Scala 1:1.000.000. "Relazione sull'attivita svolta
negli anni 1953-1963". Mineraria Somala. Maggio 1963.

1953.

Carte de la Côte Francaise des Somalis.
Institut Geographique National. Paris 1953.

1957.

Somaliland Protectorate. Geological Survey. Scale 1:125 000.
Directorate of Colonial Surveys. Surbiton 1957.(D.C.S.No.1076).

1957.

British Somaliland. Scale 1:100.000. D. Survey. War office
and Air Ministry. London 1957 (GSGS No. 4868).

1959.

Somaliland Protectorate. Scale 1:25,000. Directorate of
Overseas Surveys. Tolworth 1959. (D.O.S. No. 339 Ser. Y823).

1957-1960 AGIP MINERARIA.

Carta Geologica della Somalia. CNR. 1957 1960.

1967 E.C.

Note sur la transcription des toponymes dans
la carte su 1/100.000 du Territoire Francaise
des Afars et des Issas. "Revue Pount". No. 3.
La Societe D'etudes de l'Afrique Orientale.
Djibouti 1967.

DE AGOSTINI (NOVARA).

Somalia: 4 fogli - Brava, Merca, Dif El Uach, Eil.
De Agostini. Novara.

CANDEO,G.

Itinerario da Bardera all'Uebi Scebeli.
Scala 1:1.000.000. a colori in un solo foglio.

2. Geography (General & Descriptive) Travel and Exploration

ADEMOLLO,U.

L'opera di F. Martini e L. Dal Verme per la
conoscenze della Somalia e dell'Eritrea.
"Atti I Congresso Studi Coloniali". Vol. II.
Roma 1931.
400 p.

ADOLF,R. AND THOMPSON,V.

Djibouti and the Horn of Africa. Stanford
University Press. Stanford (California) 1968.
246 pp. ills.

AGENCE GENERALE DES COLONIES.

La Côte Francaise des Somalis. "Bulletin
Agence Generale des Colonies". Vol. XIX. Paris 1926.
349-357 pp.

AMADIO,W.

La "Pinta", la "Nina" e la "S.Maria
(dal mio diario di marcia dell'escursione nelle
isole e nella zona meridionale dell'Oltregiuba).
"L'Esploratore Commerciale". No. 3-7. Milano 1927.
44-83 pp.

ANDREE,K.

Burton's Reisen nach Medina und Mekka und das
Somaliland nach Harar in Ost Africa. Vol. 1.
Gostenoble. Leipzig 1861.
398 pp.

ANDREW,R.B.W.G.

The Somali Coasts: An account of T.A.Glover
Senegal-Somali Expedition in the Somalilands

and Eritrea. "The Geographical Journal".
London February 1934.

ANGOULVANT AND VIGNERAS.

Djibouti, mer Rouge, Abyssinia.
Librarie Africane et Coloniale. Paris 1902.

ANON.

Count Wickenberg's Journey in Somaliland.
"Geographical Journal". Vol. XII. London 1898.
78-79 pp.

―――――――

Literature of Somaliland. "Geographical Journal".
Vol. XX. London 1902.
654-655 pp.

―――――――

Surveys in Somaliland. "Geographical Journal".
Vol. XXX. London 1907.
333 p.

ANONYMOUS.

Brevi notizie sulla colonia del Benadir.
Istituto Geografico di G. De Agostini e C. Roma 1905.
19 pp.

―――――――

Da Giumbo a Bardera in barca a vapore.
"Rivista Coloniale". Roma 1906.
95 p.

―――――――

Nel Benadir. "Bollettino Societa Africana d'Italia".
Napoli 1907.
133 p.

―――――――

Distanze chilometriche tra i vari centri del Benadir.
"Rivista Coloniale". Roma 1910.
74 p.

―――――――

L'Uebi Scebeli. "Rivista Coloniale". Roma 1918.
433 p.

―――――――

La regione del medio Uebi Scebeli e la spedizione del Duca degli Abruzzi. "Bollettino Societa Geografica Italiana". Roma 1920.
440 p.

Il Territorio dei Rahanuin. "La Somalia Italiana".
No. 2. Mogadiscio 1927.

Mogadiscio. (Le Capitali del Mondo).
Gloriosa. Milano 1927.
16 pp. ills.

First list of names in Somaliland Protectorate.
Royal Geographical Society. Permanent Committee on Geographical Names. London 1928.
20 pp.

I risultati raggiunti dalla spedizione del Duca (Uebi Scebeli). "L'Oltremare". Roma 1929.
199 p.

La scoperta delle sorgenti dell'Uebi Scebeli.
"Rassegna Economica delle Colonie". Roma 1929.
489 p.

La Vallata del Giuba nella Somalia Italiana.
"Le Vie d'Italia e dell'America Latina". Milano 1929.
437 p.

La regione del medio Uebi Scebeli e la spedizione del Duca degli Abruzzi. "Bollettino Societa Geografica Italiana". Roma 1930.
440 p.

L'Oltregiuba e la Migiurtinia. "L'Italia Coloniale".
Roma-Milano 1933.
61 p.

Le isole dei Bagiuni. "Rassegna Economica delle Colonie".

Roma 1936.
379 p.

_____

Numero Speciale Dedicato alla Repubblica Somala.
"Mondo Afro-Asiatico". No. 10. T Roma 1964.
32 pp.

_____

Djibouti,son port, son arriers-pays. Supplement au
No. 182 de novembre 1965 de la "Revue Francaise de
l'elite Europeenne". Paris 1965.
34 pp.

ANSALDI,G.

Il Giuba. "La Somalia Italiana". No. 1-6.
Mogadiscio 1931.
24 p.

_____

Il Giuba. Stamperia della Colonia. Mogadiscio 1932.
35 pp.

ARC ANGELO.

A sketch of the River Juba, or Gochob, or
Gowin from a trip up the stream in 1844.
"United Service Journal".   Bombay 1844.
278 p.

AUBERT DE LA RUE,E.

La Somalie Francaise. Gallimard. Paris 1939.
162 pp.

AVANCHERS (des) P. LEON.

Esquisse geographique des pays Oromo ou Galla,
des pays Somali et de la cote orientale d'Afrique.
"Bulletin Societe Geographique". Vol. XVII. Paris 1859.
153-170 pp.

AYLMER,G.P.V.

Two recent journeys in Northern Somaliland.
"Geographical Journal". Vol. XI. London 1898.
34-48 pp.

BACQUART,H.

Etude sur le Protectorat de la Cote Somalis.
Paris 1907.

BALDACCI, G.

Il Promontorio del Capo Guardafui. "Bollettino
Societa Africa d'Italia". Fasc. No. 3-4. Napoli 1909.
56,p.

Les Somaliland Italien. Goemaere. Bruxelles 1910.
34 pp.

Le Somalie Italienne. "Revue Economique Internationale".
Bruxelles September 1911.
32 p.

BALSAN,FRANCOIS.

A'pied au Nord Somali,grenier d'aromates
des Pharcans. La Palatine. Paris 1965.
221 pp.

BARDEY.

Notes sur le Harar. "Bulletin de Geographie
Historique et Descriptive". No. 1. Paris 1897.

BARGONI,U.

Nella Terra di Nassib Bunda, lo Spartaco
della Somalia, Italiana. Marzoco. Livorno 1931.
179 pp.

BARTH,E.

L'Africa Orientale de Limpopo al paese dei Somali.
Botta. Roma 1876.

BASILE,C.

Uebi Scebeli nella Spedizione di S.A.R. Luigi di
Savoia (diario di tenda e cammino). Cappelli. Bologna 1935.
277 pp.

BASSI, U.

L'Oltregiuba. "Rivista delle Colonie e d'Oriente".
Bologna 1926.
205 p.

BAUDI DI VESME,E.

Esplorazione del paese dei Somali. "Bollettino
Societa Africana d'Italia", Napoli 1890.

Viaggio nell'interno del Paese dei Somali eseguito
nell'aprile a maggio 1890: Ricognizione da Bardera
a Scimber Berres (Uebi Scebeli). Cosmos di Guida Cora.
Torino 1889-1891.

_____

Dalla penisola dei Somali. "Bollettino Societa
Geografica Italiana". Roma 1891.

_____

Da Berbera attraverso l'Ogaden ad Imi e
nell'Harar. "Bollettino Societa Geografica Italiana".
Roma 1891.

_____

Le mie esplorazioni nella Somalia. Ministero
Africa Italiana. Ufficio Studi. Sind. Ital. Arti
Grafiche. Roma 1944.
188 pp.

_____AND CANDEO,G.

Un'escursione nel Paradiso dei Somali.
Reale Societa Geografica Italiana. Roma 1893.
7-181-294-510-632 pp.

BELLO,V.

Il Sultanato di Obbia. "Bollettino della Sezione
Fiorentina della Societa Africana d'Italia".
Firenze Aprile 1889.
37 p.

BERNUCCI,G.L.

La Somalia: la terra degli aromi.
"La Conquista della Terra". No. 9. 1940.
239 p.

BERSAIRE,H.

La côte Francaise des Somalis. "Annales Geographiques".
Paris 1943.
190-205 pp.

BERTACCHI,C.

Il Paese dei Somali. Firenze 1891.

_____

Come fu delimitato il confine dell'Oltregiuba.
"L'Oltremare". Roma 1931.
235 p.

BERTAZZO,V.

Coste e scali di Somalia. "L'Oltremare".
Roma 1929.
97 p.

BERTONELLI,F.

Sudan,Somalia e fiumi di Abissinia.
"L'Oltremare". Roma 1929.
515 p.

BIEBER.

Von Adis Abeba uber den Assabot nach Djibouti.
"Deutsche Rundschau F. Geograph. und Stat". Vol. XXX.
Viena 1907.
13-22 pp.

BOHM,R.

Die Franzosische Somalikuste. "Kolonialen Studien". 1928.
147-160 pp.'

BONASERA,F.

Le sorgenti del Giuba. "Africa". Roma 1952.
85 p.

BONCHAMPS,C. ; MICHEL,C. AND HANSEN,J.

Mission de Bonchamps de Djibouti au Nil Blanc.
"Geographical Journal". Vol.XII. London.
222p.

BONOLA,F.

Description du pays entre Zeilah et Harar.
"Bulletin Societe Geographique". Paris 1882-88.
461-462 pp.

Les explorations italiennes dans le pays
des Somalis. "Bulletin Societe Khediv Geographique".
Vol. IV. Cairo 1896.
589-602 pp.

Itineraires des explorations italiennes en Somalie
1890-1894. "Bulletin Societe Geographique". Paris 1897.
569 p.

Les explorations italiennes en Somalie.
"Bulletin Societe Geographique". Paris 1897.
569-602 pp.

BORLEE,M.

La Côte Francaise des Somalis. "Bulletin R.
Societe Belge Geographique" Bruxelles 1924.
5-25 pp.

BOTTEGO,V.

Il Giuba esplorato. "Societa Geografica Italiana".
Loescher. Roma 1895.

_____

L'esplorazione del Giuba. Societa Editrice Nazionale.
Loescher. Roma 1900.
385 pp.

_____AND FERRANDI, U.

La seconda spedizione Bottego nella Somalia
australe. Societa Geografica Italiana. Roma 1896.
510 pp.

BRACA,G.

I rilevamenti topografici della Missione dell'Istituto
Geografico Militare per la delimitazione dei confini
tra la Somalia Francese e l'Africa Italiana.
"L'Universo". Firenze 1939.
165-185 pp.

BREMOND,L.A.

Expedition scientifique et commerciale d'Obock
au royaume du Choa et au pays des Gallas. Paris 1883.

BRENNER,R.

Erkundingungen uber den Baron von der
Decken's Schieksal von Brava,der Wubuschi
und die Somalis. Poermann Mitteilungen. 1867.

_____

Die Stadte und der Nordlichen Somali Kuste.
Petermann Mitteilungen. Leipzig 1871-73.

BRUNO,A.

Una pagina di storia intorno al problema della
ricognizione dell'Uebi Scebeli. "Africa Italiana". 1915.
184 p.

BUCCHOLZER,J.

The Horn of Africa travels in British
Somaliland. (Translated from Danish).
Angus and Robertson. London 1959.
199 pp.

BUONOMO,G.

La delimitazione delle frontiere dell'A.O.I.
"Illustrazione Coloniale". Milano 1939.
30 p.

BURTON,R.F.

A Trip to Harar. "Journal of the Royal
Geographical Society". Vol. XXV. London 1855.
136-150 pp.

First Footsteps in A East Africa, Or an Exploration
of Harar. (Contribution to a discussion). "Proceedings
of the Royal Geographical Society". Vol. VII. London 1885.
641 p.

First Footsteps in Africa, Or an Exploration
of Harar. Memorial Edition. Messers Tylston & Edwards.
London January 25th, 1894.
Vol. 1. 209 pp. ills. map
Vol. 2. 276 pp. ills. map.

First Footsteps in Africa or an exploration
of Harar. Longman Brown & Co. London 1956.

First Footsteps in Africa Or an Exploration of
Harar. Routledge & Kegan Paul. Ltd. London 1966.
320 pp. ills. map.

CAMPIONI,S.

I Giam-Giam sulle orme di Vittorio Bottego.
Batteri. Parma 1960.
165 pp.

CANDEO,G.

Un viaggio nella penisola dei Somali.
"Atti 1 Congresso Geografico Italiano".
Vol. 1. 1892.
349-367 pp.

Il Giuba. De Agostini. R. Torino 1914.
64 pp.

Migiurtinia. De Agostini. Torino 1914.
64 pp.

CORRADINI,V.

Vittorio Bottego e le sue esplorazioni
africane. Grazioli Tipogr. Parma 1897.
54 pp.

CORSO,F.

Le Residenze di Balad e di Audegle. Monogr. Col.
Minist. Affari Esteri. Tipografia Min. Affari Esteri.
Roma 1912.
31 pp.

CORTI,E.

Esplorazione del Giuba e dei suoi affluenti,
compiute dal Cap. Bottego durante gli anni dal
1892-1893. "Annali Museo Civico Stoia Naturale di Genova".
Vol. XV. Genova 1895.

CORTINOIS,A.

Africa Orientale: la scoperta e le esplorzioni
geografiche nella Somalia dal 220 a.c. al 1900.
Genova (Presso l'A). 1935.
42 pp.

CROSBY,O.T.

Notes on a journey from Zeila to Khartoum.
"Geographical Journal". Vol.XVIII. London 1901.
47 p.

CUFINO,L.

Gibuti ed il suo hinterland. "Bollettino Societa
Africana Italiana". Napoli 1914.
11 p.

Nell'Oceano Indiano: Rendiconto di una missione
inviata dalla Societa Africana d'Italia (Maggio-Giugno 1914).
Napoli 1916.
200 pp.

CURI,E.

Il Principe esploratore: S.A.R. il Duca degli Abruzzi.
(Somalia Capitl. VII). Sant'Ilario. Rovereto 1935.

Un'escursione nel paese dei Somali.
Edit. Longo. Mestro 1894.
56 pp.

CANIGLIA,G.

Brevi notizie sulla Colonia del Benadir.
Istituto Geografico di DE Agostini e C. Roma 1905.
19 pp.

Il corso del nostro Giuba. "La Somalia Italiana".
No. 1. Mogadiscio 1929.

CARACI,G.

La Migiurtinia ed il territorio del Nogal secondo
recenti studi. "Rivista Geografica Italiana". Vol. XXXIV.
Roma 1927.
117-123 pp.

CARDON,G.

Chisimaio e Opia. "Nuova Antologia". Firenze 1889.
564-574 pp.

CAROSELLI,F.S.

Vittorio Bottego. "Atti del V Convegno Commercio
Italo-Africano". Genova 1956.
16 pp.

CASTELLANI,E.

Sul paese dei Gherire. "Agricoltura Coloniale".
Firenze 1938.
508 p.

CAVENDISH,H.J.H.

Through Somali, around and South of Lake Rudolf.
"Geographical Journal". Vol. XI. London 1898.
372-396 pp.

CAVICCHIONI,A.C.

Dalla Somalia Italiana all'Isola di Sant'Elena.
Libreria Beltrani di L. Cappelli. Bologna 1914.
243 pp.

CECCHI,A.

Notizie geografiche e commerciali sul protettorato
britannico della costa Somala nel Golfo di Aden.

"Memorie della Societa Geografica Italiana".
Vol. V. Roma 1896.
351-362 pp.

————————————

Da Zeila alle frontiere del Caffa.
Loscher. Roma 1887.

CECIONI,G.

La buca del Mullah. "Rivists delle Colonie Italiane".
Roma 1940.
43 p.

CERVELLI,B.

Il Duca degli Abruzzi in Somalia: la nuova
esplorzione dell'Uebi Scebeli. "Illustrazione
Coloniale". No. 10. Milano 1920.
103 p.

CHAILLE-LONG.

Notes of travel and exploration of the
river Juba. 1875.

CHENVIC,T.C.

The desert's dusty face. Blackwood & Sons.
Edinburg & London 1964.
243 pp.

CHIARINI,G.

Spedizione Italiana nell'Africa Equatoriale:
Relazione dell'Ing. G. Chiarini sulle Regioni
da Zeila a Farre. "Memorie della Societa Geografica Italiana".
Vol. 1. Roma.
180-217 pp.

CITERNI,C.

Ai confini meridionali dell'Etiopia.
Edit. Hoepli. Milano 1913.
201 pp. map.

CORA, G.

La Somalia tra Berbera ed i Bur Dap (Nogal)
esplorata dal D. Cap. Baudi di Vesme nel 1890
e posizioni geografiche determinate nella Somalia
dalle spedizioni James, Swayne, Paget, Hooper.
"Cosmos Series". No. 2. Vol.2. 1893.
244 p.

CORONARO,G.

145-155 pp.

D'ALBERTIS,E.A.

In Africa, Victoria Nyanza e Benadir.
Instituto d'Arti Grafiche. Bergamo 1906.
162 pp.

DALLA VEDOVA,G.

La spedizione Bottego: relazione sommaria.
"Bollettino Societa Geografica Italiana". Roma 1893.
14 pp.

La prima spedizione Bottego nella Somalia.
"Memorie della Societa Geografica Italiana".
Part II. Roma 1896.
510 p.

La seconda spedizione Bottego nella Somalia australe.
"Memorie della Societa Geografica Italiana".
Vol. VI. Roma 1896.

DAL VERME,L.

Il paese dei Somali. Tipografia delle Mantellate.
Roma 1889.
730 ₊p.

DE AGOSTINI,E.

Risultati scientifici di missioni compiute in Somalia.
"Atti III Congresso Studi Coloniali". Vol.V. Firenze 1937.
251 p.

DE BENEDETTI,R.

Vittorio Bottego e l'esplorazione del Giuba.
Paravia. Torino 1932.
183 pp.

DECARY,R. AND MENARD,A.

Cote des Somalis: l'Unione Francaise.
Berger-Levrault. Paris 1948.
385 pp.

DELLA VALLE,C.

I viaggi in Somalia dell'Ing. Robecchi-Bricchetti
(1888 1903). "Rivista delle Colonie Italiane".
Roma 1934.
463 p.

I viaggi in Somalia dell'Ing. Robecchi-Bricchetti
(1888-1903). "Rivista delle Colonie Italiane".
Roma 1934.
463 p.

DE MAGISTRIS,L.F.

La seconda spedizione Bottego. "Nuova Antologia".
Edit. Forzani. Roma 1899.
19 pp.

DESCHAMPS,H.

La Côte Francaise des Somalis.
Berger-Levrault. Paris 1948.
220 pp.

D'ESME,J. (pseud).

La Cote Francaise des Somalis.
Ed. du Cygne. Paris 1930.

DE RIVOIRE,D.

Obock,Mascate,Bouchire, Bassorah. Plon.
Paris 1883.

Obock (Collana Viaggi intorno al Mondo No. 118).
Sonzogno. Milano 1896.
32 pp.

DE VILLARD, U.M.

I Minareti Mogadiscio. "Rassegna Studi Etiopici".
Roma 1943.
27-30 pp.

DI GIACOMO,S.

Geografia della Somalia ad uso delle
scuole secondarie. Stamperia dello Stato.
Mogadiscio 1965.
69 pp.

Per una didattica dell'ambiente somalo.
(2nd ediz) Istituto Italiano di Cultura.
Tipografia Orientale. Mogadiscio Marzo 1968.
23 pp.

DI SAN MARZANO,R.

Dalla piana somala all'altopiano etiopico.
Ediz.dell'Azione Coloniale. Tipografia Mantero.

Tivoli 1935.
238 pp.

DONALDSON,S.A.D.

Expedition through Somaliland to Lake Rudolf:
Galla tribes. "Geographical Journal" Vol.VIII.
London 1896.
123-289 pp.

_____

Through unknown Countries: The first expedition from
Somaliland to Lake Rudolf. Arnold.London & New York 1897.

_____

Expedition durch das Somal - und Galla Land zum Rudolf-
See in dem Jahren 1894-1895. "Petermann's Mitteilungen".
Vol. XLIII. Gotha 1897.
7-15 pp.

DOWSON,V.H.W.

A short tour of Sourthern Arabia, British Somaliland and
Northern Sudan. "Royal Central Asian Journal". London 1948.
105-115 pp.

DOYLE,A.C.

Lone dhow. The Quality Book Club. London 1963.
174 pp. map.

DRACOPOLI,I.N.

Through Jubaland to the Lorian Swamp.
Seeley Service Ltd. London 1914.
309 pp.

DUBOIS,H.P.

Cheminot de Djibouti ad Addis Abeba.
Perrin. Paris 1959.
252 pp.

ELLIOT,J . A.G.

A visit to the Bajun Island. "Journal of the
British African Society". Vol. XXV. No. 97 100.
London 1926.
74 p.

ERLANGER,V. (Von).

Meine Reise durch Sud-Schoa,Galla und
die Somal-Lander. Trowitzch und Schn. Berlin 1902.
77 pp.

FALORSI,G.

L'Uebi Scebeli esplorato da S.A.R. il Duca
degli Abruzzi. "Agricoltura Coloniale".
No. 12. Firenze 1928.
443 p.

FERRANDI,U.

Notizie sulla spedizione in Somalia.
"Supplemento al B.S. Esplorazione Commerciale in Africa) 1891.
14 pp.

_____

Viaggio nella regione del Giuba.
"Esploratore Commerciale". Milano 1892.
14 p.

_____

Itinerari africani: da Lugh alla costa
(aprile 1897). Merati. Novara 1902.
62 pp.

_____

Lugh emporio commerciale del Giuba.
"Societa Geografica Italiana. Roma 1903.
429 pp.

FERRERO,A.

Sul nuovo protettorato Italiano in Africa:
costa dei Somali. Stab. Annuario d'Italia.
Genova 1890.

FOH,F.

Der Hafen von Brava an der Ostkust von Africa.
"Annalen der Hydrographie und Maritime Metereologie".
No. 5. 1881.
272-276 pp.

FORMIGARI,F.

Rapporto di Mogadiscio. Istituto Nazionale
Culturale Fascista. Roma 1938.
61 pp.

FORNARI,G.

L'Uebi Scebeli e la sua regione. "Bollettino Societa
Africana Italiana". Napoli 1906.
235 p.

_____

L'Uebi Scebeli dalle prime esplorazioni a quella
del Duca degli Abruzzi. "La Rassegna Italiana."
Vol. XXIII. Fasc. No. 128. Roma 1929.
71 p.

FOSCHINI,F.

La Somalia Italiana. Casa Edit. Rivista
di Cavalleria. Roma 1908.
107 pp.

FRANCIS,J.C.

Three months leave in Somali: being the
diaries of the late Captain J.C. Francis. 1895.
96 pp.

FRANCOLINI,B.

Aspetti della Somalia settentrionale. (Migiurtinia).
"Rivista delle Colonie Italiane". Roma 1931.
38 p.

———————————

Note sulle regione dei Migiurtini. "Atti II Congresso
Studi Coloniali". Vol. III. Napoli 1934.
265 p.

———————————

Il Basso Uebi Scebeli "Atti III Congresso
Studi Coloniali". Vol.V. Firenze 1937.
236 p.

FRITSCHE,G.E.

Die Karawanestrasse von Zeila nach Ankober und die
Kartographie der Grenzgebiete der Somali,Afar und Galla.
"Petermann Mitteilungen". Vol. XXXVI. Gotha 1890.
113-118 pp.

G.C.

Somalia. "Comm. Imp". 1937.
83 p.

GENOVIE,L.

La prima esplorazione dell'Uebi Scebeli. "Rivista delle
Colonie Italiane". Roma 1931.
534 p.

GIANNITRAPANI,L.

Il Giuba. "L'Universo". No. 9. Firenze 1926.
755 p.

GIGLI,G.

Sull'Uebi Scebeli. "Rivista delle Colonie Italiane".
Vol. IV. Roma 1930.
279-288 pp.

GIGLIOLI,M.

Importanza dell'Uebi Scebeli al confine somalo-abissino.
"Rivista di Fanteria". Roma 1935.
905 p.

GILLILAND,B.H.

Geography of British Somaliland.
"South African Geographical Journal" Aprile 1947.

GLENDAY,V.

British Somaliland. "Our Empire" No. 3. Vol. XX.
London June 1944.

GLIAMAS.

Somalia Italiana: relazione sui lavori compiuti
in Somalia dal Giugno 1910 al Giugno 1912.
Istituto Geografico Militare. Firenze.

GOEDORP,V.

Chez les Somalis. "Tour du Monde". Vol. V.
Paris 1899.
369-371 pp.

GOVERNO DELLA SOMALIA ITALIANA.

Monografie delle Regione della Somalia.

Il Giuba. (No. 1). Torino 1924.
La Migiurtinia, (No. 2,) ed il Territorio del Nogal.
Torino 1925.

Cenni sull'aspetto fisico-geografico
dell'Oltregiuba meridionale. "Rassegna Economica
delle Colonie". Roma 1929.
1270 p.

G.P.

Vittorio Bottego e la schiava Batula.
"La Voce dell'Africa". No. 4. Roma 1960.

GRANDS LACS.

Djibouti. 1947.

64 pp.

GRAE VENITZ,(von).

Italienisch Somaliland. "Die Militarische".
Welt-Heft 3. 1907.
10 p.

GRAVES,C.I.

Le Cap. Guardafui. "Bulletin Societe Geographique".
Paris 1876-1881.
29-42 pp.

Le pays des Somalis Mijjertains. "Bulletin Societe Geographique".
Paris 1876-1881.
23-27 pp.

GRAVIER,C.

Rapport sur une mission scientifique a la côte
Francaise des Somalis: Nouvelles, Articles, Mission
scientifiques et litteraires. 1906.
13 pp.

GRAZIOSI,P.

Una missione scientifica in Somalia. "Le Vie d'Italia
e del Mondo". No. 7. Milano 1935.
819 p.

GRIAULE,M.

Les resultats de la Mission
Dakar-Djibouti-Aethiopica. 1933.

GRIBAUDI,P.

Il Conte E. Baudi di Veame ed i suci due viaggi
nella Somalia. "Atti 1 Congresso Studi Coloniali".
Vol. II. Firenze 1931.
420 p.

GUILLAIN,M.

Documents sur l'histoire, la geographie et
la commerce de l'Afrique orientale. (2 vols).
Arthur Bertrand. Paris 1856.

GUILLOTAUX,E.

Madagascar et la cote des Somalis, Saint-Marie
et les Seychelles: leur role et leur avenir.
Perrin. Paris 1922.
XII, + 294 pp.

HACHETTE,R.

Djibouti au seul de l'Oriente. Redier.
Paris 1930.

HAGGENMACHER,G.A.

Reise in Somalilande. "Peterman's Mitteilungen".
Band 47. Gotha 1874.
18 p.

G.A. Haggenmacher's Reise im Somalilande 1874.
(Mit einen original-karte). Justus Perthes. Gotha 1876.
45 pp. ills. map.

HAIG,F.T.

Report of a journey to the Red sea ports: Somaliland
and Southern and Eastern Arabia. G. House. London 1890.

HARDEN,H.S.S.

Country of the mad Mullah. "Cong. Magazine".
Vol. XXXI. 1908.
241-245 pp.

HARRISON,J.J.

A journey from Zeila to Lake Rudolf. "Journal of
the Royal Geographical Society". Vol. XVIII. London 1901.
258-275 pp.

HERTIEL,J.M.

Un pays ignore: la cote francaise des Somalis.
Paris 1947.

HEUDEBERT,L.

Au pays des Somalis et des Comoriens.
J. Maisonneuve. Paris 1901.
281 pp.

HEUGLIN,(Von der).

Reise langs der Somali kuste 1859.
"Peterman's Mitteilungen". 1860.

HEUSLING,T. (Von der).

Reise in Nordost Afrika. Brunswich 1877.

HILDEBRANDT, J.M.

Auszug aus einem Bericht uber die Somali Lander.
Aden 1874.

HORSEY.

Routier des côtes sud,est et sud est d'Afrique
du Cap de Bonne Esperance au Cap Guardafui. Paris 1866.

HOYOS,G.E.

Meine und Graf Richard Coudenhove's Reise
nach Somal-lande. "Mitteilingen of the Vienna
Geographical Society". Vol. XXXVII. Viena 1894.
337-83 pp.

Zu den Aulihan: Reise und Jagderlabnisse in Somalia.
Gerold. Viena 1895.
IV, + 192 pp. ills. map.

HUNT,J.A. AND VINEY,N.M.

Gazetteer of British Somaliland (Place-Names) 1945.

ISTITUTO GEOGRAFICO MILITARE.

Relazione sui lavori compiuti in Somalia dal
Giugno 1910 al Giugno 1912. Ministero delle Colonie.
G. Bertero. Roma 1912.

Rilievi in Libia e in Somalia. G. Bertero. Roma 1914.
55 pp.

(R) ISTITUTO IDROGRAFICO.

Vedute della costa del Golfo di Aden e dell'Africa
Orientale: da Zeila a Kisimaju. Tipografia Reale
Istituto Idrografico. Genova 1902.

Vedute della costa del Golfo di Aden e dell'Africa
Orientale: da Res Dofdilla alla penisola di Afun.
Tipografia Reale Istituto Idrografico. Genova 1903.

JAMES F.L.

A journey through the Somali country to the
Webbe Shebeyli. "Proceedings of the Royal Geographical
Society". Vol. VIII. London 1885.
625-646 pp

The unknown Horn of Africa: an exploration
from Berbera to the Leopard River. G. Philip & C.
London 1888.
344 pp.

JOURDAIN,H. AND DUPONT, C.

D'Obock a Djibouti. Corbier. Paris 1933.

JOUSSEAMUE,F.

Impression de voyage en Apharreas
(côte francaise des Somalis). 2 vols.
Bailliere. Paris 1914.
Vol. 1. 699 pp.
Vol. 2. 571 pp.

KARL,A.

Burton's Reisen nach Medine und Mekka und im
Somali lande nach Harrar in Ostafrica.
Costenoble. Leipzig 1861.

KERSTEN,O.

Baron Claus von der Decken's Reisen in
Ost Afrika in den Jahren 1859 bis 1865.
Winter'sche Verlagshandlunng. Le
Leipsiz u. Heidelberg 1871.

KOETTLITZ,R.

A journey through Somaliland and Southern Abyssinia to
the Shangalla or Berta Country and the Blue Nile
and through the Sudan to Egypt. "Scottish Geological Magazine".
Vol. XVI. Edinburgh 1900.
467-90 pp.

_____

A journey through Somaliland and Southern Abyssinia to
the Shangalla or Berta Country and the Blue Nile
and through the Sudan and Egypt. "Journal of the Manchester
Geographical Society". Vol. XVI. Machester 1900.
1-30 pp.

KONSTANT,A.

Across Somaliland on foot. "Blackwood's Magazine".
Edinburgh 1934.
130 136 pp.

LAPICCIRELLA,F.R.

Luci della Somalia. Ed. Sansoni. Firenze 1960.
21 pp. ills. plates.

_____

Le luci della Somalia. Ed. Sansoni. Firenze 1960.
XXII, + 156 pp ills. plates.

_____

Le luci della Somalia. 2n Edit. Lo Scaffale. Roma 1969.
79 pp. 157 plates (multilingual annotations).

LEVA,E.

Ibn Batuta in Somalia. "Africa". No. 3. Roma 1961.
111 114 pp.

LOJERO,G.

Da Bender Beila a Gardo. "Etiopia" No. 4. 1940.
30 f.

LUIGI DI SAVOIA (Il Duca degli Abruzzi).

Le sorgenti ed il corso dell'Uebi Scebeli.
"Bollettino Societa Geografica Italiana".
Vol. VI. Roma 1929.
359 p.

_____

Alle sorgenti dell'Uabi-Uebi Scebeli.
Mondadori. Milano 1932.
227 pp.

LUSINI,A.

Mogadiscio. Numero Speciale della Rivista
"Costruire". Ottobre 1938.
65 p.

_____AND VECCHI, B.V.

La Somalia: guida informativa. Stamperia della Colonia.
Mogadiscio 1938.

MACFADYEN,W.A.

Taleh. "Geographical Journal". Vol. LXVIII.
London 1931.
125-128 pp.

MAINERI,B.

Il paese dell'incenso visitato dal Re.
"Economia Nazionale". No. 10-11. Milano 1934.
42 p.

MALLARINI,A.G.

Il Giuba, l'Uebi Scebeli e la navigabilita.
"La Rassegna Nazionale" Firenze 1910.
23 p.

_____

I nostri veri confini con l'abissinia in Somalia.

"La Rassegna Nazionale". Firenze 1910.

———————

L'Oltregiuba ed il suo fiume. "Illustrazione Coloniale".
No. 11. Milano 1924.
352 p.

———————

La nuova ripartizione regionale della nostra Somalia.
"L'Esploratore Commerciale". No. 1-2. Milano 1927.
1 p.

———————

La valle dell'Uebi. "Illustrazione Coloniale".
Milano 1929.
32 p.

MANASSEI,T.

Sul Benadir: appunti e ricordi. "La Rassegna Nazionale".
Firenze 1910.
78-88 pp.

MANISCO,G.

Noi e il bacino del Giuba. "Nazione Militare".
No. 6. Roma 1936.

MANTEGAZZA,V.

Il Benadir. Treves. Milano 1908.

MARIE,G.

La pierre a batire de Berberah. "Bulletin Societe
Geographie Eg". Ser. V. Paris 1902.
47-48 pp.

MARINELLI,G.

E. Ruspoli ed i suci viaggi nella Somalia e tra
i Galla. "Bollettino Sezione Fiorentina della
Societa Africa d'Italia". Firenze Marzo 1895.
124 p.

MARTINELLI,R.

Laggiu (Somalia). Vallecchi, Firenze 1939.
291 pp.

MASSEI,E.

In Africa per imparare: note di viaggio,impressioni
in Somalia. "Africa" No. 6-7. Roma 1956.

151 155 pp.

MATTEOTTI,G.C.

Mogadiscio e dintorni. "Le vie del Mondo".
Milano 1957.
1169-1182 pp.

M.A.V.

Somalia d'oggi. "Rassegna Espansione Commerciale".
No. 3 4. Milano 1951.
52 p.

MAZZONI,E.A.

L'Uebi Scebeli. "Atti X Congresso Internazionale
di Geografia". Roma 1915.
1235 p.

MEGGLE,A.

La Cote Francaise des Somalis.
Societe Francaise d'Edition. Paris 1931.

MENZIO,G.

Dallo Scebeli alle frontiere d'Ethiopia:
note di viaggi. "Nuova Antologia". No. 2. Firenze 1935.
530 p.

MEREGAZZI,R.

Il Commissariato del Nogal. "Rivista delle Colonie Italiane".
Roma 1927-28.
423 p.

_____

La Migiurtinia. "Rivista delle Colonie Italiane".
Roma 1928.
247 p.

_____

La regione di Obbia. "Rivista delle Colonie Italiane".
Roma 1929.
20 p.

MIGLIORINI,E.

L'opera della R. Societa Geografica Italiana nella
esplorazione della Somalia. "Atti 1 Congresso Studi Coloniale".
Vol. II. Firenze 1931.
376 p.

MILES,S.B.

On the Somali country; on the neighbourhood of
Bender Merayah. "Proceedings of the Royal Geographical Society".
Vol. XVI. London 1872.
147-157 pp.

MINISTERE DE LA DEFENCE NATIONALE.

Numero special sur la Côte Francaise des Somalis.
"Revue des Troupes de Marine". Paris Mai 1955.
32 pp.

MINISTERO DELLE COLONIE.

La foce del Giuba. Ufficio Studi.
G. Bertero. Roma 1912.
37 pp.

MOKTAR,M.

Une reconnaissance au pays des Gadiboursis.
"Bulletin Societe Geographique." Paris 1876 1881.'
5-17 pp.

——————————

Ma reconnaissance au paks des Gadiboursis.
"Bulletin de la Societe Khediviale de Geographie du Caire".
Caire 1880.

——————————

Notes sur les pays du Harar. "Bulletin de la Societe
Khediviale de Geographie du Caire". Caire 1877.

MONILE,F.

Somalia. L. Cappelli Edit. Bologna 1932.
268 pp.

MONTANDON,G.

Traversee du Massif Ethiopien, du desert Somali
a la plaine du Soudan 1909-1911. "Le Globe".
Soc. Geogr. Geneve 1912.
47 63 pp.

MORGAN,J.C.

The Horn of Africa: Somali Country.
"Corona" 9 July 1957.

MORI,A.

Nuove spedizioni italiane nel paese dei Somali.
"Bollettino della Sezione Fiorentina". Societa

Africana d'Italia. Firenze Dicembre 1892.
104 p.

Per il confine italo-etiopico in Somalia e dell'Impero etiopico.
"Rivista Geografica Italiana" 1910.
4 p.

I risultati geografici di una missione scientifica
in Somalia: missione Stefanini-Paoli.
"Rivista Geografica Italiana". Vol. XXIII. 1916.
446 p.

La spedizione del Duca degli Abruzzi per l'esplorazione
dell'Uebi Scebeli. "Rivista Geografica Italiana".
Vol. XXXVI. 1929.
83 p.

Baudi di Vesme ed i suci viaggi in Somalia.
"Rivista Geografica Italiana". Vol. XXXVIII. 1931.
39 p.

MOSCONI,B.

Il Commissariato delle Regione di confine.
"La Somalia Italiana". No. 3. Mogaidscio 1929.

MUZIO,C.

Altipiano somalo galla. Sonzogno. Milano 1925.
49 pp.

NEUMAN,O.

From the Somali coast through Southern Ethiopia
to the Sudan. "Geographical Journal". Vol. XX. London 1902.
373-401 pp.

NIUTTA,A.

Viaggio in Somalia. Italcable. Roma 1956.
74 pp.

NOBILI MASSUERO,F.

La Migiurtinia. "Italia Augusta". No. 6. 1927.
57-61 pp.

NORMAND, T.V.E.

Kisimajo: La spedizione di un Principe.
"L'Idea Nazionale". Roma 1919.

NURSE,C.G.

Journey through part of Somaliland between Zeila
and Bulhar. "Proceedings of the Royal Geographical Society".
Vol. XIII. London 1891.
657-663 pp.

PAGLIERI,N.

Esplorazioni in Somalia. "L.Oltremare". Roma 1929.
535 p.

PANTANO,G.

Nel Benadir: la citta di Merca e la
regione Bimal. S. Belforte & C. Livorno 1910.
125 pp.

_____

Qualche notizia su Hafun, Bender Cassin e Alula.
"Rivista Coloniale". Roma 1910.
41 p.

PAOLI,G.

Ricordi di Somalia. "Atti Societa Scienze
e Lettere di Pavia". Vol. III. No. 1. Pavia 1938.
72 p.

PARKINSON,F.B.

An expedition to Somaliland. "Geographical Journal".
Vol. IX. London 1897.
221 p.

_____AND DUNBAR,B.

Two recent journeys in Northern Somaliland.
"Geographical Journal". Vol. II. London 1898.
15-48 pp.

PARVIS,E.G.

Un valoroso esploratore della Somalia:
E. Baudi di Vesme. "Rassegna delle Colonie Italiane". Roma 1940.
1781 p.

PASELLI,P.L.

Somalia poco nota. "Le Vie d'Italia". Milano Dicembre 1933.

PAULITSCHKE,P.H.

Die Geografische Erforschung der Adal Lander und
Harars in Ost Afrika. Prohber. Leipzig 1884.

———————

Forschungsreise nach den Somâl - und Galla-Landern.
Leipzig 1888.

———————

Reise des Fursten Demeter Ghika Comanesti im
Somal-Lande 1895-6."Peterman's Mitteilungen".
Vol.XLII. Gotha 1896.
245-552 pp.

———————

Count Wickenberg's Journey in Somaliland.
"Peterman's Mitteilungen". No. 3. Gotha 1898.

PAVERI,F.F.

Una ricognizione dall'alto Uebi Scebeli alla
regione del Gestro. "Agricoltura Coloniale".
Firenze 1938.
529 p.

PEASE,A.E.

Some account of Somaliland: with notes on Journeys
through the Gadabursi and Western Ogaden countries,
1896-1897. "Scottish Geographical Magazine."
Vol. XIV. Edinburgh 1898.
57-73 pp.

PERHAM, M.F.

Major Dane's Garden. London 1925.

PETAZZI,E.

La Somalia Italiana. "Gerarchia". No. 78.
Stamperia della Colonia. Luglio-Agosto 1932.
18 p.

PIAZZA,G.

Un'escursione nei dintorni di Brava. "Bollettino Societa
Geografica Italiana". Roma 1908.
152 p.

———————

La regione di Brava nel Banadir. "L'Esploratore Commerciale".
Milano 1909.
39 p.

_____

Escursione a Brava, Balli, Gelib sul Giuba.
"Rivista Coloniale". Vol. VI. Roma ·1909.
181 p.

POINSOT,JEAN-PAUL.

Djibouti et la cote francaise des Somalis.
Hachette. Paris 1964.
128 pp. ills. map.

PONCINS,E.

Voyage au Choa, exploration au Somal et chez les
Danakil. "Bulletin de la Societe de Geographie".
Serie XIX. Paris 1898.
423-499 pp.

PORENA,F.

I piu grandi risultati della 2nd Spedizione Bottego.
"Bollettino della Societa Africana d'Italia". Napoli 1897.

POWELL, E.A.

Beyond the Utmost Purple Rim. New York 1925.

PROSHOGIN,N.

Guten Morgen,Afrika! Reisenotizen aus Somalia.
Veb.F.A. Brock Hause Verlag. Leipzig 1963.
193 pp. map. ills.

P.S.

Obbia ed il protettorato italiano della costa dei Somali.
Societa Africana d'Italia. Firenze 1889.
144 pp.

RAVENSTEIN,E.G.

Somali-Galla land. "Proceedings of the Royal
Geographical Society" Vol. VI. London 1884.
255-273 pp.

REPUBLIQUE FRANCAISE (AGENCE).

Côte Francaise des Somalis. 1952.

REPUBBLICA SOMALA

Guida della citta di Mogadiscio.

Ministero LL.PP. e Communicazione. Mogadiscio 1962.

REVERE,A.

La Somalia di domani. "Illustrazione Coloniale".
Milano 1932.
20 p.

Il Giuba. "Illustrazione Coloniale". No. 7.
Milano 1932.
19 p.

REVOIL,G.B.

Voyage au Cap des Aromates 1887-1878.
Dentu. Paris 1880.

Voyage au Pays des Medjourtines
(Cap Gardafui,Afrique Orientale). "Bulletin Societe
Geographie". Paris 1880.
254-269 pp.

La Vallee du Darror: Voyage au Pays des Somalis, 1880-81.
Challamel Aine. Paris 1882.
388 pp.

Voyage chez les Benadirs, les Somalis et les
Bayonns en 1882-83. Hachette. Paris 1888.

Dix mois a la côte Orientale d'Afrique:
La vallee du Daror et le Cap Guardafui. Paris 1888.
388 pp.

R.F.

Pays de Pount. "Revue Pount". No. 1.
La Societe D' etudes de l'Afrique Orientale.
Djibouti Octobre 1966.

ROBECCHI-BRICCHETTI, L.

Somalia e Benadir: Viaggio di esplorazione
nell'Africa Orientale, prima traversata della Somalia.
Aliprandi La Poligrafica. Milano 1889.
726 pp.

Itinerario del viaggio da Obbia ad Alula.
Ministero AA.EE. Roma 1891.
19 pp.

_____

La prima attraversata della penisola dei Somali
(con note di G. Dalla Vedova).
Societa Geografica Italiana. Roma 1893.
171 pp.

_____

Nell'Harar. Galli. Milano 1896.
409 pp.

_____

Nel paese degli Aromi: diario di una esplorazione
da Obbia ad Alula. F. L. Cogliati Edit. Milano 1903.
633 pp.

ROCHET D'HE'RICOURT.

Voyage sur la côte orientale de la mer Rouge
dans le pays d'Adel et le royaume de Choa.
Bertand. Paris 1841.

_____

Second voyage sur les rives de la mer Rouge, dana
le pays d'Adel et le royaume de Choa. Paris 1845.

ROMAGNOLI,M.

Impressioni di un viaggio in Somalia.
"Agricoltura Coloniale". No. 3. Firenze 1939.
131 p.

ROSSETTI,C.

La via del Basso Giuba. Bertero G. Roma 1900.
21 pp.

_____

La via del Basso Giuba. "L'Italia Coloniale".
(Estr.) Roma 1900.
11 pp.

_____

Tre note sulla citta di Mogadiscio.
"Rivista Coloniale". Roma 1906.
202 p.

ROSSETTO, V.

Memoria sulla bassa valle del Giuba e la regione
fra Giuba e Tana. Tipografia Ministero AA.EE.Roma 1890.
44 pp.

ROUIRE.

La côte francaise des Somalis et le Somaliland
britannique. "Revue de Geographie". Vol. XLI. Paris 1897.
194-203 pp.

RUSPOLI,E.

Nel paese della Mirra. Tipografia Cooperativa. Roma 1892.
70 pp.

—————————

Africa inesplorata: Somalia, Ogaden.
Tipografia della Tribuna. Roma 1893.

————————AND DAL SENO,E.

La spedizione Ruspoli: lettere. "Bollettino Societa
Geografica Italiana". Roma 1892.
71 p.

RUSSO,E.

La Residenza di Mahaddei Uen. "Rivista Coloniale".
Roma 1919.
185 p.

SALATA,F.

Il nodo di Gibuti. Industr. Grafiche Nicola
Milano 1939.
339 pp.

SALMON,C.

La Côte Francaise des Somalis.
"Bulletin Societe Francaise Topogr".
No. 3-9. 1953.

SANGUINI,M.

Vittorio Bottego. Paravia. Torino 1958.
184 pp.

SAPPA,F.

Itinerari ed attivita della missione inviata in
Somalia dal Centro di studio per la micologia del
terreno al Consiglio Nazionale delle ricerche.
Arti Crafiche P. Conti & C. Torino 1953.
7 pp.

SCHIARINI,P.

Il Sultanato di Obbia. "Bollettino Societa Geografica Italiana".
Roma 1911.
1016 p.

_____

Il Giuba da lugh a Bardera. "Bollittino Societa
Geografica Italiana". Roma 1911.
1150 p.

SCHOFF,W.H.

Cinamon,Cassin and Somaliland. "Journal of the
American Oriental Society". Vol. XL. New York 1920.
260 270 pp.

_____

The Peryplus of the Erythrean Sea:
(Originally in Old Greek language).
Longmans Green & Co. New York 1912.
323 pp.

SCORTECCI,G.

Esplorazione dello Ahl Muscat Occidentale e
centrale Somalo. "Bollettino della Societa
Geografica Italiana". No. 4-5. Roma 1958.
164-195 pp.

SERVICE D'INFORMATION DE LA COTE FRANCAISE DES SOMALIS.

Guide-Annuaire de la Cote Francaise des Somalis.
Djibouti 1959.
205 pp.

SIRACUSA, G.E.

Antonio Cecchi: da Zeila alle frontiera del Kaffa.
Paravia. Torino 1930.
366 pp.

SOCIETA GEOGRAFICA ITALIANA.

Spedizione Bottego: Communicazione della Presidenza:
"Bollettino della Societa Geografica Italiana".
Roma 1897.
9 p.

SOLTDAMMER,F.

Notice sur Obock (Golfe d'Aden) Colonie Francaise.
Armons de Riviere. Paris 1877.

SORRENTINO,G.

Relazione del comandante G. Sorrentino sulla
missione eseguita dalla Stafetta lungo la costa
del Benadir nell'anno 1892. Ministero AA.EE.
Roma 1892.
63 pp.

Ricordi del Benadir: Notiziario estratto dal
giornale di viaggio compilato durante la missione
di R. Commissario Straordinario di S.M. il Re per
il Benadir. "Bollettino Societa Africana d'Italia".
Firenze 1910.

SPEXE,H.J.

What led to the discovery of the source of
the Nile: Journal of adventures in Somaliland.
Blackwood and Sons. Edinburgh & London 1864.

What led to the discovery of the source of
the Nile: Journal of adventures in Somaliland.
(New Edition). Frank Cass & Co. Ltd. London 1967.
372 pp.

STEFANINI,G.

Risultati geografici della missione Stefanini-Paoli
in Somalia. "Atti VIII Congresso Geografico Italiano".
Vol. II. Firenze 1921.
461 p.

Risultati geografici di una Missione nella Somalia
Settentrionale Italiana (1924). "Comptez Rendu du
Congres Internationale des Geographistes". Cairo 1927.

In Somalia: note e impressioni di viaggio.
Felice Le Monnier. Firenze 1922.
343 pp.

Sui rapporti biogeografici della Somalia Italiana.
"Atti XI Congresso Geografico Italiano".
Vol. III. Napoli 1930.
211 p.

_____AND PUCCIONI,N.

Notizie preliminari sui principali risultati
della Missione R. Societa Geografica Italiana in

Somalia 1924. "Bollettino R. Societa Geografica Italiana".
Roma 1926.
12 p.

SWAYNE,E.J.E.

Expedition to Nogal Valley. 1893.

_____AND SWAYNE,N.J.E.

Report on the Reconnaissance of Northern
Somaliland: February to November 1891. Bombay 1892.

SYLAS,S.

II Sultanato Migiurtino. "Bollettino Societa
Africana d'Italia". Vol. VII. Firenze Ottobre 1902.
97-149 pp.

TANCA,G.

Per la identificazione di un luogo della
Somalia meridionale. "Atti VI Congresso
Geografico Italiano". Vol. II. Venezia 1907.
462 p.

TEDESCO ZAMMARANO,V.

Esplorazione del Basso Uebi Scebeli 1920-1921.
"Bollettino Societa Geografica Italiana".
Fasc. No. 3-6. Roma 1924.
169-245 pp.'

_____

Risultati dell'ultima spedizione 1921-22 del
basso Uebi Scebeli. "Atti IX Congresso Geografico
Italiano". (1925). Vol. 1. Genova 1925.
230 p.

_____

Tra Uebi e Giuba. "Le Vie d'Italia e del Mondo".
Milano 1933.
1483 p.

TEILHARDE, DE CHARDIN.

Lettres de voyage, 1923-1939. Grasset. Paris 1956.

TIRANT,R. AND OTHERS.

Djibouti. "La Revue Francaise". No. 182.
Imprimeries de Bobigny. Paris 1965.
11-42 pp.

TRAVERSI, R.

Sulle origini del Giuba. "Bollettino Societa
Geografica Italiana". Roma 1893.

TRAVIS,W.

The voice of the turtle. Allen & Unwin Ltd. London 1967.
203 pp. front map. ills.

TREVIS,R.

Sulle orme della secondo speeizione Bottego
da Brava a Lugh. "Rivista delle Colonie Italiane".
Roma 1931.
425 p.

UNITED STATES OF AMERICA EMBASSY (SOMALIA).

Introduction to Mogadishu. Mogadishu 1965.

VANNUTELLI,L.

Narrazione del viaggio compiuto dalla secondo
spedizione Bottego. "Rivista Marittima". Roma 1897.
14 pp.

—————————

Intorno all'ultima spedizione Bottego.
"Atti III Congresso Geografico Italiano del 1898".
Vol. 1. Firenze 1899.
221 p.

VECCHI,B.V.

Nel Nord Somalo: La Migiurtinia.
"Numero Speciale Rivista Costruire". Ottobre 1938.
71 p.

VIGNERAS,S.

Notices sur la côte francaise des Somalis.
P. Dupont. Paris 1900.
13 pp.

VOTA,G.

Somalia Italiana. "Le Vie del Mondo" Milano 1950.
21 p.

WAKEFIELD,T.

Footprints in Eastern Africa. London 1866.

WELLBY,M.S.

A trip in Somaliland. "Journal of the United
Service Institution of India." Vol. XXIV. Bombay 1895.
295-324 pp.

WHITSHED-HAWKINS.

Letters from Somali. "United Service Magazine".
No. 1. Vol. CXLVIII. 1903.
180-190 pp.

WICKENBURGH,E. (count).

Wanderungen in Ost-Africa. Viena 1899.

_____

Von Djibouti bis Lamu. "Petermann's Mitteilungen".
Vol. XLIX. 1903.
193-199 pp.

ZAGHI,C.

Enrico Baudi di Vesme-Giuseppe Candeo e l'esplorazione
della Somalia. "Annali Africa Italiana". Vol. III-IV.
Roma 1938.
1139 p.

ZANCANELLA,A.

Impressioni di Somalia: diario del regista.
"Africa". No. 7-8 Roma 1955.
221-225 pp.

_____

Da Mogadiscio alle cascate Vittoria.
"Africa". No. 4. Roma 1958.
202-205 pp.

ZAVATARI,E.

Dal Giuba al lago Rodolfo. Reale Accademia d'Italia.
Roma 1940.
34 pp.

ZICCARDI,F.

Via Veneto e la via della boscaglia somala.
"Africa" No. 11. Roma 1953.
299-300 pp.

ZOHRER,L.

Somalilander. Kurt Schroeder. Bonn 1959.
194 pp. tables. ills map.

ZOLI,C.

Notizie intorno al territorio di riva
destra del Giuba. Roma 1927.

3. Geology (General)

ALOISI,P.

Rocce della Somalia raccolte dalla
seconda missione spedizione Stefanini.
"Memoreie Societa Toscana Scienze Naturali."
Vol. XXXVIII. Pisa 1927.
132 p.

_____AND DE ANGELIS,A.M.

Geologia della Somalia: Le rocce della
Somalia. Vol. II. "Societa Geografica Italiana".
Bologna 1939.
166 pp

ANONYMOUS.

Coal from Somaliland. Imperial Institute.
Vol. XIII. 1915.
189-92 pp.

AUBERT DE LA RUE,E.

Le volcanisme en Cote francaise des
Soamlis. "Bulletin Volcanol". Vol. IV.
Paris 1938-39.
71-108 pp.

AZZAROLI,A.

Missione geologica in Migiurtinia.
"La Ricerca Scientifica". No. 2.
Anno No. 2. Roma 1957.
301-345 pp.

BERTONELLI,P.

Cenni monografici sul Paese dei
Gherire (Geologia). Mogadiscio 1937.
89 pp. ills. map.

BESAIRIE,H.

Rapport de mission geologique a la
Côte Francaise des Somalis. "Bulletin di
Laboratoire de Geologie du Service des Mines
de Madagascar". 1939.

BIASUTTI,R.

La Missione Stefanini-Paoli nella
Somalia Italiana. "L'Africa Italiana".
Roma 1916.
209 p.

BROWN,B.

Geology of North-Eastern British Somaliland.
"Quarterly Journal". Geological Society.
Vol. IXXXVII. London 1931.
259-280 pp.

CARTER,H.J.

Memoir on the geology of the South East
Coast of Arabia. "Journal" Bombay Branch
Royal Asiatic Society. Bombay 1852.

CECIONI,G.

I Bur della Somalia. "Rivista delle
Colonie Italiane". Roma 1940.
1427 p.

II crostone selciose di Bur Uen in
Somalia. "Bollettino della Societa
Geologica Italiana". Roma No. 2-3. 1940.
235 p.

CREMA,C.

Osservazioni sulla geologia del medio Soebeli
(Somalia Italiana) in base ai materiali raccolti
da S.A.R. il Principe Luigi di Savoia, Duca degli Abruzzi.
"Rendiconto Reale Accademia dei Licei", Vol. XXXII, Roma 1923.
180 p.

CUFINO,L.

I risultati scientifici della Missione
Stefanini-Paoli nella Somalia Italiana
Meridionale. "Bollettino Societa Geografica
Italiana". Fasc. No. X. Roma 1916.
847 p.

DACGUE',E.

Beiträge zur geologie des Somalilandes.
"Oberer Jur. Beitr. Palaönt. Geolo. Österr".
Unganus. XVIK-XIV XVIII. Wein & Leipzig. 1905.
119-160 pp.

DALLA VEDOVA,G.

Introduzione ai risultati geologici della
Missione Bottego al Giuba. "Annali Museo
Civico Storia Naturale di Genova". Vol. XV.
Serie II. Genova 1895.

DAINELLI,G.

Geologica dell'Africa Orientale.
Vol. IV. Reale Accademia d'Italia.
Roma 1943.
tables.

DANIELS,J.L.

A preliminary investigation of some basic
intrusions in the Hargeisa and Borama districts
of Somaliland Protectorate. Geological Society of
South Africa. Vol. 61. 1959.
1-12 pp.

DAVIS,W.M.

The freshwater Tertiary Formations of the
Rocky Mountain Region. "Proceedings of the
American Academk of Arts and Science.".
Vol. XXXV. Boston 1900.
345-73 pp.

DE ANGELIS D'OSSAT,G. AND MILLOSEVICH,F.

Seconda spedizione Bottego: Studio
geologico sul materiale raccolto da
M. Sacchi. "Societa Geografica Italiana".
Roma 1900.
X,212 pp.

DE CHARDIN,P.T. AND OTHERS.

Etudes geologiques en Ethiopie, Somalie
et Arabie Meridionale. "Memorie de la
Societe Geologique de France". Vol. IV.
Ser. No. 4-5. Paris 1930.

DREYFUSS,M.

Etude de geologie et de geographie physique
de la Côte Francaise des Somalis.
"Revue de Geographie Physique et de Geologie Dynamique".
Fasicicule No. 4. Paris 1931.
287-385 pp.

FARQUHARSON,R.A.

First report on the geology and mineral
resources of British Somaliland. London 1924.
53 pp.

———————————

The geology and mineral resources of British
Somaliland. "Mining Magazine", Vol. XXXIV.
London 1926.
265-267-329-340 pp.

GENNES DE,A. AND BONARD,A.

Les roches volcaniques du Protectorate
des Somalis. "Comptes Rendus". Vol. CXXXI,
Paris 1900.
196-198 pp.

GERBELLA,L.

Contributo allo studio della geologia
e delle risorse minerarie della Migiurtinia.
"Atti II Congresso Studi Coloniali". Vol. III.
Napoli 1936.
184 p.

GIOVANNI,C.

I Bur della Somalia. "Rivista delle
Colonie Italiane". Anne XIV. No. 10. Roma 1940.

GRAZIOSI,P.

Una missione scientifica in Somalia.
"Le Vie d'Italia e del Mondo". No. 7.
Milano 1935.
819 p.

GREGORY, J.W.

A note on the Geology of Somaliland based
on collections made by Mrs. E. Lort-Philips;
Miss Edith Cole and Mr. C.P.V. Aylmer.
"Geological Magazine". London 1896.
289-94 pp.

─────────────

The collection of fossils and rocks from
Somaliland made by Messrs B.K.N. Wyllie
and W.R. Smellie. "Geological Department
Monographe". Hunterian Museum.
Glasgow 1925.

HUNT,J.A.

Geology of the Zeila Plain, British
Somaliland. "Geological Magazine".
Vol. IXXIX. No. 3. London May-June 1942.
197-201 pp. map.

─────────────

British Somaliland. "Lexique International".
Fasc. 5a.Vol.4. Congress International Geologie.
1-27 pp.

─────────────

Note on the geology of Somaliland
Protectorate. "Colonial Geological and
Mineral Resources". Vol. 2. London 1951.
29-30 pp.

KRENKEL,E.

Abbesomalien: Abessinien und Somalien
Handbuch der Regionale Geologie.
26 Heft.,bd.VII. Heidelburg 1926.
120 pp maps.

LECKIE,R.G.E.

Preliminary report on British Somaliland.
(Extracts from "Know A. Notes on the Geology
of the Continent of Africa). London 1905.

LINO.E,.

I terreni sepolti della Somalia.
"Africa". No. 10-11. Roma 1952.

_____

I giacimenti ferriferi del Doi sfruttabili
nel quadro della granda bonifica del Giuba.
Mogadiscio 1961.
5 pp.

_____

I giacimenti ferriferi del Doi nel quadro della
bonifica del Giuba. "Africa", No. 1. Roma 1962.
35-36 pp.

MACFADYEN,W.A.

The geology of British Somaliland.
"Proceedings of Geological Society".
Vol. 87. London 1931.
87 pp.

_____

The Late Geological History of British
Somaliland. "Nature". Vol. CXXX. London 1932.
433-4 p.p.

_____

The Geology of British Somaliland.
Government of Somaliland Protectoare. 1933.
87 pp.

_____

Sand gypsum crystals from Berbera,

British Somaliland. "Geological Magazine".
Vol. IXXXVII. London November-December 1950.
409-420 pp.

MASON,J.E.

An isolated occurrence of igneous rocks
at Gorei in the Las Anod District of Somaliland
Protectorate. "Geological Magazine". Vol. 94, No. 6.
London 1957.
498-502 pp.

M'HARDY,R.A.

Somaliland. "Scottish Geological Magazine".
Vol. XX. Edinburgh 1904.
225-234;pp.

MITCHELL,L.H.

Journal official de la reconnaissance
geologique et mineralogique entre Zeilah
et Tadjourra. "Bulletin Societe Geographique".
Paris 1893.
185-225 pp.

NEVANI,A.

Meteorite (ammalite) caduta il 16/10/1919
nel territorio di Bur Hacaba nella Somalia
Italiana (Prima communicazione).
"Bollettino Societa Geografica Italiana".
Vol. XL. Roma 1921.
209 p.

PARKINSON,J.

A preliminary note on the Boramas
schists, British Somaliland.
"Geological Magazine". Vol. 69.
London 1932.
517-520 pp.

Note on the petrology of the Gadabursi
country, British Somaliland. "Geological Magazine".
Vol. 73. London 1936.
571-576 pp.

PAULITSCHKE,P.

Begleitworte zur geoolg. Routenkarte für
die Strecke von Zeyla bis Bia Waraba.
(Ost-Afrika). "Mitt,K.K. Geogr. Gessell in Wien".
Vol. XXX. Wien 1887.

PEASE,A.E.

A volcanic crater in Northern Somaliland.
"Geographical Journal". London 1898.
138-42 pp.

PELLEGRINI,L.

Si cerca il petrolio in Migiurtinia (Somalia).
"Le Vie del Mondo". No. 3. Milano 1958.
242-254 pp.

RAISIN,C.A.

On some rock specimens from Somaliland.
"Geological Magazine". Vol. V. London 1888.
414-418 pp.

———————————

Petrological notes on rocks from Southern
Abyssinia (Ogaden), collected by Rowland
Kottleby. "Quarterly Journal". Geological Society.
294-306 pp.

SOCIETA GEOGRAFICA ITALIANA.

Risultati scientifici delle Missioni
Stefanini Paoli (1912) e Stefanini-Puccioni
(1924) in Somalia: "Geologia della Somalia".
Serie I. Vol. II. Zanichelli. Bologna 1938.

SOMALILAND OIL EXPLORATION CO. LTD.

A Geological Reconnaissance of the Sedimentary
Deposits of the Protectorate of British Somaliland.
Crown Agents. London 1954.
41 pp. ills. maps.

SOMALILAND PROTECTORATE.

The Geology of the Heis-Mait Waqderia Area
(Erigavo District). Geological Survey Department.
Report No. 1. (Mason, J. E. & Warden, A. J.)
Hargeisa 1st October 1956.
22 pp. map.

———————————

The Geology of the Adadleh Area
(Hargeisa and Berbera Districts) Geological
Survey Department. Report. No. 2.
Hargeisa 1958.

———————————

Outline account of the Geology of the
proposed Dam Sites in the Dagahkureh Area

and on the Dibraweine (Hargeisa and Borama Districts).
Geological Survey Department: (Warden, A. J.)
Hargeisa December 1959.

Report on the Geology of the Berbera-Sheik Area
(Berbera and Burao districts). Geological Survey
Department. Report No. 4. (Hunt,J.A.) Printers
Hargeisa January 1960.
27 pp. map. diagrs.

Minerals and Rocks of Hargeisa & Borama
District. Ministry of Natural Resources. Department of
Geological Survey. Mineral Resources Pamphlet No. 3
(Daniels, J.L.). Pioneers Press. Hargeisa 1960.
25 pp. map.

Report on the Geology of the Las Khoreh-Elayu Area
(Erigavo District). Geological Survey Department.
Report No. 3. (Greenwood, J.E.G.W. & Stewart, J.A.B.)
Hargeisa 1960.
36 pp. maps.

Casiterite Prospect of Dalan and Asilithe-Dagahkul
Area (Geologically and topographically surveyed
by J.A.B. Stewart). Directorate of Overseas Surveys.
Tolworth 1960.
(various scales) D.O.S. (Geol) Nos. 112-14.

SOMALILAND PROTECTORATE (ANNUAL REPORTS).

Annual Report of the Geological Survey
Department for the period April 1957-March 1958.
Stationery Office. Hargeisa 11 April 1958.
18 pp.

Annual Report of the Geological Surve
Department for the period April 1958-March 1959.
The Ministry of Commerce and Industry.
Hargeisa 19th May 1959.
22 pp.

Annual Report of the Geological Survey
Department for the period April 1959-March 1960.
Pioneers Press. Hargeisa 1960.
27 pp.

Annual Report of the Geological Survey
Department of the Ministry of Commerce and
Industry for the period April 1960 - March 1961.
Hargeisa November 1961.
17 pp. tables.

SOMALI GOVERNMENT.

Annual Report of the Geological Survey
Department of the Ministry of Industry and
Commerce for the period April 1961-March 1962.
Hargeisa 1962.
25 pp. tables.

STEFANINI,G.

Saggio di una carta geologica dell'Eritrea,
della Somalia e dell'Etiopia. 2 ediz. CNR. Roma.

Osservazione geologiche nella Somalia
Italiana Meridionale. "Bollettino Societa
Geologica Italiana". Vol. XXXII. Roma 1913.
398 p.

Costituzione geologica e regime idrografico
della Somalia Italiana Meridionale.
"Atti II Congresso Internzaionale Agricol. Trop".
Vol. II. Londra 1914.
397-8 pp.

Primi risultati geologici dalla missione della
Reale Societa Geografica Italiana in Somalia (1924).
"Rendiconto Reale Accademia dei Licei". Roma 1925.
182 pp.

Sur la costitution de la Somalie Italienne
Meridionale. "Comptes Rendus" du Congress
Geologique Internationale XIII et Session,
Belgique 1922. Leig 1925.
1059-1072 pp.

Successione ed eta della serie di Lugh nella
Somalia Italiana. "Comptes Rendu", XV International
Geological Congress (South Africa). Vol. II. Section III.
(Communication No. 26) Pretoria 1930.

223-238 pp.

Sull'esistenza di rocce cristalline antiche
e di rocce eruttive recenti nella Migiurtinia
Settentrionale. "Atti di Societa Toscana Scienze
Naturali". Vol. XL. (Proc. Verb.) Pisa 1931.
3-5 pp.

TAYLOR,R.S.

Some earthquake shocks in Somaliland. "Nature".
Vol. CXXVII. London 1931.
34 p.

THOMPSON,A.B. AND BALL,J.

Report on the Dagah Shabell Oilfield
(British Somaliland). Cairo 1918.

VIAPARELLI,C.

Lo stato delle recerche petrolifere in
A.O.I. (Somalia). "Atti I Congresso Regionale
di Studi Coloniali". (1938). Napoli 1939.
693-700 pp.

WYLLIE,B.N.K.

The collection of fissils and rocks from
Somaliland. "Monographs of the Geological Department
of Hunterian Museum". Glasgow University. Glasgow 1935.

4.   Hydrology and Hydrogeology

AMMINISTRAZIONE FIDUCIARIA ITALIANA DELLA SOMALIA.

Studio per la valorizzazione delle
risorse idriche del Medio e Basso
Scebeli. AFIS. Direzione per la
Sviluppo Economico. Mogadiscio Settembre 1954.
8 pp.

AGENCY FOR INTERNATIONAL DEVELOPMENT.

Feasibility Report on Mogadiscio Water
Supply System. Hydrotechnic Corporation,
Consulting Engineers. New York July 1963.

AHMED MUDDE HUSSEIN.

New Aqueduct for Mogadiscio.
International Cooperation Administration.
Mogadiscio 8 May 1961.

AHRENS, THOMAS P.

A Reconnaissance Ground-Water Survey of
Somalia. E.R.P. Technical Assistance Mission
of Italian Government. Rome November 1951.
270 pp.

AMADEI,R.

Notizie sul programma di recerche idriche
per la pastorizia somala."Rivista di Agricoltura
Subtropicale e Tropicale". Nos. 4-6. Firenze
Aprile-Settembre 1960.
377-390 pp.

ANONYMOUS

Osservazioni idrometriche sul fiume Uebi
Scebeli presso Afgoi "Bollettino Societa
Africana d'Italia." Napoli 1911.
20 p.

———————————

Sulle sponde del Basso Giuba. "Rivista
Coloniale". Roma 1910.
154 p.

ARCHER,CHETWYND S.

Report on Hargeisa Water Supply.
Government of Somaliland Protectorate.
The Tanganyika Mission Press Kipalapla.
Tabora 1955.
26 pp.

BERTANI,G.V.

Data on New Mogadiscio Pumping Station.
Mogadiscio 3 August 1961.

BONETTI,M.

La campagna idrografica lungo le
coste della Somalia Italiana.
"Bollettino Societa Geografica Italiana".
Roma 1940.
120 p.

———————————

Lavori idrografici recentemente eseguiti
dalla R. Marina Italiana nel Mar Rosso,
nel Mar Egeo e nell'Oceano Indiano.
"Rivista Marittima". Roma 1940.
211-26 pp.

BROWN,GLENN A.

Ground Water Geology in the Vicinity
of Mogadiscio. U.S. Agency for
International Mission to the Somali Republic.
Mogadiscio July 1962.

CENTRAL AGRICULTURAL RESEARCH STATION, AFGOI.

Scebeli river water quality: 1965-1966.
USAID/SOMALI REPUBLIC. University of
Wyoming Team. Mogadiscio June 1967.
20 pp. tables.

Shabelle river water salinity measurements:
electrical conductivity in micromhos/cm 1965-1970.
Ministry of Agriculture. Mogadiscio.

CHIESI,G.

L'acqua del Benadir."Rivista
Coloniale". Vol. I. Roma 1906.

CICOTTI,G.

Studio sui problemi del corso
dell'Uebi Scebeli. AFIS. Mogadiscio 1954.
12 pp.

CORNI,G.

Ricerche idriche in Somalia.
"Illustrazione Coloniale". Milano 1931.
26 p.

DAVIS, B.G. AND HAROTH, H.F.

Water resources development project-
Somali Republic. USIAD. Mogadiscio 1963.

DE SANCTIS,G.

Il bacino idrico del Descek Uamo opera
di romana grandezza ai confini tra la
Somalia ed il Kenya. "L'Italia d'Oltremare".
Roma 1941.
28 p.

DOXIADIS IONIDES ASSOCIATES LTD.

Preliminary study on the waters of
Somalia. D.I.A. London 1961.

DREYFUSS,M.

Hydrogeologie et possibilites de
culture a la Côte Francaise des Somalis.

"Annales Scientifiques de l'Universite de
Besancon". Serie geologie. No. 16. 1962.
75-91 pp.

FAILLACE,C.

Stato delle attuali conoscenze sulle
geoidrologia della Somalia. "Rivista di
Agricoltura Subtropicale e Tropicale."
Nos. 4-9. Firenze 1960.
317-332 pp.

———————————

Le risorse idriche sotterranee dei
comprensori agricoli di Afgoi e di
Genale."Rivista di Agricoltura Subtropicale
e Tropicale". Nos. 10-12. Firenze Ottobre-Dicembre 1964.
396-417 pp.

———————————

Linee programmatiche per la
valorizzazione delle risorse idriche
in Somalia. Ministero LL.PP e
Communicazione. Mogadiscio 1962.

———————————

Surface and underground water resources
of the Shabelli Valley. Ministry of
Public Works and Communication.
Mogadiscio November 1964.
99 pp. map. charts. tables.

FANO,R.

Del regime delle acque nella Somalia
Italiana."Atti II Congresso degli
Italiani all'Estero". 1911.
1639 p.

FAVILLA,G.

Possibilita di realizzazione di
un impianto idroelettrico sul Giuba:
Considerazioni generali. Mogadiscio 1961.
17 pp.

GATTI,V.

Il basso corso dell'Uebi Scebeli: Relazione
di un viaggio dalla diga di Far Ghero alla
probabile antica confluenza col Giuba (Belet Mamo)
13 Decembre 1955-8 Maggio 1956. "Rivista di Agricoltura
Subtropicale e Tropicale". Nos. 4-9. Firenze
Aprile-Settembre 1960.

264-300 pp.

HOLLOWAY,A.E.

Portable Water Supply for
Mogadiscio: Preliminary Report.
International Cooperation Administration.
Mogadiscio 13 May 1961.

ISTITUTO IDROGRAFICO DELLA REGIA MARINA

Relazione sulla spedizione idrografica
in Somalia nell'anno 1935. Tipolitografia
dell'Istituto Idrografia della R. Marina.
Genova 1936.
14 pp.

LINO,E.

I pozzi aerei della Somalia.
"Somalia d'Oggi". No. 2. Mogadiscio 1957.
20-23 pp.

MACFADYEN,W.A.

Water supply in Somaliland. "Geographical
Journal". Vol. 78. London 1931.
124 p.

_____

The development of water supplies
in British Somaliland, 1879-1939.
Kent 20 October 1945.

_____

Water supply and geology of parts
of British Somaliland. H.M.S.C.
(Crown Agents). London 1952.

MAGLIOCCO,V.

La spedizione idrografica in Somalia
nell'anno 1935. "Societa Italiana per
il Progresso delle Scienze." Vol. XXV.
Roma 1937.
159 p.

MANNI,E.F.

Le acque dello Scebeli da Genale
ad Havai e l'Uebi Gofca. "Agricoltura
Coloniale." Firenze 1932.
217 p.

MASCARELLI,L.

La composizione delle acque
dell'Uebi Scebeli: dalle sorgenti
a Buslei e nel territorio del Villagio
Duca degli Abruzzi. "Societa Italiana
per il Progresso delle Scienze." Vol. XXV.Fasc. No. 140
Roma 1930. 75 p.

ONOR,R.

Il problema idraulico del Benadir.
"Agricoltura Coloniale". No. 7-8. Firenze 1921.
353-406 pp.

PICCINNI,G.

Le risorse idriche della Somalia.
"Etiopia". 1937.
54 p.

PIKE,R.W.

The occurence of ground water in Central
Somalia. Sinclair Somali Corporation.
Mogadishu 1959.

POUCHAN,P.

Etudes hydrologiques en Territoire
Francaise des Afars et des Iseas.
"Revue Pount". No. 3. La Societe D'etudes
de L'Afrique Orientale. Djibouti 1967.

REPUBBLICA SOMALA.

Progetto per lo studio di Corsi d'Acqua
Temporanei da sbarrare con Dighe in Terra
o in Calcestruzzo. Ministero dei Lavori
Pubblici. Ufficio Studi. Mogadiscio 24 Febbraio 1965.

SALVADEI,G.

L'alto corso del fiume Uebi Scebeli.
"L'Oltremare." Roma 1929.
197 p.

SANTANERA,S.

Regime idrico del Giuba.
"Difesa Africana". No. 7. 1940.
190 p.

SEGHETTI,D.M.

In Somalia: politica idraulica.
"Africa". Nos. 5-6. Roma 1952.
147-150 pp.

SOMALILAND PROTECTORATE.

Hargeisa Water Supply Investigation.
Howard Humphreys & Sons Ltd.
London January 1960.
109 pp.

SOMALI REPUBLIC.

Republic of Somalia: Outline of
Development Programme for Irrigation
and Hydro Power Generation. Associated
Consulting Engineers, Ltd. Karachi September 1961.
14 pp. map. diagrs. charts.

STEFANINI,G.

Relazione sulle risorse idriche della
Somalia Italiana e l'avvenire."Atti
Convegno Nazionale per il dopo guerra
delle nostre colonie." 1919.
418 p.

Il problema idraulico della Somalia.
"Agricoltura Coloniale". Firenze 1921.
539 p.

TERRENI,R.

Il Giuba e suoi problemi.
"Universo". No. 6. Firenze 1955.
957-966 pp.

THOMPSON,A.BEEBY.

Notes on water resources of
British Somaliland. "East Africa
Pamphlet." No. 41. 1918.

The water supply of British Somaliland.
"Geographical Journal". Vol. 101. London April 1943.
154-160 pp. map, ills.

TOZZI,R.

Contributo allo studio del regime idraulico
del fiume Scebeli per una razionale utilizzazione
delle piene. "Rivista di Agricoltura Subtropicale
e Tropicale" Nos. 4-9. Firenze 1960.
391-402 pp.

UNITED NATIONS DEVELOPMENT PROGRAM (SPECIAL FUND).

Project for the water control and management
of the Shabelli River Somalia. (Vol. I) General Report.
F.A.O. Hunting Technical Services Ltd. and Sir Macdonald
& Partners (London). November 1969.
141 pp. tables. map. diagrs.

_____

Project for the water control and management
of the Shabelli River Somalia.(Vol. II): The Balad
floor control and irrigation project feasibility.
F.A.O. Hunting Technical Services Ltd. and Sir Macdonald
& Partners. (London) November 1969.
69 pp. tables, map. diagrs.

_____

Project for the water control and
management of the Shabelli River Somalia
(Vol. III): The Afgoi-Mordille controlled
irrigation project feasibility study. F.A.O.
Hunting Technical Services Ltd. and Sir Macdonald
& Partners (London) November 1969.
67 pp. tables diagres.

_____

Project for the water control and
management of the Shabelli River Somalia
(Vol.IV): Water resources and engineering.
F.A.O. Hunting Technical Services Ltd. and
Sir Macdonald & Partners (London) November 1969.
203 pp. map. diagrs.

_____

Project for the water control and
management of the Shabelli River Somalia
(Vol.V): Soils and Agriculture. F.A.O.
Hunting Technical Services Ltd. and Sir
Macdonald & Partners (London) November 1969.
212 pp. tables, diagrs. map.

USONI,L. AND PARSINI,G.

Studio sulle possibilita idriche del
sottosuolo in Somalia. AFIS. Mogadiscio 1951.

WILSON,G.

Ground water geology in Somalia.
International Cooperation Administration.
(ICA) Mogadiscio June 1958.

300

5. Meteorology

BOSSOLASCO,M.

Salinita, nuclei di condensazione e
precipitazione (Somalia). "Bollettino
Comitato Geodinamico e Geofisico". Anno IV.
Nos. 1-2. 1934.

_____

Sulla struttura del vento al suolo nella
regione di Mogadiscio. Stazione Geogisica
Temporanea di Mogadiscio. Pubbl. No. 14. Torino 1936.

BROOKS,C.E.P.

The meteorology of British Somaliland.
"Journal of the Royal Meteorological Society".
London 1920.

_____AND DURST,C.S.

Winds of Berbera. Meteorological Office.
The Air Ministry. Ser. No. 336e. London 1934.
13 pp.

CENTRAL AGRICULTURAL RESEARCH STATION,AFGOI.

Rainfall and temperatures at Afgoi:Somali Republic 1965/66/
USAID/SOMALI REPUBLIC. University of Wyoming Team.
Mogadiscio June 1967.
19 pp.

CERASUOLO,F.

Cenni climatologici sulla Somalia con particolare
riferimento alle condizioni di volo.
"Rivista di Meteorologia Areonautica". No. 3. 1950.

CREDITO SOMALO.

Chart of Seasons in Somalia. Mogadishu 1967.

EREDIA, F.

La Stazione Meteorologica a Capo Guardafui.
Atti Congresso Internazionale di Meteorologia
di Stoccolma. 1931.

_____

I monsoni dell'Oceano Indiano al suolo
e in quota. "Rivista Marittima". Roma 1932.

_____

Sondaggi con palloni-piloti eseguiti nella Stazione
di Capo Guardafui (Gennaio 1932-Giugno 1933).
"Annali Ufficio Presagi". Vol. VI. Ministero Aereonautico.
Roma 1935.

Sulle osservazioni meteorologiche in Somalia.
Atti II Congresso Studi Coloniali. Vol. III. Firenze 1936.
91 p.

Le correnti aeree nel bacino imbrifero dell'Uebi Scebeli.
"Bollettino R. Societa Geografica Italiana". Ser. VII. Vol. I.
Roma 1936.
400 p.

FANTOLI, A.

Carte pluviometriche della Somalia. Ministero
Africa Italiana. Ufficio Studi. Roma 1953.

Le precipitazioni atmosferiche in Somalia.
"Rivista di Agricoltura Subtropicale e Tropicale".
Nos. 4-6. Firenze 1960.

Le precipitazioni atmosferiche in Somalia.
"Rivista Agricoltura Subtropicale e Tropicale".
Nos. 7-8. Firenze 1960.

Le precipitazioni atmosferiche in Somalia.
Istituto Agronomico per l'Oltremare.
Tipografia B. Coppini & C. Firenze 1960.
301-316 pp. tables. charts.

Contributo alla climatologia della Somalia.
Ministero Affari Esteri. O.P.I. Roma 1964
487 p.

FRITH, R.

Meteorological report in connection with U.H.F.
wireless experiments between Aden and Berbera.
Joint Meteorological Radio Panel Report No. 13.
Aden 1943.

GLOVER, P.E.

Rain water penetration in British Somaliland soils.
"East African Agricultural Journal". Vol. XVI. No. 1.
July 1950.

GRASSI,M.

Condizioni climatologiche lungo la costa somala.
"La Meteorologia Pratica". No. 2. Montecassino 1943.
38 p.

ISTITUTO AGRONOMICO PER L'OLTREMARE.

Le precipitazioni atmosferiche in Somalia.
"Rivista di Agricoltura Subtropicale e Tropicale".
Firenze 1960.

MENNELLA,C.

Il regime delle piogge in Somalia.
"Echi e Commenti". Roma 1936.
470 p.

_____

Ii clima della Somalia. "Echi e Commenti".
Roma 15 Maggio 1937.
439 p.

MILLOSEVICH,F.

Contributo allo studio sul clima di Lugh.
Societa Geografica Italiana. Roma 1903.

MOREAU,R.E.

Climatic classification from the stand point
of East African Biology. "Journal of Ecology".
London 1938.
467-496 pp.

OMODEI,D.

Osservazioni meteorologiche ed idrometriche
eseguite nel 1923 nella Somalia Italiana.
Istituto Poligrafico dello Stato. Roma 1926.
114 p.

_____

Notizie sul clima della Somalia Italiana Meridionale
e sul regime idrometrico dell'Uebi Scebeli secondo
le osservazioni fatte nelle stazioni istituite da
S.A.R. il Duca degli Abruzzi. Societa Tipo-Litografica
Ligure Oliveri. Genova 1927.
199 pp. tables. map. charts.

_____

Osservazioni meteorologiche eseguite negli anni
1928 29 nell'osservatorio meteorologhiche del
villagio S.A.R. il Duca degli Abruzzi. Tipo-Litografia
dell'Istituto Idrografico della Regina Marina. Genova 1930.
(tables.charts)

_____AND EREDIA,F.

Osservazioni meteorologiche eseguite nel 1922
nelle stazioni istituite nella Somalia Italiana
da S.A.R. il Duca degli Abruzzi. "Annali Idrografici".
Roma 1927.

OMOND,R.T.

Temperature observation in Somaliland and Abyssinia.
"Scottish Geographical Magazine". Vol. XVI. Edinburgh 1900.
490-493 pp.

PAGLIANI,S.

Sulla frequenza dei venti di diversa
velocita nella Somalia Italiana e loro
pratica utilizzazione. Istituto Poligrafico
dello Stato. Roma 1926.

PALAZZO,L.

Alcune misure magnetiche eseguite nell'Est
Africa inglese e nella Somalia Italiana.
"Annali Ufficio Centr. Meteorol. Geodinamica".
Vol. XXXVI. Roma 1910.

_____

La carta magnetica del Benadir. Ministero delle
Colonie. G. Bertero. Roma 1912.
12 pp.

_____

Misure magnetiche in Oltregiuba e Somalia nel
1926. "Memorie Ufficio Centr. di Meteorol. e Geofisica".
Ser. III. Vol. II. Roma 1930.
63 pp.

PARKINSON, J.

Climatic changes in British Somaliland.
"Nature". Vol. CXXIX. London 1932.
651 p.

PROTTI, P.

Cenni di climatologia e di nosografia della
Somalia Italiana. "Universo". No. 5. Firenze 1950.
705 p.

SOMALILAND, FRENCH.

Observatoire de Djibouti. "Bulletin Annuel du
Service Meteorologique et Climatologie". Paris 1945.

―――――――――

Resume mensuel du temps en Côte Francaise des Somalis.
"Service Meteorologique". Djibouti 1952.
(tables, charts).

―――――――――

Climatologie. "Service Meteorologique". Bulletin
Annuel". Impro. Nationale. Paris.
(tables charts).

6.   Mineralogy and Petrography

ARSANDAUX,H. AND NEUVILLE, H.

Resultats petrographiques du Voyage
de M. Maurice de Rothschild dans les
Pays Somali-Dankali et en Abssinie.
"Bulletin Mus. Hist. Natural". Vol. XI.
No. 3. Paris 1905.

ARTINI,E.

Intorno alla composizione mineralogico
di alcune sabbie ed arenarie raccolte dalla
missione scientifica Stefanini-Paoli nella
Somalia Italiana. Pavia 1915.

―――――――――

Sulla presenza della monazite nelle sabbie
e nelle arenarie della Somalia Meridionale.
"Atti Reale Accademia dei Lincei". Serie V.
Vol. XXIV. Suppl. No. I. Roma 1915.
555-558 pp.

―――――――――

Sulla composizione mineralogica di 4 campioni
di sabbia provenienti dalle dune dei dintorni
di Chisimaio nell'Oltregiuba. "Agricoltura Coloniale".
Firenze 1926.
101 p.

BRITISH SOMALILAND.

Gypsum-anhydrite. "Geological Survey Department,
Mineral Resources Pamphlet No. 1".
Hargeisa 1954.
4 pp.

FARQUGARSON,R.A.

Occurrence of phosphate minerals in
British Somaliland "Congress Geolog.
Internat. Espage Reserves Mondiale en
Phosphates". Vol. II. 1926.
611-616 pp.

HOLMES, J.R.

A Reconnaissance Survey of the Mineral
Deposits of Somalia (former Italian Somaliland):
a report of Technical Assistance Mission.
(T.A. Report No. 45-125) U.S. Operations Mission
to Italy (Rome 1957) World Mining Consultants, Inc.
New York.
56 pp. ills, map.

LUSINI,G.

Le attivita minerarie dell'Italia in
Somalia. "Africa". No. 5. Roma 1949.
133 p.

LINO,E.

Possibilita minerarie della Somalia: Rapporto
sulle prospezioni effettuate in Somalia dalla
Missione Mineraria della M.S.A. dal 1/7/1953
al 5/9/1953. AFIS. Direzione per lo Sviluppo
Economico, Servizio Geo-Minerario. Stamperia AFIS.
Mogadiscio 16 Aprile 1953.
25 pp. ills.

_____

Guida breve geo-mineraria (AFIS).
Direzione per lo Sviluppo Economico.
Servizio Geologico Minerario. Mogadiscio 1954.
23 pp.

_____

Possibilita mineraria della Somalia.
Stamperia AFIS. Mogadiscio 1956.
39 pp.

MILLOSEVICH,E.

Qualche prospettive minerarie
dell'A.O.I. (Somalia). "Rendiconti
Reale Accademia dei Lincei". Roma 1939.

MINERARIA SOMALA (AGIP).

Relazione sull'attivita svolta negli
anni 1953-1963. Mineraria Somala.

Mogadiscio Maggio 1963.
49 pp. ills. map.

MURDOCK,T.G.

The Mineral Industry of the Somali
Republic. "1963 Minerals Yearbook". Vol. IV.
(Area Report). Bureau of Maps. United
States Department of Interior. Washington, D. C. 1963.

PALLISTER, J.W.

Mineral resources of Somaliland Protectorate.
"Geological and Mineral Resources". Vol. VII.
London 1958.
154-165 pp.

UNITED NATIONS.

Report on uranium, thorium and rare earths
at Alio Ghelle Somalia prepared for the
Government of the Somali Republic by the United
Nations acting as participating and executing
Agency for the United Nations Development Programe.
Mogadiscio 1968.
49 pp.

USONI,L.

Risorse minerarie della Somalia.
"Atti del Secondo Convegno di Studi Coloniali".
Firenze 1938.

Il giacimento di stagno di magiaian
(Migiurtinia Somalia Settentrionale).
"International Geological Congress (Great Britain).
Vol. XVIII. Londra 1948.
218-222 pp.

Risorse minerarie della'A.O.I.
(Eritrea, Somalia, Etiopia). Landi Sapi.
Tivoli 1952.
553 pp.

WARDEN,A.J. AND PALLISTER, J.W.

A Gypsum/Anhydrite deposit in Somaliland.
"Mineral Magazine". Vol. 98. London 1958.
337-337 pp.

7.   Palaentology

AIROLDI,M.

Le Corallinacee del Pleistocene della
Somalia. "Paleontografia Italica".
Vol. XXXII. Suppl. No. 1. Siena 1933.
79 p.

Le Corallinacee del Miocene della Somalia
Italiana. "Paleontografia Italica".
Vol. XXXII. Suppl. No. 2. Siena 1937.
25 p.

AZZAROLI,A.

I macroforaminiferi delle serie di Garcar
(Eocene,Medio e Superiore) in Somalia e la
loro distribuzione stratigrafica.
"Paleontografia Italica". Vol. 47. Siena.
99 p.

CECIONI,G.

Ostriche Oligo-Mioceniche della Somalia.
"Bollettino Societa Geografica Italiana".
Vol. 64. Roma 1947.
80 p.

CHECCHIA,R.G.

Sui primi fossili cretacei della Somalia
Italiana. "Bollettino Reale Ufficio Geologico".
Roma 1925.
4 p.

Migliorinia: nuova genere di Echinide
dell'Eocene della Migiurtinia. "Atti Reale
Accademia d'Italia". Vol. III. Serie VII.
Roma Novembre 1941.
305 p.

Sull'esistenza del Campaniano,
Maestrichiano nella Migiurtinia. "Atti
Reale Accademia dei Lincei". Vol. II.
Serie VIII. Fasc. V. Roma 1947.
639 p.

Sull'esistenza del Maestrichtiano nella
Migiurtinia. "Atti Accademia dei Lincei".
Vol. II. Serie VIII. Fasc. No. VI. Roma 1948.
169 p.

Salenia Hawkinsi: Nuove Echinide del
Cenomaniano della Somalia. "Atti Reale
Accademia dei Lincei". Vol. IV. Serie VIII.
Roma 1948.
169 p.

Su alcuni pseudodiadominae del Cretaceo
della Somalia. "Atti Reale Accademia Nazionale
dei Lincei". Roma 1948.

Pygasteridi del Cenomaniano della Somalia.
"Atti Reale Accademia Nazionale Dei Lincei".
Vol. IV. Serie VIII. Roma 1948.
278 p.

CONNOLLY,M.

I Molluschi continentali della Somalia
Italiana. Modena 1928.

Land and freshwater Mollusca of British Somaliland.
Aden 1935.

COX,L.R.

Notes on the Post-Miocene Obstreidae
and Pectinidae of the Red Sea Region with
remarks on the Geological significance of
their distribution. "Proceedings of the
Malacological Society of London.". Vol. XVIII.
London 1929.
165-209 pp.

The Geology of the Farsan Islands, Gizan
and Kamaran Island (Red Sea Region) Molluscan
Palaeontology. "Geological Magazine". Vol. LXVIII.
London 1931.
1-3 pp.

New Lamellibranch Genera from Tethyan Eocene.
"Proceedings of the Malacological Society".
Vol. XIX. London 1931.
177-187 pp.

A contribution to the Molluscan Fauna of
the Laki and Basal Khirthar Groups of the
Indian Eocene. "Transactions of the Royal
Soceity of Edinburgh". Vol. LVII. Edinburgh 1931.

CRICK,G.C.

Notes on some fragments of Belemites
from Somaliland. "Geological Magazine".
Vol. III. New Series Dec. IV. London 1896.
296-298 pp.

_____

On the fossil Cephalopodo from Somaliland.
"Geological Magazine". London 1899.

CURRIE,E.D.

Jurassic and Eocene Echinoidae from
Somaliland. "Transactions of the Royal
Society of Edinburgh". Vol. IV. Edinburgh 1927.
411-441 pp.

D'ERASMO,G.

Avanzi di pesci delle serie di Lugh
in Somalia. "Paleontografia Italica".
Vol. XXXII. Siena 1931.
29 p.

FRENGUELLI,G.

Resti silicei di microrganismi dei
travertini della Somalia (Fossili del Pliocene
e del Pleistocene). "Paleontografia Italica".
Vol. XXXII. Suppl. No. I. Siena 1933.
67 p.

GOVERNMENT OF THE SOMALILAND PROTECTORATE.

The Mesozoic Palaeontology of British
Somaliland: (Part II of the Geology and Paleontology
of British Somaliland). Government of the Somaliland
Protectorate. January 1935.
227 pp. I-XXV plates with explanations.

GREGORY, J.W.

On the Geology and Fossil Corals and Echinids of
Somaliland. "Quarterly Journal of the
Geological Society". Vol. LVI. London 1900.
26-45 pp.

HASS,O. AND MILLER,A.K.

Eocene Nautiloids of British Somaliland.
"Bulletin AM. Museim of History". Vol. No. 99.
London 1952.
317-354 pp.

JONES,T.R.

Foraminiferal Flint from Somaliland.
"Geological Magazine". Vol. VI. New
Ser. IV. London 1899.
93-94 pp.

KIER,P.M.

Tertiary Echnoidea from British Somaliland.
"Journal of Palaentology". Vol. XXXI. No. 5.
London 1957.
839-902 pp.

LATHAM, M.H.

Jurassic and Kainozoic Corals from Somaliland.
"Transactions of the Royal Society of Edinburgh.
Vol. LVI. Edinburgh 1929.
273-290 pp.

MACFADYEN,W.A.

The Mesozoic Palaentology of British Somaliland.
"Crown Agents". London 1935.

MAYER,E.G.

Uber necomian Versteinerungen aus dem
Somalilande. Vierteljahreschr. "Naturf Gesellsch".
38bd. Zurich 1893.

NARDINI,S.

Molluschi marini e continentali del Pleistocene
della Somalia. "Paleontografia Italica".
Vol. XXXII. Suppl. No. I. Siena 1933.
169 p.

NEWTON,R.B.

On the occurence of an Indian Jurassic Shell,
Parallelodon Egertonianus in Somaliland Eastern Africa.
"Geological Magazine". Vol. III. London 1896.
294-296 pp.

———————————

The Tertiary Fossils of Somaliland
as represented in the British Museum.
"Quarterly Journal of the Geological Society".
Vol. LXI. London 1905.
155-180 pp.

NUTTAL,W.L.F. AND BRIGHTON,A.G.

Larger Foraminifera from the Tertiary of
Somaliland. ''Geological Magazine''. Vol. LXVIII.
London 1931.
49-65 pp.

OVEY,C.D.

A new Eocene species of 'Lokhartia Davies'
from British Somaliland with notes on other
species of the genus. ''Ann.Magazine Natural
History''. Ser. II. Vol. XIII. London 1947.
571-575 pp.

PARKINSON,J.

Freshwater and Land Mollusca from British
Somaliland. ''Nature''. Vol. CXXIX. London 1932.
941 p.

PARONA,C.F. AND ZUFFARDI COMMERCI,R.

Ancora sulla ''Somalia senigmatica''
(Fossili del Giuralias). ''Paleontografia Italica''.
Vol. XXXII. Suppl. No. III. Siena 1938.
11 p.

ROCHEBRUNE DE,A.T.

Observations geologiques et paleontologiques
sur la region habitee par les comalis et plus
specialment les Montagnes des Oursanguelis.

SCOTT,G.

Jurassic Cephalopoda Cretaceous Nautilus
(Petrology of Harar Province). ''Bulletin
Am. Museum of Natural History''. London 1943.

SILVESTRI,A.

Foraminiferi del Cretaceo della Somalia.
''Paleontografia Italica''. Vol. XXXII.
Siena 1932.
143 p.

———————

Foraminiferi dell'Oligocene e del Miocene
della Somalia. ''Paleontografia Italica''.
Vol. XXXII. Suppl. No. II. Siena 1937.
45 p.

———————

Foraminiferi dell'Eocene della Somalia.

(Parte I). "Paleontografia Italica".
Vol. XXXII. Suppl. No. III. Siena 1938.
49 p.

_____

Foraminiferi dell'Eocene della Somalia.
(Parte II). "Paleontografia Italica".
Vol. XXXII. Suppl. No. IV. Siena 1938.
1 p.

STEFANINI,G.

Sull'esistenza di Dictyoconoides nell'Eocene
medio della Somalia Settentrionale. "Atti di
Societa Scienze Naturali". Serie VI. Vol. V-VI.
No. 57-58. Fasc. Z. Modena 1928.
84-86 pp.

_____

Molluschi del Giuralias della Somalia:
Gasteropodi e Lamellibranchi. "Paleontografia Italica".
Vol. XXXII. Suppl. No. IV. Siena 1930.
103 p.

_____

Paleontologia della Somalia. "Paleontografia Italica".
(Anno 1931). Siena 1932.
1-246 pp.

_____

Sull'esistenza di terreni Giurassici
nella Migiurtinia Settentrionale.
"Atti Societa Toscana di Scienze Naturali".
Vol. XL. Serie V. Pisa 1931.
82 p.

_____

Cenni sulle localita fossilifere
Giurassiche della Somalia.
"Paleontografia Italica". Vol. XXXII.
Siena 1932.
35 p.

_____

Avanzi di Molluschi della 'Serie di Lugh'
in Somalia. "Paleontografia Italica".
Vol. XXXII. Siena 1932.
25 p.

_____

Introduzione alla "Paleontologia della Somalia".
"Paleontografia Italica". Vol. XXXII. Siena 1932.
1 p.

Echinodermi, Vermi Briozoi e Brachiopodi
del Giuralias della Somalia. "Paleontografia Italica".
Vol. XXXII. Siena 1932.
81 p.

Cenni stratigrafici sulle 'Serie di Lugh'
in Somalia. "Paleontografia Italica".
Vol. XXXII. Siena 1932.
17-31 pp.

Notizie sulle formazioni Plioceniche
e Pleistoceniche della Somalia.
"Paleontografia Italica". Vol. XXXII.
Suppl. No. I. Siena 1933.
55 p.

Molluschi del Giuralias della Somalia
(introduzione): Cefalopodi.
"Paleontografia Italica". Vol. XXXII.
Suppl. No. I. Siena 1933.
1 p.

Cenni sulle localita fossilifere
Oligoceniche e Mioceniche della Somalia.
"Paleontografia Italica". Vol. XXXII.
Suppl. No. II. Siena Q 1937.
1 p.

Cenni sulle localita fossilifere
Ecceniche della Somalia. "Paleontografia Italica".
Vol. XXXII. Suppl. No. III. Siena 1938.
13 p.

STUBBLEFIELD, C.J.

Some Decapodan Crustacea from Middle
Eocene of British Somaliland. "Ann. Magazine of
Natural History". Vol. XIII. Serie No. II London 1947.
505 519 pp.

TAVANI,G.

Nuove osservazioni sulle Stefaniniellidae
del Cretaceo della Somalia. "Paleontologia Italiana".
Vol. X. Pisa 1942.
15 p.

Fauna Malacologica Cretacea della Somalia
e dell'Oltregiuba. (Parte I: Lamellibranchiata).
"Paleontologia Italiana". Vol.XIII. Pisa 1948.
83 p.

Fauna Malacologica Cretacea della Somalia
e dell'Ogaden. (Parte II: Gasteropoda e Cephalopoda)
(Conclusioni). "Paleontologia Italiana". Nuova Ser. No. 8.
Vol. XVI. Pisa 1949.
1 p.

Rudiste ed altri Molluschi Cretacei della
Migiurtinia. "Paleontologia Italiana".
Nuova Ser. Vol. XVI. Pisa 1949.
1 p.

VENZO,S.

Trigonia Stefanini del Batoniano
dell'Oltregiuba, Milano 1942.
22 pp.

Ii Batoniano a Trigonia dell'Oltregiuba
Settentrionale e del Borana Orientale.
"Paleontologia Italiana". Nuova Ser.
Vol. XV. Pisa 1949.
111 p.

WEIR,J.

Jurassic fossils from Jubaland,Easte
Africa collected by V.G. Glenday and the
Jurassic Geology of Somaliland. Glasgow 1929.

WELLS, J. W.

Jurassic Anthozoa and Hydrozoa
(Palaentology of Harar Province).
"Bulletin Am. Museum of Natural History. London 1943.

ZUFFARDI COMMERCI,R.

Corallari del Cretaceo della Somalia.
"Paleontografia Italica". Vol. XXXII.

Siena 1932.
209 p.

Corallari e Idrozoi del Giuralias della
Somalia. "Paleontografia Italica".
Vol. XXXII. Siena 1932.
49 p.

Corallari Oligocenici e Miocenici della
Somalia. "Paleontografia Italica".
Vol. XXXII. Suppl. No. II. Siena 1937.
38 p.

Corallari e Idrozio Giurassici dell'Ogaden (Somalia).
"Paleontografia Italica". Vol. XXXII. Suppl. No. III.
Siena 1938.
1 p.

VIII

HEALTH AND MEDICINE

ANGRISANI,V.

Di un rarissimo caso di tifo
addominale verificatosi in
Somalia in autoctone con complicazione
miocarditica. AFIS.
7 pp.

L'alimentazione dei Migiurtini. "Archivi
Italiani di Scienze Mediche Tropicali e
di Parassitologia". Fasc. No. 10. Roma Ottobre 1953.

ANONYMOUS.

Cenni sulla patologia e climatologia della
Somalia. "Annali della Societa Medicina ed
Igiene Tropicale della Somalia." Vol. I.
Mogadiscio 1953.
15-28 pp.

ANNOVZAAI,G.

La traumatologia presso i Somali.
Chirurgia degli Organi di Movimento."
No. 4. 1939.
373-80 pp.

Appunti di ostetricia e ginecologia
somala. "Africa Orientale" No. 8. 1940.
197-206 pp.

AUDISIO,G.

L'Istituto Chimico e Farmaceutico di
Mogadiscio. "Annali della Societa di
Medicina e Igiene Tropicale della Somalia."
Vol. I. Mogadiscio 1953.
117-121 pp.

BARBIERI-ALBANI,C.

Considerazioni sulla leucodermia dei
Somali. "Rassegna Internazionale di
Chimica e Terapia." No. 3. Napoli 1940.
83-86 pp.

_____

La chirurgia presso i Somali.
"Rassegna Internazionale Chimica e
Terapia." No. 11. Napoli 1939.
478-85 pp.

BARUFFA, G.

Considerazioni sulla endemia di
lebbra in Somalia. "Annali della Societa
di Medicina ed Igiene Tropicale della
Somalia." Vol. 2. Mogadiscio 1958.
13-22 pp.

_____

La Somalia: banco di prova di nuova
terapia antilebrose. "Africa" No. 159.
Roma 1959.
188-189 pp.

_____AND MAFFI,M.

Considerazioni sull'impiego di una
derivato del Tioxantone (Nilodin)
nella cura ambulatoria di massa della
Bilharziosi (schistosomiasi) Vescicale
nella popolazione rurale in Somalia.
"Archivi Italiani di Scienze Mediche
Tropicali e di Parassitologia."
Fasc. No. 11. Roma Novembre 1958.
661-676 pp.

BELOCUROV, J.N.

Cura chirurgica della patologia
malarica epatolienale. "Notiziario

Sanitario della Somalia'' Vol. I.
Fasc. No. III. Mogadiscio 1963.
21-24 pp.

BRUNI,G.

Carie e paradenziopatie nel distretto di
Galcaio. ''Annali della Societa Medicina e
Igiene Tropicale della Somalia''.
Vol. II. Mogadiscio 1958.
26-36 pp.

CACCIAPUOTI,R.

Febbri tifo petecchiale in
Somalia. ''Annali della Societa di
Medicina e Igiene Tropicale della
Somalia.'' Vol. I. Mogadiscio 1953.
89-96 pp.

Osservazioni sul liquido cefalo
rachidiano nella febbre ricorrente
da zecche in Somalia. ''Annali della
Societa Medicina e Igiene Tropicale
della Somalia.'' Vol. I. Mogadiscio 1953.
33-40 pp.

CAMIS,MARIO.

Metabolismo basale ed alimentazione in
Somalia: primo contributo alla fisiologia
tropicale in Africa Orientale. Reale Accademia
d'Italia. Centro Studi per l'Africa Orientale
Italiana. Roma 25 Dicembre 1936.
110 pp map.

CAPPELLI,M.

La Clrochina nel trattamento della
amebiasi intestinale.''Annali della
Societa Medicina e Igiene Tropicale
della Somalia.'' Vol. I. Mogadiscio 1953.
97-103 pp.

CARLISI,F.

Sulla composizione chimica del latte
somalo. ''Giornale di Medicina Militare''.
No. 8. Roma 1937.
368 p.

CARUSILLO,G.

Nota sulla difussione del Botulismo
in Somalia. ''Notiziario Sanitaria della

Somalia." Vol. I. Fasc. No. 2. Mogadiscio
Settembre   Ottobre 1962.
59 p.

CICHITTO.

Ricerca sugli indici malarici della
Somalia Italiana."Rivista di Malariologia."
Roma 1938.

COLETTI,E. AND VEGLIO,B.

Un caso di febbre tifoide a
Mogadiscio." Notiziario Sanitaria
della Somalia." Vol. I. Fasc. No. 2.
Mogadiscio Settembre-Ottobre 1962
41-46 pp.

CONGIU,S.

Virus fisso della rabbia in
Somalia. "Annali della Societa
Medicina e Igiene Tropicale della
Somalia." Vol. 2. Mogadiscio 1958.
113-125 pp.

CONSTANT,Y.

Apercus sur la tuberculose en T.F.A.I.
(Territoire Francaise des Afars et des Issas).
"Revue Pount". No. 3. La Societe D'etudes de
l'Afrique Orientale. Djibouti 1967.

CROVERI,P.

Contributo alla conoscenza della nosografia
umana ed animale della Somalia Italiana.
"Archivio Italiano di Scienze Mediche Coloniali."
No. 3. Tripoli 1930.

DALDRI,E.

Nosografia e demografismo fra i coloni
indigeni del Comprensori di Genale.
"Archivio Italiano di Scienze Mediche
Coloniali". No. 1. Tripoli 1934.
45 p.

DE CARO,L. AND LOCATELLI,A.

Sul contenuto in vitamine A1,B1,B2,
C e D delle banane della Somalia
Italiana. "Quaderno della Nutrizione."
Vol. IV. No. 1 Capelli. 1937.
32 p.

DIAMANTI,G.

La nosografia della Regione del medio
Giuba (Residenza di Bardera). "Archivio
Italiano di Scienze Mediche Coloniali."
Tripoli 1939.
449-503 pp.

La infezione malarica nel
territorio del medio Giuba.
"Rassegna Internazionale
Chimica e Terapia". No. 9. Napoli 1939.
388-404 pp.

DI FONZO,N.

Relazione sull'attivita del reparto
otorinolaringologico della Somalia.
"Annali della Societa Medicina ed
Igiene Tropicale della Somalia."
Vol. 2. Mogadiscio 1958.
127-133 pp.

DI GENNARIO,D.

Appunti di legislazione sociale
somala: l'assicurazione obbligatorio
degli infortuni sul lavoro delle malattie
professionali. "Notiziario Sanitaria della
Somalia." Vol. I. Fasc. No. III. Mogadiscio 1963.
50-61 pp.

FABRIANI,G.

Sulla composizione chimica di prodotti
derivati dalla banana di varieta Giuba.
"I Quaderni della Nutrizione". No. 2. 1939.
19 p.

FALCONE,G.

Le manifestazioni oculari di malattie
generali in Somalia. "Archivi Italiani
di Scienze Mediche Tropicali e Parassitologia."
Fasc. No. 3. Roma Marzo 1951.

Ii cloramfenicolo in oftalmologia
tropicale."Archivi Italiani di Scienze
Mediche Tropicali e di Parassitologia."
Fasc. No. 6. Roma 1951.

Etiologia e terapia delle irido cicliti
in Somalia. "Annali della Societa

e Igiene Tropicale della Somalia."
Vol. I. Mogadiscio 1953.
57-63 pp.

FOOD AND AGRICULTURAL ORGANIZATION.

Rapport au Gouvernment Italien charge
de l'administration du Territroire sous
tutelle de la Somalie sur les resultates
de l'enquete preliminaire sur l'etat de
nutrition de la population de ce
territoire. FAO. Rapport No. 193.
Rome Janver 1954.
40 pp.

A preliminary survey of the nutritional
status of the population of Somalia.
Report to the Government of Italy.
FAO/54/2/687. Report No. 193.
Rome January 1954.

FILIPPONE,G.

La morbilita nella Somalia Italiana
nell'anno 1938. "Rassegna Sociale
Africana Italiana". Napoli 1940.
695-703 pp.

GARERO.ERNESTO.

Il problema della Tubercolosi in
Somalia. Istituto Grafico Tiberino.
Roma Gennaio 1953.
121 pp. tables.

Il metodo brasiliano della vaccinazione
con il B.C.G. Ufficio Sanita. AFIS.
Mogadiscio 1955.
26 pp.

Le basi della moderna lotta
antitubercolare. AFIS Mogadiscio 1955.
26 pp.

Lo sviluppo dell'organizzazione
sanitaria in Somalia. "Somalia
d'Oggi." No. 4. Mogadiscio 1957.
5 p.

I primi esperimenti di vaccinazione
con B.C.G. in Somalia. "Notiziario
Sanitaria della Somalia". Vol. I.
Fasc. No. III. Mogadiscio 1953.
5-20 pp.

GIGLIOLI,G.

Report on a visit to Somalia
in relation to proposed malaria
control Project. AFIS. 1955.

GIORDANO,M.

Un caso di dermatomicosi da
Penicillium crostaceum. "Archivio
Italiano di Scienze Mediche Coloniali".
Vol. XIII. Tripoli 1938.
72 p.

———————————

L'opera sanitaria della Marina
Militare Italiana in Somalia e
organizzazione del Centro Studi e
Ricerche in collaborazione con l'Istituto
di Marchiafav di Roma. Communicazione al
5 Congresso Internaz. di Medicina Tropicale e
di Paludismo. (Istanbul).
50 pp.

GIUNTA,B.

L'anchilostomiasi nell'oltre Giuba e
suoi rapporti con la colonizzazione.
Tivoli 1934.
119 pp.

GUEDEL,J.

Incidences medico-sociales de la
consommation du kat en Côte Francaise
des Somalis. "Revue Pount". No. 2.
La Societe D'etudes de l'Afrique
Orientale. Djibouti Janvier 1967.

INTRONA,SOTIR.

L'alimentazione dei Somali.
"Africa". Nos. 3-4. Roma 1954.
98-101 pp.

LE BRAS,M.

Premiers apercus sur un fleau
social: le kat. "Revue Pount" No. 2.
La Societe D'etudes de l'Afrique
Orientale. Djibouti Janvier 1967.

LIPPARONI,E.

Note ed osservazioni sulle abitudini
alimentari dei Somali e rilievi circa
le ripercussioni sul loro stato di salute
dell'attuale sistema di alimentazione.
"Archivi Italiani di Scienze Mediche
Tropicali e di Parassitologi." Fasc. No. XI.
Roma 1950.

———————————

Osservazioni sulle epidemiologie della
febbre ricorrente in Somalia. "Archivi
Italiani di Scienze Mediche Tropicali e
di Parassitologia." Fasc. No. II. Roma 1951.
12 p.

———————————

Dermatiti da zecche e dermatiti da
sostanze vegetali. "Archivi Italiani
di Scienze Mediche Tropicali e di
Parassitologia." Fasc. No. VIII. Roma 1951.

———————————

Epidemiologia malarica e lotta
antimalarica nella Zona del Villagio
Duca degli Abruzzi. "Rivista di Malariologia"
Vol. XXX. No. 2. Roma 1951.

———————————

L'alimentazione dei Somali.
"Africa". Fasc. Nos. 9-10. Roma 1951.
287 p.

———————————

Possibilita e limiti della
lotta antimalarica in Somalia.
"Rivista di Malariologia."
Vol. XXX. Roma 1951.

———————————

Un decennio di attivita dell'ambulatorio
del Villagio Duca degli Abruzzi. "Archivi
Italiani di Scienze Mediche Tropicali e
di Parassitologia." Fasc. No. VIII. Roma 1953.
34 p.

———————————

Sul Nilodin nella terapia delle
Schistosomiasi Vescicale in Somalia.

"Archivi Italiani di Scienze Mediche
Tropicali e di Parassitologia."
Fasc. No. X. Roma 1953.
8 pp.

Sulla anchilostomiasi della zona del
medio Scebeli. Societa Medicina ed
Igiene Tropicale della Somalia.
Mogadiscio 1953.
9 pp.

Ulteriore contributo allo studio
dei problemi della alimentazione dei
Somali. Presidenza del Consiglio dei
Ministri A/I. Roma 1954.
61 pp.

Il Kwashiorkor nella zona del medio
Scebeli. "Archivi Italiani di Scienze
Mediche Tropicali e di Parassitologia."
Fasc. No. VIII. Roma 1954.
17 pp.

Rilievi sul nomadismo nelle sue
correlazioni nosografiche ed
epidemiologiche in Somalia. "Archivi
Italiani di Scienze Mediche Tropicali
e di Parassitologia." Fasc. No. III. Roma 1954.
20 pp.

Ricerche e identificazione dei molluschi
principali ospiti intermedi Schistosomiasi
Vescicale in Somalia nella zona del medio
Scebeli. Societa Medicina ed Igiene Tropicale
della Somalia. Mogadiscio 1955.
5 pp.

Il ruolo della Cordeauxia Edulis, della
Eleusine Coracana e della Manihot utilissima
nella alimentazione dei Somala. "Annali della
Societa di Medicina ed Igiene Tropicale della
Somalia." Vol. II Mogadiscio 1958.
201-210 pp.

Rilievi clinici e terapeutici nella
Cheilite ulcerosa (O.Bigio). "Annali
della Societa di Medicina ed Igiene
Tropicale della Somalia."
Vol. II. Mogadiscio 1958.
135-141 pp.

MAFFI,M.

Inchiesta sulla malaria, la bilarziosi e
la treponematosi nella zona del fiume
Giuba. Relazione AFIS. Divisione Sviluppo
Sociale. Mogadiscio 1956.

———————————

Somalia paese di gente sane.
"La Voce dell'Africa". No. 1.
Roma 1957.

———————————

Quarta fasa della campagna
antimalarica in Somalia.
(Statistical and Chronological
Analysis of the Work). Mogadiscio 1957.

———————————

Notizie piu o meno sanitarie
sul distretto di Lkgh Ferrandi.
"Annali della Societa Medicina ed
Igiene Tropicale della Somalia."
Vol. 2. Mogadiscio 1958.
143-178 pp.

———————————

La singolarita del problema schistosomiasi
in Somalia e loro importanza nell'esecuzione
di una azione di lotta. "Annali della Societa
Medicina ed Igiene Tropicale della Somalia."
Vol. 2. Mogadiscio 1958.
211-219 pp.

———————————

La valorizzazione della acque del fiume
Giuba ed il problema sanitaria della
bilharziosi (schistosomissi vescicale).
"Annali della Societa di Medicina ed Igiene
Tropicale della Somalia." Vol. 2. Mogadiscio 1958.
69-74 pp.

MAGLI, P.

Brevi notizie nosografiche sull'Oltregiuba.

Italiana. (zona di afmadu). "Archivio Italiano
di Scienze Mediche Coloniali." No. 1. Tripoli 1927.
29 p.

MAHAMUD,M.

La medicina empirica somala.
"Meridiano Somalo". Mogadiscio
Gennaio 1952.

MAJMONE,B. AND TIBERIO,M.

Ricerche sulla composizione chimica, sulla
digeribilita e sul valore nutritivo di alcuni
cascami della coltivazione dei banani
(Musa Sapientum, L. Musa Cavendish, Lamb).
"Sperimentazione Agraria." Nuova Serie.
Vol. V. 1952.
133 p.

MATTEI,A.

Fauna anafeligena e malaria
nel medio Uebi Scebeli. Tipogr.
Operaia Romana. Roma 1929.
28 pp.

_____

Fauna anafeligena e malaria
nel medio Uebi Scebeli. "Annali
di Medicina Navale e Coloniali." 1932.

_____

La febbre ricorrente nella Somalia
Italiana. Tipogr. Operaia Romana.
Roma 1933.
27 pp.

MENONA,G.

Nosografia di Brava. "Giornale
Ital. Mal. Esot. Trop. e Igien. Colon."
No. 3. Vol. 65. 1930.

_____

Malaria Somala: risultati di
accertamenti microscopici.
"Giornale Ital. Mal. Esot. Trop.
e Igien. Colon." 1936.

MIRRA,G.

Notizie sull'igiene e sulla patologia
della Somalia Italiana, Meridionale.

"Giornale Ital. Mal. Esot. Trop. e
Igien. Colon". No. 6. Vol. 160. 1930.

MOISE,R.

Osservazioni sulle elmintiasi di interese
epidermologico in Somalia. "Annali Medicina
Navale e Coloniale". Anno XLIV. No. IX-X. 1938.

Politico medico-sociale nei paesi ad
evoluzione iniziali riflessi e pregiudizi
per l'organizzazione in Somalia. Istituto
Malariologia. Mogadiscio 1952.
21 pp.

Ancora sulle elmintiasi di interese
epidermiologico in Somalia.
(Anchilostomiasi ed Schistosomiasi) e sulla
adozione dei sistemi per combatterle.
"Annali di Medicina Navale Tropicale." 1952.

Il problema della malaria in Somalia e
l'importanza di una campagna di lotta.
1952.

L'incidenza della infezione da
"Plasmodium malaria" nel endemia malarica
della Somalia: inchiesta e studio
epidermiologico. Istituto Malariologia.
Mogadiscio 1953.

Attivita scientifica e pratica di
patologia e igiene tropicale del Centro
Studi e Ricerche della Marina Militare a
Mogadiscio: come premessa e contributo si
nuovi indirizzi della Sanita in Somalia.
"Minerva Medica". No. 94. 1954.
12 p.

Affezioni tropicali cosmopolite in Somalia:
illustrazione dell'attivita dell'ospedale
Antonio Cecchi Villagio Duca degli Abruzzi.
Societa Sanita Marittima di Livorno.
Livorno 1955.
47 pp.

MORETTI,I.

Valori normali della razza somala:
il calcio ematico. "Rivista di Medicina
Tropicale". Nos. 4-5. Roma 1940.
142-147 pp.

MUCCIARELLI,C.

Alcune note mediche sul Benadir.
"Bollettino Societa Geografica Italiana."
Roma 1908.
348 p.

POLIDORI,T.

I micetomi della Somalia. "Archivio
Italiano di Scienze Mediche Coloniali".
Tripoli 1936.
19 p.

POLL,M.

Contributo a letude des poissons deau
de Somalie appartenant aux genres Gobius
et Barbopsis." Bollettino dei Musei e degli
Istituti Biologici di Genova." Vol. XXI.
No. 113. Genova 1961.
59 pp.

RITUCCI-CHINNI,A.

Relazione sanitaria annuale 1916.
Tipogr. Governo. Mogadiscio 1916.
54 pp.

_____AND PIVETTI,F.

Note sull'epidemia di peste bubbonica
verificatasi in Mogadiscio nella seconda
meta 1913 e piu specialmente sul funzionamento
del Lazzaretto. Tipogr. del Governo. Mogadiscio 1916.
17 pp.

RIZZETTO,F.

Ii lebbrosario di Alessandria compie 30 anni
di vita. "Somalia d'Oggi." No. 2. Mogadiscio
Giugno 1957.
9-10 pp.

RUBERTI-FIERA,E.

La framboeisa in Somalia. Tipografia
Operaia Romana. Roma 1928.
12 pp.

RUSSO,P.

Contributo allo studio del bacino della
donna Somala. "Annali della Societa di
Medicina ed Igiene Tropicale della Somalia."
Vol. I. Mogadiscio 1953.
107-111 pp.

SCARPA,G.

Un servizio di ortopedia traumatologica in
Somalia. "Annali della Societa di Medicina ed
Igiene Tropicale della Somalia." Vol. I.
Mogadiscio 1958.
75 pp.

SERVIDORI,G.

Brevi notizie nosografiche sulla
Somalia (zona di Serenle). "Archivio
Italiano di Scienze Mediche Coloniali."
No. 10. Tripoli 1928.
625 p.

SESSA,V.

L'epatite epidemica fra le truppe nazionali
del Corpo di Sicurezza della Somalia. "Annali
della Societa di Medicina ed Igiene Tropicale
della Somalia." Vol. I. Mogadiscio 1953.
121-128 pp.

SOBRERO,L.

La rabbia del gatto in Somalia. "Notiziario
Sanitaria della Somalia." Vol. I. Fasc. No. 2.
Mogadiscio Settembre - Ottobre 1962.
55-58 pp.

_____

Dati e aspetti dei rapporti tra Malacofauna
e patologia umana ed animale nella zona del
basso Uebi Scebeli. "Notiziario Sanitaria della
Somalia." Vol. I. Fasc. No. 3. Mogadiscio 1963.
37-39 pp.

SOCIETA DI MEDICINA ED IGIENE TROPICALE DELLA SOMALIA.

Annali. Vol. I. (Anno 1953) Stamperia AFIS.
Mogadiscio 1953.
212 pp.

SOMALI REPUBLIC.

Establishment of facilities for education
and training in Somalia of the technical

categories of health project. Ministry of
Health and Labour. Mogadiscio.

_____

The integral dynamic of Health in Somalia and
its projections on Development: The long-term
Health Plan for the Somali Republic. Ministry of
Health and Labour. Mogadiscio April 1965.

SPOTO,F.

Il tracoma ed altre malattie
oftalmiche nella Somalia Italiana.
"Rassegna Italiana di Oftalmologia."
Nos. 9-10. 1939.
588-611 pp.

TALAMONTIL.

La febbre bilioso-emoglobinurica in
Somalia. Societa Medicina Coloniale.
1931.

TEDESCHI,G.

Miceti nuovi nei quadri della nosografia
somala. "Rinnovamento Medico". No. 7.
Napoli 1933.

_____AND TORTORANO,L.

Nosografia di Bulo Burti e di El Bur.
"Archivio Italiano di Scienze Mediche
Coloniale." No. 2. Tripoli 1934.
86 p.

_____AND SCALAIS.

Contributo alla biogeografia della malaria
a Bur Hacaba (Benadir). "Rivista di
Malariologia." Roma 1934.

TESTI,F.

Note su di un ofidio velenoso e su
di un colubride proteroglifo. "Archivio
Italiano di Scienze Mediche Coloniali "
Fasc. No. XI. Tripoli 1934.
81 p.

TONELLI,I.

Focolai endemo epidemici di lebbra in
Somalia. Atti del Congresso Internazionale
per la Difesa e Riabilitazione. Societa del

Lebbroso. Roma 1956.

VAGLIO,B.

Su un pemfigo epidemico osservato in
Migiurtinia e Mudugh. "Annali della Societa
di Medicina ed Igiene Tropicale della Somalia."
Vol. 2. Mogaidscio 1958.
91-97 pp.

VENERONI,C.

Nosografia medica della Somalia
Italiana. Bruni Marelli.
Pavia 1928.

VEZZOSO,V.

Servizio sanitario civile nella
Somalia Italiana. "Rinnovamento
Medico." Napoli 1936.
31 pp.

WILSON,D.B. AND NOTLEY,F.B.

Malaria in Southern Somaliland.
"East African Medical Journal."
Nairobi 1943.

WORLD HEALTH ORGANIZATION.

Bilharziasis Survey in British
Somaliland, Eritrea, Ethiopia Somalia
the Sudan and Yemen (Report by Ayad).
"Bulletin of the World Health Organization."
Vol. 14. Geneva 1956.

———————————

Tuberculosis Survey in the
Somalilands. WHO Tuberculosis
Research Office. Copenhagen
December 1956.
36 pp. charts. tables. maps.

ZAVATTARI,E.

Il lebbrosario di Gelib sul
Giuba. "L'Italia d'Oltremare."
No. 3. Roma 1928.
72 p.

———————————

Malacofauna e schistosomiasi nel
medio e basso Giuba. "Rivista di
Parassitologia." No. 4. Vol. XVII. 1956.

ZECHINI,M.

La leishmaniosi interna nella
Somalia. "Rivista di Medicina
Tropicale." No. 1. Roma 1940.
8-18 pp.

ZURETTI,S.

L'alimentazione dei Somali.
"Annali della Societa di
Medicina ed Igiene Tropicale della
Somalia." Vol. I. Mogadiscio 1953.
153-172 pp.

IX

HISTORY AND ANTIQUITY

BERNARDELLI,G.

Uno scavo compiuto nella zona archeologica
di Hamar Gergeb nel territorio di Meregh
durante l'agosto 1932. "Somalia d'Oggi".
No. 1. Mogadiscio 1957.
28 p.

BLANC,A.C. AND TAVANI,G.

Contributo alla conoscenza della preistoria
della Somalia e dell'Ogaden. "Atti della
Societa Toscana di Scienze Naturali". Vol. XLVII.
Pisa 1938-39.
133 p.

BROWN,C.B. AND BURKITT,M.C.

Stone Implements from British Somaliland.
"Man". Vol. XXXI. London 1931.
156-9 pp.

BURKITT,M.C. AND GLOVER,P.E.

Prehistoric Investigations in British Somaliland.
"Proceedings of the Prehistoric Society". London 1946.

CANIGLIA,G.

Note storiche sulla citta di Mogadiscio.
"Rivista Coloniale". Roma 1917.

CERULLI,E.

Di alcune monete raccolte sulla costa Somala.
"Rivista degli Studi Orientali". Roma 1924.
281-2 pp.

Le popolazioni della Somalia nella
tradizione storica locale. "Rendiconto
Reale Accademia dei Lincei". Vol. II. Ser. No. 6.
Roma 1926.
150-72 pp.

_____

Iscrizioni e documenti arabi per la storia
della Somalia. "Rivista degli Studi Orientali".
Vol. XI. Roma 1926.
1-24 pp.

_____

Nuovi documenti arabi per la storia della
Somalia: "Rendiconto Reale Accademia dei Lincei".
Vol. II. Ser. No. 6. Roma 1927.
392-410 pp.

_____

La Somalia nelle cronache etiopiche.
"Annali Africa Italiana". Vol. II. No. 4.
Roma 1929.
262-65 pp.

_____

Tradizioni storiche e monumenti della
Migiurtinia. "Annali Africa Italiana".
Vol. IV. Roma 1931.
153-169 pp.

_____

Vestigia di antiche civilta in Eritrea e
in Somalia. "L'Africa Orientale" Roma 1933.

_____

Noterelle somale ed al-Dimasqi ed Ibn'Arabi.
"Orientalia". No. 4. Roma 1935.
335-43 pp.

_____

La cittadina di Merca e tre sue iscrizioni
arabe. "Oriente Moderno". Anno XXIII.
No. 1. 1943.
20-28 pp.

_____

Tradizioni storiche e ricerche idriche in
Somalia. "Rassegna Sociale Africana Italiana".
Anno VI. No. 5-6. Napoli 1943.

20-28 pp.

Somalia: scritti vari editi ed inediti. Stamperia
AFIS. Roma 1957.
363 pp. ills.

Somalia (Vol. I) Storia della Somalia,
l'islam in Somalia, il libro degli Zenghi.
AFIS. Roma 1959.

CLARK,J.D.

The prehistoric cultures of the Horn of Africa:
an analysis of the stone age cultural and climatic
succession in the Somalilands and Eastern Parts of
Abyssinia. Cambridge University Press. London 1954.
374 pp. + (distribution map of prehistoric sites in
the Horn of Africa)

CURLE,A.T.

The ruined towns of Somaliland. "Antiquity".
Vol. XI. Gloucester 1937.
315-327 pp.

DE CHARDIN,T.,BREUIL AND WERNER,P.

Les Industries Lithiques de Somali
Francaise. "L'Anthropologie". Vol. XLIX.
Paris 1940.
497-522 pp.

DE MORGAN, J.

Notes d'Archaeologi Prehistorique:
(IV) Sur l'industrie de la pierrr au
Pays des comalis. "L'Anthropologie".
Vol. XXXI. Paris 1921.

EMMEPI.

Il Sultanato di Lugh nei ricordi di
V. Bottego. "Somalia d'Oggi". No. 2.
Mogadiscio 1956.
46 p.

EVANS,J.

On some paleolithic implements found in
Somaliland. "Proceedings of the Royal Society".
London 1896.

FEARON,D.

Notes on the history of Berbera.
"Somaliland Journal". No. 1. Somaliland
Society. Hargeisa 1954.
11-20 pp.

GASPARRO,A.

La Somalia Italiana nell'antichita classica.
Palermo 1910.

GAZZINI,M.

Origine e storia di Mogadiscio.
R. Montagna. Roma 1950.

GIGLIO,C.

Origine dei protettorati di Obbia
e della Migiurtinia. (Studi in onore di E. Rota).
Bari 1954.

GIOVANNI,C.

Da Harro Ualabo all'Uabi,monoliti
e tombe. "Rassegna Studi Etiopici".
Roma 1945.
131 pp.

GIRACE,A. AND PIRONE,M.

Lineamenti di una storia della Somalia,
(per le scuole secondarie). Mogadiscio 1954.
60 pp.

GLASER,E.

Die Goldlander Punt und Sasu im
Somalilande Das Ausland. Vol. XXVII-XXIX.
521-528-660 pp.

(R) GOVERNO DELLA SOMALIA.

Museo della Garesa: Catalogo.
Regia Stamperia della Colonia.
Mogadiscio MCMXXXIV-XIII.
177 pp. ills. maps.

GRAZIOSI,P.

L'eta della pietra in Somalia.
Sansoni, Firenze 1940.
89 pp. maps.

JOUVE,J.

Le musee de Djibouti. "Revue Pount".
No. 1. La Societe D'etudes de l'Afrique
Orientale. Djibokti Octobre 1966.

LEWIS,I.M.

The Somali Conquest on the Horn of
Africa. "Journal of African History".
No. 2. London 1960.
213-230 pp.

The modern history of Somaliland:
from Nation to State. (Asia-Africa Series of Modern History).
Weidenfeld and Nicolson. London 1965.
XI, + 234 pp. ills. maps.

Historical problems in Ethiopia and
the Horn of Africa. "Annals of the New
York Academy of Sciences". New York.

MAFFI, M.

Somalia e Benadir di 5000 anni fa.
"Lettura". 1908.
114-120 pp.

MATHEW,G.

The archaeological situation in East Africa (Somalia).
"Antiquity". Gloucester 1953.

MESSANA,G.

Funzionalismo architettonico degli antichi
costruttori mogadisciani. "Somalia d'Oggi".
No. 2. Mogadiscio 1956.
10 p.

Note sull'architettura mogadisciana.
"Somalia d'Oggi". No. 1. Mogadiscio 1956.
26. p.

Architettura monumentale mercana.
"Somalia d'Oggi". Mogadiscio 1957.

26 p.

_____

Le moschee di Chisimaio. "Somalia d'Oggi".
No. 4. Mogadiscio 1957.
19 p.

_____

Nella vecchia Brava. "Somalia d'Oggi". No. 3.
Mogadiscio 1957.
12 p.

MINISTERO DELLA GUERRA.

Somalia dalle origini al 1914.
Regionale. Roma 1938.
340 pp.

_____

Somalia. Vol. II (dal 1941 al 1934)
Stato Maggiore. Ufficio Storico.
Regionale. Roma 1960.
568 pp.

MOHAMED, JAMA (HABASHI).

An Introduction to Somali History
from 5000 years B. C. down to the present time.
Mogadiscio 1961.
62 pp.

_____

A History of the Somal. Mogadiscio
24th February 1963.
107 pp.

_____

A History of the Somal. 2nd edition.
Mogadiscio 1964.
139 pp.

NOMAD.

Forgotten pages: The Mad Mullah of
Somaliland. "U.E.". Vol. XVI. 1925.
76-80-137-42 pp.

PARKINSON,J.

An unsolved riddle of Africa mysterious
ruins in Somaliland. "Illustrated London News".
No. 26. London 1935.

PIRONE,M.

Leggende e tradizioni storiche dei Somali
Ogaden. "Archivio per l'Antropologia e la
Etnologia".   Vol. LXXXIV. 1954.
119-128 pp.

Appunti di storia della Somalia.
Istituto Universitario della Somalia.
Mogadiscio 1960.
78 pp.

Appunti di storia dell'Africa (II Somalia).
Anno di Studi 1960-61. Istituto Universitario
della Somalia. Facolta di Magistero. Edizioni "Ricerche". Roma.
158 pp. bibl.

REYNOLDS,B.

Somalia Museum development February 1966
to March 1966. (WS/o566.24.CLT). UNESCO.
Paris 1966.
54 pp.

ROBECCHI-BRICCHETTI,L.

Tradizioni storiche dei somali migiurtini
raccolte in Obbia. Tipografia Ministero AA.EE.
Roma 1891.
23 pp.

SETON-KARR,H.

Discovery of the evidence of the Palaeolithic
Stone Implements in Somaliland. "Journal of
the Royal Anthropological Institute". Vol. XXV.
London 1896.
271 p.

Further discovery of ancient stone implements
in Somaliland. "Journal of the Royal Anthropological
Institute". Vol. XXVII. London 1898.
93-95 pp.

Prehistoric implements from Somaliland.
"Man". London 1909.
182-3 pp.

SOMALI REPUBLIC.

Annual report for the years 1966-67-68.
National Museum of Somalia. Mogadiscio.
19 pp. tables. ills.

UZEL,B.

La fondation de Djibouti. "Revue de l'Histoire
des Colonie". No. 137.
64-75 pp.

ZAGHI,C.

Il Sultano di Zanzibar e le origini della
Somalia Italiana. "Rivista delle Colonie".
Roma 1938.

X
LANGUAGE AND LITERATURE

1.   Language and Literature

ABDULLAHI, M.F.

The best stories from the land of
Punt (Somalia). Mogadiscio 1970.

ABRAHAM, R.C. AND WARSAMA, SOLOMON.

The Principles of Somali. (2nd edition).
London 1951.
481 pp.

Somali---English Dictionary. University of
London Press. London 1966.
(2nd edition).
XVIII, 332 pp.

AHMED SHIRRE JAAMA'.

Gabayo, Maahmaah iyo Sheekooyin Yaryar.
(Poems, Proverbs and Short Stories).
The National Printers Ltd.
Mogadishu May 1965.
63 pp.

Iftinka-Agoonta (light of education). No. 1.
The National Printers Ltd.
Mogadishu November 10, 1966.

Iftinka-Agoonta (light of education). No. 2.
The National Printers Ltd.
Mogadishu November 30th, 1966.
16 pp.

Iftinka-Aqoonta (light of education). No. 3.
The National Printers Ltd. Mogadishu December 25, 1966.

_____

Iftinka-Aqoonta (light of education). No. 4.
The National Printers Ltd. Mogadishu January 25, 1967.
19 pp.

_____

Iftinka-Aqoonta (light of education). No. 5.
The National Printers Ltd. Mogadishu February 25, 1967.
11 pp.

_____AND KOZOLL, CHARLES.

An Elementary Somali Phrase Drill Book.
Mogadishu 1964.
131 pp.

_____

An Elementary Somali Drill Book.
Teachers College. Columbia University.
New York 1966.
160 pp.

ANDRZEJEWSKI,B.W.

Some Problems of Somali Orthography.
"The Somaliland Journal". Hargeisa 1954.
34-37 pp.

_____

Is Somali a Tone-Language? "Proceedings of
the Twenty-Third International Congress of
Orientalists". Royal Asiatic Society. Cambridge 1954.
367-8 pp.

_____

The Problem of Vowel Representation in the Isaaq
Dialect of the Somali. "Bulletin of the School of
Oriental and African Studies". Vol. XVII.No. 3.
University of London. London 1955.
567-80 pp.

_____

Accentual Patterns in Verbal Forms in
the Isaaq Dialect of Somali. "Bulletin
of the School of Oriental and African Studies".
Vol. XVII. No. 1. University of London. London 1956.
103-29 pp.

_____

Pronominal and Prepositional Particles in
Northern Somali. "African Language Studies".
Vol. 1. London 1960.
96-108 pp.

Notes on the Substantive Pronouns in Somali.
"African Language Studies". Vol. II. London 1961.
80-99 pp.

Speech and Writing Dichotomy as the Pattern of
Multilingualism in the Somali Republic: Report
of the C.C.T.A./C.S.A., "Symposium on Multilingualism in Africa." Brazzaville (Congo) 1962.

Poetry in Somali Society. Vol. 1. "New
Society". No. 125. London 1963.
22-4 pp.

A Somali Poetic Combat. Vol. II. Part I.
"Journal of African Languages". London 1963
15-28 pp.

A Somali Poetic Combat. Vol. II. Part II.
"Journal of African Languages". London.
93-100 pp.

A Somali Poetic Combat. Vol. II. Part III.
"Journal of African Languages". London.
190-205 pp.

_____and GALAAL,MUSSA H.I.

A Somali Poetic Combat.
Michigan State University.
205 pp.

Somali Stories (Selections from African Prose)
Traditional Oral Texts (I). Oxford Library of
African Literature. Oxford-Clarendon Press.
London 1964.
134-163 pp.

The Declensions of Somali Nouns.
School of Oriental and African Studies.
University of London. London 1964.
149 pp.

_____AND LEWIS,I.M.

Somali Poetry: An Introduction.
Clarendon Press. Oxford 1964.
167 ppp.

_____AND GALAAL,MUSSA H.I.

The Art of the Verbal Message in Somali Society.
"Neue Afrikanische Studien". Hamburger Beitrage
zur Afrika-Kunde. Bd V. Deutsches Institut fur
Afrika Forschung. Hamburg 1966.
29-39 pp.

ARMSTRONG,L.B.

The phonetic structure of the Somali.
"Mitteilungen des Seminars fur orientalische
zu Berlin". Abteilungen III. Berlin 1934.
116-61 pp.

_____

The phonetic structure of the Somali.
Gregg Press Ic. Ridgewood,New Jersey
(U.S.A.) 1964.
46 pp.

_____

The phonetic structure of the Somali.
Gregg Press. London 1964.

ARTAN,A.

Somali-Folklore (dance,music,song).
The National Theatre. Mogadishu 1971.
47 pp.

BARRY,E.

An Elementary Somali Grammar.
Tipografia Raimondi. Asmara 1937.
106 pp.

BELL,C.R.V.

The Somali Language. Longmans, Green & Co.
London 1953.
185 pp.

BERGHOLD,K.

Somali-Studien. "Zeitschrift fur Afrikanischen
und Ozeanische Sprachen. Berlin 1897.
116-61 pp.

Somali-Studien. "Zeitschrift fur die
Kunde des Morgenlandes". Vienna 1899.
123-98 pp.

BERTIN,F.

Noms et fractionnements chez les populations
de langue somalie. "Revue Pount". No. 4
La Societe D'etudes de l'Afrique Orientale.
Djibouti 1968.

BONANNI,C.

Boscaglia (Disegni di Giovanni Novaresio).
Stamperia del Governo. Mogadiscio 1957.
109 pp. ills.

Taccuino Somalo (prosa e possia tradizionale Somala).
Edizioni Scientifiche Italiane. Napoli 1960.

Poesia Somala. "Africa". No. 5. Roma 1960.
229-230 pp.

CARCOFORO,E.

Elementi di Somalo e di Ki-Suahili parlati al
Benadir. Hoepli. Milano 1912.
154 pp.

CERULLI,E.

Canti e proverbi Somali nel dialetto degli
Habar Auwal. "Rivista degli Studi Orientali".
Vol. XVII. Roma 1918.
797-836 pp.

Di alcune presunte consonanti nei
dialetti somali. "Rivista degli Studi
Orientali." Vol. XVIII. Roma 1918.
877-83 pp.

Testi Somali. "Rivista degli Studi Orientali."
Vol. VIII. Roma 1919.

Somali Songs and Little Texts.
"Journal of the African Society".
Part I. Vol. XIX. Part II. Vol. XX. Part III.
Vol. XXI. London 1919-21

Nota sui dialetti somali. "Rivista degli
Studi Orientali". Vol. VIII. Fasc. No. 4. Roma 1921.
693-9 pp.

Ii gergo delle genti di bassa casta della Somalia.
"Zeitschrift Meinhof". Amburgo 1927.
99-110 pp.

Per la Toponomastica della Somalia.
"Oriente Moderno". Vol. XI. Roma 1931.
460-7 pp..

Tentativo indigeno di formare un
alfabeto somao. "Oriente Moderno."
Vol. XII. Roma Dicembre 1932.
212-13 pp.

Qualques notes sur la phonologie Somali.
"Comptes Rendus du Groupe Linguistique
d'Etudes Chamito-Semitques". Vol. IV.
Ecole Pratique des Hautes Ecoles a la Sorbonne.
Paris 1947.
53-57 pp.

CHEDEVILLE,E.

La transcription des noms propres locaux
et sa realisation en Côte Francaise des
Somalis. "Revue Pount". No. 1. La Societe
D'etudes de l'Afrique Orientale. Djibouti Octobre 1966.

CHIARINI,G.

Raccolta di vocabulario dei Somali-Isa.
"Memoria Societa Geografica Italiana. No. 1
Roma 1897.
209-15 pp.

La transcription des noms propres locaux
et sa realisation en Côte Francaise des
Somalis. "Revue Pount". No. 1. La Societe
D'etudes de l'Afrique Orientale. Djibouti Octobre 1966.

CHIARINI,G.

Raccolta di vocabulario dei Somali Isa.
"Memoria Societa Geografica Italiana. No. 1.
Roma 1897.
209 15 pp.

CONTINI,J.

The Illiterate Poets of Somalia.
"The Reporter". Vol. XXVIII. No. 6.
New York March 14, 1963.
36-38 pp.

COSTAGUTI, M.A.

Manuale pratico di lingua somalo ad uso dei
viaggiatori nella valle di Giuba. Casa Editrice
Italiana. Roma 1909.
136 pp.

CUST,R.N.

Language of the Somali land.
Royal Asiatic Society. Bombay 1898.
95-100 pp.

CZERMAK,W.

Zur Phonetik des Somalis. "Zeitschrift fur
die Kunde des Morgenlandes". Vol. XXXI.
Vienna 1924.
82-102 pp.

Somali Texte in Dialekt der Habr-Ja'lo.
"Zeitschrift fur die Kunde des Morgenlandes.
Vol. XXXI, Vienna 1924.
113-136 pp.

Zum Gebrauch des Infinitives als 'Futurm'
in Somali. "Donum Natalicium Schrijnen".
Nijmegen Ultrecht. 1929.
182-9 pp.

DE LARAJASSE,E.

Somali-English and English-Somali Dictionary.
Kegan Paul, Trench, Trubner & Co. London 1897.
301 pp.

_____AND DE SAMPONT,C.F.

Practical grammar of the Somali language with a manual of
sentences. Kegan Paul, Trench. Trubner & Co. London 1897.
XII, 265 pp.

DE SAMPONT,C.F.

Grammaire somalie. Missione Catholique.
London. Berbera. 1905.

_____

Grammaire abregee de la langue somalie
avec exercices et conversations. R. Accademia
dei Lincei. Toma 1920.
237 pp.

DUCHENET, E.

Histories Somalis la malice des primitifs.
(Preface de Pierre Mille). Larose. Paris 1936.
VIII, 186 pp.

_____

Le chant dans le folklore Somali. "Revue du
Folklore Francais". Vol. IX. No. 2. Paris Avril-Juin 1938.
72-87 pp.

DRYSDALE, JOHN

Notes on the Somali Language for Beginners.
The Stationery Office. Hargeise 1953.
67 pp.

_____

Somali Primer, Part I. The Stationery Office.
Hargeisa 1959.
40 pp.

FERRAND,G.

Notes de Grammaire Comalie. P. Fontane et Cie.
Alger 1886.
28 pp..

FERRARIO,B.

Note di fonologia somala. "Rivista
degli Studi Orientali". Vol. XII. No. 1.
Roma 1916-18.
199-217 pp.

_____

L'accento in Somalo. "Rivista
degli Studi Orientali". Vol. XI.
Roma 1914-1915.
961-7 pp.

GALAAL,M.H.I.

Arabic Script for Somali. "Tke Islamic
Quarterly". Vol. I. No. 1. Islamic Cultural
Centre. London 1954.
114-118 pp.

_____AND ANDRZEJEWSKI,B.W.

Hikmad Soomaali. School of Oriental and
African Studies. University of London.
Oxford University Press. 1956.
150 pp.

GAL DURKA (ELIA E)

La fronda: poesie della Somalia.
Stamperia della Colonia. Mogadiscio 1929.
50 pp.

GIOVANNI, M. (DA PALERMO)

Grammatica della lingua Somala.
(Prefazione di Luigi Salol.) Tipografia
Francescana. Missione Cattolica. Asmara (Etiopia) 1914.
357 pp.

_____

Dizionario Somalo-Italiano e Italiano-Somalo.
Tipografia Francescana. Missione Cattolica. Asmara
(Etiopia). 1915.
209 pp.

HENRY,L.

Essai de Vocabularie pratique francais--
Issa (Somalis) avec prononciation figuree.
Melun 1897.

HETZRON,R.

The particle 'ba' in Northern Somali.
"Journal of African Languages". Vol. IV.
Part 2. London 1965.
118-130 pp.

HUNTER,F.M.

A grammar of the Somali language with an
English-Somali,Somali-English vocabulary.
Byculla Press. Bombay 1880.
_____

A grammar of the Somali language, together
with a short storical notice. Educational
Society's Press. Bombak 1880.

JAHN,A.

Somali Texte: gesammelt und ubersetz.
Sitzungsberichte Bd CLII. Akademie der
Wissenschaften. Alfred Holder. Vienna 1906.
136 pp.

KENADID,Y.O.

La funzione sociale del linguaggio.
"Somalia d'Oggi." No. 1. Mogadiscio 1956.
28 p.

KEWELOH,W.

Somaliade: Poesie aus dem Lande der Punt.
(Im Auftrage der Deutsch-Somalischen Gesselschaft e.V).
Verlag Az Studio. Bonn 1971.
78 pp. ills.

KING, J.S.

Somali as a Written Language.
"The Indian Antiquity" Bombay August - December 1887.
Part I: 242-3 pp.
Part II: 285-7 pp.

KIRK,J.W.C.

Notes on the Somali language with examples of
phrases and conversational sentences. London 1903.

––––––––––––

The Yibirs and Midgans of Somaliland, their
Traditions and Dialects. "Journal of African
Society". Vol. IV. London 1904.
91-108 pp.

––––––––––––

A Grammar of the Somali language with examples
in prose and verses and an account of the Yibir
and Midgan dialects. Cambridge University Press. 1905.
216 pp. + 16 correction sheets.

KLINGENHEBEN,A.

Ist das Somali eine Ton-Sprache.
"Zeitschrift fur Phonetik". Heft 5/6.
Berlin 1949.
289-303 pp.

LANG,C.

Repetition, Reduplication und Lautmalerei
in der Somali-Sprache. "Biblioteca Africana".
No. 1-2. 1925.
98-104 pp.

LAURENCE,M. (EDITOR)

A tree for poverty; Somali poetry and
prose. (Published for the Somaliland Protectorate).
Eagle Press. Nairobi 1954.
146 pp.

LEWIS,I.M.

The Gadabuursi Somali Script. "Bulletin of the
School of Oriental and African Studies." Vol. XXI.
No. 1. University of London. London 1957.
134-56 pp.

LIGHT,R.H.

English-Somali Sentences and Idioms for the
use of Sportsmen and Visitors in Somaliland.
Thacker. Bombay 1896.

MARIO,M.

L'alfabeto 'Osmania' in Somalia. "Rivista
degli Studi Orientali". Vol. X. Roma 1951.
108-21 pp.

_____

I Somali e la loro lingua. "Africa".
No. 2. Febbraio 1952.
49-50 pp.

_____

La Lingua Somalo strumento d'insegnamento
professionale. Tipofrafia Ferrari, Ocella & Co.
Alessandria (Italia) 1953.
108 pp. Bilb. ills.

_____

Terminologia medica e sue voci nella lingua somala.
Tipografia Ferrari Ocella & Co. Alessandria (Italia) 1953.
358 pp.

_____

Breve storia della lingua somala.
"Somalia d'Oggi". Mogadiscio Giugno 1957.

MINOZZI,M.T., AND TURRIN,C.P.

Dizionario Italiano-Somalo. Edizione
Grafiche A. Carcano. Milano 23 Dicembre 1961.
178 pp.

MOHAMUD,A.H. AND PANZO,B.

Afkayaga Hooyo (our mother tongue).
Edizioni Arte e Cultura. Stamperia Missione.
Mogadiscio 1960.
113 pp.

MORENO,M.M.

Nozioni di grammatica Somala. Scuola Orientale.
Universita degli Studi di Roma. Roma 1951.
141 pp.

———————

Grammatica della lingua somala. Ministero
dell'Africa Italiana. Roma 1951.

———————

Brevi nozioni di Giddu. "Rassegna
Studi Etiopici". Vol. V. No. 10.
Roma Gennaio-Dicembre 1951.
99-107 pp.

———————

La modernisation et l'unification des langues
en Somalie. "Civilisation". Vol. X. No. 1.
Bruxelles 1952.
61-66 pp.

———————

Il dialetto degli Asraf di Mogadiscio. "Rassegna
Studi Etiopici". No. 12. Roma 1953.
107-39 pp.

———————

Ii somalo della Somalia; grammatica
e testi del Benadir, Darod e Dighil.
Istituto Poligrafico dello Stato. Roma 1955.
404 pp.

———————

Il dialetto degli Asaf di Mogadiscio.
Tipografia Pio X. Roma 1955.
19 pp.

———————

Il dialetto degli Asraf di Mogadiscio.
"Rassegna Studi Etiopici". Vol. XIV.
Roma 1955-58.
108-150 pp.

NUH,O.A.

Some general notes on Somali folklore.
Mogadiscio 1970.
48 pp.

ORANO, M.

Manuale della lingua somala. U. Hoepli.
Milano 1931.

_____

Elementi per le studio della lingua somala.
U. Hoepli. Milano 1931.

_____

La lingua Somala (parlata nella Somalia
Settentrionale, nell'Ogaden e nel Benadir).
Casa Editrice Mediterranea. Roma 1936.
182 pp.

OSMAN,B.

To Be or Not to Be: The Somali Language.
"Dalka". Vol. 1. No. 12. Mogadishu June 1st, 1966.
8-9 pp.

PACE,A.

Note e discussioni sulla lingua somala.
"Somalia d'Oggi". Vol. II. No. 1. Mogadiscio
Gennaio-Febbraio 1957.
14-15 pp.

PANZO,B.

Canti Somali. "Somalia d'Oggi".
Vol. 1-2. Mogadiscio 15 Dicembre 1956.

PRESENTI,G.

Canti e ritmi arabici, somalici e Suahili.
"Bollettino della Reale Societa Geografia Italiana".
Vol. XLIX. Roma 1910.

_____

Di alcuni canti arabici e Somalici.
"Bollettino della Reale Societa Geografica Italiana".
Vol. XLIX. Roma 1912.
58-64 pp.

_____

Canti sacri e profani, danze e ritmi degli
Arabi,dei Somali e dei Suahili. "L'Eroica".
Milano 1929.

PIA,J.J.

Language in Somalia. "Newsletter of the
Center for Applied Linguistics". Vol. VIII.
No. 3. Washington, D. C. June 1966.
1-2 pp.

_____AND OTHERS.

Begining in Somali. (Drillbook). Office
of Education. U.S. Department of Health,
Education and Welfare. Washington, D. C. 1964.
210 pp.

PRAETORIUS,F.

Uber die Somali-sprache.
"Zeitschrift Deutch Morgenland Ges".
Vol. XXIV. 1870.
145 pp.

REINISCH,L.

Der Dschabartidialekt der Somali-Sprache.
"Sitzungsberichte, Akademie der Wissenschaften".
Vol. CXLVIII. Vienna 1848.

_____

Die Somali Sprache (Bd I Texte).
"Kaiserlische Akademie der Wissenschaften."
Subdarabische Expedition. Alfred Holder. Vienna 1901.
287 pp.

_____

Die Somali Sprache (Bd II, Worter buch)
Somali-Deutch-Deutch-Somali. "Kaiserlische
Akademie der Wissenschaften". Alfred Holder. Vienna 1902.
540 pp.

_____

Die Somali Sprache (Bd III, Grammatik).
"Kaiserlische Akademie der Wissenschaften.
Alfred Holder. Vienna 1903.
126 pp.

_____

Der Dschabartidialekt der Somali-Sprache.
"Sitzungsberichte Kaiserlische Akademie
der Wissenschaften". Alfred Holder. Vienna 1904.

REPUBBLICA SOMALA.

Progetto per la difesa della letteratura
orale e delle traduzioni culturali somale.
Ministero della Pubblica Istruzione. Mogadiscio
28 pp.

———————————

Il problema della linguq Somala.
"Somaliya: Antologia Storico-Culturale".
No. 7-8. Dipartimento Culturale. Ministero
della Pubblica Istruzione. Mogadiscio Giugno 1969.
266 pp.

RICCI,L.

Corrispondenza epistolare in Osmania. "Rassegna
Studi Etiopici". Vol. XIV. Roma 1959.
108-150 pp.

RIGBY,C.P.

On the Somali language. "Transactions of
the Bombay Geographical Society". Vol. IX.
Bombay 1849.

ROBECCHI-BRICCHETTI,L.

La grammatica somala del Ferrandi
Estratto dal "Bollettino Societa Geografica Italinana".
Roma 1882.
12 pp.

———————————

Testi Somali. Reale Accademia dei Lincei.
Roma 1889.

———————————

Lingua parlate somali,galla e harrari.
"Bollettino Reale Societa Geografica Italiana".
Roma 1890.

———————————

Vocabolario Harrari-Somali-Galla. Roma 1890.

———————————

La grammatica somala. Reale Societa
Geografica Italiana. Roma 1892.

———————————

Note Sulle lingue parlare somali, galla e

harrari raccolte ed ordinate nell'Harrar.
"Bollettino Societa Africana d'Italia".
Vol. XIV. Napoli 1895-7.

Materiale linguistici dell'Africa
Orientale. Napoli 1898.

SABBADINI,E.

Studi recenti di Lingua Somala in Italia.
"Africa". Vol. IX. No. 2. Roma Febbraio 1954.
56-57 pp.

SACCONI.

Vocabulary and sentences in Somali.
"L'Esploratore". Napoli 1878.
105 p.

SCHLEICHER, A.W.

Die Somali-Sprache. Berlin 1892.

Grammatik der Somali-Sprache.
Berlin 1892.

Somali-Texte (Dr. Schleicher's Somali Texte,
herausgegeben von Leo Reinisch). Alfred Holder.
Vienna 1900.
XX + 159 pp.

SMITH, A. O.

Somali Vocabulary and Useful Terms.
(Handbook). Genale (Somalia) 1943.
54 pp.

SYAD,W.

Khamsine, poems (Preface de L. S. Senghor),
"Presence Africaine." Paris 1959.
70 pp.

TILING, M. (von)

Die Vokale des bestimmten Artikels im
Somali. "Zeitschrift fur le Koloniale Sprachen".
"Zeitschrift fur Eingeborenen Sprachen". Jahrgang IX.
Berlin 1918-1919.
132-166 pp.

Adjektiv-Endungen im Somali. "Zeitschrift fur
le Koloniale Sprachen". "Zeitschrift fur Eingeborenen
Sprachen". Jahrgang X. Berlin 1919-1920.
208 240 pp.

Die Sprache der Jabarti,mit besonderer
Berucksichtigung der Verwandtschaft von Jabarti
und Somali. "Zeitschrift fur Eingeborenen Sprachen".
17-162 pp.

Somali Texte und untersuchungen zur Somali Lautlehre.
·¹ Zeitschrift fur Eingeborenen Sprachen".
No. 8. Berlin 1925. 156 pp.

VYCICHL, W.

Zur Tonologie des Somali. "Rivista degli
Studi Orientali". Vol. XVIII. Heft 3. Berlin 1928.
231-3 pp.

VYCICHL,W.

Zur Tonologie des Somali. "Rivista degli
Studi Orientali". Vol. XXXI. Roma 1956.

2.   Stories, Autobiographies, Novels, and Related Literature

AMADIO,W.

Due uomini sopra un albero: scene di caccia.
"Esploratore Commerciale". No. 12. Milano.
11-16 pp.

ARCTURUS.

Sketches in Somaliland. "Monthly Review".
London June 1907.
111-124,pp.

BARRACU,F.

Il rapimento di Hagia: Leggenda somala.
"Illustrazione Coloniale". Milano 1940.
23-25 pp.

CARLEVAROS,S.

Il racconto della Somalia (Versi).
Allegretti di Campo. Milano 1i56.
38 pp.

CAROSELLI,F.S.

Kitab Durr. Milano 1955.
96 pp.

CIPOLLA,A.

Oceano: Romanzo del Mare Indiano.
Azienda Giornalistica Libreria Editrice.
Roma 1922.
177 pp.

COLLI,I.

Il mistero nell'anima dei Somali.
"L'Eroica". Milano 1937.
487 p.

COLLINS, D.

A tear for Somalia. Jarrolds. London 1960.
192 pp. map. ills.

NURUDDIN,F.

From a crooked rib. African Writers
Series. No. 80. Heinemann. London 1970.
182 pp.

FORBES-WATSON,R.

Shifta! (Oxford Children's Library).
3rd Reprint. Oxford University Press. London 1970.
185 pp.

GRIMAUD,L.

Caccia in Somalia. Gialli Polizieschi Americani.
(Milano).
128 pp.

HANLEY,G.

The Consul at Sunset. The Reprint Society.
London 1952.
254 pp.

HELENE,DE FRANCE (S.A.R.)

Vie Errante: Sensations d'Afrique.
Francesco Viassone Editore. Ivrea 1921.
146 pp.

LAURENCE,M.

The prophet's camel bell. Macmillan & Co. Ltd.
London 1963.
242 pp ills.

MEREGAZZI,R.

Siek Siek in Somalia. Bemporad. Firenze 1927.

MITRANO,S.G.

Femmina Somala. Libreria Dekton e Tocholl.
Napoli 1933.
270 pp.

MONILE,F.

Africa Orientale. Cappelli. Bologna 1933.
201 pp.

ADAM, O.

My camel: supplementary reader. Mogadiscio 1969.
9 pp.

PERRICONE,V.A.

Mogadiscio. Stamperia della Colonia.
Mogadiscio 1929.

───────────

Ricordi Somali. Cappelli. Bologna 1936.
272 pp.

PIOVAN,F.G.

Alba Mogal: il romanzo di un esploratore africano
Antonio Cecchi. Tipografia Sant'Ilario. Rovereto 1929.
137 pp.

PIRONE,M.

Echi di voci lontane: Immagini e figure
della storia somala. Stamperia AFIS.
Mogadiscio 1956.
103 pp.

POMILLIO,M.

Un giornalista all'equatore. Vallecchi Editore.
Firenze 1933.
317 pp.

QUADRONE,E.

Pionieri, Donne, Belve. Agnelli Editore.
Milano 1934.

───────────

Somalia Italiana: Uebi Scebeli. Agnelli Editore.

Milano 1934.

Somalia Italiana: Uebi Scebeli. Agnelli Editore.
Milano 1934.

Mudundu: Cacciatori d'Ombre all'Quatore.
Marangoni Editore. Milano 1935.
239 pp.

REECE,A.

To my wife 50 camels. Harvill Press.
London 1963.
254 pp. ills.

RIBERA, A.

Antonio Cecchi. Vallechi Editore. 1940.
340 pp.

SCHREINER,C.

Nubi sugli educalipti. Tipografia Teatrale Commerciale.
Torino 1957.
256 pp.

SILLANTI,T.

Luigi di Savoia. Libreria del Littorio.
Roma 1929.
167 pp.

TEDESCO ZAMARRANO,V.

Alle sorgenti del Nilo Azzurro.
Alfieri & Lacroix. Roma 1920.

Hauertzee, mio sogno. Anonima Libreria Italiana. Roma.
205 pp.

TOM AND SANDRA BRADEN.

Stories for Somali Students. (Illustrated). Mogadishu.
135 pp.

VECCHI,B.V.

Sotto il soffio del monsone: un anno
nell'Oltregiuba. Alpes. Milano 1927.
317 pp.

Vecchio Benadir. Alpes. Milano 1930.

_____

L'Italia ai margini dell'Etiopia.
Bietti Editore. Milano 1935.
287 pp.

_____

Somalia. Marangoni Editore. Milano 1935.
229 pp.

_____

Africa nostra. Cappelli Editori. Bologna 1941.
289 pp.

VITALE,M.A.

Sotto le stelle piu lontane: romanzo coloniale.
Alfieri & Lacroix. Roma 1922.
218 pp.

WALSH,L.P.

Somali coast stories. Melrose 1937.

ZUCCA,G.

Il paese di madreperla. Alpes. Milano 1926.
311 pp.

_____

Somalia. Tosi Editore. Roma 1950.
303 pp.

_____

Il pozzo dei leopardi. "Africa". No. 7-9.
Roma 1952.

1. Customary Law

CERULLI,E.

Testi di diritto consuetudinario dei
Somali Merrehan."Rivista degli Studi
Orientali". Fasc. No. 4. Roma 1918.

Il diritto consuetudinario della Somalia
Italiana Settentrionale. "Bollettino Societa
Africana d'Italia" Napoli 1918-1919.

Cabila. "Nuovo Digesto Italiano"
Vol. II. 1937.
581-582 pp.

Destur. "Nuovo Digesto Italiano".
Vol. IV. 1938.
781 p.

Il diritto consuetudinario della Somalia
Italiana Settentrionale. Ministero della
Africa Italiana. Ufficio Studi. Roma 1951.
79 pp.

CIAMARRA,G.

Justice indigene dans la Somalie Italienne.
"Bulletin de Colonisation Comparee".
Bruxelles 1912.
385-400 pp.

COLUCCI,M.

Principi di diritto consuetudinario della
Somalia Italiana Meridionale: I gruppi sociali
el la proprieta. "La Voce." Firenze 1924.
242 pp.

"Halifa" e "Hirin". "Nuovo Digesto
Italiano". 1938.

"Wayel". "Nuovo Digesto Italiano".

1940.

"Rer". "Nuovo Digesto Italiano."
1940.

La composizione per l'omicidio e
l'origine della pena nella consuetudine
dei Somali meridionali."Rassegna Sociale
dell'Africa Italiana". No. 3. Napoli 1943.
155 p.

COPASSO, U.

Il testur somalo nel vigente ordinamento
giudiziario. "Rivista di Diritto Coloniale".
Roma 1939.
51-54 pp.

CREIGNON.

Le droit coutumier et la justice chez
les Somalienne."Revue de Geogr. Comm."
Bordeaux 1912.

CUCINOTTA,A.

Delitto, pena e giustizia presso
i Somali del Benadir. Tipograf. Unione
Editrice. Roma 1921.
30 pp.

La costituzione sociale somala. "Rivista
Coloniale". Roma 1921.
389-443 pp.

La proprieta ed il sistema contrattuale
nel "destur" somalo. "Rivista Coloniale".
Roma 1921.
241 p.

MANNI.E,F.

Le consuetudini o "destur" della
Somalia. "L'oltremare". Roma 1932.
286 p.

MELLANA,V.

L'ordinamento giuridico della Communita

somala. "Giurisprudenza Italiana".
Torino 1956.

MOHAMED, N.A.N.

Civil wrongs under customary law in
the Northern Regions of the Somali Republic.
"Journal of African Law." Vol. II. London 1967.

PERRICONE,V.A.

Il destur. "L'Italia d'oltremare".
Roma 1937.
21 p.

RAYNE, H.

Somali Tribal Law. "Journal of
the Africa Society". London 1920-21.
23-30 pp.

_____

Somali marriage. "Journal of
the Africa Society." London 1920-21.
23-30 pp.

SANTIAPICHI,S.

Il prezzo del sangue e
l'omicidio nel diritto somalo.
Dott. A. Giuffre (Editrice).
Milano 1963.
60 pp.

WRIGHT, A.C.A.

The inter-action of various systems
of law and custom in British Somaliland
and their relations with social life.
"Journal of the East African Natural
History Society." Vol. XVII. Nairobi 1943.
62-102 pp.

2.   Islamic Law

BERTOLA, A.

Confessionismo religioso e diritti
umani nella costituzione somala.
"La Comunita Internazionale." Vol. XVI.
Roma Luglio 1961.

_____

Confessionismo e diritti umani nella
costituzione somala. "La Comunita

Internazionale". Roma 1963.

BROWN,A.J.

Adoption of Islamic law in the Somaliland
Protectorate. Hargeisa 1956.

CORTE DI GIUSTIZIA DELLA SOMALIA.

Norme per i Qadi. Stamperia del Governo.
Mogadiscio 1957.

MAINO, MARIO.

La valutazione de danno alla persona
della dottorina giuridica musulmana.
Stamperia AFIS. Mogadiscio 1951.

MELLANA, V.

Diritto processuale islamico Somalo.
Tipogr. Missione Cattolica. Mogadiscio 1957.
130 pp.

————————

Diritto processuale islamico somalo.
Istituto Superiore di Diritto ed
Economia. Mogadiscio Agosto 1957.
127 pp.

————————

Alcuni aspetti storici e dogmatici del
diritto giudiziario musulmano in Somalia.
"Annuario di Diritto Comparato." Vol. XXXIII.
1958.

3. Modern (Positive) Law

AMMINISTRAZIONE FIDUCIARIA ITALIANA DELLA SOMALIA.

Leggi fondamentali per la Somalia.
Assemblea Legislativa della Somalia.
Mogadiscio 1956.

AGRESTI,L.

I meticci e la carta fondamentale
dell'Eritrea e della Somalia. "La Rivista
d'Oriente." No. 11. Napoli Novembre 1934.

ANGELONI,R.

Introduzione al Diritto Commerciale e

Bancario Somalo. Banca Nazionale Somala.
Mogadiscio 1963.
176 pp.

———————————

Diritto Costituzionale Somalo.
Dott. A. Giuffre. (Editore) Milano 1964.
336 pp.

——————————AND SANTONI.

Diritto Amministrativo Somalo.
Vol. I. Dott. A. Giuffre. (Editore)
Milano 1964.

ANONYMOUS.

Norme per l'esportazione delle pelli
secche dalla Somalia (D.G. 7846 del 25-11 1928).
"Rassegna Economica delle Colonie." Roma 1930.
160 p.

———————————

Le code du travail de la Somalie.
"Informations Sociales". No. 5. Geneva 1959.
183-187 pp.

———————————

Vote of confidence. "The Times."
London 20th June 1961.

ASSEMBLEA LEGISLATIVA DELLA SOMALIA.

Progetto di Costituzione. Comitato
Politico. Mogadiscio Maggio 1960.
XXI, 104 pp.

BERARDELLI,G.

Studi di legislazione coloniale:
(Amministrazione della giustizia nel
Giubaland prima della sua cessione all'Italia).
"Rivista di Diritto Coloniale". Roma 1939.
411-424 pp.

BARSOTTI,A.

Il codice di lavoro della Somalia.
Rassegna del Lavoro." Roma 1960.
1701-1714 pp.

BERTOLA,A.

Legislazione civile, legge sacra e diritto

consuetudinario: discorso per l'inaugurazione
dell'anno di Studi 1956-1957. Istituto Superiore
di Diritto ed Economia della Somalia. Tipografia
Ferraiolo. Roma 1957.
14 pp.

BONO,E.

Vademecum del R. Residente in Somalia.
Stamperia della Colonia. Mogadiscio 1930.
102 pp.

BRITISH MILITARY ADMINISTRATION (SOMALIA).

British Military legislation containing
proclamations and subsidiary legislation
in force on the 31st May 1943.
The Government Printer. Mogadishu 1943.
IX, 208 pp.

CASILLI D'ARAGONA,M.

Competenze facoltativa ed elettiva nell'ordinamento
giuridico somalo."Azione Coloniale" Roma 1940.
2 p.

CASSA PER LE ASSICURAZIONI SOCIALI DELLA SOMALIA.

Raccolta della legislazione concernente
la CASSA per le Assicurazioni Sociali
della Somalia: Aggiornata al 1° Gennaio 1962.
CASS. Direzione Generale. Mogadiscio 1962.
142 pp.

CIAMARRA,G.

La giustizia nella Somalia.
F. Giannini (Editore) Napoli 1914.
424 pp.

COMITATO TECNICO PER LA COSTITUZIONE.

Relazione al progetto costituzionale.
(a cura di Costanzo G. A. e Angeloni, R.)
Mogadiscio 1959.

CONTINI,P.

Integration of legal systems in the
Somali Republic."The International and
Comparative Law Quarterly." London October 1967
1088-1105 pp.

The Somali Republic: An experiment in
Legal Integration Frank Cass & Co. Ltd.

London 1969.
92 pp.

CORTE DI GIUSTIZIA DELLA SOMALIA.

Manuale di diritto e procedura penale
per i giudici distrettuali Mogadiscio 1958.

Massimario di Giurisprudenze 1956 1958
Stamperia del Governo. Mogadiscio 1959.
59 pp

COSTANZO,G.A.

Appunti sulle fonti del diritto
in Somalia. V. Ferri. Roma 1952.

Problemi costituzionali della Somalia
nella preparazione all'indipendenza
(1957 1960). Istituto Universitario della
Somalia. Dott. A Giuffre (Editore). Milano 1962.
146 pp.

COTRAN,E.

Legal problems arising out of the
formation of the Somali Republic.
"International and Comparative Law
Quarterly". Vol. 12. London 1963.

Somali Republic Supreme Court. "Journal
of African Law." Vol. 8. No. 2. London 1964.

CREDITO SOMALO.

Raccolta delle Ordinanze - Decreti-
Leggi dal 22 Febbraio 1954 al 11 Marzo
1959, riguardanti il Credito Somalo.
Credito Somalo. Mogadiscio.
133 pp.

CUCINOTTA,E.

Il diritto di naufragio nella Somalia
Italiana."Rivista delle Colonie Italiane."
Roma 1941.
369 p.

D'ANTONIO,M.

La costituzione Somala: precedenti

storici e documenti costituzionali.
Presidenza del Consiglio dei Ministri.
Roma 1962.

DI VITO,G.

Codici e leggi della Somalia: Ordinamento
doganale e leggi complementari aggiornato
al 31 Gennaio 1966. The National Printers
Ltd. Mogadiscio Gennaio 1966.
145 pp.

FLORIO,F.

Istituzioni di diritto pubblico
della Somalia. Dott. A. Giuffre. (Editore)
Milano 1963.

FOREIGN OFFICE.

King's Regulations: Somaliland
Protectorate. Berbera 1904.

_____

The Laws of the Somaliland Protectorate.
(Two volumes). London 1931.

_____

Supplement to the Laws of the Somaliland
Protectorate containing the Ordinances of
Somaliland enacted between the 1st of July
1930 and the 31st December 1932. London 1933.

FRANCA, P.

La nuova legislazione della Somalia.
"Africa". Roma 1952.
9-11 pp.

(R) GOVERNO DELLA SOMALIA ITALIANA.

Manuale per la Somalia Italiana 1912.
Tipogr. dell'Unione Editrice. Roma 1912.
301 pp.

GOVERNO DELLA SOMALIA.

Proposte per un progetto approvate dal
Consiglio Territoriale nella seduta del
1° Novembre 1958. Comitato Tecnico per
Studi e Lavori Preparatori per la Costituzione
della Somalia. Stamperia del Governo.
Mogadiscio 1959.
XVIII, 109 pp.

_____

Commentario al testo delle
proposte per un progetto di costituzione.
Comitato Tecnico per Studi e Lavori
Preparatori per la Costituzione della
Somalia. Stamperia del Governo.
Mogadiscio 1959.
316 pp.

Progetto di Costituzione. Ufficio del
Ministero per la Costituzione.
Mogadiscio 1960.
93 pp.

GOVERNO SOMALO.

Codice del Lavoro. Stamperia del
Governo. Mogadiscio 1958.
52 pp.

Legge 15 Febbraio 1961 No. 12: Referendum
per l'approvazione della Costituzione della
Repubblica Somala. Scuola Tipografica Missione
Cattolica. Mogadiscio 1961.
22 pp.

GOUVERNMENT FRANCAIS.

La Costitution de la Republique de
Somalie. "La Documentation Francaise.
Notes et Etudes documentaires". No. 3132.
Paris Octobre 1964.
14 pp.

HUBERICH,C.H.

Commercial Law of Somaliland.
"Commercial Laws of the World."
Vol. 15. 1912.

ISTITUTO SOMALO DI PUBBLICA AMMINSTRAZIONE.

Indice della legislazione Somala 1960-1966.
S.I.P.A. Mogadiscio Novembre 1967.
139 pp.

LEWIS,I.M.

Progressi costituzionali del
nazionalismo somalo. "Somalia d'Oggi."
No. 4. Mogadiscio Dicembre 1957.
11-15 pp.

MAINO,M.

Il diritto di sanare: un commento
sull'art. 24 della nuova legge sulle
assicurazioni per gli infortuni.
Stamperia AFIS. Mogadiscio.
26 pp.

MALINTOPPI.

La costituzione somala e il diritto
internazionale. "Rivista di Diritto
Internazionale." Vol. XLV. Roma 1961.

MANNI,E.F.

Manuale della Legislazione della Somalia
Italiana. Libreria del Littorio. Roma 1931.
311 pp.

MANNO,F.

Manuali di Legislazione della Somalia
1913-1929. (Vol. I,II,III,IV,V,VI,VII).
Libreria del Littorio. Roma 1931.

MELLANA, V.

Nascita di un nuovo ordinamento giuridico. No. 1.
"Somalia d'Oggi". Mogadiscio 1956.

———————————

Nozioni di diritto giudiziario Somalo.
Istituto Universitario della Somalia. Tipografia Missione.
Mogadiscio Febbraio 1957.
67 pp.

MOHAMED SCEK GABIOU.

La nostra costituzione.
Stamperia Missione. Mogadiscio Giugno 1961.
(Tri-lingual: English-Italian-Arabic).

———————————

Commento alla legislazione somala
sugli investimenti esteri. Atti del
V Convegno sui Rapporti Economici e
Commerciali con ill Continente Africano:
(Bari 13-14 Settembre 1961). Roma 1961.
15 pp.

MUHAMMED NOOR H.

The rule of law in the Somali
Republic. "Journal of the International
Commission of Jurists." Vol. No. 2. Geneva 1964.
276-302 pp.

Judicial review of administrative action
in the Somali Republic. "Journal of African
Law." Vol. 10. No. 1. London 1966.

The development of the constitution of
the Somali Republic. Ministry of Justice
and Grace. Government Printing Press.
Mogadiscio April 1969.
262 pp.

RAGGI,R.

Principi costituzionali per la
Somalia. "Eurafrica." No. 1. Roma 1953.
6-7 pp.

REPUBBLICA SOMALA.

La Costituzione. Scuola Tipografica
Missione Cattolica. Mogadiscio 1960.
35 pp.

La legislazione vigente in
Somalia: Indice analitico alfabetico
a cura di Saverino Santiapichi e di
Ahmed Mohamud Halane. Ministero di Grazia
e Diustizia. Mogadiscio Gennaio 1961.
59 pp.

Referendum Costituzionale del
20 Giugno 1961. Ministero dell'Interno.
FEAT. Torino 1963.
287 pp.

Norme sull'accertamento e sulla repressione
di violazioni delle Leggi Finanziari.
Stamperia di Stato. Mogadiscio 1966.
31 pp.

Codice Penale e Codice di Procedura Penale
con appendice di leggi complementari ed
indici. (a cura di Gabriel Di Vito). The National
Printers Ltd. Mogadiscio 4 Maggio 1967.
531 pp.

Progetto del Codice Penale Somalo: Libro 2°:
I delitti in particolare. Mogadiscio.
135 pp.

RIVISTA DI DIRITTO DEL LAVORO.

Codice del Lavoro della Somalia.
(Introduzione del Prof. Ferruccio Pergolesi).
R.D.D.L. Quaderno VIII. Dott. A. Giuffre (Editore)
Milano 1960.
53 pp.

RIZZETTO,F.

Per un codice del lavoro della
Somalia. "Somalia d'Oggi." No. 2.
Mogadiscio 1957.

ROSSETTI,C.

Manuali di Legislazione della
Somalia Italiana. Tipografia Unione
Editrice. Roma 1912.

SANTANIELLO,L.

Il problema della pena capitale
nell'Ordinamento Giuridico Somalo.
Stamperia AFIS. Mogadiscio 1957.
8 pp.

SANTIAPICHI,S.

Appunti di Diritto Penale della Somalia:
Parte Generale (Anno Studi 1961-1962).
Istituto Universitario della Somalia.
Dott. A. Giuffre (Editore). Milano 1961.
169 pp.

Lezioni di Procedura Penale. Istituto
Universitario della Somalia.
Mogadiscio Gennaio 1967.
98 pp.

SOMALI DEMOCRATIC REPUBLIC.

Index of legislation as on 28 July 1971.
Ministry of Justice and Religion. State
Printing Agency. Mogadiscio 4th August 1971.
118 pp.

SOMALILAND PROTECTORATE.

The Standing Orders of the Legislative
Council of the Somaliland Protectorate.

Gov. Printer. Aden 1957.
IV, 36 pp.

SOMALI REPUBLIC.

The Constitution of the Somali
Republic as amended to 31 December 1962.
Somali Government Press. Mogadishu 1964.

————————

Investigation and suppression of
violations of Financial Laws. State
Printing Press. Mogadishu 1966.
31 pp. (bilingual: English-Italian).

————————

The Constitution of the Somali
Republic. Scuola Tipografica Missione
Cattolica. Mogadiscio.
34 pp.

TAMBARO, I.

L'ordinamento dell'Oltregiuba.
"Annali Africa Italiana." Roma 1925.
125 p.

XII
POLITICS, GOVERNMENT, ADMINISTRATION

ABDIRIZAK, HAJI HUSSEN.

La questione dei confini dopo sei anni.
"Somalia d'Oggi". No. 1. Mogadiscio 1956.
14 p.

ADAM, F.

Handbook of Somaliland. Eyre & Spottiswoode.
London 1900.

AL. GIR.

L'Amministrazione Fiduciaria Italiana in Somalia.
"Rassegna Italiana Politica e Cultura". No. 311.
Roma Ottobre 1950.

AMMINISTRAZIONE FIDUCIARIA ITALIANA DELLA SOMALIA.

Testo della Convenzione Fiduciaria per il
Territorio della Somalia sotto Amministrazione Italiana.
AFIS. Roma Marzo 1950.
61 pp.

————————

Results and prospects of the Italian Trusteeship
Administration of Somaliland on completion of half
the trusteeshop period. Litografia Marves. Roma 1955.
42 pp.

Le prime elezioni politiche in Somalia 19 56.
Stamperia del Governo. Mogadiscio 31 Gennaio 1957.
378 pp.

Piano di trasferimento delle funzioni di governo dal
Governo Italiano al Governo Somalo. Istituto Agronomico
per l'Oltremare. Fasc. No. 3746. Firenze 1959.
16 pp.

ANON.

The Treaty with Abyssinia. "Geographical Journal".
Vol. XI. London 1898.
293-294 pp.

ANONYMOUS.

La relazione della Commissione per Alula.
"Bollettino Societa Africana d'Italia".
Napoli 1899.
11 p.

Ordinamento del Benadir: Relazione del Senato
ed alla Camera "Rivista Coloniale" Roma 1907.
115 p.

La delimitazione dei confini tra la Somalia
Italiana La Dancalia e l'Etiopia. "Bollettino
Societa Africana d'Italia". Vol. XXVII. Napoli 1908.
131-134 pp.

Documenti diplomatici: scambio di nota
22-25 giugno 1908 tra la Legazione d'Italia
in Addis Abeba e il Governo Etiopico, per regolare
le questioni di frontiera tra l'Etiopia e la Somalia
Italiana per quanto riguarda il commercio.
"Bollettino Societa Africana d'Italia". Vol. XXVII.
Napoli 1908.
221-224 pp.

L'attivita del Mullah e la sistemazione della
Somalia Settentrionale. "Rivista Coloniale".
No. 10. Roma 1910.

Coloni bianchi nella nostra Somalia.
"Rivista Coloniale". Vol. 1. Roma 1913.
53 p.

La politique anglaise au pays Somali
et l'affaire du 9 Aout. "Ren. Coloniale".
No. 12. Paris 1913.
422-424 pp.

Romolo Onor e la sua presenza in Somalia.
"L'Idea Coloniale". No. 22. Roma 1925.

Figure ed opere italiane in Somalia.
"Le Vie d'Italia e dell'America Latina".
Milano 1927.
332 p.

Tre anni di governo in Somalia: Intervista con
S.E. Guido Corni. "L'Italia Coloniale".
Roma-Milano 1931.
130 p.

L'Amministrazione Municipale di Mogadiscio:
Opere per l'organizzazione Civile in Africa
Orientale Italiana. 1939.
235-236 pp.

British Somaliland. British Society for
International Understanding. Vol. IX. No. 1.
London January 1948.
16 pp.

Inaugurazione della 1° Sessione del Nuovo
Consiglio Territoriale della Somalia.
(Discorso di Fornari). "Oriente Moderno".
No. 3-4. Roma 1952.
83-87 pp.

Somalia d'Oggi. "Rassegna Ricostruzione Italiana". 1953.
74 p.

_____

La Somalia cambia volta: Intervista con
l'On. G. Bettiol. "Eurafrica". No. 1. Roma 1954.
3-4 p.p

_____

L'azione dell'Italia in Somalia documentata alle
Nazioni Unite. "Eurafrica". No. 4. Roma 1955.
14 p.

_____

Begining of a new nation. "Time". Vol. LXVII. 1956.
40 p.

_____

Tension on Somaliland frontiers:
Part I: Unprotected British Tribes.
Part II: Ethiopian encroachments. "The Times".
London 27th and 28th February 1957.

_____

Piani etiopici per i territori della Somalia.
"Somalia d'Oggi". No. 2. Mogadiscio 1957.
26-27 pp.

_____

Towards Somali independence: British and Italian
Administration compared. "East Africa and Rhodesia".
No. 1747. London 1958.
978 p.

_____

Questo e il volto della nuova Somalia.
"Eurafrica". No. 2. Roma 1958.
14-16 pp.

_____

Somaliland. British Society for International
Understanding. Ser. No. 181. London 1959.
20 pp. ills. map.

_____

Das Regierungsprogram der Republik Somale:
Rede des Premier Ministers Abdi Rashid Ali
Sharmarke von der Nationalversammlung am 13 Aug. 1960.

"Afrika Informationsdienst". Document No. 21 and 76. 1960.

Ai Somali adesso l'avventura dell'autogoverno.
"Rassegna Espansione Commerciale". Vol. XLII.
No. 5-6. Milano 1960.
33-34 pp.

La nouvelle Republique de Somalie.
"Perspective". Paris Juin 1960.
12 p.

The Somaliland Protectorate. "Commonwealth".
No. 4. London 1960.
402-404 pp.

L'independence de la Somalie sous tutelle.
"Chronique de Politique Etrangers". No. 1-3.
Bruxelles 1961.
284-336 pp.

La Somalie independante: ensemble de 26 article
consacres a la Republique de Somalie.
"Presence Africaine". No. 3. Paris 1961.
72-248 pp.

L'affaire de Djibouti. "Revue des deux Mondes".
Paris Fevrier 1967.
321-229 pp.

La Cote francaise des Somalis de 1936
a juin 1940. "Revue Historique de l'Armee".
No. 1963-4. Paris.

ALLEGRINI,A.

L'Amministrazione Fiduciaria della Somalia.
Arte Grafiche Delle Venezie. Venezia 1951.

ALVAREZ.

Obock et Abissinie. "Revue Maritime et Coloniale".
Vol. CXXI. 1894.
59-101-295-320 pp.

APOLLONIO.

Somalia heads towards independence. "Africa Special Report"
No. 12. Washington, D C. 1958.
8 12 pp.

ARCHER,G.F.

Personal and historical memoirs of an east
African Administrator. Oliver & Boyd. London 1963.
XIV, 260 pp. ills.

ARFELLI,E.

A cinquanti anni dall'eccidio di Uarsceik.
"Azione Coloniale". Roma 1940.
6 p.

_____ATTUONI,P.

I confini della Somalia e loro vicende. "Bollettino
Societa Geografica Italiana". Roma 1953.
29 pp.

AUSIELLO,A.

Cristoforo Negri ed i precedenti dell'azione Italiana
in Somalia. "Annali Africa Italiana". Anno IV. No. 1. Roma 1943.
217 p.

BADINI-CONFALONIERI.

La bandiera ai Somali. "Eurafrica".
No. 4. Roma 1954.
1 p.

BARILE, P.

Colonizzazione fascista nella Somalia Meridionale.
Societa Italiana Arti Grafiche. Roma 1935.
222 pp.

BASSI,U.

La Somalia ed i Protettorati. "Rivista delle
Colonie e d'Oriente". Bologna 1925.
337 p.

B.C.

Ii progetto fiduciaria per la Somalia.
"Relazione Internazionale". No. 2. Milano 1950.

BECKER,G.H.

The disposition of the Italian colonies 1941-1951
(PH.D. Thesis). Universite de Geneve. Institut Univ.

De Hautes E¦tudes Internationales. Imprimerie Granchamp.
Annemasse 1952.
270 pp. bibl.

BECKIT, H.O.

British Somaliland. Oxford Survey.
British Empire. Vol. III. 1914.
299-317 pp.

BEER, E.

Ritorno in Africa (Somalia).   "Rassegna Espansione Commerciale".
No. 11-12. Milano 1949.
7 p.

BELFORTI,G.

Una grande Somalia. "Eurafrica". No. 5-6. Roma 1957.
17-18 pp.

BEMBURY,I.

Civilisation comes to the Somalis.
"Christian Science Monitor, Weekly Magazine Section". 1945.
6 p.

BENTWICH,N. (De M.)

Ethiopia, Eritrea, Somaliland. Gollancz.
London 1946.

_____

Future of the Somalis. "Contemporary Review".
London 1946.
84-87 pp.

BERNARD-DUTRIEL,M.

Djibouti: creation d'une colonie francese. 1900.
108 p. ills.

BERNASCONI,O.

L'Oltregiuba. "Rivista delle Colonie e d'Oriente".
Bologna 1927.
150 p.

BETTIOL,G.

L'Italia e il suo mandato in Somalia.
"La Voce dell'Africa". No. 2. Roma 1957.

BOLLATI, A.

Somalia Italiana. "I Commentari dell'Impero".

Unione Editrice d'Italia. Roma 1937.
214 pp.

BONACCI,G.

Lo agombro dell'interno del Somaliland e gli
interesi italiani. "Rivista delle Colonie Italiane'.
Vol. V. Roma 1910.
33-40 pp.

BORNHAUPT,C. (von)

Die deutschen Bestrebungen an der Somali-Kuste
und das englisch-italienische Abkommen vom Mai.
"Koloniales Jahrbusch". Vol. VIII. Berlin 1895.
161-171 pp.

BOURNE, H.R.F.

Story of Somali: Britain lives squandered
and treasure wasted. London 1904.
22 pp.

_____

The story of Somaliland. "East Africa Pamphlet".
No. 20. London 1904.

BOUTET, R.

Somalia d'Oggi. "Illustrazione Coloniale".
No. 1. Milano 1935.
19 p.

BRAINE,B.R.

Storm clouds over the Horn of Africa.
"International Affairs". Vol. XXXIV. No. 4. London 1958.
435-443 pp.

BRITISH MILITARY ADMINISTRATION (SOMALIA).

British Somaliland. Annual Report of the
Military Governor for the year ended 31st December. BMA.
Hargeisa 1944.

_____

Report on General Survey of British Somaliland 1945.
BMA. Aden May 1946.
62 pp.

_____

British Somaliland. "Proceedings of the first session of
the Advisory Council for the Somaliland Protectorate".
Government Press. Mogadishu 1946.
46 pp.

Report on General Survey of British
Somaliland 1946. BMA. Aden 1947.
18 pp.

British Somaliland. "Proceedings of the second
session of the Advisory Council for the Somaliland Protectorate".
(Berbera 14-18 Januark 1946). BMA. Hargeisa February 1947.
59 pp.

Annual Report by the Chief Administrator (Somalia)
for the year ended 31st December 1946. BMA.
Government Press. Mogadishu 1947.
42 pp. map.

Report on General Survey of British Somaliland 1947.
BMA. Mogadishu 1948.
26 pp.

BROWN, D.J.L.

The Ethio-Somaliland frontier dispute.
"The International and Comparative Law Quarterly".
Vol. V. Part 2. London April 1965.
245-264 pp.

BRUCATO,G.

Etiopia e Giubaland. "Illustrazione Coloniale".
No. 5. Milano 1924.
151 p.

BRUNO,L.

La Somalia alla vigilia della sua indipendenza.
"Atti dell'VII Convegno Economico Italo-Africano".
Milano 1958.
40-50 pp.

BRUNSCHWIG,H.

Une colonie inutile: Obock (1862-1888).
"Cahiers d'etudes africaines". 1er Cahier.
Paris 1968.
32-47 pp.

BULLOTTA,A.

La Somalia sotto due bandiere. Garzanti.
Milano 1949.

281 pp.

CAMERA DEI DEPUTATI.

Documenti diplomatici presentati al Parlamento
Italiano dal Ministro degli Affari Esteri.
(Somalia Italiana 1885-1895). Tipografia Camera
dei Deputati. Roma 1895.
281 pp.

CANI,R.

Il Giubaland (Monografia Societa Africana d'Italia).
Tipografia A. Trani. Napoli 1921.
60 pp.

CARLETTI,T.

Relazione sulla Somalia Italiana, 1907-1908.
Tipografia Camera dei Deputati. Roma 1910.

_____

Attraverso il Benadir. Tipografia Agnesotti.
Viterbo 1910.
247 pp.

_____

Relazione sulla Somalia Italiana per l'anno
1908-1909. Tipografia Camera dei Deputati. Roma 1910.

_____

I problemi del Benadir. Tipografia Agnesotti.
Viterbo 1912.
367 pp.

CAROSELLI,F.S.

Il Giuba e l'avvenire della Somalia.
"Rivista delle Colonie Italiane". Roma 1921.
171 p.

_____

Relazione del Governatore per l'anno 1939-40.
Stamperia della Colonia. N Mogadiscio 1941.

CASTAGNO,A.A.

Lo sviluppo politico in Somalia e nel Protettorato
del Somaliland. "Somalia d'Oggi". No. 3. Mogadiscio 1957.
25 p.

_____

The Republic of Somalia: Africa's most homogeneous state.
"Africa Special Report". No. 7. Washington, D. C. 1960.
2-4 pp.

—————————

Somalia. "International Conciliation Series". No. 522.
Carnegie Endowment for International Peace.
New York March 1959.
339-400 pp. map.

—————————

The Somali-Kenya Controversy: Implications for the future.
"Journal of Modern African Studies". Vol. 2. No. 2. 1964.
165-188 pp.

CATO,C.

British Somaliland. "Empire Review". Vol. XXX.
London 1919.
368-377 pp.

CENTRAL OFFICE OF INFORMATION. (GREAT BRITAIN).

The Somaliland Protectorate. H.M.S.O. London 1958.
11 pp. ills.

—————————

Somaliland Protectorate. "Commonwealth Leaflets".
Cam. No. 2. H.M.S.O. London 1960.
15 pp.

—————————

The Somaliland Protectorate. "Reference Division".
Reg. No. 4558. H.M.S.O. London May 1960.
17 pp. ills.

CERRINA,F.G.

Bernadir. Tipografia Ministero Affari Esteri.
Roma 1911.
190 pp.

CESARI,C.

La Somalia Italiana. Fratelli Palombi (Editori).
Roma 1935.
210 pp.

CHIESI,G.

Affari Coloniali e Consolari: Benadir, Carletti,
di Giorgio, Badolo Mercatelli, ecc. Tipografia Koschitz
e C. Milano 1909.

32 pp.

La Colonizzazione Europea nel'Est Africa:
(Italia-Inghiltera-Germania). Unione Tipografico
Editrice Torinese. Torino 1909.
814 pp. ills. maps.

_____AND TRAVELLI,E.

Le questioni del Benadkr: Atti e relazioni dei
Commissari della Societa Commerciale del Benadir.
Tipografia Bellini. Milano 1904.
384 pp.

CHIROUX,R.

Le nouveau statut du Territoire francaise
des Afars et Des Issas. "Revue de Droit des
Pays Africains". No. 719. 1° trimestre. Paris 1968.
2-47 pp.

CIALDEA,H.

La Somalia e giunta alle soglie della indipendenza.
"Italiani nel Mondo". No. 12. Roma 1958.
13-15 pp.

L'Amministrazione Fiduciaria Italiana ha avviato
la Somalia all'indipendenza. "Italiani nel Mondo".
No. 16-17. Roma 1959.
18-19 pp.

L'independenza della Somalia e l'opera'
meritoria dell'Italia. "Italiani nel Mondo".
No. 11. Roma 1960.
18-20 pp.

CIBELLI,E.

I problemi dell'Oltregiuba. "Africa".
Roma 1924.
149 p.

CIUCCI,C.

AFIS: Anno terzo. "Africa d'Oggi".
Roma 1952.

CLIFFORD,H.M.

British Somaliland-Ethiopian Boundry.

Geographical Journal. Vol. XLVII. London 1936.
289-307 pp.

COEN,G.

La seconda colonia Italiana: Il Benadir.
Unione Editrice Torinese. Torino 1909.
399 pp.

COLONIAL OFFICE (GREAT BRITAIN).

Jubaland and Northern Frontier District. 1917.

Negotiations at Rome concerning Grazing
Rights and Transit Trade in British Somaliland.
London 1937.
16 pp.

Annual report on the Somaliland Protectorate
for the year 1948. H.M.S.O. London 1949.
38 pp. ills. map.

Report on the Somaliland Protectorate for
the year 1949. H.M.S.O. London 1950.
45 pp. map.

Report on the Somaliland Protectorate for
the years 1950 & 1951. H.M.S.O. London 1952.
58 pp. ills. map.

The Haud Problem. "Africa". No. 1192. London 1956.

Somaliland Protectorate for the years 1954 & 1955.
H.M.S.O. London 1957.

Somaliland 1958 & 1959. H.M.S.O. London 1960.
78 pp. map. ills.

Report of the Somaliland Protectorate Constitutional
Conference Held in London in May, 1960. H.M.S.O.
(Cmnd. 1044). London May 1960.

27 pp.

Report of the Regional Boundaries
Commission of NFD. (Cmnd 1899). London 1962.

Report of the Northern Frontier District.
(Cmnd 1900). London 1962.

COMMANDO DEL CORPO DI STATO MAGGIORE.

Somalia: Memorie sui possedimenti e protettorati
Italiani. Tipografia Comando Corpo di Stato Maggiore.
Roma 1908.
110 pp.

COMANDO FORZE DI POLIZIA DELLA SOMALIA.

Regolamento generale delle Forze di Polizia
della Somalia. (Progetto definitivo).
Mogadiscio Luglio 1958.
268 pp.

COMMISSARIATO GENERALE DELL'OLTREGIUBA.

Notizie sul Territorio di riva destra del Giuba.
Tipografia Bettini. Mogadiscio 1925.
105 pp.

Notizie sul Territorio di riva destra del Giuba.
Roma 1927.
147 pp.

COMPAGNIA ITALIANA DELL'EST AFRICA.

La Somalia Italiana ed il suo avvenire.
Grandidier & C. Torino 1924.

CONSIGLIO,G.

Ardua Somalia. "Africa". No. 1-4. Roma 1951.
21-101 pp.

Creazione di uno Stato. "Africa". No. 6. Roma Giugno 1955.
169-172 pp.

Insistiamo,attenzione alla Somalia.
"Africa". No. 3. Roma 1956.

65-68 pp.

CONTIN,J.

Somali Republic: Politics with a difference.
"African Report". Washington, D. C. November 1964.

CORNI,G.

Relazione sulla Somalia Italiana per l'esercizio
1928 e 1929. R. Stamperia della Colonia. Mogadiscio 1929.
146 pp.

Relazione sulla Somalia Italiana per l'esercizio
1929-1930. R. Stamperia della Colonia. Mogadiscio 1931.
203 pp.

Problemi Coloniali (Eritrea e Somalia). Tipografia
del Popolo d'Italia. Milano 1933.
195 pp.

Problemi Coloniali (Eritrea e Somalia). Tipografia
del Popolo d'Italia. Milano 1933.
195 pp.

Somalia Italiana. (Volume Secondo) Editoriale Arte e Storia.
Milano 1937.
639 pp. ills.

CORSIE,A.

Purquoi la Francia doit occuper Cheik-Said.
"Revue Quest. Colonial". Vol. XXXVII. Paris 1912.
194-203 pp.

CORSI,G.

Relazione sulla Somalia Italiana per
l'esercizio 1928-29. Mogadiscio 1929.

CORTINOIS,A.

La Somalia Italiana. Biblioteca Patrie Colonie.
Casa Editrice Vallardi. Milano 1913.
174 pp.

COSSU,F.

Relazione sull'Ogaden. "Archivio Affari
Politici e Civile". Sezione Pol. Cat. II. CL.V.No. II. 1936.

COSTA,M.G.

L'Oltregiuba durante l'occupazione Italiana: Tesi di
Storia e Legislazione Coloniale. Universita degli Studi
di Firenze. Facolta di Scienze Sociali e Politiche.
Firenze 1959-1960.
171 pp.

COSTANZO,G.A.

Problemi della nuova politica coloniale:
La formazione delle classi medie autoctone
nelle tre Somalie. Jovene Edit. Napoli 1955.
60 pp.

_____

La politica Italiana per l'Africa Orientale 1914-1919.
Istituto per l'Oriente. Roma 1957.
218 pp.

_____

Somalie sous tutelle italienne: l'evolution politique
de la Somalie durant les six premieres annees de
l'administration italienne. "Civilisations". Vol. VI.
No. 2. Bruxelles.
301-309 pp.

_____

La Somalia al termine dell'Amministrazione Fiduciaria.
Istituto Italiano per l'Africa. Roma 1960.
61 pp.

C.R.

Pensiamo al Benadir. "Rivista delle
Colonie Italiane". Roma 1907.
70 p.

D'AGOSTINO,O.P.

Francia contro Italia in Africa (Gibuti).
La Prora. Milano 1939.
53 pp.

_____

La tutelle italienne en Somalie. "Revue Coloniale Belgique".
Bruxelles 1952.
283-285 pp.

D.A.N.

Quarto rapporto italiano sull'amministrazione
della Somalia. "Eurafrica". No. 3. Roma 1954.
7-8 pp.

DAVIS,H.

Resurrection in Djibouti. "Saturday Evening Post".
CCXVI. 1943.
17 p.

DEGLI ALBERTI,G.

Appunti sulla Somalia settentrionale. "Rivista
delle Colonie Italiane". Roma 1906.
105 p.

DELLA VALLE,C.

Carlo Citerni e la delimitazione dei confini
Italo-Etiopici in Somalia. "Rivista delle Colonie Italiane".
Roma 1935.
238 p.

———————

Le origini della Somalia Italiana al Parlamento (II):
La Societa Commerciale del Benadir (1900-1905).
"Annali Africa Italiana". Roma 1939.
299-312 pp.

DE LA RUE,A.

La Somalie Francaise. Gallimarch.
Paris 1937.
162 pp.

DEL PRETE.

Lineamenti dell'Amministrazione Fiduciaria
in Somalia. Bari 1959.

DE MARINIS.

Discorsi Parlamentari: Ordinamenti del Benadir:
Pelriscatto dei porti della Somalia Meridionale-
Proposto del credito e Banca Coloniale-Accordo
Franco-Italiano per l'Etiopia e questione di Lugh.
Tipografia Camera dei Deputati. Roma 1906-07.
211 pp.

DE MARTINO,G.

Ii programma per la Somalia. "Rivista delle
Colonie Italiane". Roma 1910.
545 p.

———————

Relazione sulla Somalia I 'anno
1910 (appendice). Tipografia Camera dei Deputati.
Roma 1911.
159 pp.

La Somalia Italiana nei tre anni del mio Governo.
Tipografia Camera dei Deputati. Roma 1912.
211 pp. tables.

La Somalia nostra (Conferenza). Istituto Italiano
d'Arte Grafiche. Bergamo 1913.
114 pp.

DE RIVOIRE,D.

Les Francais a Obock. Picard et Kaan. Paris 1887.

DE VECCHI,C.M.

Delimitazione del confine tra Somalia
e Somaliland. "La Rassegna Italiana".
Vol. XL. Fasc. No. 210. Roma 1935.
802 p.

Orizzonti d'Impero: 5 anni in Somalia.
Mondadori. Milano 1935.
378 pp.

DI VALLOIA,G.

Nella Somalia Italiana. "Illustrazione Coloniale".
No. 1. Milano 1924.
20 p.

DRAKE-BROCKMAN,R.E.

British Somaliland. Hurst & Blackett, Ltd.
London 1912.
344 pp.

DRUETTI,G.

La Somalia Italiana. "Atti 1° Congresso Studi Coloniali".
Vol. VII. 1931.
2 p.

DRYSDALE,J.

The Somali Dispute. Pall Mall Press.
(World Affairs Special Series). London 1964.
183 pp. map.

EMMEPI.

Documenti della situazione somala. "Africa". No. 1.
Roma 1954.
21-23 pp.

EXPOSITION COLONIALE INTERNATIONALE (PARIS).

La côte francaise des Somalis. Presse Coloniale Illustree.
Paris 1931.

FELICE,O.S.

II Benadir ignorato. Bernardo Lux. Roma 1914.
204 pp.

FENN. C.

Bloodness victory in French Somaliland.
"Tarvel". Vol. LXXXI. 1943.
16 19 pp.

FILESI,T.

La Somalia come e e come era. "Africa". No. 2.
Roma 1948.
41 p.

_____AND COSTANZO,G. AND BIGI,F.

La Somalia al termine della Amministrazione Fiduciaria.
Istituto Italiano per l'Africa. Roma 1960.
480 pp.

FILONARDI,V.

Considerazioni sulla Somalia Italiana.
Stab. Tipografico Italiano. Roma 1893.

FINAZZO,G.

L'Italia nel Benadir: L'azione di
Vincenzo Filonardi 1884-1896. Ateneo. Roma 1966.
480 pp.

FOREIGN OFFICE (GREAT BRITAIN).

Italian Somaliland (A handbook). Historical Section
of the Foreign Office. Ser. No. 128. H.M.S.O. London 1920.
VI, + 27 pp.

_____

French Somaliland (A handbook). Historical Section
of the Foreign Office. Ser. No. 109. H.M.S.O. London 1920.
VI, + 28 pp.

_____

British Somaliland and Sokotra (A handbook).
Historical Section of the Foreign Office.
Ser. No. 97. H.M.S.O. London 1920.
VI, + 39 pp.

The Somalilands" Problems of the Horn of Africa.
"Africa". R. No. 4101. London.

Treaty between the United Kingdom and Italy regulating
certain questions concerning the boundaries of their
respective territories in East Africa/ London 1924.
10 pp.

Agreement concerning claims of certain British and
Italian protected persons and colonial subjects arising
out of raids and incidents on the Anglo-Italian Frontier
in Somaliland, Bihen, 2 September 1930. London 1931.

Memorandum on Political Affairs in the Somaliland
Protectorate. London 1926.

Report on the disposal of the former Italian
colonies in accordance with the terms of the Treaty
of Peace with Italy of 1947. H.M.S.O. London 1953.
47 pp.

FORNARI,G.

La nuova missione dell'Italia in Africa:
La tutela della Somalia. "Rassegna Italiana di
Politica e di Cultura". Anno XXVIII. No. 319. Roma Giugno 1951.
16 pp.

La Somalia nei primi due anni di amministrazione fiduciaria
italiana. (Estr. "La Communita Internazionale, Vol. VII. Fasc. No.
3. 1952). Cedam. Padova 1952.
17 pp.

FOUR POWER COMMISSION OF INVESTIGATION FOR THE FORMER ITALIAN
COLONIES.

Report on Somaliland (2 vols). London 1948.

GADOLA,A.

Il nostro ritorno in Somalia. "Rassegna Espansione Commerciale."
No. 5-6. Milano 1950.
21 p.

GALLUCCI,S.

La Somalia Italiana. Scuola Tipografia Istituto
Pavoniano Artigianelli. Milano 1936.
135 pp.

GARELLI (MAGGIORE).

Somalia Italiana: Situazione interna del
Distretto di Balad. Tipografia Ministero AA.EE.Roma 1912.
11 pp.

GASPARINI,F.

Pionieri italiani in Somalia. "Le Vie del Mondo".
No. 6. Milano 1936.

GIACCARDI,A.

L'opera del Fascismo in Africa. Vol. II.
Mondadori, Milano 1938.
128 p.

GIANNINI,A.

L'ultima fase della questione orientale 1913-1932.
Roma 1933.

GIAVOTTO,M.

Sul Benadir (Conferenza). "Estraz. Atti VII
Congresso Geografico Italiano". 1910-1911.
41-121 pp.

GILMOUR,T.L.

Abyssinia: the Ethiopian railways and the Powers;
being a narrative record of recent events in the
Ethiopian Empire nearly affecting the relation between
Great Britain and France and the maintenance of the
Entent Cordiale. London 1906.
92 pp.

GIORDANO,N.

Dai viaggi dei pionieri d'Africa alla indipendenza
della gente Somala. "Universo". No. 4. Firenze 1958.
509-518 pp.

GIORIO,C.

Relazione generale politica amministrativa
economica del Commissariato dei Migiurtini.
Dante. 15 Luglio 1937.

GODEL-LANNOY.

Das Gebiet des Dschub-Flusses und dessen
Dependenz von Zanzibar. "Mitteilungen der Geogr. Gessellsch".

VIena 1871.
267-272 pp.

GOULED,H.

Ma vie politique pendant treize annees, 1949-1962.
Roneo. Djibouti 1963.
145 pp.

GOUVERNMENT FRANCAIS.

La Côte Francaise des Somalis. "La Documentation Francaise".
"Notes et Etudes Documentaires". No. 1321. Paris Avril 1950.
16 pp.

——————————

Notes d'ensemble sur la Côte Francaise des Somalis.
Ministere de la France d'Outer-Mer. Paris 1956.
125 pp.

——————————

La Côte Francaise des Somalis. "La Documentation Francaise".
"Notes et Etudes Documentaires". No. 2774. Paris Avril 1961.
52 pp.

——————————

Consultation du 19 mars 1967 de la population de
la Côte Francaise des Somalis; rapports de la
Commission de controle et de la Commission de
recensemente et de judgement. "La Documentation Francaise".
"Notes et Etudes Documentaires". No. 3393. Paris Mai 1967.
17 pp.

GOVERNMENT OF ETHIOPIA.

The Ethio-Somalia frontier problem. Ministry of
Information. Addis Abeba 1964.
35 pp. maps.

GOVERNO DELLA SOMALIA.

Le prime elezioni politiche in Somalia 1956.
Stamperia del Governo. Mogadiscio 1957.
378 pp.

——————————

Ufficio Elettorale Centrale: Decisione sui reclami.
Stamperia Missione Cattolica. Mogadiscio 1964.
15 pp.

GOVERNO DELLA SOMALIA ITALIANA.

La Somalia Italiana. Treves. Milano 1929.

47 pp.

Notiziario Politico. Anno III. No. 1. Mogadiscio
Gennaio 1930.

GUCCIARDINI,F.

Eritrea e Somalia. Tipografia Camera dei Deputati.
Roma 1910.
7 pp.

GUGLIELMONT.T.

Di ritorno della Somalia. "Africa".
No. 10-11. Roma 1951.
267 p.

HAJI FARAH A.O.

La Somalia alla vigilia della propria indipendenza.
"Atti del IX° Convegno Economico Italo-Africano,Milano
Giugno 1960". Istituto Agronomico per l'Oltremare.
Fasc. No. 36 52. Firenze 1960.
41 pp.

HAMILTON,J.A.L.

Somaliland. Hutchinson & Co. London 1911.
XV, + 366 pp.

HENRIQUE,L.

Les Colonies Francaises (Obock). Paris 1899.

HESS,R.L.

Italian Colonialism in Somalia. University
of Chicago Press. Chicago 1966.
234 pp. ills.

HUNTER,F.M. AND FULLERTON,J.D.

Reports on Somali Land and the Harar Province.
Government Central Branch Press. Semla 1885.

HUNT,J.A.

Report on General Survey of British Somaliland.
Mogadiscio 1945.
17 pp. maps. diagrs.

A General Survey of the Somaliland Protectorate 1944-1950.
(C.D. & W. Scheme D. 484) The Crown Agents for the Colonies.

London 1951.
203 pp. maps, ills. tables. charts. diagrs.

INGER,S.

Italy and Somaliland. "Italian Affairs". Vol III. 1954.
561-572 pp.

INTER NATIONES.

Somalia and Germany: a pictorial souvenir of the State
Visit of H. E. Aden Abdulla Osman, President of the
Somali Republic to the Federal Republic of Germany
April 6 - 16, 1965. Bonn 1965.

IRACI,L.

Per una demistificazione del colonialismo
italiano, il caso della Somalia. "Terzo Mondo."
Milano Marzo 1969.

IRVING, K.

Area Handbook for Somalia. Supt. of Documents.
U. S. Government Press. Washington, D. C. 1969.
455 pp.

ISLAO MAHADALLE.

Discorso all'O.N.U. il 6 Ottobre 1949.
Stamperia Romana. Roma 1949.
8 pp.

ISMAY,H.L.

Somaliland 1884-1919. "United Service Institution".
Vol. LIII. 1932.
91-109 pp.

ISTITUTO COLONIALE ITALIANO.

Notizie sul Benadir. Tipografia dell'Unione.
Roma 1909.
19 pp.

ISTITUTO ITALIANO PER L'AFRICA.

La Somalia al termine dell'Amministrazione
Fiduciaria. Roma 1960.
61 pp.

ISTITUTO STUDI POLITICA INTERNAZIONALE.

L'Africa Orientale: illustrazione storico-geografica.
(Somalia, Costa dei Somali, Somalia Inglese). Vol. II.
Mondadori, Milano 1936.
519 672 pp.

ISTITUTO UNIVERSITARIO DELLA SOMALIA.

International Cooperation in Africa: Report of
the Study Congress held at Mogadiscio from 14 to 16
January 1960. Dott. A. Giuffre. Milano 1960.
498 pp. ills. (Multi-lingual: English,Italian,Arabic).

ITALIAN TRUSTEESHIP ADMINISTRATION OF SOMALILAND.

Results and prospects of the Italian Trusteeship
Administration of Somaliland on completion of half
of Trusteeship Period. New York June 1955.
42 pp.

_____

Report of the Italian Government to the General
Assembly of the United Nations on its Trusteeship
Administration of Somalia 1959.

ITALICUS.

L'opera compiuta in Somalia da Maurizio Rava.
"La Rassegna Italiana". Fasc. No. 206. Roma 1935.
648 p.

JARDINE,D.

Somaliland: Cinderella of Empire. "African Society".
Vol. XXIV. London 1925.

JOELSON,F.S.

East Africa Today: an intimate description of
Kenya Colony, British Somaliland. 1928.
420 pp.

JOHNSON, J.W.

Historical Atlas of the Horn of Africa. Mogadishu 1967.
15 pp. ills. maps.

JOUBERT,J.

La question de Cheik-Said: un Gibraltar francais
abandonne. "Revue Question Coloniale". Vol. XXXVII. Paris 1912.
72-76 pp.

LABROUSSE,H.

Une tentative d'implantation russe en Cote Francaise
des Somalis en 1889: l'affaire de Sgallo.
"Revue Pount". No. 5. La Societe D.'etudes de l'Afrique
Orientale. Djibouti 1968.

LAMY,R.

Le destin des Somalis. Cahiers de l'Afrique et

de l'Asie. Editions Peyronnet. Paris 1959.
163-212 pp.

LATHAM-BROWN,D.J.

The Ethiopia-Somaliland Frontier Dispute.
"International and Comparative Law Quarterly"
London April 1956.

Recent Developments in the Ethiopia-Somaliland Dispute.
"The International and Comparative Law Quarterly".
London January 1961.

LAVISON,R.

Lotta di influenze in Somalia.
"Somalia d'Oggi". No. 4. Mogadiscio Dicembre 1957.
24-27 pp.

La Somalie d'hier e d'aujoudhui. "Revue Militare
de Information". 1957.
7-33 pp.

LAWRENCE,S.F.

Somaliland under Italian Administration.
Woodrow Wilson Foundation. New York 1955.

LEFEVRE,R.

Politica Somala. Cappelli. Bologna 1933.
240 pp.

Passato, presente ed avvenire in Somalia.
"Rivista delle Colonie Italiane". Roma 1935.
103 p.

LE NOUVEAU LAROUSSE ILLUSTRE'.

Benadir-Somalia. Vol. VII. Paris.
211 pp.

LE POINTE,H.

La colonisation francaise au pays des Somalis.
Jouve. Paris 1914.
99 pp.

LESSING,P.

La chute de l'Empire fasciste en Afrique Orientale
en 1941. "Historia-Magazine". No. 17. Paris Fevrier 1968.

449-459 pp.

LEWIS, I.M.

Progressi costituzionali del nazionalismo Somalo.
"Somalia d'Oggi". No. 4. Mogadiscio 1957.
11 p.

————————

Modern political movements in Somaliland. International
African Institute (Memorandum XXX). "Reprinted from Africa.
Vol. XXVII. No. 3. July 1958 and No. 4. October 1958).
Oxford University Press. London 1958.
41 pp.

————————

Problems in the Development of Modern Leadership and
Loyalties in the British Somaliland Protectorate, and
U.N. Trusteeship Territory of Somalia. "Civilisations".
Vol. X. Bruxelles 1960.

————————

Pan-Africanism and Pan-Somalism. "The Journal of Modern
African Studies". Vol. 1. No. 2. London 1963.
147-161 pp.

————————

Pan-Africanism and Pan-Somalism. University of London.
Institute of Commonwealth Studies. "Reprint Series". No. 17.
14 pp.

————————

The Somali Republic since independence. "World".
No. 3. Vol. 19. London April 1963.
7 pp.

LEZZI, E.A.

Cenni sulla Somalia inglese. "Africa Italiana".
Vol. XXIV. Roma.

LOTI, P.

Obock en passant. "Revue Politique et Litteraire".
Paris 26 Fevrier 1887.

LUCHINI, R.

Somalia indipendente. "Rivista Geografica Americana".
No. 241. 1955-1956.
8 pp.

LUIGI DI SAVOIA (IL DUCA DEGLI ABRUZZI).

Conferenza sulla Somalia. "Rivista delle Colonie Italiane".
Roma 1920.
403 p.

LUPIS,G.

Di ritorno della Somalia. "Africa". No. 10-11.
Roma 1951.
267 p.

LYTTON,N.A.S.

The stolen desert: A study of Uhuru in North East Africa.
Macdonald. London 1966.
252 pp. ills. map. bibl.

MACCHIORO,G.

Relazione sulla Somalia Italiana per l'anno
1908-1909. Tipografia Camera dei Deputati. Roma 1910.
114 pp.

MAFFI,Q.

Le elezioni amministrative in Somalia.
"Africa". no. 3-4. Roma 1954.
97-98 pp.

MALACCHINI,M.

Il passato e il presente nella Somalia Italiana.
Verona 1922.

MANASSEI,T.

Le prime colonie d'Italia: Eritrea, Somalia.
Istituto Geografico De Agostini. Novara 1912.

MANTEGAZZA,V.

Il Benadir. Treves. Milano 1908.

MANZOLI,G.

Relazione sulla colonie del Benadir: Stato
attuale e lavori da compiersi. P.B. Bellini.
Milano 1910.
72 pp.

MARIAM,M.W.

The background of the Ethio-Somalia boundry dispute.
Berhanena Selam P.P. Addis Abeba 1964.
83 pp. maps. Bibl.

MARIANI,V.C.

L'Italia in Africa: il mandto Italiano in Somalia.
"Espansione Commerciale". No. 3-4. Milano.
57-58 pp.

_____

La futura Somalia indipendente. "Rassegna di Espansione
Commerciale". No. 11-12. Milano 1952.
21-24 pp.

MARSHALL,A.D.

Somalia: un esperimento delle Nazioni Unite.
"Somalia d'Oggi". No. 1. Mogadiscio 1957.
44 p.

MARSTON,T.S.

Britain's imperial role in the Red Sea area
1800-1878. The Shoe String Press. Hamden, Connecticut 1961.
XIV,550 pp.

MARTIN,C.J.

The Somali Republic. (The British Survey).
The British Society for International Understanding.
"Main Series". No. 203. London February 1966.
20 pp.

MARTINEAU.

La Côte Francaise des Somalis. Edition Geographiques
Maritimes et Coloniales. Paris 1931.

MARTINO,E.

Due anni in Somalia. Stamperia AFIS.
Mogadiscio 1955.
162 pp.

MARTINOLI,G.

Premesse e promesse della Somalia. 1928.
30 pp.

MASI,C.

L'Eritrea e la Somalia nella storia politica
e diplomatica della nazione italiana.
"L'Africa Orientale Italiana". Roma 1933.

MAUGINI,A.

La Somalia Italiana. "Rivista Agricoltura
Tropicale e Subtropicale". No. 10-12.
Firenze Ottobre-Dicembre 1947.

221-233 pp.

_____

Ritorno in Somalia. "Rivista di Agricoltura
Tropicale e Subtropicale". Firenze 1950.

M.B.

Documenti della situazione somala.
"Africa". No. 1. Roma 1954. 21-22 pp.

MERCATELLI,L.

Progetto di ordinamento della Somalia
Italiana Meridionale. Roma 1905.
27 pp.

MEREGAZZI,R.

La Somalia Italiana. "Italia Coloniale".
Roma-Milano 1928.
235 p.

_____

L'amministrazione Fiduciaria Italiana della
Somalia (AFIS). Dott. A. Giuffre. Milano 1954.
191 p.p.

MICHELOTTI,P.

Un protettorato nella Somalia rifiutato
da Rudini. "Antischiavismo". No. 3. 1929.

MILLE,P.

Djibouti clef de l'empire francaise.
"Le Temps". 1939.

MINISTERE DE LA FRANCE D'OUTERMER.

La Côte Francaise des Somalis. Paris 1950.

(R) MINISTERO AFFARI ESTERI.

Protettorato Italiano sul Sultanato di Obbia
e sui territori di Grand e Uadi Nogal. Tipografia
Ministero AA.EE. Roma 1890.
126 pp.

_____

L'Africa Italiana al Parlamento Nazionale 1882-1905.
Tipografia Unione Coop. Editrice. Roma 1907.
989 p.

_____

Memorie,comparse e sentenza per la liquidazione della
Societa anonima Commerciale Italiana per il Benadir.
Tipografia Berbero e C. Roma 1907-1910.
148 pp.

Relazione della Commissione d'inchiesta sul
dissidio Carletti di Giorgio. Tipografia
Ministero Affari Esteri. Roma 1909.
20 pp.

La Foce del Giuba: Negoziato fra l'Italia ed
l'Inghilterra 8-15 Luglio 1911. G. Bertero. Roma 1912.
37 pp.

MOCHI,L.

La Somalia Italiana (Benadir) e il suo avvenire.
Paravia. Napoli 1896.
41 pp.

MOHAMED F. SIAD.

Le elezioni in Somalia. "Africa".
No. 1-2. Roma 1956.
16-17 pp.

La Somalie a mi chemin vers l'indipendence.
"Eurafrica". No. 3. Roma 1955.
40-42 pp.

Somalia e Occidente. "Africa".
No. 3. Roma 1958.
69 p.

La vita politica somala nella democrazia tradizionale.
"Somalia d'Oggi". Anno II. No. 1. Mogadiscio Gennaio-
febbraio 1957.
2 p.

MOHAMED A. OMAR.

Che cos'e la Somalia. "Africa d'Oggi". Roma 1952.

MONDAINI,G.

All'alba della Somalia Italiana:
Emilio Dulio Governatore. "L'Italia d'Oltremare".

Roma 1933.
584 p.

MONILE,F.

Somalia. L. Capelli Edit. Bologna 1932.
268 pp.

MORGANTINI,A.M.

Somalie sous tutelle italienne 1956-1957.
"Civilisation". No. 3. Bruxelles 1958.
429-445 pp.

MORI,A.

La Somalia Italiana nella storia e nella
colonizzazione dello A.O.: Programma corso svolto
negli anni scolastici 1902-03-04.
12 pp.

_____

L'azione coloniale dell'Italia nella Somalia:
il periodo delle esplorazioni. "Bollettino Societa
Geografica Italiana". Vol. IV. Roma 1903.
532-560 pp.

_____

Il Benadir: Cenni e Notizie. Bemporad. Firenze 1911.
30 pp.

_____

Terre e Nazioni in Africa (Somalia).
Vallardi. Milano 1936.
87-127 pp.

MUCCIARELLI,C.

Hanno dominato i Portoghesi nel Benadir.
"Bollettino Societa Africana d'Italia". Napoli 1908.
8 p.

MYLIUS.

L'Italia nel Benadir. Lombardi. Milano 1895.

OBERLE', P.

Afars et Somalis: le dossier de Djibouti.
Presence Africaine. Paris 1971.
296 pp. map. ills. bibl.

ONOR,R.

La Somalia Italiana. **Edit.Irene Onor.
Bocca.** Torino 1925.

OSS,M.

Il Benadir e il suo avvenire. "L'Oltremare".
Roma 1929.
456 p.

PANKHURST,E.S.

Ex-Italian Somaliland. Philosophical Library.
London 1951.
460 pp. maps. ills.

PANTANO,G.

Nel Benadir: la citta di Merca e la regione
Bimal. Belforte. Livorno 1910.

---

23 anni di vita Africana: Eritrea,
Somalia, Libia. Casa Editrice Milit. Ital.
Firenze 1932.
359 pp.

PESENTI,G.

Le origini, i primordi, gli sviluppi
della Somalia (Conferenza). Reale Stamperia
della Colonia. Mogadiscio 1939.
19 pp.

PESTALOZZA,G.

Il Sultanato dei Migiurtini. Tipografia
Ministero AA.EE. Roma 1901.
43 pp.

PIACENTINI,R.

Il protettorato italiano della Somalia
settentrionale. Coop. Ital. 1911.

Il protettorato della Somalia Italiana.
Popolo Romano. Roma 1911.

PIAZZA,G.

Il Benadir. Bontempelli ed Invernizzi.
Milano 1913.
408 pp.

PIAZZI,D.

La Somalia di ieri e quella di oggi.
"Illustrazione Coloniale". No. 1. Milano 1929.
47 p.

PICCIOLI,A.

Gibuti la freccia nel fianco. "Rassegna Storica
Risorgimento". Vol. XXI. 1934.
74-124 pp.

PIRONE,M.

Somalie sous tutelle italienne. "Chronique Culturelle".
Vol. VIII. No. 4. Bruxelles 1958.

_____

Somalie sous tutelle italienne. "Chronique Culturelle".
No. 1. Vol. IX. Bruxelles 1959.

_____

La Somalie a la veille de l'independance.
"Chronique Culturelle". Vol. X. No. 2. Bruxelles 1960.

_____

Somalia: politica dal luglio 1960 al luglio 1961.
"Africa". No. 3-4. Roma 1961.
107-111 pp.

PISTOLESE,G.E.

L'acquisto dell'Oltregiuba. "La Rassegna Italiana".
Vol. XXXIV. Roma 1933.

PIVATO,M.

La nostra colonia del Benadir. C. Ferrari Edit.
Venezia 1914.
73 pp.

POINSOT, JEAN PAUL.

Ainsi nquit Djibouti. Serie de 23 articles
publies dans le Reveil de Djibouti du 10 octobre
1959 au 12 mars 1960. Djibouti 1960.

_____

Djibouti et la Côte francaise des Somalis.
(Album illustre de 55 photos). Hachette. Paris 1964.

POLLACCI,G.

Studi sulla Somalia Meridionale (a cura della S.A.B.I.)Genova.

Societa An. d'Arti Grafiche S. Bernardino. Siena 1935.
73 pp.

POMILIO,M.

Somalia nell'anno X. "L'Africa Italiana". Roma 1932.
60 p.

POWELL-COTTON,D.

Notes on Italian Somaliland.
(MSS British Museum and Pitt Rivers Museum-Oxford).

RAVA,M.

Somalia (Luglio 1931-Luglio 1934).
R. Stamperia della Colonia. Mogadiscio 1934.
275 pp.

La Somalia e sua posizione nell'impero.
"Rivista delle Colonie Italiane". Roma 1937.
671 p.

Alcune verita sul Benadir. "L'Italia all'Estero". 1939.
237-249 pp.

RAYNE,H.A.

Sun,sand and Somalis: leaves from the note-book
of a district commissioner in British Somaliland.
London 1921.
223 pp.

REECE,G.

The Horn of Africa. "International Affairs". Vol. XXX.
No. 4. London October 1954.
440-449 pp.

REPUBBLICA ITALIANA (Official).

Relazione sulle attivita del Ministero delle
Colonie. (Somalia). Roma 1918.
129-159 pp.

Relazione della VII Sezione della Commissione del
dopo guerra: Questioni Coloniali (varie relazioni sulla Somalia).
R. Ministero delle Colonie. Tipografia Camera dei Deputati.
Roma 1919.
322 pp.

I progressi della Somalia sotto l'Amministrazione
Fiduciaria Italiana. Presidenza del Consiglio dei
Ministri. "Documenti di Vita Italiani". No. 4. Roma 1952.
285-294 pp.

Il terzo rapporto all'O.N.U. sull'Amministrazione
Fiduciaria Italiana: L'opera compiuta per preparare
la Somalia alla indipendenza. Presidenza del Consiglio
dei Ministri. "Documenti di Vita Italiana". No. 26.
Roma 1954.
1999-2004 pp.

L'Italia e la Somalia: i risultati di 4 anni di
Amministrazione Fiduciaria. Presidenza del Consiglio
dei Ministri. "Documenti di Vita Italiana". No. 34.
Roma 1954.
2637-2642 pp.

L'ultimo rapporto all'O.N.U. sulla Somalia. Presidenza
del Consiglio dei Ministri. "Documenti di Vita Italiana".
No. 46. Roma 1955.
3509-3606 pp.

Amministrazione della Somalia durante 1956.
Presidenza del Consiglio dei Ministri.
"Documenti di Vita Italiana". No. 73. Roma 1957.
5757-5764 pp.

Supplemento al rapporto 1958 sulla Amministrazione
Fiduciaria della Somalia concernente il periodo 1-1-31-5 1959.
Roma 1959. (Ministero Affari Esteri).
14 pp.

L'Amministrazione Fiduciaria della Somalia e i rapporti
dell'Italia con la Repubblica Somala: Relazione presentata
al Parlamento Italiano dal Ministro per gli Affari Esteri,
On. Antonio Segni. Ministero degli Affari Esteri. Istituto
Poligrafico dello Stato. Roma Ottobre 1961.
208 pp.

Italia e Somalia: Dieci anni di collaborazione.
Presidenza del Consiglio dei Ministri. Istituto
Poligrafico dello Stato. Roma 1962.
211 pp.

La Somalia durante l'Amministrazione Fiduciaria Italiana.
Presidenza del Consiglio dei Ministri.
"Documenti di Vita Italiana". No. 134. Roma 1963.
10493-10504 pp.

REPUBLIQUE FRANCAISE.

Côte Francaise des Somalis   1955.
Jibuti 1956.
125 pp.

REPUBLIQUE ITALIENNE. (Official)

Rapport du Gouvernement Italien a l'Assemblee
Generale des Nations Unies sur l'Administration
de la Somalie Places sous la Tutelle de l'Italie,
Avril 1950 - Decembre 1950. Ministere des Affairs
Etrangeres. Istituto Poligrafico dello
Stato. Rome 1951.
335 pp. maps, tables, charts, ills.

Rapport du Gouvernement Italien a l'Assemblee
Generale des Nations Unies sur l'Administration
de la Somalie Places sous la Tutelle de l'Italie, 1951.
Ministere des Affairs Etrangeres. Istituto Poligrafico
dello Stato. Rome Avril 1952.
396 pp. maps tables, charts, ills.

Rapport du Gouvernement Italien a l'Assemblee
Generale des Nations Unies sur l'Administration
de la Somalie Places sous la Tutelle de l'Italie, 1952.
Ministere des Affairs Etrangeres. Istituto Poligrafico
dello Stato. Rome Avril 1953.
404 pp. maps, tables, charts ills.

Rapport du Gouvernement Italien a l'Assemblee
Generale des Nations Unies sur l'Administration
de la Somalie Places sous la Tutelle de l'Italia, 1953.
Ministere des Affairs Etrangeres. Istituto Poligrafico
dello Stato. Rome Mai 1954.
528 pp. maps, tables charts ills.

Rapport du Gouvernement Italien a l'Assemblee
Generale des Nations Unies sur l'Administration
de la Somalie Places sous la Tutelle de l'Italie, 1954.
Ministere des Affairs Etrangeres. Istituto Poligrafico
dello Stato. Rome Mai 1955.
367 pp. maps, tables, charts, ills.

Rapport du Gouvernment Italien a l'Assemblee
Generale des Nations Unies sur l'Administration
de la Somalie Places sous la Tutelle de l'Italie, 1956.
301 pp. maps, tables, charts, ills. (Rome 1957)

Rapport du Gouvernement Italien a l'Assemblee
Generale des Nations Unies sur l'Administration
de la Somalie Places sous la Tutelle de l'Italie, 1957.
Ministere des Affairs Etrangeres. Istituto Poligrafico
dello Stato. Rome Juin 1958.
291 pp. maps tables, charts, ills.

Rapport du Gouvernement Italien l'Assemblee
Generale des Nations Unies sur l'Administration
de la Somalie Places sous la Tutelle de l'Italie 1958.
Ministere des Affairs Etrangeres. Istituto Poligrafico
dello Stato. Rome Juin 1959.
315 pp. maps, tables, charts, ills.

Rapport du Gouvernement Italien a l'Assemblee
Generale des Nations Unies sur l'Administration
de la Somalie Places sous la Tutelle de l'Italie, 1959.
Ministere des Affairs Etrangeres. Istituto Poligrafico
dello Stato. Rome Mai 1960.
375 pp. maps, tables, charts,ills.

Renseignements Supplementaires su Rapport 1959
sur l'Administration de Tutelle de la Somalie concernant
la periode 1er Janvier-30 Avril 1960. Ministere des
Affairs Etrangers. Rome Juin 1960.
16 pp.

RILEY,B.

Term paper on Foreign Policy of Somalia.
Johns Hopkins University. 1964.

RIVERI,C.

Relazione sulla Somalia Italiana. Ministero delle Colonie.
Ufficio Studi. Roma 1922.

Relazione al 10 Ottobre 1921 sulla situazione generale
della Somalia Italiana. Sind. Italiano Arti Grafiche. Roma 1924.
104 pp.

Relazione annuale sulla situazione generale
della Colonia 1910-1921. Sind. Italiano Arti Grafiche.
Roma 1930.

RIVLIN,B.

The United Nations and the Italian colonies.
Carnegie Endowment for International Peace.
New York 1950.
IV, + 114 ⊦p. maps.

ROBECCHI BRICCHETTI,L.

Dal Benadir: Lettere alla Societa Anti-Schiavista.
La Poligrafica. Milano 1904.
286 pp.

_____

Somalia redenta. "Antischiavismo". No. 3. 1906.
68-71 pp.

ROBERTAZZI,B.

II Somaliland e l'Unione Somala. "Universo".
No. 5. Firenze 1960.
1017-1030 pp.

RODD, J.R.

Social and diplomatic memories (second series 1894-1901).
Arnold. London 1923.

ROLLINI,G.

L'Oltregiuba nel primo anno di occupazione italiana.
"La Rassegna Italiana". E Roma 1927.
81 p.

_____

L'Oltregiuba nella sua realta e nel suo avvenire.
"La Rassegna Italiana". Roma 1927.
187 p.

ROMANI,A.

La nuova realta Somala: Un popolo verso
l'indipendenza. (Conferenza tenuta a Firenze
nel Salone Brunellesco il 16 Giugno 1959). Roma 1959.
12 pp.

ROSA,U.

Somalia. "La Voce dell'Africa". No. 20.
Roma 1961.
4-5 pp.

ROSENTHAL, E.

The fall of Italian East Africa. London 1941.

ROSSETTI,C.

La colonizzazione italiana del Benadir.
Bertero G. Roma 1900.
33 pp.

———————————

La Colonia del Benadir. (Opuscolo). 1907.

ROUARD, DE CARD.

Les possessions francaise de la côte orientale
d'Afrique. "Revue Generale de Droit International
Public". Pedone. Paris 1899.

ROZIS,A.

Le protectorat de la Côte des Somalis.
"Mois Col. ". Vol. III. 1905.
454-460 pp.

———————————

A la côte des Somalis et en Ethiopie:
rapport de la Mission Rozis. "Mois Col".
Vol. VI. 1908.
21-37 pp.

RUSSO,E.

La residenza di Mahaddei-Uen. Monogr. I Colon.
Istituto Coloniale Italiano. Tipografia Unione
Coop. Editrice. Roma 1919.
27 pp.

SALEM,O.

La Somalie, hier et aujord'hui. "Presence Africaine".
Vol. III. Paris 1961.

SALOMONE,F.

Governo Somalo in Somalia. "Africa".
No. 4-5 Roma 1956.
96-97 pp.

SAYRE,F.B.

United States views on staggering problems in
Somaliland. "Bulletin of the U. S. Department of State".
Vol. XXV. Washington, D. C. 1951.
32-34 pp.

SCERNI,P.

Lo Sviluppo della Somalia. "Rivista delle Colonie
e d'Oriente". Bologna 1927.
119 p.

SEARS,M.

Statement on Somaliland. "Bulletin of the U.S.
Department of State". B. Vol. XXXI. Washington, D. C. 1954.
34 p.

SERRAZANETTI,M.

Considerazioni sulla nostra attivita coloniale
in Somalia. La Rapida. Bologna 1933.
26 pp.

––––––––––––––

La politica indigena in Somalia. Bologna 1934.

SFORZA,C.

La Missione dell'Italia in Somalia.
Menaglia. Roma 1950.

SILBERMAN,L.

The Frontier of Somalia. Hargeisa 1960.
417 pp.

––––––––––––––

Why the Haud was Ceded."Cahiers D'Etudes Africaines".
Vol. II. Paris 1961.

SOMALI INSTITUTE OF PUBLIC ADMINSTRATION.

Orientation course for foreign experts working
in Somalia: Perspectives on Somalia. SIPA. Mogadiscio.
128 pp. tables. map. Appendices.

––––––––––––––

A Directory of Senior Government Officials. SIPA.
Mogadiscio October 1967.
25 pp.

––––––––––––––

Training Manual of Office Procedure. SIPA.
Mogadiscio May 1, 1967.
87 pp. tables.

––––––––––––––

Report on Clerical Training Centre Hargeisa. SIPA.
Mogadiscio September 1967.
76 pp.

_____

An O and M Study of the Mogadiscio International
Airport: report prepared by participants of the
1st O&M Course. SIPA. Mogadiscio November 1967.
39 pp.

_____

SIPA first management development course for the
senior officers (graduates) of the government of
Somalia, Nov. 4, 1967 - Feb. 1, 1968. SIPA. Mogadiscio 1968.

_____

Manual of **registry** and filing procedures. SIPA.
Mogadiscio 1968.

_____

Reading Binder: O&M Course, Sept. 16 Nov. 11, 1967.
SIPA. Mogadiscio 1967.

_____

Manual of registry and filing procedures. SIPA.
Mogadiscio 1968.
34 pp.

_____

An O and M Study of the Mogadiscio Municipality:
Report prepared by participants of the 3rd O & M Course.
SIPA. Mogadiscio January 1969.
54 pp.

_____

Inspection Manual. SIPA. Mogadiscio January 1969.
10 pp.

SOMALILAND PROTECTORATE (OFFICIAL)

Somaliland Protectorate. Mills & Co. Coventary 1925.
11 pp.

_____

Code of regulations for the guidance of civil officers
in the Protectorate service. 1st Edition. Waterlow & Sons Ltd.
London 1928.
XXII, 106 pp.

_____

Somaliland Protectorate: General Orders 1936.
Waterlow & Sons Limited. London 1936.

Report on General Survey of Somaliland Protectorate, 1948.
Hargeisa 1948.
17 pp.

Report on General Survey of Somaliland Protectorate 1949.
(British Somaliland). Hargeisa October 1950.
42 pp.

Inquiry into the future organisation of town councils.
(Report and Appendices). Hargeisa 1952.
83 pp.

Commission on the Civil Service (Report 1953-54).
Government Printer. Hargeisa 1954.
181 pp. tables.

Revised conditions of service. Hargeisa 1954.

Report of a commission to review the salaries of
the civil service. Hargeisa 1956.
162 pp. tables.

Somaliland Protectorate: (a Handbook).
The Information Office. Hargeisa 1956.
16 pp. ills. maps.

Annual report on the administration of British Somaliland for
the year ended 31st December 1954. Cowasjee Dinshan & Bros.
(Printers) Aden 1957.
88 pp.

Agreement between the Government of the United Kingdom
of Great Britain and Northern Ireland and the Government
of Ethiopia relating to certain matters connected with the
withdrawal of British Military Administration from the
territories designated as the Reserve Area and Ogaden,

London November 1954. H.M.S.O. London 1955.
5 pp.

Somaliland Protectorate (A Handbook).
Information Office. Hargeisa 1957.

Commission of Inquiry into Unofficial Representation
on the Legislative Council (Report). Hargeisa 1958.
78 pp. tables. diagrs.

Commission on Representational Reform. (Report) Apr-May 1959.
Hargeisa 1959.
55 pp. tables. map.

Commission on the Somalisation of the Civil
Service (Report). Hargeisa January 1959.
100 pp.

Somalisation Policy. (Chief Secretary's Report to the
Legislative Council).
Hargeisa October 19th, 1959.

SOMALI REPUBLIC (OFFICIAL).

Ordinamento del Personale Civile dello Stato.
Mogadiscio 1962.
43 pp. tables.

Police Force: 12th Anniversary. Mogadiscio 20th December 1962.
63 pp. (Blingual: English and Italian).

The Somali Peninsula: A new light on imperial motives.
Ministry of Information. Mogadishu 1962.
137 pp. maps. (Printed in London 1962 by Steaples Printer).

La Peninsule de Somalie: Une lumiere nouvelle sur
les motifs imperialistes. Service de l'Information.
Mogadishu 1962. (Printed in Paris 1962 by Danel, Oaris-Little)
222 pp. carte.

The Issue of the Northern Frontier District: a report
on the events leading to the severance of diplomatic
relations between the Somali Republic and the
United Kingdom. Ministry of Information. Government Printer.
Mogadishu May 1963.
92 pp. map.

Ambasciate e Legazioni Estere in Somalia. Ministero
degli Affari Esteri. Mogadiscio 15 Agosto 1963.
95 pp.

Discorso Programmatico in occasione della presentazione
del nuovo Gabinetto di S.E. l'On. le Abdirizak Haji Hussen
Primo Ministro e Presidenza del Consiglio dei Ministri.
Assemblea Nazionale. Mogadiscio 9 Luglio 1964.
60 pp.

Programma del secondo Governo di S.E. l'On. le
Abdirizak Haji Hussen Presidente del Consiglio
dei Ministri. Mogadiscio 15 Settembre 1964.
52 pp.

La Repubblica Somala e l'organizzazione dell'unita
Africana. Sezione Pubbliche Relazioni. Ministero
degli Affari Esteri. Tipo-Lit. Missione. Mogadiscio 1964.
58 pp.

The Somali Republic and the Organization of
African Unity. The Public Relations Section
Ministry of Foreign Affairs. Tipo-Lit. Missione.
Mogadiscio 1964.
56 pp.

Ambasciate e Legazioni Estere in Somalia Aprile 1965.
Dipartimento del Protocol. Ministero degli Affari Esteri.
Mogadiscio 1965.
71 pp. Index.

Somalia: A Divided Nation seeking reunification.
The Public Relations Service. Ministry of Information.
Hofbuchdruckerei J. F. Carthaus. Bonn April 1965.
55 pp. ills. maps.

French Somaliland in true perspective. Ministry of
Information. Government Press. Mogadiscio 1966.
20 pp.

_____

Premier's "meet the people tour" of all regions of
the Somali Republic from 28th November to 17th December 1966.
Government Printing Press. Mogadiscio.
55 pp. ills. maps.

_____

Report of the Commission on National Broadcasting.
Ministry of Information. Mogadiscio July 1966.
108 pp.

_____

Report of the Commission on Government Printing.
Government Press. Mogadishu March 1966.
35 pp.

_____

French Somaliland: A classic colonial case:
(events leading to the referendum March 19th 1967).
Ministry of Information. Government Press.
Mogadishu March 1967.
38 pp. ills. maps.

_____

Dichiarazioni Programmatiche di S.E. Mohamed Ibrahim
Egal Presidente del Consiglio dei Ministri. Tipo-Lit.
Missione. Mogadiscio Agosto 1967.
59 pp.

_____

Diplomatic List. Ministry of Foreign Affairs.
Protocol Department. Mogadiscio January 1967.
75 pp.

SOMALI DEMOCRATIC REPUBLIC (OFFICIAL).

My Country and My People: The collected speeches of
Major-General Mohamed Siad Barre, President of the
Supreme Revolutionary Council, October 1969-October 1970.
(Vol. 1). Ministry of Information and National Guidance.
Mogadishu October 1970.
98 pp.

————————

My Country and My People: The collected speeches of
Major-General Mohamed Siad Barre, President of the
Supreme Revolutionary Council, October 1970-October 1971.
Ministry of Information and National Guidance.
Mogadishu October 1972.
218 pp.

————————

Speech of the President of the Supreme Revolutionary
Council of the Somali Democratic Republic on the occasion
of May Day 1972. The Ministry of Labour and Sport.
State Printing Press.
79 pp. ills.

————————

New Era (No. 7.) Somalia in the World Community.
Ministry of Information and National Guidance.
Mogadishu 1972.
50 pp. ills.

————————

Broadcasting Handbook. Ministry of Information
and National Guidance. Mogadishu October 1972.
65 pp. ills.

SORRENTINO,G.

Condizione in cui trovasi la colonia del Benadir
nel 1897 e suo probabile avvenire. "Bollettino
Societa Africana d'Italia". Fasc. IX.X.XI.XII.Napoli 1907.
184-209-241-266 pp.

————————

Ricordi del Benadir (a cura Soc. Africana d'Italia).
Tipografia Golia. Napoli 1912.
149 pp.

STAFFORD, J. H.

The Anglo-Italian Somaliland Boundry.
"Geographical Journal". Vol. LXXVIII. London 1931.
102-125 pp.

STEFANINI,G.

STEFANINI,G.

I possedimenti italiani in Africa: Libia,
Eritrea, Somalia. Bemporad. Firenze 1923.
254 pp.

STRAZZA,S.

La Somalia nel quadro dell'Impero.
"L'Italia d'Oltremare". Roma 1938.
240-272-292-326 pp.

SULEYMAN,I.A.

Ungarns Kolonie im Somalilande. Buchdruckerei
der Voster Lloyd Gesellschaft. Budapest 1904.
111 pp.

SUMMERS, G. H.

Somaliland. "Empire at War'. Vol. IV. 1924.
565-569 pp.

SYAD,W.

La Somalie a l'heure de la verite.
"Presence Africaine". No. 3. Paris 1961.
74-97 pp.

T.F.

Mandato sulla Somalia e l'istituto
del "Trusteeship". "Relazione Internazionale".
Milano 1950.

TITTONI,T.

Discorso del Ministero AA.EE. on. Tittoni
sulla questione del Benadir. Tipografia Camera
dei Deputati. Roma 1908.
38 pp.

TOSCANO,M.

Francia ed Italia di fronte al problema di Gibuti.
Quaderni dello Studio Fiorentino di Politica Estera.
Vol. V. Firenze 1939.
55 pp.

TOUVAL,S.

Somali Nationalism: international poltics and
the drive for unity in the Horn of Africa. Harvard
University Press. Cambridge 1963.
214 pp.

TULI,S.

La visita a Roma del Presidente della Repubblica Somala.
"Italiani nel Mondo". No. 19. Roma 1963.
17-19 pp.

U.B.

Nella Somalia Italiana. "L'Africa Italiana".
Roma 1915.
239 pp.

UNITED NATIONS ORGANIZATION.

Project d'accord de tutelle pour le Territoire
de la Somalia sous Administration Italienne.
Rapport Speciale du Conseil de Tutelle. New York 1950.

_____

Texte de l'accord de tutelle pour le Territoire de la
Somalie sous Administration Italienne. New York 1950.
15 pp.

_____

Draft Trusteeship Agreement for the Territory of
Somaliland under Italian Administration Special Report
of the Trusteeship Council. General Assembly Official
Records. 5th Session. Suppl. No. 10. New York 1950.
11 pp

_____

The Trust Territory of Somaliland under Italian Administration.
New York 1952.
343 pp

_____

Rapporto della Missione di Visita delle Nazioni Unite
per i Territori della Africa Orientale - 1951.
(Inviato con lettera del Presidente De Marchena al
(Segretario Generale delle Nazioni Unite del 22 Dicembre 1951).
Somalia sotto l'Amministrazione Italiana. New York 11 Gennaio
1952. 65 pp.

_____

The Trust Territory of Somaliland under Italian Administration.
Report prepared jointly by the Government of Italy, United
Nations Technical Assistance Administration, the FAO, the
UNESCO and the WHO. New York 1952.
IX, + 343 pp.

_____

Report of the UN Visiting Mission to Trust Territories

in East Africa, Somaliland under Italian Administration.
UN Trusteeship Council. New York 1952

———————

Report of the United Nations Advisory Council for the
Trust Territory of Somaliland under Italian Administration.
New York 28 April 1953.

———————

Half way to independence: Somaliland under Italian
Administration. "United Nations Review" , July 1954.
Department of Information. New York, 1954.
II, 30 pp. ills.

———————

Cinque anni di Amministrazione Fiduciaria Italiana
sulla Somalia. Dipartimento dell'Informazione Pubblica.
New York 1954.
27 pp.

———————

Report on Somaliland under Italian Adminstration together
with related documents (United Nations Visiting Mission to
Trust Territories in East Africa 1954). Trusteeship Council.
Official Records. (16th Session). Suppl. No. 2. New York 1955.
IV, + 67 pp

———————

Report on Somaliland under Italian Administration together
with related documents (United Nations Visting Mission to
Trust Territories in East Africa 1957). Trusteeship Council.
Official Records. (22nd session). Suppl. No. 2. New York 1958.
IV, + 39 pp.

———————

Renseignements sur le territoire des Somalis; examen du
Comite Special de l'independence et mesures prises par lui.
New York 1958.

———————

Conditions in Somaliland under Italian Administration.
Trusteeship Council. New York 1960.
35 pp.

UNIVERSITA' DEGLI STUDI DI FIRENZE.

Amministrazione Fiduciaria dell'Italia in Africa.
Centro di Studi Coloniali. Firenze 1948.
415 pp.

VECCHI,B.V.

Migiurtinia. Fratelli Bocca. Torino 1933.
208 pp.

Somalia, Vicende e Problemi. Milano 1934.

Somalia, Vicende e Problemi. Milano 1934.

Somalia di Ieri e di Oggi. "Africa". Roma 1952.

VEDOVATO,G.

L'accord di Amministrazione Fiduciaria della
Somalia. "Idea". Roma Marzo 1950.

Accordi di Amministrazione Fiduciaria Internazionale.
Tipografia Toscana. Firenze 1951.
165 pp.

La Somalia di fronte al '60 "Estrat. dalla Rivista
di Studi Politici Internazionale". Annl XXVI. No. 2. 1959.
Poligrafico Toscano. Firenze 1959.
47 pp.

L'Italia di fronte alla Somalia e all'Africa.
"Italiani nel Mondo". No. 19. Roma 1959.
9-11 pp.

La Somalia: Stato Indipendente. "Rivista di Studi
Politici Internazionali". Anno XXVII. No. 3.
Firenze Luglio-Settembre 1960.
323-329 pp.

Questioni ed aspetti attuali del nuovo stato
Somalo: discorso pronunciato alla Camera dei
Deputati nella seduta del 2 Marzo 1961. Roma 1961.
17 pp.

Accordi Italo-Somali: discorso pronunciato alla
Camera dei Deputati, nella seduta del 24 Gennaio 1962.
Roma 1962.
18 pp.

VICINANZA,G.

La Somalia Italiana. De Rosa e Polidori (Editori).
Napoli 1910.
257 pp.

VIOLATI-TESCARI,F.

Al Benadir. "Rivista Coloniale". Roma 1908.
668 p.

VITALE,M.A.

La Somalia Italiana. "Africa Italiana". 1923.
26 p.

VITALI,V.

La Somalia: Azione del Governo. "Numero Sepciale
di Rivista Costruire". Roma Ottobre 1938.
48 pp.

VITALI,M.

Sulla via di ritorno. Capello. Milano 1947.
72 pp.

ZADOTTI,V.

Collaborazione Italo-Americana in Somalia.
"Africa". No. 10. Roma 1954.
264-267 pp.

ZAGHI,C.

Luigi Robecchi-Bricchetti nel Harar e
nella Somalia. "L'Oltremare". Roma 1932.
115 p.

ZOLI,C.

Relazione generale dell'Alto Commissario per
l'Oltregiuba. Sind. Italiano Arti Grafiche. Roma 1926.
211 pp.

Oltregiuba: notizie raccolte a cura del Commissariato
Generale nel primo anno di occupazione Italiana 1925-1926.
Sind. Italiano Arti Grafiche. Roma Febbraio 1927.
370 pp.

                            RELIGION

BERGNA,C.

L'arrivo dei francescani in
Somalia. "La Somalia Cristiana."
Mogadiscio 1940.
35-37 pp. ills.

CERULLI,E.

Note sul movimento musulmano
in Somalia. "Rivista degli Studi
Orientali." Vol. X. Fasc. No. 1.
Roma 1923.
1 p.

COMITATO DI FESTEGGIAMENTI.

Festeggiamenti in onore di S. Ecc.
Mons. F.V.Filippini - Vescovo Vicario
Apostolico di Mogadiscio: A sua Eccellenza
Mons. F.V. Filippini nel XXV di Episcopata.
Mogadiscio 29 Giugno 1958.
ills.

EBY, O.

Sense and incense. Herald Press.
Scottdale. Pennsylvania 1965.
160 pp. ills. map.

FERRAND,G.

Les comalis: Materiaux
d'etudes sur les pays mussulmans.
Leroux. Paris 1903.

GAIBI,A.

II MULLAH: breve stroia di
flaso Messia. "Rivista Coloniale."
Vol. XXII. Roma 1927.
200-226 pp.

LEWIS, I.M.

The names of God in Northern
Somaliland."Bulletin of the
School of Oriental and African
Studies." Vol. XXII, Part 1.
University of London. 1959.
135-140 pp.

_____

Sufism in Somaliland: a study in

tribal Islam. "Bulletin of the School
of Oriental and African Languages."
Vol. XVIII. London 1956.

PARROCCHIA DI S. ANTONIO DI PADOVA (CHISIMAIO).

La Voce del Giuba: "Bollettino Parrocchiale
Mensile." Anno XIV. No. 1. Chisimaio 1 Gennaio 1965.
27 pp.

La Voce del Giuba: "Bollettino Parrocchiale
Mensile". Anno XIV. No.2. Chisimaio 1 Febbraio 1965.
25 pp.

XIV

STATISTICS AND MULTI-PURPOSE STATISTICAL SURVEYS

SOMALI REPUBLIC (OFFICIAL)

Statistical Abstract of Somalia. No. 1. 1964.
Statistical Department. Planning Directorate.
Mogadiscio December 1964.
66 pp. (Bilingual:English-Italian).

Statistical Abstract of Somalia. No. 3. 1966.
Statistical Department. Ministry of Planning
and Co-ordination. Mogadiscio June 1968.
134 pp. (Bilingual: English-Italian).

Statistical Abstract of Somalia. No. 5. 1968.
Statistical Department. Ministry of Planning
and Co-ordination. Mogadiscio May 1969.
136 pp.

Statistical Abstract of Somalia. No. 6. 1969.
Statistical Department. Ministry of Planning
and Co-ordination. Mogadiscio December 1970.
82 pp. (Bilingual: English-Italian)

Statistical Abstract of Somalia. No. 7. 1970.
Statistical Department. Ministry of Planning
and Co-ordination. Mogadiscio November 1971.
139 pp. map. (Bilingual: English-Italian).

Quarterly Statistical Bulletin. No. 1. 1965.
Statistical Department. Planning Directorate.

Mogadiscio Aprile 1965.
32 pp. (Bilingual: English-Italian).

Quarterly Statistical Bulletin. No. 2. 1965.
Statistical Department. Planning Directorate.
Mogadiscio July 1965.
39 pp. (Bilingual: English-Italian)

Quarterly Statistical Bulletin. No. 3. 1965.
Statiscal Department. **Planning Directorate.**
Mogadiscio October 1965.
41 pp. (Bilingual: English-Italian)

Quarterly Statistical Bulletin. No. 1. 1966.
Statistical Department. **Planning** Directorate.
Mogadiscio Aprile 1966.
42 pp. (Bilingual: English-Italian)

Quarterly Statistical Bulletin. No. 2. 1966.
Statistical Department. Ministry of Planning
and Co-ordination. Mogadiscio July 1966.
42 pp. (Bilingual: English-Italian)

Quarterly Statistical Bulletin. No. 3. 1966.
Statistical Department. Ministry of Planning
and Coordination. Mogadiscio October 1966.
42 pp. (Bilingual: English-Italian).

Somali Statistics. Monthly Bulletin. January 1967.
Statistical Department. Ministry of Planning
and Co-ordination. Mogadiscio.
8 pp.

Somali Statistics. Monthly Bulletin. February 1967.
Statistical Department. Ministry of Planning and
Co-ordination. Mogadiscio.
7 pp.

Somali Statistics. Monthly Bulletin. March 1967.
Statistical Department. Ministry of Planning and
Co-ordination. Mogadiscio.

10 pp. (Bilingual: English-Italian)

Somali Statistics. Monthly Bulletin. May 1967.
Statistical Department. Ministry of Planning
and Co-ordination. Mogadiscio.
11 pp. (Bilingual: English-Italian)

Somali Statistics. Monthly Bulletin. June 1967.
Statistical Department. Ministry of Planning
and Co-ordination. Mogadiscio.
11 pp. (Bilingual: English-Italian)

Somali Statistics. Monthly Bulletin. July 1967.
Statistical Department. Ministry of Planning
and Co-ordination. Mogadiscio.
10 pp. (Bilingual: English-Italian)

Somali Statistics. Monthly Bulletin. August 1967.
Statistical Department. Ministry of Planning
and Co-ordination. Mogadiscio.
15 pp. (Bilingual: English-Italian)

Somali Statistics. Monthly Bulletin. September 1967.
Statistical Department. Ministry of Planning
and Co-ordination. Mogadiscio.
8 pp. (Bilingual: English-Italian)

Somali Statistics. Monthly Bulletin. October 1967.
Statistical Department. Ministry of Planning and
Co-ordination. Mogadiscio.
9 pp. (Bilingual: English-Italian)

Somali Statistics. Monthly Bulletin. November 1967.
Statistical Department. Ministry of Planning and
Co-ordination. Mogadiscio.
16 pp. (Bilingual: English-Italian)

Somali Statistics. Monthly Bulletin. December 1967.
Statistical Department. Ministry of Planning. Mogadiscio.
8 pp. (Bilingual: English-Italian)

Somali Statistics. Monthly Bulletin. January 1968.
Statistical Department. Ministry of Planning and
Co-ordination. Mogadiscio.
14 pp. (Bilingual: English-Italian)

———————————

Somali Statistics. Monthly Bulletin. February 1968.
Statistical Department. Ministry of Planning and
Co-ordination. Mogadiscio.
13 pp. (Bilingual: English-Italian).

———————————

Somali Statistics. Monthly Bulletin. March 1968.
Statistical Department. Ministry of Planning
and Co-ordination. Mogadiscio.
9 pp. (Bilingual: English-Italian).

———————————

Somali Statistics. Monthly Bulletin. Aprile 1968.
Statistical Department. Ministry of Planning and
Co-ordination. Mogadiscio.
8 pp. (Bilingual: English-Italian)

———————————

Somali Statistics. Monthly Bulletin. May 1968.
Statistical Department. Ministry of Planning
and Co-ordination. Mogadiscio.
18 pp. (Bilingual: English-Italian)

———————————

Somali Statistics. Monthly Bulletin. June 1968.
Statistical Department. Ministry of Planning
and Co-ordination. Mogadiscicio.
18 pp. (Bilingual: English-Italian).

———————————

Somali Statistics. Monthly Bulletin. July 1968.
Statistical Department. Ministry of Planning
and Co-ordination. Mogadiscio.
16 pp (Bilingual: English-Italian)

———————————

Supplement to the July 1968 Issue of Somali Statistics:
Multi-purpose Survey of Baidoa District February-April 1968.
Statistical Department. Ministry of Planning and Co-ordination.
22 pp.

———————————

Somali Statistics. Monthly Bulletin. August 1968.

Statistical Department. Ministry of Planning and
Co-ordination. Mogadiscio.
30 pp. (Bilingual: English-Italian).

Somali Statistics. Monthly Bulletin. September 1968.
Statistical Department. Ministry of Planning and
Co-ordination. Mogadiscio.
14 pp. (Bilingual: English-Italian)

Somali Statistics. Monthly Bulletin. October 1968.
Statistical Department. Ministry of Planning and
Co-ordination. Mogadiscic.
15 pp. (Bilingual: English-Italian).

Somali Statistics. Monthly Bulletin. November 1968.
Statistical Department. Ministry of Planning
and Co-ordination. Mogadiscio.
18 pp. (Bilingual: English-Italian).

Somali Statistics. Monthly Bulletin. December 1968.
Statistical Department. Ministry of Planning
and Co-ordination. Mogadiscio.
21 pp. (Bilingual: English-Italian)

Supplement to the December 1968 Issue of Somali
Statistics: Multipurpose Survey of Brava District,
July and November 1968. Statistical Department.
Ministry of Planning and Co-ordination. Mogadiscio.
29 pp.

Somali Statistics. Monthly Bulletin. January 1969.
Statistical Department. Ministry of Planning and
Co-ordination. Mogadiscio.
24 pp. (Bilingual: English-Italian)

Somali Statistics. Monthly Bulletin. February 1969.
Statistical Department. Ministry of Planning and
Co-ordination. Mogadiscio.
44 pp. (Bilingual: English-Italian).

Somali Statistics: Monthly Bulletin. March 1969.
Statistical Department. Ministry of Planning and
Co-ordination. Mogadiscio.
9 pp. (Bilingual: English-Italian).

Somali Statistics. Monthly Bulletin. April 1969.
Statistical Department. Ministry of Planning
and Co-ordination. Mogadiscio.
16 pp. (Bilingual: English-Italian).

Somali Statistics. Monthly Bulletin. May 1969.
Statistical Department. Ministry of Planning
and Co-ordination.
        (Bilingual: English Italian).

Somali Statistics. Monthly Bulletin. April 1969.
Statistical Department. Ministry of Planning
and Co-ordination. Mogadiscio.
16 pp. (Bilingual: English-Italian).

Somali Statistics. Monthly Bulletin. May 1969.
Statistical Department. Ministry of Planning
and Co-ordination. Mogadiscio.
15 pp. (Bilingual: English-Italian)

Somali Statistics. Monthly Bulletin. June 1969.
Statistical Department. Ministry of Planning
and Co-ordination. Mogadiscio.
24 pp. (Bilingual: English-Italian)

Somali Statistics. Monthly Bulletin. July 1969.
Statistical Department. Ministry of Planning
and Co-ordination. Mogadiscio.
21 pp. (Bilingual: English-Italian)

Somali Statistics. Monthly Bulletin. August 1969.
Statistical Department. Ministry of Planning
and Co-ordination. Mogadiscio.
26 pp. (Bilingual: English-Italian).

Somali Statistics. Monthly Bulletin. September 1969.
Statistical Department. Ministry of Planning

and Co-ordination. Mogadiscio.
17 pp. (Bilingual: English-Italian)

Somali Statistics. Monthly Bulletin. October 1969.
Statistical Department. Ministry of Planning and
Co-ordination. Mogadiscio.
23 pp. (Bilingual: English-Italian)

Somali Statistics. Monthly Bulletin. November 1969.
Statistical Department. Ministry of Planning and
Co-ordination. Mogadiscio.
23 pp. (Bilingual: English-Italian)

Somali Statistics. Monthly Bulletin: December 1969.
Statistical Department. Ministry of Planning and
Co-ordination. Mogadiscio.
44 pp. (Bilingual: English-Italian)

Somali Statistics. Monthly Bulletin. January 1970.
Statistical Department. Ministry of Planning and
Co-ordination. Mogadiscio.
31 pp. (Bilingual: English-Italian)

Somali Statistics. Monthly Bulletin. February 1970.
Statistical Department. Ministry of Planning and
Co-ordination. Mogadisco.
18 pp. (Bilingual: English-Italian)

Somali Statistics. Monthly Bulletin. March 1970.
Statistical Department. Ministry of Planning and
Co-ordination. Mogadiscio.
15 pp.   (Bilingual: English-Italian)

Somali Statistics. Monthly Bulletin. **April 1970.**
Statistical Department. Ministry of Planning and
Co-ordination. Mogadiscio.
 12 pp. (Bilingual: English-Italian)

Somali Statistics. Monthly Bulletin. May 1970.
Statistical Department. Ministry of Planning
and Co-ordination. Mogadiscio.

16 pp. (Bilingual: English-Italian)

Somali Statistics. Monthly Bulletin. June 1970.
Statistical Department. Ministry of Planning
and Co-ordination. Mogadiscio.
10 pp. (Bilingual: English-Italian)

Somali Statistics. Monthly Bulletin. July 1970.
Statistical Department. Ministry of Planning
and Co-ordination. Mogadiscio.
19 pp. (Bilingual: English-Italian)

Somali Statistics. Monthly Bulletin. August 1970.
Statistical Department. Ministry of Planning
and Co-ordination. Mogadiscio.
25 pp. (Bilingual: English-Italian)

Somali Statistics. Monthly Bulletin. September 1970.
Statistical Department. Ministry of Planning
and Co-ordination. Mogadiscio.
25 pp. (Bilingual: English-Italian)

Somali Statistics. Monthly Bulletin. October 1970.
Statistical Department. Ministry of Planning and
Co-ordination. Mogadiscio.
27 pp.   (Bilingual: English-Italian)

Somali Statistics. Monthly Bulletin. November 1970.
Statistical Department. Ministry of Planning and
Co-ordination. Mogadiscio.
26 pp.   (Bilingual: English-Italian)

Somali Statistics. Monthly Bulletin. December 1970.
Statistical Department. Ministry of Planning and
Co-ordination. Mogadiscio.
18 pp. (Bilingual: English Italian)

Somali Statistics. Monthly Bulletin. January 1971
Statistical Department. Ministry of Planning and
Co-ordination. Mogadiscio.
31 pp. (Bilingual: English-Italian)

Somali Statistics. Monthly Bulletin. February 1971.
Statistical Department. Ministry of Planning
and Co-ordination. Mogadiscio.
45 pp (Bilingual: English-Italian)

Somali Statistics. Monthly Bulletin. March 1971.
Statistical Department. Ministry of Planning
and Co-ordination. Mogadiscio.
30 pp. (Bilingual: English-Italian)

Somali Statistics. Monthly Bulletin. April 1971.
Statistical Department. Ministry of Planning
and Co-ordination. Mogadiscio.
33 pp. (Bilingual: English-Italian)

Somali Statistics. Monthly Bulletin. May 1971
Statistical Department. Ministry of Planning
and Co-ordination. Mogadiscio.
27 pp.

Somali Statistics. Monthly Bulletin. June 1971.
Statistical Department. Ministry of Planning
and Co-ordination. Mogadiscio.
24 pp. (Bilingual: English-Italian)

Somali Statistics. Monthly Bulletin. July 1971
Statistical Department. Ministry of Planning
and Co-ordination. Mogadiscio.
36 pp. (Bilingual: English-Italian)

Somali Statistics. Monthly Bulletin. August 1971.
Statistical Department. Ministry of Planning
and Co-ordination. Mogadiscio.
43 pp. (Bilingual: English-Italian)

Somali Statistics. Monthly Bulletin. September 1971.
Statistical Department. Ministry of Planning
and Co-ordination. Mogadiscio.
33 pp. (Bilingual: English-Italian)

Somali Statistics. Monthly Bulletin. March 1972.

Statistical Department. Ministry of Planning
and Co-ordination. Mogadiscio.
45 pp. (Bilingual: English-Italian)

Somali Statistics. Monthly Bulletin. April 1972.
Statistical Department. Ministry of Planning and
Co-ordination. Mogadiscio.
43 pp. (Bilingual: English-Italian)

Somali Statistics. Monthly Bulletin. May 1972.
Statistical Department. Ministry of Planning and
Co-ordination. Mogadiscio.
39 pp. (Bilingual: English-Italian)

Somali Statistics. Monthly Bulletin. June 1972.
Statistical Department. Ministry of Planning
and Co-ordination. Mogadiscio.
37 pp. (Bilingual: English-Italian)

Somali Statistics. Monthly Bulletin. July 1972.
Statistical Department. Ministry of Planning
and Co-ordination. Mogadiscio.
41 pp (Bilingual: English-Italian)

A Multi-Purpose Statistical Survey of the Hargeisa
Town April-June 1962. Statistical Service.
Mogadiscio April 1964.
42 pp.

Report on a Multi-Purpose Survey of the Borama
Town 30 April-5 June 1963. Statistical Service.
Mogadiscio August 1964.
19 pp.

Report on a Multi-Purpose Survey of Zeila Town.
Statistical Service. Mogadiscio 1964.
22 pp.

Report on Demographic Survey of Mogadishu, July 1967.
Statistical Department. Ministry of Planning and
Co-ordination. Mogadiscio November 1970.
42 pp.

The Multi-Purpose Survey of Kisimayo District.
Statistical Department. Ministry of Planning
and Co-ordination. Mogadiscio. March 1969.
35 pp.

_____

The Multi-Purpose Survey of Coriolei District.
Statistical Department. Ministry of Planning
and Co-ordination. Mogadiscio. 1969.
23 pp.

_____

The Multi-Purpose Survey of Gelib District.
Statistical Department. Ministry of Planning
and Coordination. Mogadiscio April 1969
27 pp.

_____

The Multi-Purpose Survey of Afmedou District.
Statistical Department. Ministry of Planning
and Co-ordination. Mogadiscio 1969.
27 pp.

_____

Pilot Sample Survey on rural population and their
livestock in Bardera District in June 1971.
Statistical Department. Ministry of Planning and
Co-ordination. Mogadiscio June 1972.
5 pp. appendices.

XV

TELECOMMUNICATION

AMMINISTRAZIONE FIDUCIARIA ITALIANA DELLA SOMALIA.

Principali norme regolamentari sulla organizzazione
e sul funzionamento degli uffici postali e telegrafici
e delle stazioni radiografiche della Somalia.
Ispettorato Poste e Telecommunicazioni.
Mogadiscio Novembre 1953.
65 pp. tables.

ANONYMOUS.

Miglioramento delle communicazione postali
con la Somalia Italiana. "Le Vie d'Italia".
Milano 1931.
226 p.

NICCHIARDI,B.

La Radiotelegrafia al Benadir. "Rivista Marittima".
Roma 1909.
18 p.

SARACENI.

Benadir e Somalia Italiana nella Posta e
nella Filatelica. Palermo 1921.

SOMALI REPUBLIC. (OFFICIAL)

The need of the Somali Republic in Telecommunication.
Public Works Division. Mogadiscio November 1961.

XVI

TOURISM

BRANCA,A.

Turismo venatorio. III Fiera della Somalia.
"Numero Unico". Mogadiscio Settembre-Ottobre 1955.
50-55 pp.

FUNAIOLI, U.

Proposte per lo sviluppo del turismo venatorio in Somalia.
"Rivista di Agricoltura Subtropicale e Tropicale".
No. 4-9. Firenze Aprile-Settembre 1960.
666-669 pp.

GERMAN PLANNING AND ECONOMIC ADVISORY GROUP(SOMALIA)

Reconnaissance study on the situation and the development
possibilities of tourism in Somalia. Mogadiscio December 1966.

PELLEGRINI,L.

Turismo in Somalia. "Le Vie d'Italia".
No. 8. Milano 1953.
1041-1051 pp.

VENATOR.

Un serio contributo al turismo venatorio in Somalia.
"Bollettino Mensile della Camera di Commercio,
Industria e Agricoltura della Somalia". No. 1-6.Mogadiscio 1957.

VIENNA HOSPITALLA.

Feasibility Study for the Development of Tourism in Somalia.
Vienna Hospitalla Consulting Engineers and Architects.
Vienna July 1969.
79 pp. drawings. graphs.

XVII

TRANSPORT

AGENCY FOR INTERNATIONAL DEVELOPMENT.

Air Transport Study Somali Republic. AID.
Mogadiscio 1962.
19 pp.

ANONYMOUS.

Les communications entre Djibouti et Addis-Ababa.
"La Geographie". Vol. X. Paris 1904.
295-300 pp.

La ferrovia del Benadir e la politica ferroviaria
delle nostre Colonie. "Rivista Coloniale". Roma 1918.
442 p.

La valorizzazione della Somalia ed i trasporti con
l'Italia. "L'Italia Coloniale". Roma-Milano 1929.
217 p.

La grande arteria Mogadiscio-Bender Cassin.
"Le Vie d'Italia e dell'America Latina". Milano 1932.
173 p.

La rete stradale della Somalia. "Annali Africa Italiana".
No. 4. Roma 1934.
333 p.

B.A.

Carbonizzazione e trasporti automobolistici in Somalia.
"Il Legno." Milano 1929.
418 p.

BARBERIS,L.B.

Navi bananiere. "Monogr. No. 3. "Ministero delle Colonie.
Roma 1936.
107 pp.

BASTOGI,G.

La messa in valore della Somalia: trasporti rapidi.
"Illustrazione Coloniale". No. 16. Milano 1920.
293 p.

BECATTI,G.

La flotta banaiera italiana. "La Rassegna Italiana".
Roma 1939.
399 p.

BIGAZZI, G. P.

Programmi dell'Impero: la ferrovia della Somalia.

"L'Oltremare". No. 1. Roma 1939.
17 p.

————————————

I fiumi della Somalia e loro funzioni nell'economia somala.
"Rassegna d'Oltremare". No. 2. Genova 1940.
3 p.

BUONOMO,G.

La ferrovia Mogadiscio-Lugh. "Bollettino Societa
Africana d'Italia". Firenze 1910

————————————

La funzione di Alula (Capo Guardafui).
"Bollettino Societa Africana d'Italia". Firenze 1902.

————————————

Il faro di Capo Guardafui. "L'Africa Italiana". 1923.
68 p.

————————————

Le tre porte della Somalia. "Illustrazione Coloniale".
No. 6. Milano 1927.
207 f.

————————————

Imperio sul 'Oceano Indiano: Il porto Re Vittorio
"Illustrazione Coloniale" Milano Agosto 1940.
32 p.

CAPPELLO,E.

L'avvenire del Benadir in rapporto al suo
sistema fluviale. Congresso Coloniale di Asmara.
Asmara 1905.
297 p.

CHIESI,G.

La politica delle communicazioni nella Somalia Meridionale.
"Rivista Italiana di Communicazioni e Trasporti". Roma 1907.

CIBELLI,E.

Per il traffico bananiero nazionale. Tuminelli e C.
Roma 1938.
246 pp.

C. R.

La navigazione al Benadir. "Rivista Coloniale". Roma 1907.

427 p.

DE BERNARDO,L.

Studio per la costruzione di un pontile all'ancoraggio
sud della baia di Chisimaio. Stamperia AFIS. Mogadiscio 1955.
8 pp.

ENTE AUTONOMO PORTUALE DELLA SOMALIA.

Handbook. Mogadiscio 1965.

FAVILLA,G.

Studio di massima per la stabilizzazione dell'anello
stradale Afgoi-Baidoa-Gelib-Chisimaio-Afgoi.
Stamperia AFIS. Mogadiscio 10 Giugno 1955.
9 pp.

FIDEL,C.

Djibouti et le Chemin de fer Franco-Ethiopien.
"Revue Question Coloniale". Paris 1916.
120-123 pp.

FIORETTI,M.

I compiti imperiali dei porti somali.
"Azione Coloniale". Roma 3 Ottobre 1940.

FRANCOLINI,B.

Ferrovie della Somalia Italiana. "Illustrazione Coloniale"
No. 11. Milano 1930.
18 p.

FRENCH SOMALILAND (OFFICIAL).

Convention conclude le 6 fevrier 1920 entre le
Protectorate de la Cote francaise des Somalis et
la Compagnie imperiale des chemins de fer ethiopiens. 1920.

GIAVOTTO,M.

Gli ancoraggi del Benadir: sulla necessita di
lavori portuali. Officina Poligrafica Italiana. Roma 1909.
27 pp.

_____

Gli ancoraggi del Benadir e la necessita di lavori
portuali nella nostro Somalia Meridionale.
"Rivista Marittima". Roma 1909.

GOUVERNMENT FRANCAIS.

Djibouti et le chemin de fer franco-ethiopien.

"La Documentation Francaise". "Notes et Etudes
Documentaries" No. 112. Paris 1945.

––––––––––––

Traite franco ethiopien du 12 Novembre 1959 relatif
au chemin de fer Djibouti-Addis Abeba. "La Documentation
Francaise". "Notes et Etudes Documentaires" No. 2658.
Paris Avril 1960.
15 pp.

GOVERNO DELLA SOMALIA ITALIANA

Le strade della Somalia Italiana. Istituto Poligrafico
dello Stato. Roma 1931.
33 pp map.

––––––––––––

Le strade della Somalia Italiana. "Rassegna Economica
delle Colonie". Roma 1931
132 p.

GRANDI,B.

La quarta porta dell'Impero: Chisimaio.
"Geopolitica". Milano 1939
291-296 pp.

INTERNATIONAL COOPERATION ADMINISTRATION.

Rapporto sull'aviazione civile nella Repubblica Somala.
ICA. Mogadiscio 1962.
57 pp.

ITALIAN TRUSTEESHIP ADMINISTRATION OF SOMALIA.

Kisimayu Project. Consultants Alpina. Milano.

JONES, K. P.

Rapporto sull'aviazione civile nella Repubblica Somala.
Organizzazione Dell'Aviazione Civile Internationale
Mogadiscio 1962.
53 pp.

JOUTEL,G.G.

Le port de Djibouti. "Rens. Col". 1928.
635-641 pp.

LEFEVRE,R.

Le communicazioni stradali in Somalia.
"L'Oltremare". Roma 1933.
45 p.

MAGNINO,L.

Le communicazioni stradali nello sviluppo della
Somalia Italiana. "Illustrazione Coloniale"
No. 10. Milano 1933.

MALLARINI,A.

Le vie acquee della Somalia Italiana e il loro avvenire.
"Riforma Marittima". Napoli 1911.

MASSARI,A.

Genova-Mogadiscio. Corbaccio. Milano 1932.
263 pp.

MERENDA,L.U.

Le strade ferrate della Somalia Italiana.
"Illustrazione Coloniale". No. 3. Milano 1939,
50 p

(R) Ministero   AA.EE.

Progetto per la costruzione di un faro al Capo Guardafui
e di un fanale a Punta Alula. Direzione Affari Coloniali.
Reale Istituto Idrografico. Roma 1905.

(R) MINISTERO DELLE COLONIE.

Le strade della Somalia Italiana. "Rassegna Economica
delle Colonie". No. 12. Roma 1931.

MOSCONO,G.C.

Il servizio automobilistico militare in Somalia
"Rivista di Fanteria". No. 6. Giugno 1927.

NAUTA.

Ras Guardafui: movimentata storia di un faro.
"L'Oltremare". No. 2. Roma 1962.
17-24 pp.

NAUTILUS.

Bananiere. "Rassegna d'Oltremare". No. 8. Genova 1937.
366 p.

ONOR,L.

La applicazione della mototrazione alla lavorazione ed
ai trasporti con speciale riguardo alle condizioni del Benadir.
Roma 1917.

ORTOLANI,M.

Gibuti. "Bollettino Societa Geografica Italiana". Roma 1935.

480-499 pp.

PALUMBO,A.

La rete stradale della Somalia Italiana.
"Illustrazione Coloniale". No. 8-9
Milano 1932.

PELLEGRINISCHI,A.V.

Il nuovo porto di Mogadiscio. "L'Oltremare". Roma 1934
94 p

PEROZ.

Le chemin de fer Ethiopien et le Port de Djibouti
Impr. P. Leve. Paris 1907
31 pp.

POTTIER.

Le chemin de fer franco-ethiopien. "Encyclopedie mensuelle
d'Outre-Mer'. Paris Mars 1954.

POZZI, M.

Camionabili e carovaniere in Somalia. "L'Oltremare". Roma 1930
263 p,

QUEIROLO,E.

La nuova grande strade Mogadiscio-Bender Cassim.
"Rivista delle Colonie Italiane". Vol. IV. Roma 1930
138-151 pp.

REINECKE,F.G.

Port Survey in Somalia: East Africa. U. S. Operations
Mission to Italy. Rome 1954.
40 pp.

RENT.

Le antiche strade commerciali attraverso l'Etiopia.
"Bollettino Societa Africana d'Italia." Firenze 1891.
100-107 pp.

RENY, (DE) E.

Un chemin de fer dans la Somalie Italienne
"Rens. Col." 1911
61-63 pp

ROSSETTI,C.

La navigazione al Benadir. Istituto Coloniale Italiano
Roma 1907.

SCOGNAMIGLIO, L.

Le linee bananiere Italiane "Geopolitica" No. 1
Milano 1941
20 p.

SOMALI AIRLINES.

Relazioni e Bilancio dell'esercizio 1965.
Mogadiscio 24 Giugno 1966.
18 pp.

_____

Relazioni e Bilancio dell'esercizio 1967
Mogadiscio 20 Giugno 1968.
10 pp.

SOMALI REPUBLIC (OFFICIAL).

Scialambot - Gelib Road: Feasibility Report
Italconsult. Rome June 1963.
104 pp tables charts. diagrs.

_____

Progettazione esecutiva degli aero-porti regionali
di Chisimaio, Baidoa, Belet Uen, Galcaio, Burao, Bosaso
(Interim Report) Italconsult. Roma Maggio 1963

_____

Programme for the construction of bridges in the
Somali Republic. Ministry of Public Works and
Communications. Mogadishu 1965.

_____

Primo Seminario Nazionale del Settore
Marittimo e Portuale. Ministero Communicazione
e Trasporto. Mogadiscio 1965.

_____

Progetto della ricostruzione della strade
Giohar-Belet Uen. Ministero LL.PP. Mogadiscio Novembre 1966.

_____

"Yours in service", Souvenir Independence Day
July 1st 1966. Ministry of Communication and
Transport. Tipografia Missione. Mogadiscio July 1st 1966
31 pp ills.

_____

Progetto della ricostruzione della strada

Scialambot-Merca. Ministero LL.PP. Mogadiscio Gennaio 1967.

———————

Report on Bridge over the River Juba near Lugh Ganana
Preliminary **Design**. Ministry of Public Works. Mogadishu.

———————

Progetto di massima di rifacimento e raddoppio
della rotabile tra mogadiscio ed Afgoi. Ministero LL.PP.

SOMALI PORTS AUTHORITY.

Brochure. Insutrie Grafiche della Somalia. Mogadiscio
15 pp chart.

SON,F.

Origine et developpement de Djibouti. Paris Colonial.
Paris 1914
32 pp.

STEFANINI,G.

Gli sbocchi della Africa di nord-east
nell'Oceano Indiano. "Rivista Geografica Italiana'"
Vol. XXIV. Paris 1917
272 p.

U. S. ARMY ENGINEER DIVISION,

Specification for construction for port facilities
Phase II of Kismayu Project. Mediterranean Corpos of
Engineers, APO. New York March 1966
tables, charts. diagrs. designs.

———————

Mogadiscio port improvement study. U.S.A.E.D.
Leghorn (Italy) August 1963
79 pp tables. charts.

VALORI, F.

I porti della Somalia. "Rivista Coloniale" No. 1
Roma 1939
427 p.

———————

II problema ferroviario della Somalia Italiana.
"Rivista di Ingegneria Ferroviaria". No. 2.
Roma 1951.

VAN DYKE,J.A.

Road Study in Somalia. U. S. Operations Mission
to Italy. Rome 1953.
106 pp.

ADDENDUM A

I. AGRICULTURE

AGRICULTURAL RESEARCH

ANONYMOUS.

Analisi dei campioni di terreni della regione Scidle prelevati
dal Prof. Scassellati-Sforzolini nella Missione 1919/20.
"Annali S.A.I.S.". Vol. L. (1929/29) Genova 1929.
131 p.

CASTELLANO,G.

Umidita del terreno irriguo nel comprensorio della S.A.I.S.
"Annali SAIS". Genova 1930.

Relazione sui risultati ottenuti nell'analisi di vari campioni
del terreno del comprensorio della SAIS. "Annali S.A.I.S."
Genova 1930.
11 p.

CENTRAL AGRICULTURAL RESEARCH STATION, AFGOI.

How to grow upland rice in Somalia. USAID/SOMALI REPUBLIC.
University of Wyoming Team. Mogadishu November 1968.
5 pp.

ISTITUTO SUPERIORE AGRARIO DI MILANO.
Analisi di 24 terreni della S.A.I.S. Laboratorio di Chimica
Agraria.
"Annali S.A.I.S." Vol. I. (1927/29). Genova 1929.
315 p.

SACCO,T.

Ricerche sul succo di Citrus hystrix Do subsa acida (Roxab)
Bonavia var. abyssinica (Riccobono). "Staz. Sperimentale
Industrie Essenze e Profumi". No. 1.
3 p.

SCURTI.

Relazione sui resultati ottenuti dall'analisi di vari campioni
di terreno della Somalia. "Annali S.A.I.S.." Genova 1929.
19 pp.

VERONA,P. AND PINI,G.

Reperti microbiologici su di alcuni terreni della Somalia.
"Agricoltura Coloniale". Firenze 1934
516 p.

AGRICULTURE (GENERAL)

BIGI,F.

II Giuba: esempio ed orientamento dell'autonomia dell'
agricoltura indigena della Somalia. "Atti II Convegno Studi'
Coloniali".
Firenze 1947.
303 p.

RONCATI,R.

L'istruzione agraria in Somalia. "Rivista di Agricoltura Subtropicale e Tropicale". Nos. 4-9 Firenze Aprile-Settembre 1960.
244-252 pp.

ROSSOTTO,C.

La redenzione della terra somale e l'autarchia
L'opera dell'A.R. il Duca degli Abruzzi. "Collana Quaderni
Agricole". No. 25. G. Volani. Torino 1940.

SEKALLY,R.

Raccolta di note sull'importanza del ramie e sulle sue esigenze
di coltivazione. Stamperia del Governo. Mogadiscio 8 Aprile 1957.
99 pp.

_____

II ramie. "Somalia d'Oggi". No. 2. Mogadiscio 1957.

SUKERT,E.

Note pratiche preliminari sulla coltura del ramie in Somalia.
Stamperia AFIS. Mogadiscio 1955.
7 pp.

BANANA

ANONYMOUS.

Sviluppi dell'industria bananiera in A.O.I. "L'Italia

d'Oltremare". No. 11. Roma 1940.
172 p.

BIGI,F.

Problemi della bananicoltura somala in vista della liberal-
izzazione del mercato bananiero italiano. "Rivists di Agricoltura
Subtropicale e Tropicale. Nos. 7-9. Firenze 1966.

ROSSI,U.

L'industria bananiera e le sue vicende produttive. "Atti del VII
Convegno Economico Italo-Africano". Milano 1958.
111-120 pp.

CAMPOSAMPIERO,A.

L'industria delle banane in Somalia. "Rivista delle Colonie
Italiane". Roma 1933.

HORTICULTURE

RAGAZZINI,P.

Considerazioni sulle possibilita di produzione industriale della
papaina Somala. "Rivista di Agricoltura Subtropicale e Tropicale"
Nos. 4-9. 556-570 pp.

IRRIGATION

MANFREDI,C.

Regolazione dell'Uebi Scebeli. "L'Ingegnere". 1936
490 p.

Regolazione dell'Uebi Scebeli. "L'Ingegnere". 1938.
760 p.

S.A.I.S.

Quesiti riguardanti l'interrimento del fiume Uebi Scebeli a
monte delle opere di derivazione e dei canali d'irrigazione e
l'impianto di prosiciugamento. "Annali SAIS". Genova 1931.
125 p.

OIL SEED

BECCARI,F.

La produzione ed utilizzazione industriale dei semi oleosi in
Somalia. Istituto Agronomico per l'Oltremare. Fasc. no. 4282.
Firenze 1956.
7 pp.

V. ECONOMICS

BANKING AND MONEY

SOMALI NATIONAL BANK (BULLETINS)

Bulletin Nos. 31-32. July-December 1972. Economic Research and
Statistics Department. Mogadiscio 1972. State Printing Agency.
56 pp. Stat. Tables. (Blingual: Somali English)

Bulletin Nos. 33-34. January-June 1973. Economic Research and
Statistics Department. Mogadiscio 1973. State Printing Agency.
50 pp. Stat. Tables. (Blingual; Somali-English)

Bulletin No. 35. July 1973. Economic Research and Statistics
Department. Mogadiscio 1973. State Printing Agency.
48 pp. Stat. Tables. (Blingual: Somali-English)

Bulletin No. 36. December 1973. Economic Research and Statistics
Department. Mogadiscio 1973.
15 pp Stat. Tables. Appendices. Charts.

Bulletin No. 37. May 1974. Economic Research and Statistics
Department. Mogadiscio 1974.
18 pp. Stat. Tables. Appendices.

CENTRAL BANK OF SOMALIA.

Bulletin No. 38. November 1974. Economic Research and
Statistics Department. Mogadiscio 1974. State Printing Agency.
46 pp. Stat. Tables.

SOMALI NATIONAL BANK (Annual Reports)

Annual Report and Statement of Account 1971. 11th Financial Year
1 Jan. - 31 Dec. 1971.
27 pp. Stat. Tables.

Annual Report and Statement of Account 1972. 12th Financial Year
1 Jan. - 31 Dec. 1972.
57 pp. Stat. Tables.

Annual Report and Statement of Accounts 1973. 13th Financial Year
1 Jan. - 31 Dec. 1973.
50 pp. Stat. Tables.

CENTRAL BANK OF SOMALIA.

Annual Report and Statement of Accounts 1974. 14th Financial
Year 1 Jan. - 31 December 1974. State Printing Agency.
Mogadiscio. 56 pp. Stat. Tables.

SOMALI COMMERCIAL BANK (Bulletins)

Bulletin 1972-1973. State Printing Agency. Mogadiscio
October 1973. 47 pp. Ills. Stat. Tables.

Bulletin 1973-1974. State Printing Agency. Mogadiscio October
1974. 84 pp. Stat. Tables. Ills.

_____(Annual Reports)

1972 Balance Sheet and Profit and Loss Account for the Year
Ended 31st December 1972. State Printing Agency. Mogadiscio.
12 pp. Stat. Tables.

1973 Balance Sheet and Profit and Loss Account for the Year
Ended 31st December 1973. State Printing Agency Mogadiscio.
14 pp. Stat. Tables.

1974 Balance Sheet and Profit and Loss Account for the Year
Ended 31st December 1974. Research and Statistics Department.
10 pp. Stat. Tables. Map.

SOMALI DEVELOPMENT BANK

Fourth Annual Report January-December 1972. State Printing
Agency. Mogadiscio June 1973.
26 pp. Stat. Tables. Charts. Ills. Plates.

Fifth Annual Report and Statement of Accounts for 1973.
1st January - 31 December 1973. Mogadiscio.
25 pp. Stat. Tables.

Sixth Annual Report and Statement of Accounts for 1974.

1st January-December 1974.
32 pp. Stat. Tables.

BANKING AND MONEY (Additions)

SOMALI SAVINGS AND CREDIT BANK   (Bulletins)
(CASSA DI RISPARMIO E CREDITO DELLA SOMALIA)

Bulletin. First Half Year January-June 1973.
Research and Statistics Department. Mogadiscio 1973.
10 pp. Stat. Tables.

_____

Bulletin. First Half Year January-June 1974.
Research and Statistics Department. Mogadiscio 1974.
10 pp. Stat. Tables.

_____(Annual Reports)

Bilancio dell'Anno 1971 Primo Esercizio. Mogadiscio.
8 pp. Stat. Tables. Appendices.

_____

Annual Report and Accounts of 1972. Second Year. State
Printing Agency. 41 pp. Stat. Tables. ills. Map.

_____

Report and Accounts for the Year Ended 31st December 1973.
State Printing Agency. Mogadiscio.
32 pp. Stat. Tables.

_____

Report and Accounts for the Year Ended 31st December 1974.
State Printing Agency. Mogadiscio 1975.
32 pp. Stat. Tables. Plates.

INDIA/FAO SEMINAR ON AGRICULTURAL BANKING.

Somali Democratic Republic. State Bank Staff College.
Hyderbad(India) August 1973.
7 pp. Stat. Tables. Map.

INTERNATIONAL MONETARY FUND.

19th Annual Report on Exchange Restrictions, 1968.
IMF. Washington, D. C. May 13, 1968.
493 pp. (Somalia: 370-373 pp)

_____

20th Annual Report on Exchange Restrictions 1969.
IMF. Washington, D. C. May 6, 1969.

538 pp (Somalia: 403-406 pp),

21st Annual Report on Exchange Restriction 1970.
IMF. Washington, D. C. May 7, 1970.
572 pp. (Somalia: 432-435 pp.)

22nd Annual Report on Exchange Restrictions 1971.
IMF. Washington, D. C. May 5, 1971.
495 pp. (Somalia: 369-381 pp)

23rd Annual Report on Exchange Restrictions 1972.
IMF. Washington, D. C. May 5, 1972.
500 pp. (Somalia: 376-378 pp)

24th Annual Report on Exchange Restrictions 1973.
IMF. Washington, D. C. May 25, 1973.
556 pp. (Somalia: 415-417 pp)

25th Annual Report on Exchange Restrictions 1974.
IMF. Washington, D. C. April 25, 1974.
504 pp. (Somalia: 379-381 pp)

26th Annual Report on Exchange Restrictions 1975.
IMF. Washington, D. C. May 16, 1975.
548 pp. (Somalia: 417-419 pp.)

ECONOMIC DEVELOPMENT PLANS

SOMALI DEMOCRATIC REPUBLIC (OFFICIAL)

Development Programme 1971-1973. Progress of Implementation:
1971 & 1972, And Programme; 1973. Ministry of Planning and
Co-ordination. Mogadiscio, January 1973.
121 pp. Stat. Tables.

Five Year Development Programme 1974-1978. Ministry of Planning
and Co-ordination. Mogadishu, 1974.
298 pp, Stat. Tables.

Five Year Development Programme: Manpower Requirement 1975-1978.

General Directorate of Planning and Co-ordination. Planning
Department.
Mogadishu 1975.
Vol. I. 123 pp. Stat. Tables. Charts. Graphs.
Vol. II. 28 pp. Stat. Tables. Charts. Graphs

Annual Development Plan 1976. Directorate General of Planning
and Co-ordination. Planning Department. Mogadishu January 1976.
52 pp. Stat. Tables.

FINANCE AND FOREIGN AID

MOHAMED JAMA (HABASHI)

Economic Survey of Somalia, 1955-1969. Third Edition. No. 3.
(Privately printed). Mogadiscio 1970.
88 pp. Stat. Tables.

NUCLEARE SOMALA (SPA)

Annual Report and Statement of Accounts at 31 st December 1971.
Mogadiscio. 23 pp. Stat. Tables.

SOMALILAND PROTECTORATE (OFFICIAL)

Grants-in-aid of the administration of the Somaliland Protectorate.
Arrangements for financial control (1965). (Cmnd. 9666).
6 pp.

SOMALI DEMOCRATIC REPUBLIC (OFFICIAL)

Revised Programme of Assistance Required to the drought
Stricken-Areas of Somalia. Directorate General of Planning
and Co-ordination. Mogadishu, January 1975.
63 pp. Stat. Tables. Ills. Plates.

UNITED NATIONS DEVELOPMENT PROGRAMME

Co-operation with Somalia. UNDP. Mogadiscio October 1973.
30 pp, Stat. Tables. Ills. Plates.

INDUSTRY AND MANUFACTURERS

SOMALI DEMOCRATIC REPUBLIC (OFFICIAL)

Handicrafts of Somalia. (Editors Abdisalam H. Adam and Rughia Siad).
Ministry of Industry Publications. Tipo-Lito Missione.
Mogadiscio 1972. 22 pp. Ills. Plates.

Industrial Production 1970. Ministry of Planning and
Co-ordination. Central Statistical Department. Mogadiscio March
1972. XXXVI,45 pp. Stat. Tables.

Industrial Production 1971. Ministry of Planning and
Co-ordination. Central Statistical Department. Mogadiscio
August 1972.
VI,47 pp. Stat. Tables.

Industrial Production 1972. Ministry of Planning and
Co-ordination. Central Statistical Department. Mogadiscio
March 1974. 58 pp. Stat. Tables.

Industrial Production 1973. Directorate General of Planning
and Co-ordination. Central Statistical Department.
Mogadishu October 1975.

LABOUR ECONOMICS AND CONDITIONS

SOMALI DEMOCRATIC REPUBLIC (OFFICIAL)

Manpower Survey Project. (4 Vols.) Ministry of Labour and
Sports. Labour Department. Mogadiscio August 1972.

VOL. I.   The Manpower Implications of Current Development
             Strategies.
             290 pp. Stat. Tables.

VOL II.   Classification of Establishments by Size, Industry
             Location. Classification of Workers by
             Occupation, Industry Group and Location.
             490 pp. Stat. Tables.

VOL. III.   Directory of Private Establishments Having Five
             or More Workers.
             90 pp. Stat. Tables.

VOL. IV.   Classification of Occupations and Classification
             of Industries.
             39 pp. Appendices.

Quarterly Labour Statistics. Bulletin No. 3 & 4. July-
September 1972. October-December 1972. Ministry of Labour
and Sports. Statistical Section. Labour Department.
Mogadiscio December 1972. 38 pp. Stat. Tables. Charts.

TRADE AND COMMERCE (Additions)

AMBASCIATA D'ITALIA IN MOGADISCIO.

Notizie utili per l'operatore economico Italiano Repubblica
Democratica della Somalia. Cura dell'Ufficio Commerciale.
28 pp. Stat. Tables. Map. Ills. Plates.

AGRICULTURAL DEVELOPMENT CORPORATION.

Annual Report 1972-73. ADC. Mogadiscio.

Stat. Tables. Diagrs. Charts.

CHAMBRE DE COMMERCE ET D'INDUSTRIE(DJIBOUTI)

Bulletin Periodique Fevrier 1974. Djibouti 1974.
16 pp. Stat. Tables.

Bulletin Periodique Mai 1974. Djibouti 1974.
11 pp. Stat. Tables.

SOMALI DEMOCRATIC REPUBLIC (OFFICIAL)

Foreign Trade Returns Year 1970. Ministry of Planning and
Co-ordination. Central Statistical Department. Mogadiscio
August 1971. 437 pp. Stat. Tables. (Bilingual: Italian-English)

Foreign Trade Returns Year 1971. Ministry of Planning and
Co-ordination. Central Statistical Dept. Mogadiscio August 1972.
487 pp. Stat. Tables. (Bilingual: English-Italian)

Foreign Trade Returns Year 1972. Ministry of Planning and
Co-ordination. Central Statistical Dept. Mogadiscio August 1971.
437 pp. Stat. Tables. (Bilingual: Italian-English)

Foreign Trade Returns Year 1971. Ministry of Planning and
Co-ordination. Central Statistical Dept. Mogadiscio August 1972.
487 pp. Stat. Tables. (Bilingual: English-Italian)

Foreign Trade Returns Year 1972. Ministry of Planning and
Co-ordination. Central Statistical Department. Mogadiscio
November 1973. 517 pp. Stat. Tables. (Bilingual: Italian-English)

Foreign Trade Returns Year 1973. Ministry of Planning and
Co-ordination. Central Statistical Department. Mogadiscio
November 1975. 477 pp. Stat. Tables. (Bilingual: Italian-English)

Foreign Trade Returns Year 1974. Directorate of Planning and
Co-ordination. Central Statistical Department. Mogadiscio
December 1975.
387 pp. Stat. Tables. (Bilingual: English-Italian)

NATIONAL BANANA BOARD.

ENB Statistiche 1970. Anno 1970. Mogadiscio.
Prosp. 33 pp. Stat. Tables. Charts. Graphs. (Bilingual: English-
Italian)

_____

ENB Statistiche 1971. Anno 1971. Mogadiscio.
Stat. Tables. Charts. Graphs. (Blingual: English-Italian)

_____

WMU Statistika 1972. Sannado 1972. Statistics and Programs
Department: Mogadiscio.
34 pp. Stat. Tables. Charts. Graphs. (Tri-lingual: Somali-
Italian-English)

_____

WMU Statistika 1973. Sannad 1973. Statistics and Programs
Department.
Mogadiscio.
20 pp. Stat. Tables. Charts. Graphs. (Tri-lingual: Somali-
Italian-English)

_____

WMU Statistika 1974. Statistics and Programs Department.
Mogadiscio.
28 pp. Stat. Tables. Charts. Graphs (Tri-lingual: Somali-
Italian-English)

VI. EDUCATION

SOMALI DEMOCRATIC REPUBLIC (Official)

Our Revolutionary Education: Its Strategy and Objectives.
Ministry of Information and National Guidance.
State Printing Agency. Mogadishu June 1974.
52 pp. Stat. Tables. Ills. Plates.

_____

Statistics of Education in Somalia 1972/73. **Ministry** of
Education. Department of Planning. Mogadishu, July 1973.
69 pp. Stat. Tables.

_____

Annual Report 1973 and Statistics of Education in Somalia
1973-1974. Ministry of Education. Mogadiscio.
86 pp. Stat. Tables. Charts. Graphs.

VII. GEOLOGY & GEOGRAPHY

GEOLOGY (General)

SOMALI REPUBLIC (OFFICIAL)

Report on the Geology of the Area North of Hargeisa and
Laferug (Hargeisa and Berbera Districts). Geological Survey
Report. No. 7. (Mason, J. E.) Hargeisa 1962.
34 pp.

LINO,E.

Cenni sui materiali di costruzione della Somalia. Direzione
per lo Sviluppo Economico. Mogadiscio 1956.

MINERALOGY

ALFOSSO,A.

Le risorse di ferro e manganese in Africa Orientale. "Atti I
Congresso Regionale di Studi Coloniali". 1938. Napoli 1939.
669-675 pp

DOLGYKH,M.

Exploring Somalia's Mineral Wealth. New Africa. Nos. 5-6.
London 1968.
13 p. Map.

HYDROLOGY AND HYDROGEOLOGY

CASTELLANO,G.

Analisi di alcuni campioni di acque prelevate dai pozzi del
Comprensorio della SAIS. "Annali SAIS". Genova 1931.
105 p.

Variazioni della composizione dell'acqua dell'Uebi Scebeli dal
10/3/1930 al 25/4/1931. "Annali SAIS". Genova 1931.
166 p.

CATERINI,S.

Il problema idraulico in Somalia. "Agricoltura Coloniale".
Firenze 1923. 132 p.

MASCARELLI,L.

Relazione sulla potabilita o non potabilita di alcuni x campioni
di acque dei pozzi della SAIS. "Annali SAIS". Genova 1931.
92 p.

Relazione di analisi di sei campioni di acque prelevate da pozzi
delle Azienda della SAIS. nel Villagio Duca degli Abruzzi.
"Annali SAIS". Genova 1931.
97 p.

SPIGNO,A.

Pozzi tubolari nel letto dell'Uebi Scebeli per rifornimento
di acqua potabile "Annali SAIS". Genova 1931.
157 p.

STEFANINI,G.

Il problema idraulico in Somalia (Replica alla lettera di
S. Caterini). "Agricoltura Coloniale". Firenze 1923.
136 p.

METEOROLOGY

SWALLOW, J.C.

The Somali current, some observations made abroad R.R.S.
Discovery during August 1964. Int. Indian Oc. Expl. Coll. Reprints IV.

_____AND BRUCE,J.G.

Current Measurements off the Somali Coast during the Southwest
Monsoon of 1964. Deep Sea Research 1966. Vol. 13.
861-888 pp.

STOMMEL,H. AND WOOSTER, W.S.

Reconnaissance of the Somali Current during the Southwest
Monsoon. Int. Ind. Oc. Expl. Coll. Reprints III.
Contribution No. 190.

WARREN,B. STOMMEL,H. AND SWALLOW,J.C.

Water Masses and Patterns of Flow on Somali Basin during the
Southwest Monsoon of 1964. Deep Sea Research 1966. Vol. No. 13.
825-860 pp.

X. LANGUAGE AND LITERATURE

ADAM,HUSSEIN M.

A Nation in Search of a Script: The Problem of Establishing a
Natural Orthography for Somali. (M.A. Thesis). University of
East Africa. Makerere,1968.

AHMED MOHAMED.

"Shah" A Somali Game. "The Somaliland Journal" I.N.2.
Hargeisa 1955. 110-113 pp.

ANDRZEJEWSKI,B.W.

Speech and Writing Dichotomy as the Pattern of Multilingualism
in the Somali Republic. Symposium on Multilingualism C.C.T.A./
C.S.A. Brazzaville 1962.
177-81.

The Art of the Miniature in Somali Poetry. African Language
Review. No. 6. 1967.
5-16 pp.

Reflections on the Nature and Social Function of Somali Proverbs.
African Language Review. No. 7. 1968.
74-85 pp.

The Role of Broadcasting in the Adaptation of the Somali
Language to Modern Needs. Language Use and Social Change:
Problems of Multilingualism with Special Reference to Eastern
Africa. (Ed. W. H. Whiteley). Oxford University Press. London
1971. 262-73 pp.

_____AND GALAAL,MUSA.

A Somali Poetic Combat. Journal of African Languages. II.N.2.,3.
1963. 15-28, 93-100 and 190-205 pp.

_____AND MOHAMED FARAH ABDILLAHI.

The Life of 'Ilmi Bowndhe,a Somali Oral Poet Who is Said to have
Died of Live' Journal of the Folklore Institute. Indiana
University. Vol. IV. 2/3. Indiana. 1967.
73-87 pp.

ANDRZEJEWSKI,B.W.,STRELCYN,S. AND TUBIAN,J.

The Writing of Somali; Somaliya:Antologia Storico-Culturale,7-8.
(II Problema della lingua Somala,I.)Ministry of Education.
Cultural Department. Mogadishu 1969.
215-34. (Reprint of Unesco Limited Distribution Report W/S
0866.90 CLT. Paris 1966.

GALAAL,MUUSE,H.I.

Somali Poetry. German Review of Economic, Cultural and Political
Affairs in Africa and Madagascar. VII. N.2. 1966.
43-6 pp.

JOHNSON,JOHN WILLIAM.

The Development of the Genre "Heello' in Modern Somali Poetry.
(P.PHIL.Thesis).School of Oriental and African Studies.
University of London. 1971.

The Family of Miniature Genres in Somali Poetry. Folklore Forum
Folklore Forum Society. V.3. Indiana.
Bloomington 1972.
79-99 pp.

Research in Somali Folklore. Research in African Literatures.
Vol. IV. N.1. 1973.
51-61 pp.

Heellooy,Heelleellooy: The Development of the Genre 'Heello' in
Modern Somali Poetry. Research Center for the Language Sciences.
Indiana. Bloomington 1974.

HASSAN,SHEIKH MUMIN.

Leopard Among the Women: Shabeelnaagood, A Somali Play. Transl.
with an Introduction by B.W. Andrzejewsi. Oxford University Press.
London 1974.
230 pp. Bibl.

OMAR AU NUH.

Songs that Derive from Folk Dances. New Era. N. 7. Mogadishu 1972.
19-21 pp.

PIRONE,MICHAEL.

La Lingua Somala e i suoi problemi. Africa. V.XXII.N.2.Roma 1967.
198-209 pp.

KEWELOH,WERNER (Collector and Translator)

Somaliade Poesie aus dem Lande der Punt. Gesammelt und
ubertragen von (Werner Keweloh) mit Zeichnungen von Peter Giesel.
Herausgeben von Manfred H. Oblander. Im Auftrage der Deutch-
Somalischen Gesellschaft e V. Verlag AZ Studio. Bonn November 1971.
78 pp. ills.

ZHOLKOVSKY,A.K.

Somaliisky Rasskaz "Ispuitanie Proritsatelya".
(Opuit Porozhdayushchevo Opisaniya.) Narodui Azii Afriki.
No. 1. Moscow 1970.
105-15 pp.

XII. POLITICS. GOV. AND AMINISTRATION

H.M.S.O. (BRITAIN)

Protocol Between the Government of Her Britannic Majesty and of
His Majesty the King of Italy for the Demarcation of their
Respective Spheres of Influence in Eastern Africa signed at
Rome March, 24 and April 15, 1891. H.M.S.O. London May 1891.
7 pp.

Agreement Between the Government of Great Britain and France with

Regard to the Somali Coast February 1888. H.M.S.O. London June 1894. 4 pp.

Protocol between Great Britain and Italy Respecting the Demarcation of their Respective Spheres of Influence in Eastern Africa signed at Rome May 5, 1894. Treaty Series No. 17.C.17388. H.M.S.O. London. 1894.
10 pp.

SOMALI DEMOCRATIC REPUBLIC (OFFICIAL)

My country and my people. Vol. II: The Collected Speeches of Major-General Mohamed Siad Barre, President, The Supreme Revolutionary Council. Mogadiscio 1971. Ministry of Information and National Guidance. 218 pp.

National Campaigns, 1971-1972; A Record of Activities. Ministry of Information and National Guidance. Khartoum. 1972. 192 pp.

Speech of the President of the Supreme Revolutionary Council of Somali Democratic Republic on the occasion of May Day, 1972. Ministry of Labour and Sport. Mogadiscio 1972.

Broadcasting Handbook. Broadcasting Department. Mogadiscio 1972. 65 pp.

Diplomatic List July - 1973. Protocol and Public Relations Department. Ministry of Foreign Affairs. Mogadiscio. 111 pp.

The Role of Our Socialist Women: **An Active Role in Nation-**Building. Ministry of Information and National Guidance. Mogadishu June 1974.
34 pp. ILLS. Plates.

Revolutionary Somalia in the eyes of the World-A Real Assessment of our Revolutionary Actions. Ministry of Information and National Guidance. Mogadishu June 1974.
53 pp. Ills, Plates.

Somalia's Socialist Revolutionary Construction 1969-1973.
Ministry of Information and National Guidance. State
Printing Agency. Mogadishu October 1973.
210 pp. Ills. Plates.

SOMALI INSTITUTE OF PUBLIC ADMINISTRATION

Notes on Labour Administration. Training Course for Labour
Inspectors. (Prep. by Salvatore Cimmino V.) SIPA. Mogadiscio 1971
31 pp.

Report on Local Government in Somalia. (Prep. By Abdalla Ali
Gadalla). SIPA. Mogadiscio 1972.
49 pp.

Appraisal of Administrative Capability in Somalia, 1970-1972; in
connection with the first over-all review and appraisal of
progress in implementing the international development strategy.
SIPA. Mogadiscio 1972.
28 pp.

Duties and responsibilities of personnel officers working in
Ministries/Public Agencies. SIPA. Mogadiscio 1972.
20 pp.

Elementary Statistics for Supervisors. (Prep. by Mohamed Aslam
Niaz). SIPA. Mogadiscio 1972.
12 pp.

List of functions of public agencies in Somalia. SIPA.
Mogadiscio 1972. 20 pp.

Report on sixth orientation course in public administration for
top and middle management officers held in Somalia April-May 1972.
SIPA. Mogadiscio 1972.
14 pp.

The Writing of Reports. (Prep. By Mohamed Aslam Niaz.)
SIPA. Mogadiscio 1972.
23 pp.

Role of Supervisor. (Prep. by Mohamed Aslam Niaz.).
SIPA. Mogadiscio 1972.
7 pp.

SUMMIT CONFERENCE OF EAST AND CENTRAL AFRICAN STATES.

Summit Conference of East and Central African States. 7th
Mogadiscio, 1971. Mogadishu Declaration, 18-20 October, 1971.
Mogadiscio 1971. 13 pp.

XIV. STATISTICS AND MULTI-PURPOSE STATISTICAL SURVEYS

SOMALI DEMOCRATIC REPUBLIC (OFFICIAL)

Monthly Statistical Bulletin, August 1972. Ministry of
Planning and Co-ordination. Central Statistical Department.
Mogadiscio. 37 pp. Stat. Tables. Map.
(Bilingual: English-Italian)

Monthly Statistical Bulletin, September 1972. Ministry of
Planning and Co-ordination. Central Statistical Department.
Mogadiscio. 51 pp. Map. Stat. Tables. (Bilingual: English-
Italian)

Monthly Statistical Bulletin, Combined Issues October,
November, December. Ministry of Planning and Co-ordination.
Central Stat. Dept. Mogadiscio.
95 pp. Stat. Tables (Bilingual: English-Italian)

Monthly Statistical Bulletin, January, February and March,
Combined Issue 1973. Ministry of Planning and Co-ordination.
Central Stat. Depart. Mogadiscio. 65 pp. Stat. Tables. Graphs.
(Bilingual: English-Italian)

Monthly Statistical Bulletin, July August and September,
Combined Issue 1973. Ministry of Planning and Co-ordination
Central Statistical Department. Mogadiscio.
51 pp. Stat. Tables. Graphs.

Monthly Statistical Bulletin, October, November and December
Combined Issue 1973. Ministry of Planning and Co-ordination.
Central Statistical Department. Mogadiscio.
59 pp. Stat. Tables.

Monthly Statistical Bulletin,January,February, and March
Combined Issued, 1974. Ministry of Planning and Co-ordination.
Central Statistical Department. Mogadishu.
77 pp. Stat. Tables. (Bilingual: Somali-English)

Statistical Bulletin April 1974. Ministry of Planning and
Co-ordination. Central statistical Department. Mogadiscio.
18 pp. Stat. Tables; (Bilingual: Somali-English).

Statistical Abstract No. 9. 1972. Ministry of Planning and
Co-ordination. Central Statistical Department. Mogadiscio
December 1973.
167 pp. Stat. Tables.

Statistical Abstract No. 10, 1973. General Directorate of
Planning and Co-ordination. Central Statistical Department.
Mogadiscio September 1975.
132 pp. Stat. Tables.

Pilot Survey of Nomadic Population, using Hiloes as source
of water, Bardere District, Gedo Region. Ministry of
Planning and Co-ordination. Central Statistical Department.
Mogadiscio December 1973.
52 pp. Stat. Tables.

Pilot Sample Survey on Rural Population and their Livestocl
in Bardere District in June 1971. Ministry of Planning and
Co-ordination. Central Statistical Department. Mogadishu June
1972. 18 pp. Appendices. Stat. Tables.

ADDENDUM B

DARDANO, A.

Aerometria dell'Oltrebiuba (Biubaland).
"Bollettino Societa Geografica Italiana."
Roma 1924.
268.

DE ROSSI, G.

Venti e correnti dominanti nell'Oceano Indiano
dal 1872 al 1881. Forzani. Roma.

EREDIA, F.

Sul clima della Somalia Italiana Meridionale.
Ministero delle Colonie.   (Rapporti e Monografie Coloniali)
No. 14. G. Bertero. Roma Ottobre 1913.
48 pp.

_____

Sul soleggiamento a Mogadiscio.
"Bollettino Informazione." Ministero delle Colonie.
Roma 1919.
189 p.

_____

Contributo alla distribuzione delle piogge in Somalia.
"Agricoltura Coloniale." Firenze 1921.
72 p.

_____

Influenze del regime dei monsoni su quello
delle piogge nella Somalia Italiana.
"Bollettino Societa Meteorologica Italiana."
Torino 1926.

_____

Le precipitazioni acquee nella Somalia Italiana
nel 1923 e nell'andamento medio annuale.
Stab. Poligrafico dello Stato. Roma 1926.
10 pp.

AGENCE DE LA FRANCE D'OUTRE-MER.

La Côte Francaise des Somalis. Paris 1950.
21 pp. ills. map.

MORI, A.

Il viaggio del Cap. Bottego nel Bacino del Giuba.
"Natura ed Arte." Milano 1894.

Le spedizioni italiane nella penisola dei Somali.
"Bollettino Sezione Fiorentina." Societa
Africana d'Italia. Firenze Gennaio 1894.
107 pp.

SOMALI REPUBLIC (OFFICIAL)

Somali Statistics. Monthly Bulletin. October-December 1971.
Statistical Department. Ministry of Planning
and Co-ordination. Mogadiscio.
77 pp. (Bilingual: English-Italian)

Somali Statistics. Monthly Bulletin. January 1972.
Statistical Department. Ministry of Planning
and Co-ordination. Mogadiscio.
43 pp. (Bilingual: English-Italian)

Somali Statistics. Monthly Bulletin. February 1972.
Statistical Department. Ministry of Planning and
Co-ordination. Mogadiscio.
31 pp. (Bilingual: English-Italian)

Statistical Abstract of Somalia. No.2. 1965.
Statistical Department. Planning Directorate.
Mogadiscio February 1966.
128 pp. (Bilingual: English-Italian)

Statistical Abstract of Somalia. No.4. 1967.
Statistical Department. Ministry of Planning
and Co-ordination. Mogadiscio June 1968.
140 pp.

SOMALI INSTITUTE OF PUBLIC ADMINISTRATION.

A Directory of Senior Civilian Officials of the
Somali Republic (First Edition). SIPA. Mogadiscio 1st August 1965.
33 pp.

CAMERA DEI DEPUTATI.

Atti parlamentari --- Documenti relativi alle
condizioni ed alla amministrazione del Benadir,
dal 1899-1903. Tipografia Camera dei Deputati. Roma 1903.
183 pp.

LIPPARONI, E.

La sifilide in Somalia: Rilievi
epidemiologici e clinici statistici,
note critiche. "Archivi Italiani di
Scienze Mediche Tropicali e di Parassitologia."
Fasc.No.III. Roma 1951.
22 pp.

TAVANI, G.

Fauna Malacologica Cretacea della Somalia
e dell'Ogaden. (Parte I: Lamellibranchiata).
"Paleontologia Italiana." Vol.XIII. Pisa 1948.
83 p.

MASCARELLI, L.

Relazione di analisi di due campioni di acqua prelevate in Somalia dal
fiume Uebi Scebeli presso il Villagio Duca degli Abruzzi.
"Annali SAIS." Genova 1931.
104 p.

OREGLIA DI S. STEFANO, L.

La Somalia Italiana. Tipografia Palestina di G. Bosis E. Rossi.
Torino 1915.
85 pp.

TILING, M. (von)

Jabarti Texte. "Zeitschrift fur Eingeborenen Sprachen."
Vol. XV. Berlin 1925.
50-64-139-158 pp.

––––––––––––

Ein Somali-Texte von Muhammed Nur.
"Zeitschrift fur Eingeborenen Sprachen."
Vol. XVIII. Heft 3. Berlin 1928.
231-3 pp.

REPUBLIQUE ITALIENNE (OFFICIAL).

Rapport du Gouvernement Italien a l'Assemblee
Generale des Nations Unies sur l'Administration
de la Somalie Places sous la Tutelle de l'Italie, 1955.
Ministere des Affairs Etrangers. Istituto Poligrafico
dello Stato. Rome Avril 1956.
273 pp. maps, tables, charts, ills.

SOMALI DEMOCRATIC REPUBLIC (OFFICIAL)

Monthly Statistical Bulletin, April, May and June Combined Issue 1973.
Ministry of Planning and Co-ordination. Central Stat. Dept.
Mogadiscio.
65 pp. Stat. Tables (Bilingual: English-Italian)

Statistical Abstract No. 8. 1971. Ministry of Planning
and Co-ordination. Central Statistical Department.
Mogadishu August 1972.
XII, 175 pp. Stat. Tables.

ERRATA

Page 87	Duplication of entries under DE VILLARD, U.M.
Page 236	Duplication of entries 1910 ISTITUTO IDRO-GRAFICO DELLA R. MARINA through 1910: (Carta magnetica del Benadir).
Page 345	Duplication of entries under CHEDEVILLE, E., and CHIARINI, G.
Page 355	Duplication of entries under VYCICHL, W.
Page 358	Duplication of entries under QUADRONE, E.: (Somalia Italiana: Eubi Scebeli).
Page 386	Duplication of entries under CORNI, G.: (Problemi Coloniali).
Page 422	Duplication of entries under VECCHI, B.V.: (Somalia, Vicende e Problemi).
Page 430	Duplication of entries for SOMALI STATISTICS. MONTHLY BULLETINS APRIL & MAY 1969.
Page 455	Duplication of entries for FOREIGN TRADE RETURNS AUGUST 1971 & 1972.